AFTER EMPIRE

AFTER EMPIRE

THE CONCEPTUAL TRANSFORMATION
OF THE CHINESE STATE,
1885–1924

Peter Zarrow

Stanford University Press
Stanford, California

Stanford University Press
Stanford, California

Printed in the United States of America on acid-free,
archival-quality paper

Library of Congress Cataloging-in-Publication Data

Zarrow, Peter Gue, author.
After empire : the conceptual transformation of the Chinese state,
1885–1924 / Peter Zarrow.
pages cm
Includes bibliographical references and index.
ISBN 978-0-8047-7868-8 (cloth : alk. paper) —
ISBN 978-0-8047-7869-5 (pbk. : alk. paper)
1. Monarchy—China—History—20th century. 2. China—
History—1861–1912. 3. China—History—1912–1928. 4. China—
Politics and government—19th century. 5. China—Politics and
government—20th century. I. Title.
DS761.Z36 2012
951'.035—dc23
2011039936

Typeset by Bruce Lundquist in 10/15 Sabon

Cover illustration: The calendar poster on the cover of this book
welcomes the new republic and national unity, displaying the
boy emperor Puyi (center), Sun Yat-sen (upper left), Li Yuanhong
(upper right), and two women revolutionaries, Cao Daoxin
and Xu Wuying (below). The lower half illustrates various
revolutionary scenes, including foreign sympathizers (lower left).

Contents

Preface

This is a study primarily of political thought. I began with a set of simple questions. How did the Chinese people stop believing in the emperor in the late Qing period and decide to overturn a monarchical system that could be traced back over two thousand years—in some respects over three thousand years? Did the foreign origins of the Qing dynasty (1644–1912) really weaken it after 260 years of rule? What made it possible to suddenly imagine a Chinese state without the emperor—what conditions of political possibility had emerged by the end of the nineteenth century? For millennia the monarchy had held a central position in any conception of Chinese politics and culture: how could it be replaced? And whatever replaced it, did ideas about the monarchy collapse and disappear, or did they continue to influence the shape of the post-imperial political order? How did the monarchy manifest itself in the daily lives of people as its institutional basis broke down? What did the court do to makes its presence known and press claims to its indispensability? Above all, how were these claims attacked? How did new republican rituals come to replace the old imperial rituals after 1912?

These questions turned out not to be so simple and led to further questions. What does it even mean to speak of a "belief in" the emperor—supposedly "Son of Heaven" and possessor of Heaven's mandate—while it was no secret that emperors were all-too-fallible men? Was it the Qing's policies or the entire emperor system that proved incompatible with the changes China was undergoing in the late nineteenth and early twentieth centuries? If the Qing had been Han Chinese instead of Manchu, would it have survived in some form? Yet put another way, the question is not how the Qing failed but how did popular attitudes change so that its overthrow made sense? Could new political institutions ever replace the numerous functions that the emperor (or the idea of the emperor) performed? Once the emperor was no longer, did this create a sudden vacuum? Or was the monarchy already so outmoded that its fall simply cleared the ground for the construction of better institutions?

I am sure these are important questions—not the only important questions about China around the turn of the twentieth century, but certainly among them. I am less certain I have answered them well. At the least, a focus on how Chinese proposed that the state should be reconstructed offers new perspectives on a familiar modern story: from subject to citizen, slavery to liberty, and ignorance to enlightenment. In another, older version, from colonial oppression to national independence. This is a story with special resonance in America, but it is known everywhere; it is a story claimed by all revolutions and by all colonized peoples. It has long supplied our story of modernity: from the unthinking traditional to rationality, or from superstition to science and secularism. Or in less optimistic terms, to disenchantment of the world and cold utilitarianism, to social institutions of disciplinarity and governmentality.

These are well-known "stories," and I do not intend to deny their truths but to suggest that they imperfectly capture the discursive frameworks of Chinese modernity. The Revolution of 1911 replaced a monarchical system with a republic. The republic was heavily flavored with the taste of military dictatorship and soon fell into warlordism, but the ideal of republicanism continued to motivate intellectuals and activists. At the same time, the range of beliefs that had surrounded the emperorship survived the revolution: the need for enlightened rulers, the power of sageliness, the paternalistic responsibilities of the educated classes, and a moralized cosmology. The 1911 Revolution could not have happened unless large numbers of people were prepared to accept an emperor-less world, but it did not only overthrow entrenched views: it built on them as well.

China's rejection of millennia of dynastic rule was a product of world historical trends—as Chinese intellectuals often argued at the time—but it followed a twisting and turning path. This path led from one set of beliefs about relations among the sacred, political legitimacy, and textual authority to, eventually, a new set of beliefs if not a new common faith. It does not matter whether we call these beliefs stories, myths, or the discovery of the rational, though it does matter that the revolutions of twentieth-century China vehemently claimed to operate in the name of civilization and rationality. Chinese elites and commoners moved from a belief in the cosmic and charismatic role of the emperor to deep-seated skepticism in the course of just two generations in the late nineteenth and early twentieth centuries. The traditional emperorship had affirmed moral values held by the whole community; the collapse of the monarchy was therefore a significant part of widespread cultural crisis. The fall of the last dynasty, the Qing, represented the collapse not just of a single dynasty but of the entire imperial system, though this was not clear to all in the immediate wake of the revolution. The whole cultural edifice of the imperial system declined together, including: first, the coercive powers of the imperial court vis-à-vis local society; second, the civil service examination system that recruited the bureaucracy and reaffirmed the cultural capital of the gentry; and third, the immense system of classical (sacred) learning upon which the exams were based.

"Story" singular is surely a misleading description of this book. I have pursued tangents and explored byways, or at least started down them: one issue does lead to another and to yet another. Still, this study focuses on changes in Chinese views of the emperorship from the early essays of Kang Youwei (1858–1927) in the 1880s, perhaps the first writings to fundamentally challenge the monarchy, to the expulsion of the last Qing emperor from the Forbidden City in 1924 in an atmosphere of iconoclasm. I discuss other figures of the intellectual stature and creativity of Kang in the pages that follow, especially his disciple Liang Qichao (1873–1929). I see Liang as a particularly eloquent and sensitive bellwether who reflected and anticipated key ideas of the age. But this is not an intellectual biography of the journalist-scholar Liang. Rather, in addition to major figures, I cite the works of students, anonymous editorialists, and textbooks, and I look at political movements and political rituals in order to understand a great transformation.

The theocratic nature of the monarchy—the emperor's cosmic role as the pivot between Heaven and Earth and as the provider of peace and order among humans—became rapidly attenuated not just among a tiny minority of radicals but among the urban classes generally. Theocratic modes of thought we might call "imperial Confucianism" were replaced by such radically new modes of thought as evolutionism and utilitarianism and notions of democracy. This happened first among intellectuals and students educated in the new schools that educational reformers had begun to establish by the 1890s, next spread among merchants, Overseas Chinese, and the urban classes generally, and finally (and only partially) among the petty landlords and peasants of rural China. At first, these new modes of thought undermined the foundation of the monarchy without being able to replace them. Then the end came quickly. The ease with which the Chinese monarchy fell was perhaps only apparently less traumatic than the English or French Revolutions of the seventeenth and eighteenth centuries. Indeed, as we know, it long proved impossible to fashion a new, stable system of government on the ruins of the old. It is also worth noting the political strength that monarchical movements maintained even into the 1920s, especially in northern China and Manchuria. Finally, then, this study in a more preliminary way also touches on the effects that the fall of the monarchy had on Chinese culture.

A topic like this is not amenable to exhaustive treatment. At least, I cannot claim to have read every relevant document, or even more than a small fraction of political pamphlets, official memorials, memoirs, newspaper accounts, and essays in political philosophy of the period. Further research would certainly enrich our picture of the age and might alter my argument. Some of the journalistic essays discussed in this book might be regarded as the late Qing equivalent of blogging: they represent breadth rather then depth, they are quick and often excited reports of only partially digested new readings, they are responses to other essays by friends and enemies, and they are replete with personal put-downs and point-scoring. But they are serious, and they reflect earnest attempts to understand a revolutionary milieu.

Oddly, in the many years I have been pursuing this topic, no one ever asked me about my personal feelings toward monarchism. Could I be a closet monarchist? This perhaps seems absurd, yet we live in a society saturated with monarchical longings. Even venerable democratic societies long for a leader who can solve all their problems. In popular culture, the *Return of the King* (part three of Tolkien's ring cycle) found a rapt audience for its "good king" ideology at the beginning of the twenty-first century. The Feast of Christ the King is celebrated by many Christians. Actual monarchies are alive and well in many parts of the world. It is true that the old notions of divine right, chakravartin kingship, sage-rulers, sun goddess descendants, and the like have lost much of their magic. It is true that the line between kingship and kleptocracy is pretty thin. But it is also true that peoples from around the world, including those of industrial powers and oil-rich sultanates, continue to identify one way or another with their kings, which is to say largely father-to-son inheritance of a right to reign if not rule. Europe alone includes several kingdoms, a grand duchy, a duchy, and two principalities, not to mention the papacy (an elected monarchy). There are four monarchies in Southeast Asia, at least four in Africa (not counting subnational monarchies), and several in the Mideast, Oceana, and Asia, including Japan.

However, the fact remains that monarchy is not what it once was, and its cosmological basis disintegrated in the French Revolution. Somewhat over a century later, between 1905 and 1912, democratic revolution came to the Ottoman empire, Iran, Mexico, Portugal, and Russia, as well as China. (Other countries also had democracy movements that could claim varying degrees of success.) If kingship survived or revived in some of these cases, it was also remade. Monarchism became associated with conservatism and reaction. It provided a basis of reactionary ideology in the wake of the French Revolution if not even earlier. Precisely because of this, though, we can think of monarchism as sometimes providing the basis of resistance—resistance above all to the modernizing nation-state embedded in the capitalist world-system. This has been a resistance not, of course, limited to syphilitic old aristocrats, but has frequently fueled popular revolt by offering an image of a more stable and arguably fairer world. Monarchism has been a powerful source of identity, and again not merely for aristocrats, in tumultuous times. No longer linked to cosmological sources of power, it is linked to collective consciousness and serves nationalism.

Most of human history—from the origins of Neolithic farming to the coming of the Industrial Revolution—was shaped by kings. Even the most venerable of democratic societies is short-lived compared to the millennia of human experience with kingship. The choice to do without a king is thus a momentous decision. The first remaining kingdom of the twenty-first century to become a republic was Nepal, a kingdom created through conquest some 250 years previously. The Nepalese royal house abdicated in 2008 as required by a vote by a special assembly after years of guerilla resistance, a Maoist insurgency that took over ten thousand lives, widespread discontent, economic collapse, and family dysfunction (the abdicating king, King Gyanendra, took the throne in 2001 on the death of his brother King Birendra, when the crown prince killed Birendra and most of the royal family and then shot himself). Nepal's path to republicanism, far from assured at this writing, was rocky indeed. So has China's been.

Romanization and Characters: Chinese and Japanese names are given surname first. Romanization of Chinese follows the Hanyu pinyin system for Mandarin, except for names better known in other forms (such as Sun Yat-sen for Sun Yixian, Sun Zhongshan). In quoting from Western writings, I modify their original romanization of Chinese words into Hanyu pinyin; I do not alter titles or names in citations. The List of Characters uses traditional characters, as were used in the period under discussion; citations follow the traditional or the simplified characters of the work being cited.

Acknowledgments

Over the many years of this study's preparation, I have accumulated many debts. Institutional support has come from the National Science Council in Taiwan, the Australian Research Council, Center for Chinese Studies (Taiwan), Institute of Advanced Studies (Princeton), the National Endowment for the Humanities (USA), the Vanderbilt University Research Council, the American Philosophical Society, and the Foundation for Scholarly Exchange (Fulbright-Hays Exchange Program). I am grateful to those institutions not merely for financial support but for throwing me into contact with kind and stimulating colleagues (sometimes the same colleague). I have been talking about the parts of this study on too many occasions to list precisely, but suffice it to say I am particularly grateful for criticism and advice received at the Institute of Modern History (Academia Sinica), the University of New South Wales, Indiana University, the University of California at Santa Barbara, Harvard University, the University of Heidelberg, Sichuan University, Leiden University, Beijing University, Fudan University, East China Normal University, and the Institute of Modern History (Chinese Academy of Social Sciences), as well as the peripatetic meetings of the Chinese Studies Association of Australia, the Historical Society for Twentieth-Century China, and the Association of Asian Studies (U.S.). It is impossible to imagine better colleagues than at the Institute of Modern History, Academia Sinica, where I have had the privilege of finishing this study. At these sites and others, numerous scholars have given me the benefit of their knowledge and insights on numerous points. Really, it would be impossible to name them all. The publisher's anonymous readers were thoughtful and thorough, and I am in their debt as well. Paul Katz corrected some of my ideas about religion. An ad hoc reading group carefully went through the penultimate draft and gave me many good ideas, some of which I was able to incorporate into the book and some of which I was not. So for helping me improve the book and for giving me more to think about, I am grateful to my colleagues Chiu Peng-sheng, Chen Hsi-yuan, Huang Ko-wu, Lu Miaw-fen, Shen Sung-chiao, Lin Chih-hung, and Wang Chaohua. That also applies to the careful editing of Richard Gunde. Finally, this book would not have been possible without the help of my longtime research assistant, Miss Jodie Hung, and my new research assistant, Mr. Yeh Yi-chun (who created the Bibliography and fixed numerous errors in the Notes), even while the remaining faults of commission and omission remain my responsibility.

AFTER EMPIRE

Introduction

WINTER SOLSTICE 1914. In the pre-dawn cold of Beijing, President Yuan Shikai left the presidential palace for the Temple of Heaven, where he presided over sacrificial rites to Tian (Heaven) in the name of the nation. As recorded by the American ambassador, Paul Reinsch, Yuan "drove surrounded by personal bodyguards over streets covered with yellow sand and lined threefold with soldiers stationed there the evening before."[1] (Yellow represented the generative principle of the universe in traditional cosmology and was long associated with the imperial family.) Accompanied by a number of his ministers, high officials, and generals, Yuan was joined at the Temple of Heaven by the ritual experts: "the sacrificial meatbearers, the silk and jade bearers, the cupbearers, and those who chanted invocations." Yuan changed into his sacrificial robes in a tent set up on the grounds, and washed his hands. He then signed a ceremonial board with prayers to Heaven in red letters. (Tian, or "Heaven," was both a kind of supreme deity and a way of talking about cosmological processes.) Yuan ascended the altar itself, facing north on the second platform, kneeling and bowing four times. His retinue moved ahead to the first platform with the items of sacrifice. The sacrificial firewood was lit, and then Yuan moved to the first circle, lifted the tray of silk, which was then placed on a table. He returned to the second circle for another round of bowing; then the sacrifice of meat and the reading of prayers followed in the same way. Music, dancing (or posturing), and incense accompanied the ceremonies. Yuan offered several prayers, calling on Tian to accept the sacrifices being offered, to protect the nation, and to renew the world. The president then partook of wine and meat, symbolizing the blessings he received from Tian on behalf of the people. Finally the jade was offered to Tian and all the items burnt.

The president's decision to carry out sacrifices to Heaven, so redolent of ancient imperial practice, fueled rumors that he was plotting to found a new dynasty and become emperor. When Yuan did indeed try to found a new dynasty the following year, he insisted that his would be an updated emperorship, a constitutional monarchy, a dynasty suitable for a dynamic nation-state. Yet Yuan's would-be emperorship ended in defeat and ignominy. Given Yuan's undoubted power—his control of the military and political bureaucracies, his stifling of dissent—how was it possible his emperorship was stopped in its tracks? For that matter, how could a leader as savvy (and ruthless) as Yuan have so misread the political situation as to self-destruct? What was wrong with founding a new dynasty anyway? Another way of putting the question: Why was Yuan unable to reverse the Revolution of 1911, for all its manifest failures?

Many answers of varying specificity can be given to these questions. The levers of government at Yuan's disposal were already creaky. Self-avowed republicans were enraged by Yuan's betrayal of the Republic. And even among politically active segments of China's population who had brought themselves to accept Yuan's presidential autocracy, few could tolerate the notion of a new dynasty. Even if Yuan had hollowed out parliamentary and local government institutions, abandoning their shells seemed a big step backward. Besides, the Revolution of 1911 had made instant constituencies like adding hot water to make instant noodles, and political gentlemen guarded their constituencies. Similarly, top military officials personally loyal to Yuan were not pleased to see their relationship unilaterally changed, nor the eventual prospect of Yuan's son becoming emperor. China did still have monarchists, but they identified themselves as loyal to the Qing dynasty (1644–1912). Including some figures of considerable influence in Beijing, they could tolerate the Republic, but if there was going to be a restoration of monarchism, it had to be the Qing house that was restored. Finally, the foreign powers, particularly Japan, opposed Yuan's monarchism and gave aid and comfort to his enemies.

Yet at a deeper level, the answers to these questions really revolve around the fact that the time of monarchy had passed. The opposition to Yuan, though multifarious and far from liberal-minded, shared an understanding that the 1911 Revolution was essentially irreversible. Yuan's sacrifices to Heaven appeared no less exotic to educated Chinese, and even more bizarre, than to the American ambassador. Admittedly, the monarchy's death is easier to see in retrospect than at the time: this is the historian's advantage. Yuan's was not the last attempt to revive it. And while outright restorationism was rare—though it persisted throughout the century—the complex of ideas we can call "imperial Confucianism" shaped efforts to build new political systems into the twenty-first century.

All the same, something deep in the political culture changed forever in 1911. The bonds that held together the Chinese imperial system had been under strain for several generations, and finally burst apart in a brief but violent explosion. The fall of the Qing dynasty was not the first time a dynasty had been overthrown in China's long imperial history, but it was the first time a republic was established. In going to the Altar of Heaven, Yuan was obviously trying to build up a claim to the throne. The Qing emperors had offered sacrifices to Tian at the Temple of Heaven, one of several sacred precincts in the districts surrounding the capital. But the meanings associated with Heaven had changed—not totally and not overnight—but irreversibly nonetheless. For a number of years the Temple of Heaven had been used by U.S. marines for football games. The marines had been stationed in Beijing since helping to put down the Boxer Uprising at the beginning of the century. Yuan, too, had contributed to the desecration of imperial precincts. In 1913 he had taken the presidential oath at the Hall of Supreme Harmony in the Imperial City. This was the main site where the Qing emperors had held court behind high walls. Now, ordinary citizens bought tickets to enter the Imperial City, climb around the Hall, and gawk at sights once reserved only for court officials and foreign emissaries. This implied something about the end of the emperor-subject relationship that no foreign invaders ever could. By the time of the third anniversary of the Republic, in 1914, Yuan opened a museum to display art and relics collected by the Qing emperors—the predecessor of today's Palace Museums in Beijing and Taipei—which again firmly placed the imperial order in the past.

This book describes some of the ways Chinese political culture changed at the turn of the twentieth century. "Political culture" here refers to the systems, ideologies, and assumptions that shape power. Later chapters define imperial Confucianism more precisely, measure the intellectual dimensions of the constitutionalist movement and the 1911 Revolution, examine attempts to legitimate the new political order, and discuss how republicanism was imagined. With or without a revolution, the traditional imperial system was doomed. The *system*, not any particular emperor or dynasty, had come to be seen as autocratic and despotic, inherently incapable of responding to the challenges of the day, and opposed by its very nature to the creation of modern citizens. For, it was felt, the imperial forms had to be rooted up if China was to become the rational, dynamic, and civilized nation-state that it needed to become if it were to survive in a dangerous world. This was the view of both those who supported and those who opposed violent revolution. In a sense, the task they set themselves was no less than the creation of China itself out of the moribund empire. Once the revolution had taken place, there was no going back, as Yuan Shikai learned to his cost.

The fires of nationalism and statism in China were set ablaze in the late nineteenth century and continued to burn across the twentieth century and beyond. By "statism," I mean the view that the state—the institutions of governance—is the ultimate locus of sovereignty, self-legitimating, and the highest source of good. Statism is compatible with republican institutions but may also justify dictatorial ones. In either case, it focuses on the relationship between the state and the individual citizen, who is defined by "rights and duties." This was key to the new political discourse that arose during the late Qing. Citizenship was inseparable from national identity, the second great key to late Qing discourse. Nationalism was about creating "Chinese," as distinct from "men of Qing." The empire, which was a multinational project, was not compatible with the concept of a "people" who more or less shared common blood and a common culture and who were collectively the subject of history. In this view, what counted in history was not one great dynasty succeeding another but the formation of a Chinese people who could stand equally with the other peoples of the world. No people could stand without a state. And so the logic of nationalism led to statism, and ultimately a view of the sovereign state as the subject of history.

"AFTER EMPIRE"

The title of this book refers to "after empire," but I am not claiming that China today has nothing in common with the old empire. I am claiming that by the 1890s, Chinese elites were beginning to think about what would come after empire. By "empire" I mean the traditional dynastic state. I also mean to distinguish empire from the modern nation insofar as empires tend to claim universal rule in some sense; to in fact rule over diverse peoples bound together in their loyalty to the monarchy; and to mix patrimonial kingship with a legal-bureaucratic system of civil rule. Naturally, in those cases when nations are formed out of empires, they inherit a good deal even while rejecting imperial structures.[2] I am not claiming that intellectuals of the late Qing abandoned the civilizing mission (*jiaohua*) of Confucian culture, and it is obvious that the Republic of China was founded in the twentieth century as a multinational state—though how this was conceived still needs explaining. I *am* claiming late Qing intellectuals could no longer imagine a future in which the form of the state was monarchical or made claims to universal rule. On the contrary, they came to imagine a state composed of citizens. This book is thus about political modernity. The 1911 Revolution marked an enormous political rupture, the result of social, cultural, economic, and institutional changes underway for a generation or more. The questions it raised and the tensions it brought to the fore still preoccupy Chinese today; political modernity is an unfinished project.

All history-writing is simultaneously an attempt to get at the history of the thing and part of an ongoing conversation among historians. This book is intended for general readers with little background in Chinese studies, though some knowledge of the state of the world at the turn of the twentieth century is assumed. I hope that the people and ideas discussed here are understandable to a reader who has never heard of Yuan Shikai or Liang Qichao. All the same, I am writing in a tradition of scholarship on China. From time to time in the pages below, I will comment on the previous findings of historians. The issues I examine are not new. In the 1960s, Joseph Levenson noted the dramatic disjuncture between traditional China as a universal empire, or the Tianxia ("all under Heaven"), and the modern nation-state with its demands to a particular identity.[3] The formula of Levenson's *Confucian China and Its Modern Fate* was perhaps a bit too pat, but it inspires the pages that follow. One way to clarify the issues it raises is to focus on the concept of sovereignty. As Levenson also pointed out, the shift from culturalism to nationalism meant that the very meaning of tradition had to change: whatever modern Chinese felt about the classical texts, the tradition could no longer be taken for granted.

Radicals attacked Confucian morality on grounds hitherto unavailable; conservatives defended it with new arguments; all possessed a new understanding that alternatives existed. Of course, as the pages below will also show, there was never a unitary and unchanging "tradition" in the first place; the Chinese tradition had long had great scope for self-critique, which played a major part in intellectual life at the turn of the twentieth century. Rethinking the Chinese past was as important for intellectuals, I believe, as learning about Western achievements.

Fifty years after Levenson's work was published, the Chinese scholar Wang Hui finished his equally magisterial *Rise of Modern Chinese Thought*.[4] We can set Wang's optimistic rise against Levenson's grim fate, though that is not precisely what Wang meant. To some extent we can set today's paradigm of modernity against yesterday's modernization theory. The latter was about a single program all nations had better join; the former, especially for Wang, is more a set of possible conditions now open to us. If Levenson was writing in the context of the Cold War, Wang was writing in the context of the collapse of communism (but also the collapse of China's democracy movement of the 1980s), the crises of global capitalism, and the growing wealth of China. Wang begins his story of modern Chinese thought with the intellectual revolution of the Song dynasty in the tenth and eleventh centuries. Wang's view that the Song period saw many features of the modern is not eccentric. Many scholars have pointed to the modernity of the Song's political centralization, bureaucratization, and corresponding decline of landed aristocrats; its economic commercialization; and its nationalist sentiment; as well as its intellectual innovation. The Song is important to Wang not only because Song and later Ming (1368–1644) thinkers approached modernity in some sense, but because their development of a kind of transcendental concept of "Heavenly principle" (natural patterns and coherence, *tianli*) created new capacities for self-criticism. This concept was furthermore, he contends, one of the important tools available to late Qing intellectuals in their pursuit of reform. This is surely true, but it tends to gloss over the sharpness of the break with traditional thinking that late Qing intellectuals forged. As well, one of Wang's concerns is to excavate the history of Chinese critiques of global capitalism. The problem here obviously is that Song critics of merchants and commercialization were not criticizing global capitalism but something entirely different. Nor did the late Qing intellectuals, insofar as they were critical of what I would prefer to call imperialist capitalism, hold many reservations about economic modernization.

Wang and Levenson share the view that the major problematique of modern Chinese history is the move from empire to nation. In Levenson's terms, this amounted to the move from universal culture to particular tradition. In Wang's terms, however, universalism was not forgotten but reinvented in the concept of "universal principle" (*gongli*), which was something like the modern scientific form of *tianli*. I will follow Wang in pursuing the multiple meanings of *gongli* and *gong* ("public") in the pages below, even while focusing on their contribution to a specifically Chinese state.

An important topic implied but not explicitly discussed in Levenson and Wang is the precise relationship between the monarchy and culture during this transition from empire to nation. Or more precisely, the significance of the collapse of the monarchy for Chinese culture. Since the monarchy had been central to Confucianism for so long, Yü-sheng Lin and Hao Chang have suggested that its collapse led to a cultural crisis that encompassed the entire "orientational order."[5] That is to say, since the emperor was a universal, mediating force between Heaven and Earth, without his charismatic presence, ethico-political values were divorced from the cosmic order and a kind of collective mental chaos resulted. However, this interesting theory has never received systematic analysis, and my findings suggest it can be used only with great care. Cultural crisis there may have been, but it did not affect all persons equally, and even those most affected by it found ways to adjust to the new world. For many, as we will see, cultural crisis was welcome, for it was part of the process of seeking inclusion. The fall of the monarchy did have something to do with gender equality and generational rebellion. The rise of citizenship discourse did have something to do with creation of a more open public sphere. In the wake of the 1911 Revolution, outside of specific pockets of loyalists, there was little nostalgia for a political institution that had come seem irredeemably corrupt. While many people retained a degree of respect and affection for the cultural bases of that institution, traditional morality was under heavy fire. It seems the urban classes generally were in the process of working out new terms and concepts eclectically derived from Confucianism, Buddhism, and Western science and commerce (especially utilitarianism) that could be used to make sense out of a rapidly changing world. Already by the time of the 1911 Revolution, new means of constructing authority and power had emerged.

I try to highlight the terms of debate in the pages below. Chapter 1 begins the discussion of political reformism with Kang Youwei. Kang was a man caught between his vision of deeply radical and even utopian change and his belief that in some sense the emperor was the only source of political legitimacy. He also worked out a set of proposals that became the intellectual inspiration for the 1898 reform movement. When reformers won the ear of the emperor in the summer of 1898, they produced a cascade of imperial edicts that would have fundamentally changed the traditional bureaucratic system of governance. However, the Empress Dowager, who still held real power, soon called an abrupt and violent end to the reforms. Chapter 2 turns to Kang's disciple Liang Qichao, who announced his abandonment of Confucianism in the wake of 1898, and began to advocate more vigorous steps to turn China into a nation-state constituted by its citizens. Chapter 3 broadens the perspective to examine the sources of concepts concerning state sovereignty and constitutionalism in late Qing legal translations and other texts, as well as Liang's evolving statism. But it is important to remember that powerful men opposed any reform that seemed to challenge the Confucian moral order, and Chapter 4 examines their position. Chapters 5 and 6 turn to the revolutionary movement, which was based on ideas of national identity forged through race and history, as well as on republicanism. The effects of the 1911 Revolution are examined in Chapters 7 and 8, which focus on the discourses surrounding republican state-building through its new rituals and legitimating ideologies. Before heading off to the fields of political debate, however, this introduction concludes with a brief look at the Qing state, the baseline for my study.

THE QING MONARCHY

The Qing had come to power in the mid-seventeenth century, a Manchu royal house leading multiethnic armies out of Manchuria to conquer what was left of the crumbling Ming dynasty, and also Mongolia and much of central Asia and Tibet. With its vast conquests and non-Han ruling house, the Qing was in some ways a new kind of empire. The Manchus distinguished themselves legally and socially from the "Han" people, the vast farming population and gentry elites of China proper (that is, essentially the Ming dynasty territory, which lay south of the Great Wall and east of the plateaus and deserts of Central Asia).[6] The Qing imperial construction under a series of unprecedentedly powerful and strong-willed emperors created stability and prosperity, but many Han Chinese never quite shook off the shame of conquest—though at the same time most understood the Qing's legitimacy in orthodox terms. "Foreignness" was secondary to the consolidation of power, especially since the Qing affirmed Confucian orthodoxy and brought Han elites into the highest levels of the bureaucracy. Claims to universal rulership based on cultural mastery were never expressed more strongly and systematically than by the Qianlong emperor (r. 1768–1795).[7]

From the point of view of Chinese elites and peasants of the old Ming dynasty, the Qing was but the latest of a series of ruling dynasties. Since antiquity, the Chinese kingship stood at the center of the state and of society and, in a sense, the cosmos as well. The ideology of monarchism was constantly being modified, but it never recognized the legitimacy of a politics that did not originate in the court. The historical Chinese kingship was built on extraordinarily strong social and ideological foundations. It was long intertwined with Confucianism, yet its origins lay in the ancient Shang-Zhou shamanism of the first state formations of the second millennium BC. In later centuries Confucianism adopted some of the ancient rituals and cosmologies, developing both an essentially new legitimation for the kingship and a radical critique of it. Eventually military elites turned to Confucianism, or at least used Confucian advisers, and the intellectual tension of its sacred texts generally tilted to high conservatism. But the radical potential of the Confucian critique remained. Essentially, by claiming that imperial authority rested on "virtue" (de), Confucians set themselves up to judge precisely how virtuous a given political regime really was. The emperor and his bureaucracy also held a central place in the popular imaginary. Indeed, the emperorship not only rested on official ideology, rhetoric, and ritual, but also had a central place in orthodox (Confucian) views of society and the cosmos, and in popular beliefs as well. One of the strengths of the imperial institution was its adaptability and its ability to be nearly all things to nearly all persons.

By rooting kingship in virtue, Confucians had given a role for the emperor to play in politics and ritual. The Chinese emperorship, in combining the bureaucratic-military leader (secular) and the sacred cosmological leader (religious), was nonetheless a singular role. "Virtue" in this sense was not so much an inner and certainly not an otherworldly goodness but rather far-sighted devotion to the good of the people, that is, maintenance of a stable social order. If the emperor was not virtuous, he could be criticized, but it was literally impossible to imagine a legitimate system not headed by a virtuous emperor. First, regardless of whether Heaven was seen as an anthropomorphic high god or cosmic processes, the emperor was the "son of Tian" (*Tianzi*) and possessed "Tian's mandate" (*Tianming*). Second, in a firmly patriarchal society, the analogy between the head of the household and the head of the empire was frequently and explicitly drawn. The state was the family writ large; the family was the bulwark of the state operating under similar moral principles. The overarching virtue of filial piety lay at the core of subjecthood within the family and state alike. Confucianism, then, provided a blanket of beliefs and moral imperatives that covered both the state structure and society. The absolute moral demands of the "Three Bonds" (*san'gang*) stipulated hierarchical obligations between ruler and minister, father and son, and husband and wife. The family and the imperial state were not parallel but mutually imbricated. The emperor embodied the patriarchal ideal, for example, with his dozens or hundreds of wives and concubines. He also came to exemplify filial piety, behaving with perfect devotion to Heaven and to his ancestors.

The Chinese kingship depended on a cosmos that is orderly and whose essential order can be made understandable. If there is no order to the cosmos, the monarchy loses its foundations. Ritually, the Chinese emperor sought to guarantee order by linking Heaven, Earth, and Humanity. In the historiographical tradition, the emperor stood at the opposite pole of much-feared chaos (*luan*). Late imperial emperors laid a claim to the incredibly ancient achievements of their predecessors: the patterns set by the entirely virtuous rulers of the golden age or "Three Dynasties" (Xia-Shang-Zhou). Achievements such as fire, houses, fishing, farming, and not least imperial rule—or civilization itself—were understood to have resulted from superior and virtuous insight into the workings of the cosmos. Order was invented by the first sage-kings (*shengwang*) and maintained by succeeding emperors. Dynastic legitimation or "orthodox succession" (*zhengtong*) depended on a sense of cyclical time. A new royal house emerged when failure to heed virtues rooted in the cosmos was righted and the proper balance restored.

Hierarchy is inherent in kingship, which establishes distinct statuses. There is one king and many subjects, but subjects are not equal in their subjecthood. Rather, individuals measure themselves against each other in terms of their access or imaginary closeness to the king. In China, formal aristocracy or nobility of blood came to be of relatively little importance, especially after the Han dynasty (206 BC–AD 220), but the social hierarchy was deeply embedded in lived experience. Late imperial law privileged family heads over junior members, men over women, and gentry over commoners. At the same time, the ideology of the civil service examination system was meritocratic, and "gentry" was legally defined by exam success.[8] That is, officialdom was to be open to (male) talent regardless of family origins (with some exceptions). Meritocratic logic was no threat to the Chinese kingship, not least because it was firmly subsumed within the ideology of the cosmic and social hierarchy.

What is striking about the Chinese kingship is that over time most forms of legitimacy were not discarded but layered over with new ones.[9] The archaic kingship was universal insofar as it claimed to rule "all under Heaven." This actually meant an uninhibited center, from which all else spiraled out to create concentric circles of decreasing power and prestige. (This is from the emperor's point of view, of course.) Much later, the emperor claimed to be a "sage" (*sheng*), a personage of such mystical power that his inner virtue would radiate out to transform the entire world. In comparative terms, the remarkable feature of the Chinese kings was their linkage of sacred and mundane power in their persons. The emperor functioned both as chief priest (and a numinous or charismatic figure in his own right) and as head of the bureaucracy, including the military.[10] The notion of the Chinese emperor as numinous or charismatic needs qualification. The emperor was never worshipped as a god—which in the Chinese context would mean that sacrifices were made to him. However, emperors embodied both traditional authority and charisma.[11] Chinese imperial charisma promised not to make a new society but to reestablish communal unity and social—ultimately cosmic—order. Emperors claimed the power to regulate cosmic forces and performed numerous rituals to do so, and were thus charismatic in the sense they derived their authority neither from tradition nor the law. They never claimed to stop change but strove to regulate it.

The Chinese emperor was, up to a point, an ever-present symbol of power. Much of popular religion revolved around representations and elaborations of the emperor. Local temples and even household altars linked communities to a spiritual hierarchy of numerous gods that paralleled the officials of imperial bureaucracy.[12] In the popular imagination, too, as formed by quasi-historical tales and operas, the emperor was dragon spirit, warrior hero, successor to the founders of civilization itself. His personal name became taboo upon his succession to the throne. Time itself was named through the use of dynastic and official royal era years. Yet the emperor himself was often nearly invisible, and the gods that represented him were not the most important gods for most of the people. The emperor lived behind walls behind walls behind yet more walls. Perhaps this walled-in existence highlighted his centrality, his power all the more terrible for being restrained until needed—hidden like the river dragon of fertility and flooding that he claimed association with. Access to court rituals was strictly limited. This remained true as late as 1908 when the Empress Dowager and the Guangxu emperor were entombed in the Qing's mausoleums.[13]

This is to say the emperor was also represented by absence, however paradoxical this may sound. Few persons were allowed into the inner court where the emperor was surrounded by the ritual and panoply of imperial symbolism, an absence that licensed the imaginations of the people. While the European tradition of kingship tended to embody power as visibility, the Chinese emperor's image was not circulated.[14] European kings showed up on coins and made numerous displays of public splendor; Chinese emperors were shrouded. Most importantly, they were *imagined* through symbols and myths such as dragons, gods like the "Jade Emperor," and Heaven itself. The ritual activities of officials deliberately mimicked those of the emperor, only in county and prefectural cities instead of the capital. The locality thus served as microcosmos to the macrocosmos of the empire. True, the emperor received his ministers and foreign ambassadors bearing tribute. Many of the rituals he performed had select audiences, and many of his actions were recorded by special officials in the Diaries of Rest and Repose.[15] The Qing emperors Kangxi and Qianlong even made several progresses across their realm—though, again, ordinary commoners were not supposed to lay eyes on them. Nonetheless, it was the Chinese emperor's absence that linked him to cosmic powers as much as did the public symbols of his position.

Qing emperors celebrated numerous "miscellaneous" and "middling" sacrifices, but only four "grand sacrifices": to the imperial ancestors, in the Grand Temple at the spring and autumn equinoxes; to the gods of Land and Grain, at their altar to the west, during the first ten days of the second and eighth month; to the Earth, at the Square Pool to the north at the summer solstice; and to Heaven (Tian), at the Altar of Heaven to the south at the winter solstice.[16] The imperial presence thus marked the four directions, encompassing the realm in microcosm.[17] Angela Zito, in her study of grand sacrifice under the Qianlong emperor, suggests that the sacrifices at the Altar of Land and Grain acted as a display of the imperium: while the emperor sacrificed in Beijing, these same sacrifices were simultaneously carried out by officials at the provincial, prefectural, and county levels.[18] The other grand sacrifices, however, were carried out by the emperor (or his delegate) alone. The ancestral sacrifices at the Grand Temple, as opposed to more private ancestral sacrifices within the palaces, "displayed" the emperor as a paragon of filial piety, a critical legitimating device. Of all the emperor's ritual activities, arguably the most important was the Sacrifice to Heaven at the winter solstice. It was in his sacrifices to Heaven that the emperor acted out his role as the sole and irreplaceable link between Heaven, Earth, and Humanity, as well as his filiality. The heart of sacrificial rituals lay in offerings to the spirits, and commoners made sacrifices just as did the emperor. But commoners made sacrifices to their ancestors, local gods, and sometimes other spirits. If they presumed to worship Heaven, they were deemed traitors and usurpers.

There was always a certain tension between family and state, despite all the attempts of the state to contain the myriad families of the realm. Nonetheless, the state aspired to the seeming naturalness of the family. In the vast Qing empire, governed at the top by a Manchu nobility, the ruling house used different languages of rule for the different parts of its realm.[19] A Buddhist language of rule substituted for the Confucian bureaucratic norms of Han China in Tibet and Mongolia, and Qing emperors presented themselves as bodhisattvas. Even so, the notion of imperial grace (*en*, *ze*, *chong*) returns us to the family. Whether Mongol prince, Manchu servant, or Han official, one ritually acknowledged the imperial grace, a favor literally beyond the recipient's capacity to ever repay, though one should devote one's life to the effort to be deserving. And what was the debt to imperial grace but the veneration one owed to one's father? The Mongol poet Kheshigbatu (1849–1917) noted that "The merciful and righteous grace of the Lord Emperor's state and realm / Is like the nourishing kindness of parents who did give you birth."[20] It seems the language of grace depended again on the analogy between the emperor-father and the biological father, for one's very existence depended on both.

This was a language that began to be disputed in the last decades of the Qing. But this was not the first time the imperial political tradition was fundamentally rethought. Late Qing intellectuals themselves rediscovered writings from the first decades of the dynasty—writings that had been prompted by the fall of the Ming dynasty. The great scholars and Confucian masters Huang Zongxi (1610–1695) and Gu Yanwu (1613–1682) maintained their "loyalism" to the Ming but circulated reform proposals that they had to know would benefit the Qing. Their political writings were rediscovered in the nineteenth century. The resolute opposition to ignoble barbarian contamination found in the anti-Manchu writings of Lü Liuliang (1629–1683) and Wang Fuzhi (1619–1692) also impressed later radicals.

Most important for efforts to reconceptualize the state in the late decades of the Qing was Huang Zongxi's book on the nature of kingship, *Plan for the Prince*, which the Qing had banned.[21] Huang's examination of the monarchy as it really was left it naked and shivering in the cold wind of his criticisms. True, Huang's ideas should be seen in the context of his times and in the ongoing development of Neo-Confucianism, not as a precursor to democratic thought.[22] Yet neither was he alone in his disillusionment with the institution of the kingship. We can thus read

Plan for the Prince as exemplary of its age and, perhaps, the limit case of Confucian cosmological skepticism. Huang condemned the Qin dynasty, which had unified the "warring states" in 221 BC, as the turning point in the history of the kingship. Before: sage-kings who lived to serve the people. After: tyrants who treated the realm as their private property and the people as their slaves. Huang's notion of public service was not new. But as Theodore de Bary stresses, Huang's originality lies in his efforts to describe laws, institutions, and models (*fa*) that transcend any specific dynastic practices, institutions based on the sage-king ideal but designed for the very different world of his own times.[23] Huang began his work with a description of a primitive world closer to Hobbesian nightmare than Rousseauan dream. Then the sage-kings, with great effort and personal sacrifice, invented the institutions that made common life and mutual benefit possible.

However, with those who later became princes (*renjun*) it was different. They believed that since they held the power over benefit and harm, there was nothing wrong in taking for themselves all the benefits and imposing on others all the harm. They made it so that no man dared to live for himself or look to his own interests. Thus the prince's great self-interest took the place of the common good of the realm. . . . He looked upon the world as an enormous estate to be handed on down to his descendants, for their perpetual pleasure and well-being. . . .

This can only be explained as follows: In ancient times [the people of the realm] were considered the master (*zhu*), and the prince was the tenant. The prince spent his whole life working for the realm. Now the prince is master and the people are his tenants. That no one can find peace and happiness anywhere is all on account of the prince. In order to get whatever he wants, he maims and slaughters the people and breaks up their families—all for the aggrandizement of one man's fortune.[24]

Huang was not alone. Even stronger thoughts were expressed by the somewhat less distinguished provincial scholar Tang Zhen (1630–1704).[25] Tang recorded a conversation with his wife in which he said:

"All the emperors from the Qin dynasty on were bandits. . . . In the case of men killing a single person and robbing him of his clothes and grain, they would be regarded as bandits. Yet there are those who go about killing all men under Heaven and taking away their clothes and their food, as well as their other belongings. And you don't call them bandits?"

My wife asked me, "When the entire nation falls into chaos, is it really likely that it may be pacified without shedding a single drop of blood?"

[I replied,] "To bring order back to a state in turbulence, bloodshed may indeed be necessary. . . . [But] if all they did was to ruin every village on their way, to harass every market town they happened to pass and to massacre every city that they entered, what in the world was the excuse for their savage activities? . . . While corpses and skeletons were still exposed in the wild, and before people could stop weeping or their tears had dried, the conqueror of the land was already dressing in the emperor's gowns, riding in his majesty's carriages, and arriving at the splendid hall to receive greetings and salutes of joy."[26]

Though his language was a little more restrained, Huang Zongxi did not hesitate to attack the established notion of loyalty. The minister's true calling was his duties to the realm, not to the emperor. Huang made two important moves. First, his emphasis on "laws" or institutions was a break with Song and Ming thought. And second, Huang clearly separated the person of the ruler from his job description. Thus did Huang summarily dispatch the hereditary monarchy. Little of its sacred aura remained. True, even desacralized and turned into but one of several political institutions necessary to a functioning society, Huang's monarchy could claim roots in the sage-king ideal. But now, in Huang's view, China needed bottom-up institutions, decentralized decision-making, sites for the development of public opinion such as schools. This was certainly not democracy, as late Qing intellectuals sometimes thought, but it reflected a fear of despotism that they found echoed their own concerns. Huang also ratified their own sense of historical destiny: their higher loyalty to themselves and to China.

THE LATE QING CONTEXT

By the late nineteenth century the Qing was suffering from three great weaknesses. First, the royal family, imperial kin, and elite military leaders maintained their identity as Manchus, distinct from Han Chinese and benefiting from legal and political privileges. The Qing managed the

Manchu-Han relationship with considerable skill throughout the eighteenth century, but old anti-Manchu feelings broke out again in the nineteenth century. Second, the Empress Dowager Cixi (1835–1908) embodied the highest political power in the realm from the 1860s right through to her death, but as a woman she had no right to such power whatsoever. This situation created a political reality that was difficult to assimilate into orthodox rituals or morality.[27] Third and most fundamentally, the Qing proved unable to protect China from foreign onslaught. This reminds us of the contingencies of history. *If* the Qing had been better able to resist the foreign pressure or, more realistically, had been more adept at working with the foreigners and pursuing domestic reform, it might have survived in constitutional form. Or, *if* there had been a "native" Han Chinese dynasty with leaders better able to meet popular expectations, possibly that dynasty could have worked out a compromise to remain a constitutional monarchy. Still, if revolutionary republicanism was not inevitable, a fundamental change of state structures and ideology was. We should also note that as early as the eighteenth century, certain intellectual trends—the rise of textual studies (*kaozheng*), substantial learning (*shixue*), and statecraft pragmatism (*jingshi*)—all played a role in desacralizing the monarchy. The textual authenticity of the classics, if not their ultimate message, was under attack.[28] As well, the older concern with "orthodox succession" had disappeared, possibly because as a conquest dynasty the Qing found the entire topic too disturbing.

Nonetheless, well into the nineteenth century the growing presence of Western merchants in coastal enclaves, and even the Opium War of 1839–1842, were no real threat to the Qing. The Taiping Rebellion, which raged across southern and central China through the 1850s to 1864, was a real threat. Yet it was the threat of peasant armies invading the capital, not a serious intellectual challenge to the governing ideology. The Qing, supported by the gentry class, was eventually able to defeat the Taipings. The "gentry" here refers to provincial elites who reproduced themselves through landholding, commercial interests, and above all success in the civil service examinations that generated the court's officials. At the same time, foreign threats continued to loom. The Self-strengthening (*ziqiang*) Movement led by certain officials in the 1860s sought to defend the dy-

nasty against both domestic and foreign dangers, and it created an infrastructure for gentry political involvement and for Western learning. Space
considerations prevent a detailed examination of the changes involved,
but I will highlight a few of the new institutions on which the radicals of
the 1890s were to build.[29] Under the pressures of "domestic chaos and
foreign invasion," interest in Western military technology turned into a
broader interest in the scientific and economic bases of that technology,
and finally into an interest in Western social and political institutions.
Through the 1880s, provincial and court elites by and large sought to import Western technologies while preserving Chinese cultural values and
the social system intact.

But many gentry were alarmed by what they saw as a growing gap
between high officials in Beijing and themselves, as they dealt with local
problems. The "road of speech" (*yanlu*) or, more prosaically, channels of
communication to the emperor, was a time-honored political value. The
classics, with their idealized yet often fallible kings, emphasized the importance of good and frank advice. The implication was that the imperium was as much the responsibility of good mediators as good emperors.
Mediators were to tell the king what he needed to know of the world and
tell the world what the commands of the king were. In the early nineteenth
century the scholar Wang Boxin (1799–1843) recalled the ancient Three
Dynasties (*sandai*) as an era when "rulers and ministers" and "sages and
worthies" spoke straight to one another, holding nothing back.[30] Toward
the end of the century, his essay was reprinted in one of the statecraft
compendia of the age. Even more important for Wang than the advice to
be given the emperor were the officials who would shape his commands
into written edicts, edicts that would inspire his officials, his soldiers, and
his people. Imperial edicts, when properly done, had an almost mystical
power—like a force of nature—to clarify lawful order, remove suspicions,
retain knowledge of effective rule, and broadcast virtue.

Speech was thus a two-way road, and Kang Youwei's appreciation of
imperial charisma was in accord with Wang's appraisal of the power of imperial words, as we will see in the next chapter. Late Qing reformers urged
opening the road of speech so that nothing would block the links between
rulers and ruled. Barbara Mittler has shown how advocates of the establish-

ment of newspapers in the 1890s rested their arguments on the importance
of the road of speech.[31] And as Lloyd Eastman suggested, the ideological
battles of the 1870s and 1880s were fought along the road of speech. At that
time, the road was heavily traveled by low-ranking officials and non-official
gentry who vociferously criticized the reformers of the day and sought more
militant anti-Western policies.[32] When the Empress Dowager Cixi decided
on peace after a brief and controversial war with France in 1885, however,
she closed the road. Writers of unsolicited memorials were punished.

But not for long. The radical reformers of the 1890s that I discuss in
the pages below insisted on being heard. They owed much to an earlier
generation of reformers and malcontents, though this was a debt they were
reluctant to acknowledge. A decade after the Sino-French War, in 1895 the
Qing was handily defeated by the Japanese military in a war over influence in Korea. To the radical reformers, this defeat signified the failure of
the Self-strengthening reforms of the past three decades.[33] The Guangxu
emperor opened the road of speech again in 1898. When Cixi crushed the
reform movement that year, the road closed. But now the metaphor of
the new state imaginary was no longer the "road of speech" but "popular power" (*minquan*). In a sense, this entire book is about the transition
from the road of speech to popular power.

The last several decades of the nineteenth century saw the emergence
of wonderfully hybrid institutions designed to promote Western learning.
Newspapers were first established by Westerners for Westerners and their
Chinese associates. *Shenbao* was founded under British ownership in 1872
as an entirely commercial enterprise but was largely Chinese-written.[34]
Even earlier, by the 1860s, missionary publications began—tentatively—
to move beyond purely evangelical purposes to tell their readers about
the world.[35] The first translation projects had begun in the Opium War
period. Governor-general Lin Zexu (1785–1850) was stationed in Guangzhou in 1839 with the impossible task of dealing with the opium problem.
Whether out of intellectual curiosity or intelligence needs, he sponsored
translations of basic works such as the *Encyclopaedia of Geography* by
Hugh Murray (1779–1846).[36] Between 1843 and 1860, the new treaty
ports produced 434 translations of Western works, about three-quarters
Christian proselytizing and most of the rest scientific.[37] Between 1860 and

1900, the number of works about the West and translations produced by missionaries, the Qing government, and private scholars exploded. And their nature began to change. Of some 555 translations, for example, science and technology still dominated (387 works), but some 123 works dealt with subjects we would classify as the humanities and social sciences. Shanghai became the center of Chinese intellectual life, not least because it was protected from the Taipings and the other problems of the countryside, and the foreign concessions offered a degree of safety from Qing censorship.[38] There, as well, the Jiangnan Arsenal was founded in 1866, not only hiring foreign engineers to teach weapons-making but launching a scientific translation bureau.[39]

A department for foreign affairs, as demanded by the Western powers, was instituted in 1861 as the Zongli yamen. In turn, the Zongli yamen founded the Tongwenguan ("Interpreter's College") as its foreign languages school.[40] Originally, only Manchus were allowed to enter, but that soon changed. Other Tongwenguan were established in Shanghai in 1863, Guangzhou in 1864, and Fuzhou in 1866. The Tongwenguan were never able to attract the best students because they offered no guarantee of a career in officialdom. Still, many graduates were able to enter China's embryonic diplomatic corps, and scholarships attracted some bright but impoverished boys. Sciences were added in 1867, and the Tongwenguan began to be funded directly from the foreign-run Customs Service. The curriculum grew to include mathematics, chemistry, astronomy, physics, physiology, and international law, as well as English, French, Russian, German, and Japanese. The Tongwenguan thus served as a basis for the more fully modernized higher schools and universities that would be built after the turn of the century. Meanwhile, like the Jiangnan Arsenal, it also sponsored translation projects to bring Western works to the attention of Chinese scholars. At least as important as these state projects were the private entourages of leading officials, who needed their own secretariats. As long as the Empress Dowager Cixi and the court mustered little enthusiasm for reform, most Self-strengtheners found employment with provincial governors such as Li Hongzhang (1823–1901) and Zhang Zhidong (1837–1909), who directly or indirectly also often supported the newspapers, arsenals, and schools that harbored Western learning.

In encountering Western learning, many late Qing intellectuals claimed to find its origins in ancient China. Some said that ancient Chinese knowledge, from mathematics to democracy, had found its way to the West, where it had been implemented in ways unknown in China. Indeed, the eighteenth century had already seen a revival of ancient "heterodox" schools of learning that Western knowledge could be mapped onto. (This was a by-product of the rise of textual studies.) The theory of Chinese origins perhaps served as psychological recompense for victimization at the hands of Western imperialists;[41] perhaps as part of a way of understanding concepts that were, at root, quite unfamiliar, that is, as a comparative mode of analysis; perhaps as a calculated rhetorical device designed to gain acceptance of foreign ideas. At any rate, as Xiong Yuezhi notes, the theory served as a bridge to Western learning.[42]

To find the origins of Western ideas in ancient China was a way to domesticate them. It was not necessarily to approve of them. Late Qing intellectuals often said that Christian doctrines and myths were derived from Buddhism (a view widespread as early as the mid-nineteenth century) or from Mozi (founder of a school of thought of the fourth century BC whose anti-Confucian doctrines were said to have spread westward after being rejected in China).[43] A case in point is the diplomat, poet, and reformer Huang Zunxian (1848–1905), writing in the late 1880s in perhaps the heyday of the "Chinese origins" theory. He thought that Christianity in essence and, in all, about 70 percent of Western learning were derived from Mozi.[44] The notion of individual autonomy (*renren you zizhu quanli*) came from Mozi. The notion of a unique God came from Mozi, as did "love thy neighbor." Huang did not think these notions were particularly good, but he granted that they had their advantages. He thought that Western societies had used these notions to achieve a certain stability. Their relatively egalitarian politics promoted their progress in a world of competition. And at the same time the fear of God made their people law-abiding. But all China needed, according to Huang, was Western technology, and since Western technology was originally invented by Chinese, it would be easy to adopt.[45] Zhang Zhidong, a leading official of the day, was to capture this hope in a famous formula: "Chinese learning for the essence and Western learning for its utility" (*Zhongxue wei ti, Xixue wei yong*).

In addition to missionary schools, the Tongwenguan, and the arsenals, Western learning began to infiltrate the traditional private academies. Li Hongzhang founded several institutions devoted to Western learning of one kind or another in the 1870s and 1880s, as did Zhang Zhidong in the 1880s and 1890s. These institutions focused on professional training, such as in engineering and above all military science, but increasingly included courses in mathematics and the natural and physical sciences as well as languages and other humanities. Perhaps more significant as a barometer of changing mainstream opinion, gentry in several locations also established schools with Westernized curriculums—one count finds 107 such privately established schools by 1900.[46] Missionary schools expanded much more dramatically, totaling almost 2,000 by 1890 (including perhaps 300 girls' schools) with some 40,000 students.[47] Finally, in 1902 the court itself inaugurated a state school system that, however small, worked to define "learning" in the last years of the Qing, teaching sciences alongside Confucian ethics.

Meanwhile, study societies had become common by the late 1890s.[48] The Study Society for Strengthening [the country] (Qiangxuehui) was founded by Kang Youwei in 1895 with the participation of numerous officials. The society was only the first of at least several hundred like-minded groups by 1898, with some 10,000 members in total. These numbers jumped to over 700 groups with 50,000 members by the end of the Qing. Although many were ephemeral (like the Study Society for Strengthening itself) and not necessarily political, most advocated gentry involvement in at least local affairs. Study societies emphasized a certain equality of members and civility of discourse. By the end of the Qing, many study societies were dominated by students. The most flourishing societies could boast their own publishing houses and libraries.

Study societies, state and private schools, the arsenals, officials' secretariats, the new media—such institutions provided homes for politically interested students and gentry. I call such persons "intellectuals" in this book. Though the term was not in use at the time, it captures the searching and independent stance taken by the thinkers I consider.[49] This is not to say they always saw themselves as oppositional figures, nor that they considered themselves a group with common interests. But they had a new social base in the new media and the new schools in the late Qing. They operated in the newly opened public sphere and did not, by and large, have official careers. The spread of so-called Western learning since the 1860s was slow but penetrating. It changed the relationship between educated persons and the state, and the traditional state would not survive.

CHAPTER I

Kang Youwei's Philosophy of Power and the 1898 Reform Movement

O N SEPTEMBER 28, 1898, six men were summarily executed in Beijing. They became known as the "six noble men" (*liu junzi*) or martyrs, symbols of selfless dedication to reform. They were arrested and held for trial, but their trials were cut short as the court panicked that a supposed plot against the Qing, or at least against the court faction surrounding Empress Dowager Cixi, was in the works. At least one of the martyrs, Tan Sitong, chose not to flee but deliberately gave up his life to inspire his countrymen. Thus ended the "hundred days of reform" of 1898. Cixi put the Guangxu emperor (r. 1875–1908), her hapless nephew, under house arrest on an island in a lake in the Imperial City.

Other reform leaders fled into exile. The most important of these were Kang Youwei (1858–1927), the intellectual godfather of the reform movement, and his disciple Liang Qichao (1873–1929). They immediately wrote accounts of the reform movement that became potent political weapons in the battles for the minds of the Chinese that followed.[1] More important for us here are the questions of how the reform movement came to embody ideas that had been fermenting for a decade or more; why it scared Cixi; and where it might have been leading. The "hundred days of reform" in 1898 was the culmination of a movement dedicated to fundamental institutional change since the early 1890s and fueled by the shock to public consciousness of China's defeat at the hands of Japan in a struggle for influence in Korea.[2] The "hundred days" shook China's political institutions to the core, but less because of the proposed reforms themselves than the new philosophy that lay behind them.

Winning the ear of the Guangxu emperor and his top advisers in the spring of 1898, the reformers, led by Kang Youwei, drafted edicts to establish government bureaus to support agriculture, industry, and commerce; a postal system; a modernized military; a new university; and a more transparent fiscal system. Although proposals to modernize the educational and examination systems raised concerns among men who had spent their life-times studying the Confucian classics, concrete reforms remained modest. In late August, the emperor moved to reorganize the central government and abolish certain posts. In terms of the edicts themselves, even here there was nothing to challenge Manchu political supremacy or the position of the court. Yet in a nervous atmosphere—factional plotting, secret policy-making, racial tension between Han Chinese and Manchus, and military defeat and humiliation—antennas were super-sensitive to danger. Guangxu moved to enlarge the right to memorialize the throne. On the one hand, this was hardly a revolutionary step; there was a long tradition of Con-fucian pieties about keeping open the "road of speech." But on the other hand, it was a blow to the highest of the emperor's ministers, to whom alone Qing dynastic law had traditionally given the right to memorialize. If anything, such a change would broaden the emperor's authority, limit-ing the ability of his ministers to control his access to knowledge—a very old problem in Chinese statecraft theory. But it also reflected the calls of younger, reformist gentry to be heard, as we will see below. At any rate, in the reforms of 1898 themselves there was nothing about a constitution or establishing local assemblies, much less a national parliament. The re-forms represented ideas that many moderates had long supported. How-ever, it is true that Guangxu seemed to be moving in an ever more radical direction by the end of the summer, announcing his intention to carry out future political changes.[3] As well, Kang's personal support of a constitu-tion and parliament and his attacks on "the institutions of the ancestors" were well known. When Guangxu moved to appoint leading reformers to high ministerial positions, the conservatives moved decisively against him.

Cixi's "coup d'état" assured that her men would remain in the top po-sitions at court, in the provinces, and in the military. The reforms, such as they were, were entirely abrogated. Cixi had stepped back from day-to-day control of administration in favor of Guangxu in 1889, but she had remained the ultimate arbiter of policy and appointment. Now she resumed full power. Even moderate voices for reform were cowed. There is no tell-ing whether Cixi and her advisers really believed an anti-Manchu plot was underway, but they were right to be nervous about the future. The reform movement had been built on an explosive growth of open and openly

politicized literati clubs and journals and academies—various study societies—after 1895. These groups, sometimes with only the barest of links
to officialdom, challenged the court's right to limit social forces and determine policy behind closed doors. But Cixi was also shortsighted to oppose
reform. After 1898, it was the Manchu court that had to struggle to prove
its legitimacy. After 1898, new forms of political engagement and new
standards of state-society relations were considered legitimate by China's
townspeople and young literati.

The reformers lost their heads, or at least their domiciles, but won the
argument. For since 1898, leaders have had to justify their rule in terms
of representing the nation. Throughout the twentieth century even the
most dictatorial regime has claimed to rule in the name of the people. By
1898, when reformers asked what made the West strong, they focused on
a perhaps paradoxical combination of "popular power" (minquan) and
wealthy governments. Popular power did not necessarily imply enfranchis-
ing ignorant masses, but it was a loose way of talking about democratic
ideas and constitutional government as seen in the West and Japan. As
Xiong Yuezhi notes, it was crafted to legitimate calls for reconstituting
the Qing state.[4]

The reform movement engaged in a creative appropriation, based at
this point on limited knowledge of the West shaped by largely Confucian
moral goals, of the nation-state, of mass citizenship, of constitutionalism
and representation, and of commercial development. It is true that for
both practical and theoretical reasons, the reformers sought no changes in
China's lineage-based rulership. Practically, they hoped for the support of
the court to reshape the bureaucracy and were in no position to challenge
its authority. Theoretically, they favored using all the autocratic powers
of the emperor along the lines of their interpretations of Peter the Great
and the Meiji emperor. But "popular power" shifted the terms of discourse
by linking the "people" (min) as active political agents to the basis of the
state. The very ambiguity of "popular power" proved to be a persuasive
factor in reconceptualizing the legitimate state, as sovereignty (zhuquan)
shifted from the monarchy to the populace, however defined, in the eyes
of radical literati. In other words, the discursive center of the polity moved
from the dynastic house to the nation. The 1898 reform movement marked

a pivotal moment in the creation of a distinctively *Chinese* national identity defined in political terms that implied a future of full-fledged political rights and participation of citizens. The question of the emperor's relation both to the state and particularly to the nation suddenly emerged as urgent and troubling to any reform agenda.

The move to radical reform had deep roots. Structural, long-term stresses on the political system provoked a few literati to begin questioning the balance of power between court and locality, or between central government and literati. A sense of crisis had been building up since the end of the eighteenth century, long before military losses to the foreign powers began to chip away at Chinese sovereignty in the 1840s.[5] Some of its problems seemed disastrous but not deep-seated: the elderly Qianlong emperor had allowed court favorites to engage in massive corruption. Some of these crises were broader—the White Lotus Rebellion, which began in the late 1790s and blazed for eight years in central-northwest China. In no small part fostered by pervasive corruption that weakened the Qing's armies, the rebellion was nonetheless successfully put down once a new emperor came to the throne and was able to clean house. But only a few scholars of the day realized that the crisis was structural. Above all, a demographic explosion beginning in the eighteenth century had left too many farmers struggling to survive on too little land. Also, the size of government had not kept up with the growing population.[6] This made it more difficult to maintain efficient administration and encouraged the growth of local "subbureaucracies" outside of the official civil service system. Nor could the regular civil service keep up with the over-production of educated men. Many members of the lower gentry engaged in business or managed public projects such as schools or irrigation works. Philip Kuhn has perceptively noted that collectively they were becoming an incipient national elite, and they maintained ties to official circles.[7] The Qing's proscriptions against factionalism were rapidly falling apart.

Such problems were slow to ripen, however, and in spite of the numerous threats of the nineteenth century, the Qing survived. The political structure finally became destabilized during the 1890s for four reasons. First, the rise of Cixi had already created two foci of power, the Empress Dowager and the young emperor, neither of which was fully legitimate by

itself, as Marianne Bastid has shown.[8] Second, the Sino-Japanese War of
1894–1895 had not merely resulted in a shocking defeat, but an unprecedented indemnity and loss of territory—not merely the loss of offshore
islands and claims to suzerainty over bordering states, but lands that had
been incorporated into the Qing provincial bureaucracy.[9] The Treaty of
Shimonoseki granted Japan an indemnity of 200 million taels of silver
(ten times the indemnity the Qing had been forced to pay the Western
powers in both Opium Wars a generation earlier), Taiwan, and the Liaodong Peninsula. Russia, concerned over the threat of a Japanese presence
in Manchuria, and backed by Germany and France (the "Triple Intervention"), forced Japan to relinquish the Liaodong Peninsula, for which
the Qing then agreed to pay an additional 30 million taels. This sum being considerably more than the Qing's annual revenues, Japan offered a
convenient financing plan, though at a high rate of interest. By the early
1900s, a quarter to a third of government revenues went to repay foreign
debts. The annual payments were enough to cripple such half-hearted
Self-strengthening reforms as the Qing wished to pursue. The prospective
loss of Liaodong, though averted, led directly to a new phase of foreign
demands—the "scramble for concessions"—for direct and indirect control
over strategic coastal areas and for rights to build mines and railroads. In
other words, not the mere fact of defeat but ongoing crises weakened the
Qing government in the late 1890s and opened the road to radical reforms.

Third, by 1898 the factions revolving around the emperor and the
Empress Dowager had expanded beyond mere court politics, and represented a new ideological divide among the gentry. This factional struggle
was a precipitating cause of the 1898 reforms, as the emperor's faction
reached out to politically marginal scholars like Kang. And fourth, the
very reforms advocated in 1898 marked a contradiction at the very root
of the attempt to reconceptualize the state. The emperor was, on the one
hand, to be all-powerful and all-wise, pushing reforms to completion
against obscurantist opposition; on the other hand, he was to be literally
self-effacing, creating new power structures that would replace the court
with literati-government and ultimately acknowledge that sovereignty lay
in the people. The logical consequence of this intellectual tension was that
if the emperor proved incapable of implementing reforms, then he was

expendable. The failure of the 1898 reform movement led to the rise of a revolutionary movement. Although Kang Youwei never wavered in his belief in constitutional monarchy, others became less certain that a constitutional system needed a monarch at all.

SAGE KANG

Kang was a native of the province of Guangdong, a precocious student, and a man who assigned himself the mission of saving China.[10] Guangdong, though long prosperous thanks to its key position in the Qing's international trade and its tropical farmlands, was peripheral to Qing culture and scholarship until the nineteenth century.[11] Perhaps this was a good basis for producing political radicals. Kang was perhaps the most influential politico-philosophical writer of the 1890s in China, and he was one of the key figures in the project of creating modern Chinese thought. Kang was born to a locally prominent family that had produced several successful examination candidates. He was heir to a somewhat eclectic style of Neo-Confucian thinking associated with Guangdong scholars. Given Kang's precociousness, his beloved grandfather, and after his grandfather's death the family collectively, expected him to study for the examinations. The Chinese civil service examination system, it is important to remember, was not a single test but a long series of local, provincial, and capital examinations that took most men half a lifetime to conquer, if they ever conquered it. Kang achieved initial examination success early, which gave him the official status of scholar, or low-ranking gentry, but the provincial *juren* degree eluded him until 1893. He then won the capital *jinshi* degree in 1895, ironically just as he was protesting the Qing court's agreement to sign the humiliating Treaty of Shimonoseki. Kang's teacher Zhu Ciqi (1807–1881) emphasized both individual moral rectitude and engagement with the world. Kang appreciated Zhu's emphasis on true—moral—learning, rather than crude preparation for the civil services exams. Zhu Ciqi took a deliberately eclectic approach to the major schools of scholarship. The dominant new school of the eighteenth century had been Han Learning, an attempt based on philological methods to strip away the accretions of later exegesis and determine exactly what the classics had really meant.[12] Han Learning scholars tended to despise the Song Neo-Confucians for their textual misreadings and also for excessive moralizing. They relied heavily on Han dynasty exegesis, which was after all closer in time to when the classics were written. Han Learning was thus opposed to Song Learning. But philology was dangerous. The research of Han Learning scholars produced two unexpected results. First, it revealed that many passages in the classics were forged—that is, were clearly interpolations that had been written as late as the Han dynasty. This was not entirely a new suspicion, and it did not amount to a challenge of the fundamental veracity of the classics as such. The second unexpected result, however, was to have momentous consequences in the hand of Kang Youwei. That was the rediscovery of a long-forgotten school of Confucian thought, the New Text Learning, which had originally flourished in the hands of such Han dynasty scholars as Dong Zhongshu (179–104 BC). I will discuss the basic tendencies of New Text Learning below; here, it is simply important to note that many of the political reformers of the mid-1800s and even earlier were adherents of the school. It seemed to justify activism.

For Zhu Ciqi, at any rate, Han Learning philology was a useful technique for textual analysis but in danger of becoming sterile; Song Learning moral principles were necessary to a good life as long as they did not descend into airy pontificating. For Zhu, then, the Han-Song debate of the eighteenth century was pointless; the point was to take practical steps to improve the world. Zhu's statecraft views connected scholarship to real-world activism. (A statecraft school of thinking had arisen by the turn of the eighteenth century that was little concerned with either philosophical or textual questions, though it was associated with New Text scholars; it focused on the hands-on policies of bureaucratic governance such as irrigation, tax collection, currency, and the like.) The examinations still demanded thorough knowledge of Song Neo-Confucianism. But that a budding scholar would familiarize himself with Han Learning and philological analysis went without saying, and Kang was trained in textual exegesis.

In 1901 Liang Qichao said that Kang was the Martin Luther of Confucianism, that is, the man who put Confucianism back on its rightful path.[13] Kang himself would say no less. Kang's confidence in his mission seems so complete, and stories of his intellectual arrogance so numerous, that we can fairly say he had a messiah complex. Put in a more Chinese way, he frankly sought to become a "sage" and seems to have thought he succeeded; he sought to save the world. In the wake of the debacle of 1898, Kang was exiled with a price on his head. In 1899 he established the Society to Protect the Emperor (Baohuanghui), dedicated to reinstating Guangxu as China's rightful ruler. Over the next few years, he traveled the world, raising money from Chinese communities, writing voluminously, and even becoming something of an international celebrity.

What motivated such a man? Kang's conviction in his sagehood is revealed in his "chronological autobiography." He wrote this from time to time, perhaps like an occasional journal, until 1898, with additions made in 1927.[14] It is clear that Kang's self-image as a sage gave him intellectual confidence and political courage. He recounted that he was born in the eleventh month of his mother's pregnancy (delayed parturition is a classic feature of the lives of men with special purpose). He emphasized that in studying with Zhu Ciqi he found a model not just of the pursuit of scholarship but of moral character. Zhu emphasized the need to help humanity and the need for the individual to follow four moral standards: filiality, integrity, self-restraint, and introspection.[15] At the age of only 20, Kang had resolved to become a sage, or at least conceived the goal to be possible. He was inspired by Zhu to reach an exalted state of mind, transcending the secular world and "living" among the great men of the past. The eldest son, Kang reported that he gave up worldly ambitions for the delights of scholarship—reading feverishly and writing essays for Zhu's approbation. This was also the time when Kang married, about which he reported little beyond his somewhat prudish refusal to allow the traditional teasing of the bride. Kang's first teacher had been his grandfather, and he was deeply moved by the old man's death. Kang mourned him with passionate devotion to outmoded rituals. At the same time, his grandfather's death was freeing.[16] Kang could now abandon his conventional studies. He confidently dismissed the entire corpus of the great Confucian scholar Han Yu (763–824) as shallow. He practiced meditation and studied Buddhism. He returned home when his uncles threatened to cut off his allowance. Kang mixed the sublime with the mundane in a way that showed the nature of Confucian sagehood, with one foot planted in spiritual exercises but the other foot planted firmly in this world.

Kang continued to live with utmost filiality, save for his reluctance to focus his studies on exam success. He fantasized about teaching in America or establishing a "new China" through colonization in Brazil, but was prevented by lack of resources and the fact that he could not leave his mother.[17] He *did*, however, leave his mother for a political career in 1895, and his politics forced her into exile in 1898. He never told her that his younger brother had met a martyr's death in 1898. Risking one's own life might be seen as unfilial, but devotion to humankind was also a kind of higher filiality in Kang's eyes. According to his memoirs, in 1887 and 1888 Kang feared for his life when he criticized Cixi for using public funds to rebuild the Summer Palace, which Western troops had destroyed in 1860. "But then I thought, life and death are predestined. If I am to save the world, how can I withdraw now?"[18]

Over the next few years Kang continued to broaden his horizons through reading, including more and more translated Western works, meeting missionaries, visiting Hong Kong and Shanghai, and starting a school of his own. His sense of himself as a savior remained strong. By the mid-1880s, he had begun writing. He maintained good relations with local officials in Guangzhou, but his criticisms of national figures were potentially dangerous. His books were banned in the 1890s. On several occasions Kang recorded his belief that all his setbacks and dangers would be resolved by fate, or the will of Heaven. In 1893, Kang reported, he went into battle against local bandits and their gentry protectors.[19] Others did indeed die, but not Kang. Kang's confidence was the mirror image of his fatalism. His mission required him to risk not merely his own life, but trust in fate justified the larger risks.[20] Kang wrote that he was compelled by compassion and humanity to involve himself in public issues. Yet Kang's record of his life was scarcely one of unalloyed public concerns. He had several enjoyments, perhaps mostly prominently tourism. In the wake of 1898 he was to become one of the world's greatest travelers, but even earlier he seems never to have missed a chance to visit a temple or a lake.

THE EMPEROR: POWER AND RESTRAINT

Kang wrote the first systematic synthesis of his political and philosophical ideas in the mid-1880s.[21] In *A Complete Book of Substantial Truths and Universal Principles* Kang presented a kind of geometrical proof of his views, using scientific axioms to delineate absolute moral truths.[22] This was a universalistic vision of the public good. Using the Confucian value of benevolence (*ren*), he proclaimed the equality of humanity as well as a notion of individual autonomy (*ge you zizhu zhi quan*). Already challenging traditional norms, Kang stated that marriages should be freely entered into and subject to change; children should be raised in public nurseries with no filial obligations (nor would parents have obligations toward their children); and sages and teachers would have no special authority.[23] Kang's vision of the king was that of a mediator (*zhongbao*), chosen by the people for their own protection as two individuals chose a mediator in a dispute.[24] Kang had criticisms of democracy but generally supported the idea of popular elections of officials who would carry out administrative functions. To grant a monarch unlimited powers (*junzhu weiquan wu xian*) was not only to construct an artificial system but also to contravene the axioms of geometry. In other words, despotism was a man-made institution that also lacked any basis in justice. In a superior system, elected officials would themselves be regarded as sovereigns, implying that potentially anyone could be king. Kang argued that "power belongs to all" (*quan guiyu zhong*), and we can infer that he was already thinking in terms of political equality.

However, at the same time, in his *Esoteric and Exoteric Essays of Master Kang*, Kang presented a vision of an absolute and highly active monarchy.[25] He defined the sage as one who possessed transformative powers. That is to say, sagely rulers can manipulate and control people to do whatever they want. At the same time, they must understand the circumstances and trends (*shi*) around them in order to lead and correct. China is uniquely suited for this task,

not because of China's huge territory or its large population or its abundant natural resources, but because of the supremacy of imperial power (*junquan duzun*). This supremacy is indeed not stolen from circumstances, nor is it teased out of profit, but rather it is achieved through the accumulation of the benevolence (*ren*) of the founding emperors, the righteousness (*yi*) of the Han, Tang, Song, and Ming dynasties, and the promotion of honorable rewards by millions of sages and worthies over millions of years.[26]

Kang was not exalting the supreme power of the emperor for its own sake, but noting that it could be used to supplement deficiencies in the bureaucracy, the populace, or the military. It is also clear that the emperor should only have the best interest of his people in mind; he should not act for his own benefit. But how can he act at all? Kang's first chapter is entitled "Hepi," a reference to the *Classic of Changes* (Yijing), which links sagely wisdom, powers, and action to the needs of the people and to the essence of change.[27] Referring to a commentary believed to be written by Confucius, "hepi" refers most literally to the opening and closing of a gate, which is associated with the fundamental cosmic principles of Reception (*kun*) and Creation (*qian*), which is to say, primal generative energies. Their interaction, or the alternation of rest and movement, thus defines "change" (*yihe yipi wei zhi bian*). But "hepi" further implies strategies, magical powers, and the techniques of rewarding virtue and punishing evil. Following the ancient "Legalist" thinkers Guanzi and Shang Yang, Kang said that the "way of the sages is to take care of the people and correct their virtue" and create prosperity.[28] Furthermore, this is not merely what a king does; it is what a king *is*: "The distinction between the hegemon and the true king lies solely in the mind-and-heart. When the mind is sincerely devoted to the people and one leads them to wealth and power, this is the kingly way. When the mind is obsessively devoted to oneself, and one leads the self to wealth and power, this is the method of the hegemon."

At the same time, the root of kingly behavior is not mysterious but simply the "mind that cannot bear to see suffering." Suffering requires action to cure it. Rotten old customs are deeply rooted. Kings must therefore use power. By no means did Kang think the people would naturally follow the king willy-nilly; rather, kings must use "the method of rewards and punishments" (*kaise zhi shu*) to threaten and coerce.[29] This, too, defines the sage, and at this point in his argument Kang referred to the Confucian classics: "Restrain the people with rites, pacify the people with music," making them good and joyful without their even knowing how this came to pass. "Thus it is said, 'The people can be made to follow [the Way] but not to understand [it].'"[30] Governance follows from punishing evil and rewarding good; the loyalty of the masses derives from benefiting them. Kang cited numerous historical cases of kings not only gaining and retaining power through "rewards and punishments" but also of converting entire populations—to Buddhism in the case of Emperor Wu of Liang, to Western customs in the case of the Meiji Emperor, and even to new clothing and hair styles in the case of Empress Ma of the Ming. Kang was thus talking about a good deal more than what we normally mean by political power.

Rulers need an understanding of history and the models of the past, a knowledge of techniques of administration, a sense of priorities, and the ability to assess the present situation. Kang here promoted an activist style of ruling that went against the grain of Qing orthodoxy. Although the "mind that cannot bear suffering" lies at the root of government, rulers cannot be merciful to evil-doers. Whereas earlier scholars had criticized the harshness of Ming Taizu (r. 1368–1398), Kang thought that Taizu's severity in punishing malfeasance demonstrated his love of the people. The lesson was that only after the system was reformed could one "nourish the people with magnanimity."[31] Then will commoners obey the laws, the talented rush forward to prove their merit, and culture flourish. The powers of the ruler will be virtually unlimited. He can encourage and nourish talent; build schools; spread knowledge; develop infrastructure, industry, commerce, and farming; train armies; and clarify the "rites and music" (i.e., reform the government). When the nation becomes wealthy and strong, domestically customs will be uplifted and externally foreigners will be subjugated. This will be the time to "avenge the anger and shame of our ancestors, recover China's culture [or Confucianism, lit. "sacred teachings," *shengjiao*], preserve the sacred ethical relations (*shenglun*) from imminent destruction, and save the kingship (*wangjiao*) from gradual disintegration."[32]

Passages such as these can be understood in terms of the Confucian statecraft tradition, as Hao Chang suggests, or of Legalist influences, as San-pao Li suggests.[33] Both are present. The point here, however, is that Kang does not so much exalt the monarchy as exalt power—or, more precisely, transformative power—itself. It is true that he associates this power with the traditional kingship represented by the sage-king (*shengwang*) ideal and the historical dynasts. This leads Kang to assert the supremacy of the monarch, and his prose is redolent, in the final analysis, of the Confucian ideal of the "kingly way," which Kang used to glorify imperial power. Nonetheless, as in mainstream Confucianism, his final concern is the welfare of the people and the morality of rule. Kang treats the realm of rulership, perhaps, as amoral in the sense that the ends justify brutal means, but he does not in fact treat the political realm as in any way autonomous. Those ends are determined by the moral principles of society. In that sense, the kingship is instrumental. It is historically determined, and there is little indication in these passages that Kang treated it as rooted in the nature of the cosmos. He has preserved the omnipotent, almost magical kingship, but separated it from its old moorings. A later essay in the volume of "Master Kang's" writings clarifies this point. Kang borrowed Dong Zhongshu's distinction between benevolence (*ren*), associated with others, and righteousness (*yi*), associated with the self.[34] But unlike Dong, Kang emphasized the contradictory aspects of the two virtues, "benevolence" representing regard for others, unselfishness, and egalitarianism while "righteousness" represented self-regard and hierarchy. The traditional Chinese reverence for the ruler over the subject, the male over the female, and the noble over the base all represented "righteousness" and, more to the point, should be replaced with more egalitarian attitudes. Kang thus clearly preferred benevolence, Buddhist egalitarianism, and even the Mohist "universal love" (*jian'ai*) to the traditional Confucian regard for righteousness. In regard to the monarchy, he concluded that a king should behave with universal love even though the people could be self-regarding.[35] The moral responsibilities of the ruler thus demanded his administrative perfection; equally, rulership was infused with moral meaning.

Kang was concerned with the history of governing insofar as it offered models of imperial decisiveness; he showed no such interest in institutions. The monarch must be devoted to the welfare of the nation, and that in turn required fundamental, sweeping change. Change, in turn, is dictated by and must be in accord with circumstances and trends, even while it is the test of leadership. Kang simultaneously suggested that in some ultimate sense the monarch and the people are equal and also that for the time being the king stands far above the nation. Kang's activist emperor possessed charisma in the sense of possessing almost-but-not-quite magical powers. Kang did not discuss the mythical sage-kings such as Yao and Shun or later dynasts such as Ming Taizu as anything but human, but because these particular men "could understand the trends and penetrate into people's minds" and because they knew the "methods of power," they could do anything.[36] The sage-kings were both real and a-real for Kang, as for others. History treated them as real, if hazy, figures of a very distant antiquity. In this lineage, the last sage-king, Yu, founded the first actual dynasty, the Xia, and in turn the Xia dynasty was the first of the great "Three Dynasties" of the golden age: the Xia, the Shang, and the Zhou. Collectively, the sage-kings founded both civilization and the state.

Kang's was still ultimately a moral and even spiritual vision of leadership, because Kang firmly planted the monarchy in the soil of benevolence and selflessness. If there seems to be a contradiction between what in the end boils down to his fairly traditional conception of the monarchy and his strong egalitarianism, this was resolved for Kang in the stringent moral demands he placed on the person of the monarch rather than the institution of the monarchy.

Yet any sense of the imperial personality disappeared under the weight of the responsibilities Kang assigned to him. If imperial charisma for Kang, as noted above, was derived from human skills of a rather incredible order, another part was derived from the mind-and-heart rooted in benevolence. Kang wrote as a vicarious adviser or prime minister to the king, and there is much in his approach, in terms of both style and substance, that had a long Confucian pedigree. He speaks of the ruler in the most exalted language. Kang's ruler was, in his capacities, more than an ordinary person who happened to hold a certain post, but he was also less than an ordinary person, stripped of desires and required to deny himself ordinary pleasures. Ordinary people could behave selfishly; not the ruler. Perhaps Kang was implying that the ruler's charisma stemmed from his lack of self-regard. Yet the ruler nonetheless remained a ruler; he did not *represent* the people. Kang's emperor was the sole, personal focus of sovereignty.

In these early essays Kang did not separate the state from the person of the ruler nor, for all his egalitarianism, did Kang treat the people with any great respect. If anything, Kang considered it their duty to be passively transformed; after that, they conceivably might form a nation. Kang's thought moved on two separate planes. He desired fundamental reform, including reform of the monarchy, even while he would strengthen the institution, not least by recalling its cultural resources to it. Kang maintained a "more or less conciliatory attitude toward the existing political order," as Kung-chuan Hsiao put it.[37] Kang justified his regard for the Qing monarchy through a synthesis of Confucian statecraft and Legalist ideas. Yet Kang's ultimate goals—and the ancillary consequences of his activism—were radical. For Kang, there was no contradiction between conservative and radical tendencies, as long as he ascribed different goals to different parts of the future. The real tension in Kang's thought was between means and ends.[38] For the near future, he could not envision a Chinese state except as the creature of the emperor. Yet as Young-tsu Wong has pointed out, Kang's ultimate purpose in his early writings was not to exalt the ruler but to press for reform from the top.[39]

Kang was in fact promoting reform in a new way. He was not praising imperial power for power's sake. It is true that he adopted a lyrical and allusive language of charismatic transformation. And this was already something quite different from the mainstream of Confucian gradualism. Both Kang's faith in charisma and his notions of fundamental institutional change, as we will see below, departed from the major currents of Han Learning, Neo-Confucian metaphysical and moral principles, and even statecraft thought, which assigned little initiative to the emperor. Kang's simultaneous condemnation of despotism was not in tension with his faith in charisma but defined it. Kang's emperor did retain two central values of the classics: benevolence and righteousness.

Kang's stress on activism and wholesale, transformative change was a profound challenge to the status quo. Kang claimed to find historical precedents for his ideas, but Kang's ideas were more than a little tinged with the heterodox Legalist tradition, his interpretations of Confucian texts were highly innovative (as we will see below), and in effect he urged that China adopt foreign institutions. As well, a possibly unintended but necessary consequence of Kang's reinterpretation of the role of the Chinese emperor was to show that the rulership could be consciously reformulated. The search for the roots of monarchism led not merely to its exaltation but also to the questioning of its purpose in both moral and utilitarian perspectives. The implication that an immoral monarchy was not legitimate could not be ignored. Kang was able to reconcile disparate views—Confucianism, statecraft thinking, Legalism, even Mohism—within an ideal kingship, but he had less to say about other institutions that might support reform.[40] Thus rulership for Kang lay in meeting challenges, creating (undefined) institutions, and overcoming danger.[41]

Kang had reconceptualized the state precisely by ascribing charismatic powers to the emperor, who would reform institutions. The association between the New Text school and statecraft concerns from the early nineteenth century virtually guaranteed that Kang, emerging from this tradition, would pay a great deal of attention to institutions. Beginning in 1888, Kang wrote out his proposals in memorials to the emperor. According to Qing law, only high-ranking officials could memorialize the emperor, but Kang used channels among his friends in officialdom, thus not straying too far outside the law. It seems clear neither Cixi nor Guangxu saw any of Kang's memorials until 1898, but these memorials reveal some of the specific proposals of the radical reformers. Kang's early memorials went so far as to urge a parliament. His was not the only voice advocating a more or less constitutional system of government with some separation of powers among deliberative bodies, administrators, and judicial officers, but his ideas were the most far-reaching. And they were grounded in Confucian logic. Parliaments, Kang assured the emperor, allowed sovereign and people to deliberate together, fostering communication and forging consensus, and not incidentally encouraging people to pay their taxes. Kang argued that democracy (loosely defined in this way) strengthened the nation while autocracy weakened it, because autocratic government was inherently divisive. Examples: France falling to revolution and Poland falling apart, while "Western countries" and Japan moved from strength to strength. If Kang's ideas for specific reforms did not go much beyond those of a number of his contemporaries, his condemnation of autocracy was sharper than theirs.

Kang's views of the state in the mid- and late 1890s contrasted in significant ways with his earlier views. Like other reformist thinkers, he treated a parliament as a means for promoting national unity, connecting ruler and people, but Kang also offered a picture of the emperor outside politics and administration, yet no longer above the nation. In Kang's words, the essence of a parliamentary system was that "the ruler and the citizens discuss the nation's politics and laws together."[42] If, according to the separation of powers, parliament makes the laws, legal officials adjudicate them, and the government administers them, then what does an emperor do? "The ruler remains in general charge" (*renzhu zongzhi*). Not only did Kang thus preach the doctrine of Western-style constitutional monarchy, but he also clearly implied that the emperor, though establishing the constitution, is also subject to it. Under such a system the government "represents" the emperor, who is sacred but without responsibility and (thus?) forms "one body" with all the citizens.

Rulership here is attenuated and edging toward the symbolic rather than practical. Nonetheless, Kang claimed that this was a recipe for strengthening China. In his famous petition to the throne of May 1895 opposing the proposed peace terms with Japan, Kang had complained of the growing gaps between ruler and officials and the officials and the people.[43] This charge had long been fundamental to the reformist position, but here Kang elaborated: a unified country was strong and orderly while in autocratic countries the people did not participate in government but only fought with each other and sought to benefit themselves.[44] Another lesson Kang drew was that unity and assimilation under the great umbrella of benevolence should prevent ethnic differences from emerging, at least on the political level. Kang thus tried to allay Manchu fears of reform, while he also implied that the institution of a parliament (or constitutionalism generally) would unite not only ruler and people but also the people themselves.

Kang cited the mythical sage-kings Yao and Shun to show that in ancient times China was governed with a democratic spirit but—tellingly—noted that the ancient kings lacked the institution of a parliament to assure cooperation between ruler and people. At the same time, Kang promised Guangxu that his sacred rule (*shengzhi*) would surpass that of the earlier dynasties and even spread beyond the governing of China itself.[45] The *mode* of Kang's reformism of the 1890s continued a long pattern of radical proposals made in the name of the systems of the Three Dynasties and the virtues of the "Former Kings."[46] But its content was unprecedentedly thoroughgoing. Kang actually believed that the institutions of the Three Dynasties were not so much historical fact as Confucian prophecy awaiting fulfillment, as we will see below. The real paradox is that at the height of the reform movement in 1898 Kang had no political choice but to emphasize monarchical power (*junquan*). In a June memorial, for example, Kang returned to language reminiscent of his "Hepi" chapter, reminding Guangxu of the emperor's "inexhaustible powers," his duty to take action, and his ability to change customs and arouse the people.[47] There were two great examples of reforming monarchs that Kang found abroad that we now turn to.

THE MEIJI EMPEROR IN THE CHINESE REFORMIST IMAGINATION

In the midst of the summer of 1898 Kang urged Guangxu to take Peter the Great of Russia and the Meiji emperor of Japan as his models. Peter the Great showed what a strong emperor could do to modernize a backward nation.[48] He had fearlessly traveled abroad, learned the latest techniques and theories in a wide range of disciplines, and returned home to crush conservative opposition. However, Russia had indisputably reverted to autocracy, or indeed never left it. Meiji Japan was a better model of successful political modernization, and the details of the Restoration of 1868 certainly better known. True, Chinese reformers spoke of the emperor as playing a larger role in leading the reforms of the 1870s and 1880s than we now know was actually the case, but they had a good grasp of what those reforms consisted of. They followed late Meiji accounts that glorified the Japanese emperor, and saw in them lessons on how to instill patriotic identity, industrialize the economy, and build a strong military—as well as achieve a constitutional political order. Since few Chinese had direct experience of Japan in the 1890s, to an extent it could be used—invented even—as a utopian projection in a larger critique of the Chinese political and social status quo.[49]

That is to say, Meiji Japan seemed to be a place where both administrative efficiency and top-down reforms, on the one hand, and "self-government" and "public opinion," on the other, were reconciled. The Meiji emperor united the bureaucracy and the nation in support of progressive policies and symbolized this national reconciliation. It may seem surprising that the Chinese reformers saw anything useful or even familiar in the Japanese *tennōsei* ("emperor system"), with its imperial line unbroken, its misty origins in the age of the gods, and its numinous nature. But the continuity of national and cultural identity promised through the person of the emperor appealed greatly to these early Chinese observers. The Meiji emperor seemed to offer change and continuity at the same time. And the very triumph of the Meiji proved that successful reform was possible in the teeth of conservative opposition.

Concrete knowledge of Japan was quite limited until the 1890s. None of China's radical reformers had even visited there. The most important source of information was the extensive notations on contemporary Japanese society, politics, and culture by the Qing diplomat Huang Zunxian, who also maintained extensive personal contacts with leading reformers.[50] Serving in the Qing's Tokyo legation from 1877 to 1882, Huang became close to many leading Japanese intellectuals and literary figures. They could share their interests in poetry and other matters through written "brush conversations" (*bitan*), educated Japanese being trained in Chinese classical literacy even if unable to speak a word of Chinese. Huang himself was sharply critical of any kind of radical reform and "Western" ideas. He published a collection of poems on "Japanese affairs" in 1879, which was read in China as much for the information the poems offered on Japan as for their literary quality. Huang's massive "treatise" on Japan was finished by 1890, but, though hardly radical in tone, it met with the court's disapproval, and even a reformist official like Li Hongzhang (1823–1901) refused to publish it. It was, however, published in the crisis following the Sino-Japanese War in 1895 and republished again in 1898. Indeed, by the 1890s, there were dozens of Chinese accounts of Japan and translations from the Japanese.

Kang presented his lengthy *Study of Japan's Reforms* to Guangxu in the spring of 1898.[51] As early as his first memorial of 1888, Kang had cited the Meiji reforms, and he later remarked that China could follow Japan's example in ten years.[52] Japan, he thought, had adapted the essentials of Western civilization to its own purposes, and China could learn much about the West through Japan. But Kang's new book was much more systematic than his earlier observations. It took the form of a chronology covering the first twenty-four years of the Meiji period—from the Restoration to the constitution—to which Kang interpolated his explanatory and hortatory annotations. Kang's interest in Japan and his study of the Meiji reforms have received considerable scholarly attention.[53] Here, I simply want to draw out the implications of the Meiji example for Kang's effort to rethink the state. One way to judge Kang's work is in terms of its appeal, calculated or not, to the Chinese emperor, and Guangxu was indeed apparently impressed. Overall, a number of central themes emerge from the *Study of Japan's Reforms*. Perhaps the most basic premise, explicitly stated over and over again, was that the world had entered an age of international competition. In such a ruthless environment it followed that the state needed to select the best men to work for it and give the emperor a wide range of advice, divide the branches of government for greater efficiency, strengthen local government, provide social order and policing, and improve the schools and make the most recent scholarship available through translations. Not surprisingly, Kang gave the emperor a major role in the reform process and the renewed state that would follow. But he was also reconceptualizing the monarchy along more passive and spiritual lines whereby the emperor would select the best men and largely heed their advice. The emperor was to be no mere symbol: he retained ultimate sovereignty and power, but he delegated. By standing above political battles, the emperor could unite with the people and thereby unify the nation.

As we have seen, Kang's main objection to autocracy was the gap it created between ruler and ruled, a gap that led to national paralysis. In his *Study of Japan's Reforms*, Kang repeatedly used two tropes to describe Japan before the Meiji: these were images of difference, distance, and chasms on the one hand, and of being closed, shut down, and isolated on the other. The great accomplishment of the Meiji emperor had been to bridge the gaps among the Japanese and to end Japan's isolation. The Meiji emperor could then symbolize and maintain the unity of the national community. Since China's political habits were about the same as Japan's, Kang assured Guangxu, China could simply learn from Japan's accomplishments and mistakes to make the reform process even easier: as easy as turning the imperial palm.[54]

Kang began the *Study of Japan's Reforms* familiarly enough by noting in the preface that all around the world conservative states were failing because the monarch separated himself from the people.[55] A few countries like Japan, however, had prospered by pursuing reform as the monarch was able to open up channels between himself and the people (*junzhu neng yu min tong*). Japan had succeeded in spite of foreign pressures, the shogun's usurpation of power, rampant feudalism, and the reduction of the ruler to titular status. By opening up the political system to good men and widespread discussion, sending Japanese out to inspect the rest of the world, bringing in foreign advisers, and building a national school system, the Meiji reforms had led to great improvements. However, Kang thought, the reforms had remained limited as long as the classes remained divided (*zun bei you ge*). What Kang had in mind was not a modern understanding of socioeconomic classes but the gap between rulers and ruled. The solution was to proceed with the complete destruction of "feudalism" (*fengjian*) and to empower local officials to act as middlemen between those above and those below them in order that "popular sentiment" be made known.

For Kang, the Meiji Restoration's "Charter Oath"—which Kang regarded as a set of pledges made by the emperor upon taking the throne—was key to understanding the success of the Meiji state.[56] Sinifying the story for his intended audience—Guangxu—Kang said the Meiji emperor had sacrificed to Heaven in order to show his seriousness. The oath not only announced to all the general direction the new government intended to take, but it also fostered national unity. It made the nation the concern of everyone, condemned the obstructive tactics of the conservatives, raised the flag of reform, abolished the old forms of exaltation and the "divisions between high and low," formed the citizenry into a "single body," and selected the best ways of doing things from around the world. According to Kang, the Meiji emperor's sincerity affected the entire society down to its meanest elements; the highest goal was no less than the sharing of the emperorship itself (*shang zhi yi gong tianwei*). More practically, Kang found, the oath was a successful promise to open up government to all men of talent and to extend public opinion. He also judged that the emperor's later edicts encouraged loyalty and righteousness.[57] By way of contrast, Kang feared that the Chinese emperor was in constant danger of isolation and losing track of what was going on—or in other words becoming trapped by conservative officials.[58] Kang thus praised the Meiji emperor for his tours of the nation and for his meetings with various elements of Japanese society. This was tantamount to a transformation of traditional social values. Such a transformation could only be led by the emperor.[59]

Nonetheless, Kang did not urge that China immediately adopt all of the reforms that had taken Japan thirty years to implement. He pointed out that, while the Japanese settled affairs by general discussion and voting, the Chinese were not ready for this.[60] In time, because of the emperor's love of his people, he would enlighten them through schooling, and once enlightened they would learn how to run local assemblies and eventually a national parliament.[61] Self-government was one of Japan's strengths, but Japan's example also heightened Kang's faith in monarchism. No matter how capable and progressive his ministers and no matter how completely the gaps between upper and lower were shrunk, the emperor retained two essential functions: to unify the people and to control them.[62] The emperor did this by punishing the evil and rewarding the good, as well as by teaching and nourishing. In turn, the people would love him like a parent and respect him like a teacher.

Such an emperor, as Wang Xiaoqiu has pointed out, needed to be a firm and activist leader.[63] Yet Kang's approach rested on the assumption that in reality the emperor's powers were always *limited*, not unchecked. Emperors needed to tour the nation, to explain and persuade, to gradually bring the people into the political process through education, and above all to find good men to staff their bureaucracies. It is therefore misleading to assume Kang was merely supporting monarchical institutions as against constitutional ones.[64] In reconceptualizing the state, there were at least two steps Kang saw needed to be taken: first, to build a modern reformist autocracy, and only second, to move on to parliamentarism. In trying to create dynamic leadership out of an apparently moribund imperial court, Kang called on all the resources available to him, including China's golden age. Peng Zezhou has emphasized the resonances between Kang's description of the Meiji political structure and ancient Chinese political forms, a point not neglected by Kang himself.[65] However, for all of Kang's references to the superior ways of the Former Kings, he also studied the modern monarchies of Britain, Germany, Russia, and, above all, Japan.

NEW TEXT VISIONS OF THE STATE

How did Kang inspire the explosion of reformist energies from 1895 to 1898? Partly by his brilliance and charisma; partly by his forced, even arbitrary rereadings of the sacred classics.[66] Though provoking massive reaction, as we will see, Kang's classical hermeneutics inspired his disciples and lent the reform effort a kind of religious legitimacy without which it would never have found a hearing at court. Also, Kang was a master of playing politics at the edges of the system. He refused to work for any of the reform-minded governors, who often hired progressives for their private staffs. For all of his friendships among officials, cultivated with some success in spite of his eccentric behavior, Kang sought to break out of the political channels of the day. In 1895 he organized a petition drive, in the form of yet another memorial to the emperor, protesting the Treaty of Shimonoseki. The petition-memorial was signed by perhaps a thousand aspiring candidates collected together in Beijing for the *jinshi* examinations. This is to say that it was signed by men who had already achieved high status. It was, simply, an act of elite protest, based on the moral stature of Confucian gentlemen.

But the bulk of Kang's time was devoted to textual exegesis of the Confucian classics, creating a peculiar scriptural hermeneutics that justified his faith in progressive reform. Kang made all of his proposals for reforming the dynastic institutions in the name of Confucian doctrine. He was simultaneously working on a detailed scheme for a utopian future that, while leaving anything remotely recognizable as Confucianism far beyond, was still rooted in his peculiar vision of Confucianism. For example, Kang envisioned a future without families, but insisted he was correctly interpreting the prophecies of Confucius. As far as Kang was concerned, he was Confucius's true disciple, and Confucius had been the sage—sacred leader and gift from Heaven, "uncrowned king" (*suwang*)—who left a secret blueprint for the future. In fact, it was Kang who was the prophet.

Kang's reinterpretation of Confucianism, its roots in New Text hermeneutics, and its political thrust are well discussed in the scholarship.[67] Here, it needs to be emphasized that the core of Kang's belief system was simply a faith in progress. This was not the social Darwinist progress-through-competition that so conquered Chinese minds at the end of the century.

Rather, it was generally derived from Western, and specifically missionary, optimism and from Kang's appreciation of the sheer modernity of places like Hong Kong and Shanghai. He saw beyond their fantastic physical plants to their new institutions and even a kind of spiritual modernity. Kang then attached this general notion of progress to a sense of how history proceeded through discrete stages, the specific features of which he derived from Confucian classics. In the distant future, he foresaw the "Datong" or utopian commonweal. Chinese (and others), he felt, were not ready to hear about the Datong, which he began to sketch out perhaps as early as the mid-1880s. But he told his disciples some of what he was thinking by the mid-1890s, and his *Book of the Commonweal* (Datong shu) that we now have was probably mostly written in the early 1900s. We will return to the Datong below; here, the point is Kang's acute sense of the need for each historical age to work out the institutions and social arrangements that are appropriate for it.

The notion that each distinct age has its appropriate set of institutions had been integral to the New Text school of Confucianism since the early 1800s.[68] In brief, the New Text school harked back to an ancient dispute. After the attempt of the Qin ruler to destroy Confucian texts when he came to power in 221 BC, two sets of the classics emerged in the Han dynasty. The "New Text" were written in contemporary characters, based on what scholars remembered. The "Old Text" had allegedly been discovered in their hiding places, such as Confucius's old home, written in pre-Han script. By no means were the textual differences vast; many Han scholars used both, while in time, the Old Text versions tended to predominate. The New Text tradition was more closely associated with mystical interpretations of Confucius and efforts to unearth the hidden meanings of the classics. In this view, the classics were written by Confucius and contained esoteric messages to future generations. In contrast, Old Text interpretations assumed Confucius had mostly "transmitted" rather than written the classics, which were ancient records: sacred in their way but with no mystical significance. As we have noted, with the rise of philological research in the eighteenth century, it was possible to show systematically precisely how much of the traditional canon was written after the postclassical era and therefore *not* by Confucius.

Through most of the Qing, this scholastic exercise did not displace what was essentially a scriptural tradition. Kang, however, stridently attacked the entirety of the Old Text canon in a book published in 1891, *An Examination of the Forged Classics of the Xin Dynasty* (Xinxue weijingkao). It was his contention—not original with him but made into a systematic accusation for the first time—that what generations of Chinese literati had taken as their canon of knowledge for two thousand years was but a set of forgeries designed by Han scholars to support the political usurpation of one Wang Mang, who had founded the short-lived Xin dynasty (AD 9–23).[69] This of course meant that the classics had to be completely reinterpreted, a job for none other than Kang. Then in 1897 Kang published his *Confucius as Institutional Reformer* (Kongzi gaizhi kao), the argument of which is evident from its title. Confucius, for Kang, was of course more than a mere reformer, even a great one like, say, the Meiji emperor. Confucius was the "uncrowned king." But what on earth did this mean?

It meant that Confucius had received the Mandate of Heaven (*Tianming*) to reform the institutions of his day in preparation for a new dynasty. He was the last of the true sage-kings and the only one not to have actually become king. Kang's point was that, if read properly, the classics reveal the future. They describe three fundamental stages of human progress, which Kang associated with primitive chaos, more orderly but still vulnerable forms of political control, and something like utopian consensual democracy. Kang adopted the fundamental notion of progress from the West, but he made sense of it on the basis of two ancient texts. The first of these was central to the New Text school, the *Gongyang Commentary* (*zhuan*) on the *Spring and Autumn Annals* (Chunqiu). Even Old Text scholars believed that the *Spring and Autumn Annals* had been written by Confucius, and hence it was always regarded as one of the classics. By itself, it was an extremely sparse and concise chronicle of the doings of the court of the state of Lu and other kingdoms between 772 and 481 BC. It acquired a number of commentaries, which were read to explain how the entries in the *Annals* reflected Confucius's own moral and political judgments. Of these commentaries, the *Gongyang* was picked up by the New Text school as offering a more philosophical, or at least more esoteric, engagement with Confucius's intentions. The *Gongyang*'s meanings were supposedly encoded in ways only adepts could understand.

By the early nineteenth century, the text was central to statecraft thinking, giving practical thoughts about reviving the infrastructure and reforming the tax system, for example, a philosophical, even metaphysical base. The "esoteric dicta and sublime meanings" (*weiyan dayi*) of the *Gongyang Commentary* left room for creative interpretation. Yet the commentary's judgments also often displayed an acute awareness of political realities and a kind of moral relativism: leaders were expected to understand the trends of their times and act accordingly. For example, in tumultuous times a minister might legitimately betray his ruler if it meant the kingdom would survive. The *Gongyang* tradition also spoke of sets of institutional change (*gaizhi*), providing Kang with a classical rationale for reform proposals beyond his eccentric vision of Confucius. Kang was thus indebted to the notion of the "three unities" (*santong*) that Dong Zhongshu had explicated. The "three unities" linked cosmological forces with historical institutions as well as powerful symbols with their appropriate age and dynasty. All followed the workings of Heaven, and so each dynasty has its own appropriate set of institutions.

But the most useful aspect of the *Gongyang* for Kang was its notion of Three Ages (*sanshi*), into which the *Spring and Autumn Annals* had supposedly been divided. In Han dynasty discourse, one interpretation of the Three Ages emphasized that Confucius had distinguished between an ancient past based on records; a recent past for which he had witnesses; and the contemporary age, which he personally witnessed. In the Gongyang school's theory of history, then, events were transmitted, heard, or seen. Another strand of Gongyang thinking, however, said that Confucius had ascribed historical events to different epochs or ages. The first age was a time of Disorder (*juluan shi*), the second age Emerging Peace (*shengping shi*), and the third age Great Peace (*taiping shi*). This was not necessarily a vision of progress, and New Text adherents of the nineteenth century continued to place it largely within an overall historical framework of cycles or even devolution. It was Kang who insisted that the Three Ages described slow but unending linear progress. Or not precisely unending, since perfection would eventually be reached. Key to Kang's vision was another classical work, the "Liyun" chapter of the classic the *Book of Rites* (Liji), which spoke of the "movement" (*yun*) of the rites (*li*) in terms of two systems that could conceivably refer to two epochs: the Lesser Peace (*xiaokang*) and Datong, which Kang associated with the Emerging Peace and the Great Peace ages, respectively. The "Lesser Peace" described a world where virtue was inculcated and policed, a world, in other words, of brutal rulers and inflexible rituals and rules not unlike our own. The Datong described a time when the "Great Way prevailed": all lived in peace, rulers were virtuous, the strong took care of the weak, and crime was unknown. Again, most readers assumed the Datong might have existed in a better past, while Kang simply turned this schedule around.

As far as Kang was concerned, Confucius had laid out the road to ideal political institutions in his discussions of the ancient sage-kings.[70] The point here is not that Kang's classical hermeneutics were arbitrary.[71] Rather, he combined a rigorous scheme of historical progress with his faith in the prophetic foresight of Confucius. Kang essentially posited a new originary moment in the history of human civilization. There was an ancient and shadowy time before Confucius, but this was a semi-organized society (still in the age of chaos); Confucius himself created order—that is, the "emerging peace"—although this was still not the ideal system. For Kang as for earlier Chinese scholars, political and social organization was marked by order (*zhi*). Assuming that the classics were designed by Confucius to institute reform, Kang did not regard them as a source of historical data. At the least, he thought the details of the systems of the Xia and the Shang dynasties were already unrecoverable by Confucius's time.[72] Thus Kang implied that the supposedly earlier Yao and Shun merely represented the ideas of Great Peace, or democracy, that were yet to be carried out.[73] Indeed, Kang was prepared to begin the story of real history only with Yu and the Xia dynasty, in the wake of the great floods that according to legend had once inundated the land.[74] When Confucius appeared a millennium later, he acted as a de facto emperor by showing how to create proper institutions. In this way, Kang ignored the traditional Golden Age (of the Three Dynasties) and replaced Yao, Shun, the Duke of Zhou, and the other sage-kings with the single personage of Confucius.

In this sense Chinese civilization began with Confucius, whose persona was highly mystical indeed:

Heaven having pity for the many afflictions suffered by men who live on this great earth, [caused] the Black Emperor to send down his semen so as to create a being who would rescue the people from their troubles—a being of divine intelligence, who would be a sage-king, a teacher for all the ages, a protector of all people, and a religious leader for the whole world [that is, Confucius]. Born as he was in the age of chaos, he proceeded, on the basis of this chaos, to establish the pattern of the Three Ages, progressing with increasing refinement until they arrive at universal peace.[75]

On whether the present day was one of Disorder or Lesser Peace, Kang was inconsistent, but his vision of the future was worked out in detail. Kang Youwei's *Book of the Commonweal* is perhaps China's only full-fledged utopia.[76] Certainly, it was the first attempt to work out how a perfectly egalitarian society would function based on first principles.[77] It is difficult to say how his utopianism, which he long kept private with his disciples, related to his political reformism.[78] Nonetheless, at least it is clear that Kang's linear view of history, combined with his fundamental faith in the virtue of cosmic benevolence (*ren*), created a space for utopianism. Hao Chang has pointed to the roots of Kang's moral vision in *ren*, in particular a strand of Confucianism that equated *ren* with Heaven itself.[79] Kang's *Commonweal* describes a stable social order. Notwithstanding his immediate loyalty to the Qing, Kang imagined a future without kings. The Datong was in essence a religious vision, both because Kang believed this progress had been prophesied by Confucius, and because it was imbued with the virtue of *ren*. For Kang, the cosmos was itself moral, and so if progress was conceived as a natural process, it tended toward moral perfection.

Ren could simply be seen as the natural human capacity or tendency to have compassion for all beings. For all beings were equally born out of an organic cosmos, children of Heaven. In the political sphere, egalitarianism was thus the first principle or, as Kang had once phrased it, axiom. The *Commonweal* begins with a lengthy account of human sufferings, ranging from happenstance such as floods, to social conditions such as poverty as well as existential conditions such as old age. Kang then claims that the cause of suffering resides in "boundaries" ranging from nations and classes to species and the transmission of suffering. Abolition of these boundaries will lead to unity, equality, independence, productivity, peace, and joy. The rationality and logic of both the organization of the *Commonweal* and its social conception are striking: Kang moves from individual to family, nation, race, and planet, following the same, relentless, homogenizing move from his basic premise that boundaries cause suffering to his vision of their abolition.

Evolution was the magic carpet of progress. "The evolution of national boundaries from division to unity is a natural tendency," Kang claimed.[80] The innumerable states of China's legendary period had shrunk to three thousand states at the beginning of the Shang, to two hundred or so by the Spring and Autumn period, and so forth. In the future, as democracy spread around the globe, states would form alliances, beginning perhaps with a unified western Europe and a unified northern and southern America, and Russian domination of eastern Europe. World government, democratic and federalist, would ensue. Kang also noted the contraction of the world due to new forms of transportation such as airplanes.

Kang thus explained how the Datong would emerge out of present circumstances, long and arduous though the voyage would be. He did not simply outline an ideal world. The present, however, disappeared in this scheme. Kang discussed the past and the future in considerable detail, but it is as if the present moves by too quickly to be noted. At the same time, of course, the future is not infinite. The moment would come when the Datong is reached. At that moment, time would have to stop, for by definition there could be no further "evolution." This is because *ren* for Kang was a transcendental ideal, and therefore timeless. In the final Datong, although there is some scope for individual differences, there is very little room for accidents or change. And yet this is not entirely true. Kang also proclaimed that one day people would "leave behind" the Datong, that people could leave behind their own humanity to pursue the arts of achieving immortality, buddhahood, and finally roaming the heavens.[81] At this point, Kang is no longer talking about human society at all.

While obviously making a huge break with Confucian society, Kang's *ren* did continue to link him with the universalist assumptions of Confucianism. He had no doubt that moral values rooted in the cosmos applied to all persons. But Kang relativized morality along the time axis, even while this led to the homogenization of identities or the abolition of group "boundaries." This move was made possible, as John Fitzgerald points out, by allowing subjecthood only to the world as a whole.[82] Individuals, nations, and classes possessed only temporary validity as historically contingent subjects. Indeed, it may not even have been the world that possessed subjecthood for Kang. As Hao Chang notes, the cosmos was for Kang a living organism, and hence naturally prone to process and growth.[83] Kang believed that progress moved on both the material and moral levels. Of material progress, few had any doubts after the wonders of the nineteenth century, though the question of moral progress remained open. However, it remains useful to see Kang's ideas as operating on "two levels," not a single continuum.[84] Kang's utopianism served as a critique of his own contemporary society and a spur to work for progress, while his own gradualism was so gradual as to make him one of the founders of modern Chinese conservatism.

There was a link between Kang's version of monarchism and his universalistic understanding of Confucianism. The "emperor" transcended race, nationality, and even territory in Kang's New Text interpretation, and this strengthened a pluralistic "Chinese" identity under the Qing, as Wang Hui has pointed out.[85] Perhaps we can add that in principle Kang was ready to move from a Confucian universalism that still had place for the monarchy to a more transcendent universalism, even while he understood the time was not ripe for this move. In other words, Kang's New Text universalism implied a further project at the level of the world, and even ultimately the cosmos. In this sense, Kang's monarchism and his Datong thought existed in parallel universes, while they were also temporally connected. By justifying reform in universal terms, Kang implied that monarchical power could be unlimited and indeed was rooted in cosmic forces. Yet his vision of the Datong was nothing less than a complete critique of power in all its forms.

∽

Kang's radical Confucian reformism made its last stand in 1898: little notion of imperial charisma survived its defeat, though the monarchy lasted a further dozen years. Reformers—and revolutionaries—turned increasingly to various sorts of secular, popular organization to build a more open and adversarial politics, relocating the myth of sovereignty to "the people." New Text Confucianism came to seem, at best, irrelevant. Kang had pushed the classical tradition to the point it imploded. Skepticism over the authenticity of the textual tradition ultimately left Confucius exposed. And the imperial state was left equally exposed. For Kang's transcendental New Text language claimed to find progressive forces rooted in the cosmos itself. He shifted these immanent forces away from the emperor and relocated them in the historical-sacred person of Confucius. This was a critical step in expanding the scope of the "public" (*gong*), because Confucius had never been the sole property of the state. As we will see in the next chapter, "public" was deeply embedded in reform discourse. Kang next separated the polity from the emperor. It then became a relatively small step for others to separate sovereignty from the emperor and place it in the people, the state, or the nation. These were all realms of the "public."

The reform movement of the 1890s was partly, but only partly, about building up the "wealth and power" of the Chinese state. It was fundamentally about redefining the state. The reformers were capable of advocating strong imperial rule and certainly doubted the ability of the Chinese people to rule themselves. Yet, equally certain, they opposed despotism; they foresaw and promoted democratization. Reformers seized upon the long-standing links between the sage-king ideal and the image of the populace as the foundation of the state (*minben*) in Mencius. Mencius, a leader of the Confucian school in the fourth century BC, taught that the ruler should serve his people on both practical and moral grounds. *Minben* thought could be a weapon for criticizing autocracy, though it could not offer an alternative to kingship. Yet for the radical reformers the historical kingship was also a symbol of the decadence and dissipation of an entire civilization. By historicizing the kingship as they did, the reformers separated it from one of its traditional charismatic bases, that of sagehood. They began to move away from the traditional cosmology.

Yet if the emperor were to become a committee chairman of a desacralized state, what would become of the basis of legitimacy? The failure of the reformers in 1898 thus had an intellectual dimension. In addition to the political opposition of the bureaucracy, the suspicions of the Manchu nobles, and the naïveté of the reformers themselves, reform intellectuals grappled with a fundamental contradiction: they wanted to use the "private" powers of the emperor to create the "public." The strong sage-king promoted by Kang Youwei in the 1880s had shrunk to a relatively feeble symbol by the time the institutional reform movement of the late 1890s got underway. The emperor, as we will further see in the next chapter, was stripped of his sagehood, to use the old Confucian political language. And in a new language of political neologisms and translated concepts, sovereignty was being constructed around the people and the state. The political implications of desacralizing the monarchy were perhaps not all discernible in 1898, but they were soon to become manifest. The new political discourse did not so much *allow* as *mandate* wider policy discussion.

CHAPTER 2

Liang Qichao and the Citizen-State

K ANG YOUWEI'S most illustrious disciple was soon to outstrip his teacher in fame and influence. Liang Qichao was born to an educated but relatively poor family in Guangdong.[1] After an orthodox early education, Liang won the prestigious *juren* degree at 17 and became Kang's disciple. Kang's teachings filled Liang with enthusiasm, opening up a new world. The two men continued to work together from that point to the early 1900s. Something of Liang's precocity—and an attendant superficiality—was to remain with him through the twists and turns of his intellectual life. As he remarked more than once, one could easily refute his new ideas by reference to his old ideas. Yet even as he liked to try new ideas on for size, Liang did not veer between extremes; rather, he tacked through difficult winds toward a consistent objective: strengthening China by building a strong citizenry in a constitutional framework. Kang taught Liang New Text doctrines, the moral imperatives to action of the Wang Yangming school,[2] and the beauties of the Datong future. Kang's teachings became the first basis of Liang's evolving political philosophy, but not the last.

The radical Confucians of the 1890s had taken as their rallying cry: "Protect the country, protect the race, and protect the Teaching" (*baoguo, baozhong, baojiao*). These were somewhat ambiguous, perhaps conflicting goals. The meaning of *guo*—country, nation, state, and mostly plainly *dynasty*—in traditional usage was the farthest from clarity. The reformers were beginning to conceive *guo* as a collective identity, and from the viewpoint of Cixi, say, this implied a conflict between the Chinese and the Qing dynasty. The reformers claimed there was no conflict because the interests of the dynasty and the *guo* were the same. At this time, the basic meaning of *zhong*—race, kind—seems to have been a way to speak of "Chinese" in the most general sense as subjects of the Qing empire, though it too was to open the chasm between Han and Manchu. In any case, from Cixi's

56

viewpoint, again, what mattered was loyalty to the dynasty, not collective identity of any kind. Finally, the *jiao* or "teaching" of the reformers was, simply, Confucianism: but prophetic Confucianism or the Confucianism of the old family-state?

"Protect the country, protect the race, and protect the Teaching." This apparently innocuous slogan represented radical and controversial demands in 1898. Four years later, Liang Qichao rejected it. Or more precisely, he boiled it all down to the singular need to protect the nation.[3] By 1902, Liang thought that "protecting Confucianism" was no longer necessary: a religion or teaching (*jiao*) was something that protected people; it was not something that people protected. More critically, Liang understood that *baojiao* was a response to Christianity that sought to make Confucianism more like a Western religion. He now disapproved of this and had little use for religions at all. They were historically regressive because they had led to unnecessary struggles as well as dogmatic refusal to pursue the truth. In his reading of Western history, Liang saw a historical process in which Christian superstitions were declining as the forces of science and liberty spread.[4] China obviously, then, had no use for such superstitions. Furthermore, Liang proclaimed that one reason for the progress of civilization lay in the intellectual freedom that had emerged since the Renaissance. The religionization of Confucianism was thus neither necessary nor desirable, especially if the figure of Confucius was going to be used to suppress dissent. This was not to abandon Confucianism entirely. Liang claimed Confucianism, properly understood, was at heart ethical philosophy and statecraft (a position farther from Kang Youwei's could hardly be imagined).

Nor was "protecting the race" necessary, Liang proclaimed on even simpler grounds. For "race" was extremely vague: did it refer to the Yellow race or to the Chinese (*Huazhong*)? If the former, then it included the Japanese and other races, and did not amount to protection of China. If it referred to a putative Chinese race, then this was indeed a people suffering from exploitation and oppression, but in what sense were the Chinese a "race"? To protect them was not a matter of racial consciousness. Rather, one and only one thing was necessary: a strong state. To speak of protecting the race was thus superfluous, as this would result automatically from protecting—strengthening—the state.

In this way, Liang walked away from Confucian hermeneutics, even New Text heroics. "I love Confucius but I love the truth more. I love my elders, but I love my country more. I love my friends, but I love liberty more." More conciliatorily, he added, "I also know that Confucius loved the truth, and that my elders and friends love our country and love liberty even more than I do. Thus I am confident and I am also contrite."[5] To set off "truth" and "Confucianism" against each other in this way suggests that Liang was seeking a new epistemology. And indeed, he was never again to offer a proof by citing the classics, even though he continued to find much wisdom in them. Yet Liang hedged this apparent opposition with so many qualifications that we can at most conclude his rejection of New Text was not so much a grand epistemological shift as one of many moments in such a shift that the reform generation as a whole was experiencing. Henceforth, arguments about what should be done had to rest on other logics, not appeals to the classics.

According to Liang's *Autobiography at Thirty*, his first sense of the world outside China came when traveled through Shanghai on his way back home from attempting the metropolitan exams in Beijing.[6] He bought the world atlas *Yinghuan zhilüe*, and he met Kang Youwei. Kang assured Liang that all his old learning was useless. The experience was like having cold water poured over his head. Liang lost his bearings and could not sleep. Formally becoming Kang's disciple, Liang focused on Wang Yangming learning of the mind-heart, history, and some Western learning.[7] Only then did Liang "finally understand what learning was." He read widely, ranging from Buddhism to translated Western works, and developed an ambition utterly new: to become a journalist. With the backing of the reformist statesman Zhang Zhidong, Liang began writing for the journal *Shiwu bao* ("Chinese Progress") in 1896—the start of Liang's long journalistic career—and joined the faculty of the Shiwu xuetang (Academy of Current Affairs) in Changsha, Hunan. There he became friends with Tan Sitong (1865–1898), to whom we will return in the pages below. They discussed Tan's *On Cosmic Benevolence* (Renxue) and studied Buddhism.

Liang's autobiography reveals something of the psychological tensions that the reformers faced. Like Kang, Liang found the demands of filial piety, understood as the most complete expression of personal goodness, difficult to reconcile with public duties. While Kang sought a kind of refuge in indefatigable tourism, Liang often fantasized about escape. He was to lead a life divided between political activism and scholarship. Arguably, Liang was not very successful at either, but he did lead a generation into the thickets of Western learning. Be that as it may, Liang reveals that while he was publicly "loyal" to the Qing, he taught his students at the Shiwu xuetang of the racial differences between Han and Manchu.[8] This was tantamount to saying the Qing was an illegitimate dynasty. Liang furthermore stridently supported democracy and called the emperors traitors (minzei) and killers. In this mood, Liang said China's entire history had produced not a single "true king" (wang) in Confucius's sense and only a few hegemons (that is, strong leaders at least capable of defending the borders and preserving the peace). But just earlier, in the wake of the Sino-Japanese War, Liang had written in a poem: "The emperor is foolish; he does not hear my calls / My high-minded ideas are of no use."[9] This is the voice of the neglected but loyal remonstrator.

Through the 1898 reform movement, Liang continued to affirm Confucianism (baojiao), and maintained a commitment to Kang's vision of universal world harmony. He read early versions of Kang's Book of the Commonweal with enthusiasm, and he was deeply influenced by Buddhism and its promise of universal salvation.[10] However, by 1902 Liang had not only rejected Confucian epistemology, as we have seen, but vehemently attacked universalism in the name of nationalism. In the wake of the 1898 debacle Liang had fled to Japan, and his entire worldview began to shift as he became familiar with the world of Japanese scholarship and Japanese translations of Western works. As we will see in detail below, what was to remain of Liang's Confucianism were standards of personal morality. Liang himself did not know where all this was going, but it is at least clear that his use of Confucian morality was thoroughly divorced from the imperial institution.

ON THE NECESSITY OF THE IMPERIAL STATE

From the mid-1890s to the end of the decade, Liang Qichao used Kang's evolutionary notion of the Three Ages to explain the historical role of the monarchy. Liang had also begun his wide reading in Western history and politics but not yet accepted social Darwinism.[11] Evolution, in Liang's hands, explained how the monarchy had developed. Liang believed that the origins of the Chinese kingship lay not in the Age of Disorder (as had Kang) but with the following Age of Emerging Peace, while democracy would come with the Age of the Great Peace.[12] The earliest Age of Disorder was marked by "multiple lords": tribal and feudal-aristocratic systems. Monarchism represented a higher stage of civilization than did feudalism. Liang completely junked the sage-king founders of civilization, writing in a more naturalistic mode of warring tribal chieftains, cruel lords, harsh punishments, high taxes, a caste system, and even slavery. Confucius, however, emerged to lead China to the next stage of civilization—that is, monarchism. Confucius, according to Liang, had criticized the hereditary lords, promoted independent farmers, and conveyed his future vision of the Great Peace. Liang felt that disunity led to weakness as rulers pursued their selfish interests (*jun zhi siyou*) by encouraging their peoples to fight each other. This is why the unitary kingship constituted at least the Emerging Peace that saw relatively little warfare and other disturbances.

Thus did Liang follow the New Text school's adulation of Confucius, praising the "uncrowned king" for rescuing China from the worst excesses of aristocratic misgovernment, showing how to strengthen the state by recruiting the talented into a civil bureaucracy, and encouraging a smallholder economy that made it all possible. Liang distinguished between sagehood, associated with Confucius, and kingship, associated with more prosaic purposes. Nonetheless, the order-creating capacities of the former were in the service of the latter.[13] According to Liang, Confucius tried to "carry out the affairs of the emperor," though it could also be said Confucius was using the emperor.[14] The emperor fulfilled a specific historical role as the focal point for Chinese unity. By equating monarchism with the Age of Emerging Peace, Liang moved China up the evolutionary scale. The next step was the Age of the Great Peace, which was to say democracy, though it was not easy to say when this step might be taken.[15] Constitutional monarchy stood as a kind of transitional phase between the two, Liang believed, and if China was not on the verge of Great Peace, it was perhaps ready to begin a new transition in that direction.

Clearly, an evolutionary interpretation of the Three Ages provided the basic operating framework of Liang's reformism in the late 1890s. He believed, like Kang, in a kind of historical determinism: there was no use in pushing history faster than it could move, but when the time was right, trying to stop progress was futile. Yet Liang was already working out a new kind of relationship between ruler and people. Democracy was essentially a higher stage of unity, related both to communal property (*gongchan*) and the unity of the masses (*hezhong*). This could take a vaguely racial or ethnic cast. Liang's 1897 essay on "Grouping" began by emphasizing that the ruler should be "a member of the same group as the people."[16] Still, Liang's main point was that once a particular stage was reached, no country could revert to a simpler, less advanced political form. What, then, of contemporary political forms? Was it even possible to determine the historical stage in which China and the world currently found themselves? The vision of a world beyond China was important, for Liang emphasized that the laws of history were universal. Broadly speaking, it made no sense that different parts of the world could coexist in different stages. Thus Liang argued that even republics like the United States and France were not in fact in the Age of Great Peace yet, since major powers like Britain and Russia were still monarchies, and significant portions of the globe remained tribal. The world as a whole, marked by selfish struggles between nations, was thus a world of chaos. The age of Great Peace might be far, far in the future.[17] Westerners realized the virtues of the "public" to a degree, but they were still mired in struggles between nations, families, and individuals. Liang concluded: China needed the West's knowledge of legal matters but the West needed (China's) "sage law" to finally civilize the whole world.[18]

In the meantime, however, what of China's monarchy? When was democracy to replace it? Liang was not to answer these questions directly in the few years leading up to 1898. In fact, he vacillated between sharp criticism of the monarchy and a call for popular participation in government on the one hand, and an appreciation of the special powers of the king and a fear that the Chinese people were simply not ready for democracy on the other. Like Kang, Liang judged rulership on the basis of ultimate or moral standards, but Liang emphasized the "public" (*gong*), which was conceptually related to the practical question of grouping, rather than benevolence (*ren*), which remained open to a more spiritual interpretation. Through the 1890s, Liang maintained his loyalty to the monarchy as an institution, to the Qing dynasty specifically, and to Confucianism (*baojiao*), but his political critique grew increasingly sharp and even bitter.

Liang's case *for* the monarchy was made most convincingly in his first major essay, "General Discussion of Reform," published serially over 1896 and 1897.[19] Here, Liang assigned an essential role to the emperor. This is how Liang chose to oppose conservative prejudice against altering the "inviolable" ways of former kings: "Those who cannot create laws are not sages, and those who cannot act according to the times are not sages." Indeed, this rule applies not only to the founders of new dynasties but to all rulers. Without change, inertia will lead to weakness, but if leaders consider their faults and change, "this is renewal of the kingship" (*si wei xinwang ye*).[20] Like Kang Youwei, Liang emphasized the historical innovations—*in response to the trends of the day*—of dynasts from the earliest times through the Qing itself. Liang considered this responsiveness to be the essence of sagehood, and if Kang claimed Ming Taizu as a sage, Liang added the Kangxi and Yongzheng emperors to the list. Replying, in effect, to the conservative charge that the reformers were slavish imitators of the West, Liang proclaimed that a characteristic of sages was that they felt no shame in learning from others.

Liang's was still very much a top-down vision. It is worth noting that another of Kang's disciples, Mai Menghua (1874–1915), wrote even more explicitly in favor of a disciplinary state. In an essay addressing the question "Should China Follow Monarchy or Democracy?" Mai praised the monarchy as the best way to achieve reform.[21] Mai, who was one of the most active of the reform proponents, argued that the essence of sovereignty (*daquan*) lay in the "ability to create a political system, to establish new precedents, and to kill people or let them live." For Mai, power was indivisible. The key point was not that the Chinese people were backward, though this was a consideration, but that (legitimate) power stemmed from the top, in attending to the needs of the people. Mai's analogies were to the way individuals ran their lives, unless they lost control; or the way family heads ran their families, unless they allowed the servants to take over. When kings command the empire, the people depend on them, but if they lose power, then corrupt officials will emerge and the nation will lack the (sovereign) power it needs to survive. "Democracy," according to Mai, describes the situation when rebels emerge and all seize power for themselves. This disaster occurs when the king neglects his duties and loses or gives up his power.

Mai did not rule out the bare possibility that democracy might be workable, but this required the entire population first be equipped to manage its own affairs. Meanwhile, at least, China needed the discipline of the Western nations with their population registers, efficient tax systems, compulsory education, health and safety regulations, meritocratic civil services, and stable currencies. Mai looked to the West and saw not freedom but efficiency, order, and unity. He looked at China and saw not despotism but laxity, corruption, and favoritism. The Confucian family model of government remained the core of Mai's political thinking. As in the contemporary West, "the Former Kings ruled by taking the people as their children and themselves as parents and taking the people as their students and themselves as teachers." This was the medicine Mai prescribed for contemporary China.

Mai's arguments spoke to critics of reform who feared Western "democracy" would weaken the state. But by stressing the disciplinary nature of the Western state structure, Mai was turning "monarchical power" into a notion of state sovereignty rather than anything specifically tied to a personal imperium. Aside from the single reference to the Former Kings, Mai did not celebrate the monarchical institution in anything like the terms Kang or even Liang used. Liang too favored a disciplinary and educational state, but extended his concerns to broader themes of national unity. Liang demanded cooperation and an end to discrimination between the Manchu and Han peoples. The corollary to this was to end divisions between ruler and people. Both propositions rested on the assumption of the "righteousness of making the empire public" (*gong tianxia zhi dayi*).[22]

In trying to prove that the Manchus had nothing to fear and much to gain from reform, Liang did not treat the Qing emperor as a Manchu king. Rather, the emperor is a kind of embodiment or symbol of the group. The meaning of "group" (*qun*), for Liang, was based more on history and culture than "race." The group was a nation defined by the state rather than ethnicity. Liang praised the putatively reformist tendencies of the present emperor ("sagacious, benevolent, indomitable, and unobstructed") and cited the historical contrast between the English and French revolutions in regard to the monarchy. The English kings—in Liang's view—compromised with popular demands and so the imperial system survived and England had peace, prosperity, and an empire. In France, however, monarchical and aristocratic obduracy led to disaster. In other words, China's national unity depended on reform rather than revolution, moderation and compromise rather than extremism, and monarchism rather than republicanism.

Even as Liang's politics remained cautious, however, his worldview was increasingly radical. Aside from his growing affinity for racial analysis, there can be no doubt that for Liang the kingship had already become attenuated. For all his rhetorical flourishes, and for that matter for all his skepticism about the capabilities of the Chinese people as such, he nonetheless looked outside of the monarchy for the main motive force for reform. Specifically, Liang seemed to place most of his hopes in the gentry-activists (*zhishi*), and a great deal of his "General Discussion of Reform" focused on institutional reforms in education, the civil service, and the role of the gentry. This implied a sense of bottom-up as well as top-down reform. Nonetheless, Liang retained a real fascination with the charisma of the monarchy. He stated that given China's great population, abundant minerals, fertile soils, and intelligent people, "when monarchical power is uniform (*junquan tongyi*), the emperor need fear no obstacles in whatever he wishes to establish."[23] Liang also had to support the monarchy for lack of other options. Democracy or republicanism he considered premature given the backwardness of the Chinese people, whom he called "ignorant" and "weak" though certainly educable.[24] Thus in his short essay "An Examination of Ancient Parliaments," Liang presented the institution in terms long familiar to the reform movement: not as a body that allowed policy to be made by the people but as a technique of "uniting" the ruler and the people in order to concentrate their powers.[25]

Nonetheless, Liang was already indulging in some sharp attacks on the institution of kingship itself, most frankly in a letter to Yan Fu in 1897.[26] Although Liang denied that China's history was fundamentally inferior to that of the West, he accepted Yan's judgment that the reasons for the decline of the "yellow race" boiled down to rulership (*junzhu*).[27] Furthermore, "The strength of a nation stems ultimately from democracy. This is the nature of democracy. Monarchism is simply selfishness (*si*) while democracy is simply public-mindedness (*gong*). Public-mindedness is the ultimate standard of governance while selfishness is rooted in humanity."[28] In equating the monarchy with selfishness, Liang was not saying that selfishness was entirely wrong but rather that private interests had no place in the public realm. As well as signifying selfishness, *si* referred to the entire realm of the self and the private, a realm Liang also wanted to strengthen. Liang criticized a strand of traditional Confucian thought that emphasized the moral value of self-control or "self-suppression" (*keji*), and he noted that selfishness was, after all, natural. He thus urged that a balance be struck between *gong* and *si*. Liang started with the proposition that the Chinese people were still ignorant and aimless. To unify them, they needed to be given a focus, so to speak, that was already popular. Liang remarked that the emperor provided such a focal point in spite of the harmfulness of the institution.[29] But he wanted this focus to be gradually broadened until the people learned to trust the reformers. The implication was that eventually the unified populace would trust and rule themselves. The question was whether under the immediate circumstances it was or was not the historical role of "monarchical power" to transform the people.

The ancient dichotomy between *gong* and *si*—the general realms of public and private—was thus central to Liang's views of the monarchy. But it was also related to another reformist assumption. The reformers tended at times to dismiss China's entire post-Qin history as a kind of wrong turn, a two-thousand-year detour. One point was to use the ancient past to attack the recent past, but more was involved as well. To denigrate the Han and the Tang along with the traditionally despised Qin was to attack, above all, dynastic kingship itself. If the relationship between Confucianism and monarchism had never been entirely easy, still the reformers were attacking imperial Confucianism as it had developed over the centuries. This is, of course, one reason why conservatives and even less radical reformers were so shocked by Kang and Liang. The only kingship that generations had known was at stake. Referring to the pre-Qin past, Liang proclaimed:

"The Former Kings treated the empire as public, and thus did they manage affairs. Later ages treated the empire selfishly, and thus they [merely, at best] prevented problems."[30]

What Liang meant, as he explained in his 1896 essay "China's Weaknesses Are Due to Preventing Problems," was that the duty of rulers was to actively take care of the people, not simply try to maintain the status quo, or "prevent problems." This attitude simply arose from selfishness.[31] As rulers became isolated and ignorant, chasms developed so that the ruler treated his officials like animals and officials regarded the ruler as a mere commoner. For two thousand years, laws became stricter while politics and education declined, and "monarchical power became ever more exalted" (*junquan ze rizun*) as national prestige decreased. People were left helpless; oppressors (*minzei*) intensified their exploitation.[32] The entire system, in Liang's reading, became more and more elaborate, with the emperor isolated from the people and the bureaucrats tripping over one another. The emperor's isolation not only led him to make mistakes but weakened the popular spirit (*minqi*) and the state, leading to the loss of unity (*qun*). Thus Liang despised emperors who called themselves "I the one man" or "I the solitary one" to separate themselves from the people.[33] But he held on to an image of a Golden Age when the Former Kings regarded the empire as a "public realm" and when the rulers of the various kingdoms (*guo*) were close to their peoples but still unified under the Son of Heaven (*ge qin qi min er shang tong yu Tianzi*).[34] Something like this should be revived today, Liang said.

Selfish monarchs produce weak nations, but when the populace exercises its rights and powers (*quan*), according to Liang, it produces strong nations.[35] Such powers cannot be exercised by one person, since no single individual is strong or wise enough for such responsibilities. The "Former Kings" thus understood that equality was essential. Yet, again, Liang did not condemn selfishness totally: it was the monarch who needed to be completely selfless, while the people needed to be "selfish" in the sense they would insist on their rights. Liang derived rights from the Western doctrine of autonomy (*zizhu zhi quan*).[36] He acknowledged that autonomy, with its emphasis on duties and rewards, represented a kind of selfishness. But without this selfishness, citizens would have no basis on which to exercise their rights. As long as no one seizes the rights-powers of others, these rights-powers accumulate to form a strong nation. Such rights-powers should be subject neither to struggle, which harms others, nor to neglect, which harms oneself. If neither the emperor nor the people are willing to assume responsibility, the result is disaster. Yet if one party pushes the struggle for power to the utmost selfishness, this too results in powerlessness.

An even sharper defense of popular power, "Reform of the Various Nations Stems from the People," was penned in 1898 by Ou Jujia (1870–1911), another of Kang's disciples.[37] Without directly attacking the Confucian basis of authority, Ou Jujia offered one of the clearest defenses of popular power. Like Liang and even Kang Youwei himself, Ou cited the advantages of communication and unity between high and low. However, this did not mean that Ou believed China was actually ready for democracy; indeed, he too emphasized the ruler's dual role in taking care of the people and maintaining order. He too followed the hoary family model of government. Ou defined the ruler in terms of his ability to unite the people (*neng qunmin wei zhi jun*). The ruler formed "one body" with the people, representing the collectivity, and was himself *composed* by combining the people (*he zhongmin er cheng jun*), just as in physics bodies are composed by combining particles or as in politics nations are formed by combining clans. At the same time, Ou drew a distinction between ruler and "king." The true king does not actively unite the people but seems to draw them to himself: "those to whom the people come are called king" (*min suo guiwang wei zhi wang*).[38]

Ou's approach to the kingship, emphasizing national integration over the "wealth and power" of the state, came close to Liang Qichao's position. Where Ou went beyond other reformers, however, was in the lessons he drew from China's immediate dire circumstances. If the king had lost power, like a father who could no longer feed or educate his children, the solution lay not in some attempt to revive long-lost institutions but in creating new ones. With proper education and ethics, the people themselves could be energized to renew the nation. Reform in China was the responsibility of the people, not the leaders. Witness the political successes of the West, which were due to its peoples, not its rulers. Logically enough, Ou concluded that the people were therefore to blame for the failure to reform. Ou's was a bleak vision. He took some hope in the historical fact that the peoples of the West were once equally backward, but he noted that Chinese culture could hardly revive while China was being enslaved by those very same Western powers.

Following Kang, then, disciples like Ou and Liang firmly separated sagehood from the kingship. Only Confucius was the "uncrowned king" and sage. At the same time, sagehood remained the goal of good men, and their role was to help the king. Liang exalted Confucius for his attempts to "carry out the matters of the emperor" at a time of general decline, that is, to reform the age.[39] Now, how could Confucius, a mere commoner, speak of such matters as rituals and regulations? Because, being a sage, though writing in a respectful and indirect fashion, Confucius understood the need to save the world from chaos and to clarify universal principles (*gongli*).[40] According to the radical reformers, Confucius sought to influence and "use" the king, but he did not glorify kingship for its own sake. Charges that Confucius sought to usurp power were mistaken—although Confucius surely could have seized power had he wanted to. If reformers were modeling themselves on Confucius, they were promising loyalty to the throne, but a critical loyalty.

For Liang Qichao, both kings and sages were necessary, but it was only Confucius who possessed the "great virtue and magnificent achievements of a founder of a Teaching." Liang also noted that Confucius was a lawgiver. While Kang had praised particular emperors as lawgivers, Liang claimed that Confucius's own greatness resided in his use of laws to establish order in the Age of Disorder, as well as looking ahead to the laws for the ages of Emerging Peace and Great Peace.[41] Today, Liang urged, China needed to pursue the study of the law because it was through laws that the group was linked together to form a political community. Intelligent emperors in ancient times had recognized this truth, but it was a wisdom that had been forgotten after the Qin. Even as the population increased, laws were simplified and no attempt was made to keep them up to date. Turning to the *Spring and Autumn Annals*, then, Liang claimed its emphasis on rites (*li*) was the equivalent of universal principles or truths (*gongli*), which in the West were used to circumscribe power.

Thus for Liang what distinguished Chinese civilization was not the institution of the monarchy but the perfection of sagehood. The sage possessed
many of the attributes of the king. He was a lawgiver and retained great
charismatic powers, influencing events as he recognized and responded to
contemporary trends. Nonetheless, the sage only worked through indirec-
tion, and Liang never imagined that sages were so plentiful that they could
replace real, historical or existing, kings. More clearly than Kang, Liang
linked the Chinese emperor with the nation or "group." The dichotomies
shifted as well. If Kang's emperor was to be *benevolent* rather than *righteous* while Liang's emperor was to be *public-minded* rather than *selfish*,
what change has occurred? The key factor was probably Kang's universalism. Although Kang certainly stressed the need for reforms to make China
strong, he still spoke largely in terms of the universal, cosmic kingship.
Liang, on the other hand, though in the 1890s still devoted to an ultimately
universal vision for all humanity, pictured an emperor more clearly Chinese.

LIANG QICHAO, MEIJI JAPAN, AND BEYOND

Like Kang Youwei, Liang found the very model of the modern monarch
in the massive reforms Japan undertook in the 1870s and 1880s. Unlike
Kang, he remained in Japan for most of the period from 1899 to 1911,
learned to read Japanese, and became personally acquainted with Japanese
scholars and political figures. But Liang's essential opinion of Japan had
been formed by the mid-1890s. In his "General Discussion of Reform,"
Liang had contrasted two sorts of nations: conservative and progressive.[42]
Nations that failed to change—no matter how venerable their civilizations,
notable their past accomplishments, or extensive their territories—would
perish, "gobbled up" by stronger powers. This was the story of India,
the Ottoman empire, Africa, and Poland. Accumulated evils—the weight
of tradition—frustrated reforms. On the other hand, according to Liang,
Russia under Peter the Great became stronger after he traveled abroad
and brought foreign technology back to Russia. Germany was unified
under the Prussian military. And now Japan, in the thirty years since the
Meiji Restoration, had even seized the Liuqiu (Ryukyu) Islands and Taiwan. Liang was saying, in effect, that the Qing's enemy should become the
Qing's teacher. Its recent historical experiences were like China's: it faced

extinction at the hands of the Russians, Germans, and Americans. But unlike China, Japan had recovered through thoroughgoing reform.[43] Change came willy-nilly, but only if people were directing it along the right path could it preserve the country, the race, and Confucianism.[44]

The Meiji Restoration suggested not only a model for practical reforms but an entirely new way of thinking about emperorship. Liang especially admired Japan's modern educational system, but he noted that political cultivation was the true foundation of reform.[45] On the one hand, Liang condemned despotism, but on the other he associated reforms with the renewal of the kingship and extension of its powers.[46] Liang called on the emperor to unite the nation. "Viewed from the righteousness of making the empire public, then all the people of the nation have the duty to love and worry about the nation, and so divisions between Manchu and Han and between ruler and people (*junmin*) are not permissible."[47] Liang was not, of course, publically advocating democracy but rather seeking to remind the emperor of his duty.[48]

Liang's interest in the Meiji emperor lay neither in his political powers nor in his symbolic value, but precisely in his openness to change for the sake of the national community. Liang's sole reference to the Meiji emperor himself in this work comes in a passage equating the Qing's great emperors Kangxi and Yongzheng with such modernizing monarchs as Russia's Peter the Great and Germany's Wilhelm I, as well as the Meiji emperor.[49] Here is where Japan fit, although incidentally, into Liang's larger scheme, derived from Kang Youwei, of the king-as-sage. The essence of sagehood was a kind of active flexibility. Sages act according to the times, they understand the trends of their age, and if necessary they can build new institutions to deal with them. This is the core of Liang's argument against conservatism. Japan's Tokugawa shogunate (1603–1868) should serve China as a warning of the evils of obscurantism, for it fell because the government became isolated from the people.[50] The Meiji's special spirit, in contrast, came from the unifying role of the emperor.

The Meiji proved there was nothing intrinsically "Western" about reform. However, Liang contrasted the Japanese and Chinese responses to the West. The Japanese traveled to Europe to investigate conditions firsthand and applied what they had learned when they returned to their own country, whereas the Chinese traveled to Europe merely to buy off-the-shelf military technology.[51] Similarly, when Japanese students who had been sent abroad for their studies returned home, they were given suitable positions, while in China returning students were slighted.[52] Liang even contrasted the differences between the Japanese and Chinese governments' methods of hiring foreign experts. The Japanese had begun by making greater use of foreign advisers but quickly phased them out, whereas the Chinese continued to find them essential, unable to grasp that the point was to learn from them and then get rid of them.[53] As for the learning of government (zhengxue), Liang believed that a nation with competent generalist administrators would be able to put more specialized talents to good use, while a nation with all the technical training in the world but lacking good administrators would waste that training. On the one hand, this could be read as an attack on the old Self-strengthening Movement of the 1870s and 1880s; on the other hand, Liang was defending traditional education in the classics, philosophy, and Chinese history. Combined with Western administrative methods, these would produce good government. This approach, he claimed, was precisely the foundation of Japan's success. The Japanese leaders had understood that as reform depended on education, so education in turn needed to emphasize governing. In other words, the Meiji reforms had been predicated on the understanding that government and law (zhengfa) were the basis of the nation (liguo zhi ben).[54]

The symbolic functions of the Meiji emperor and his association with the unity of the national community appear to have been equally clear to Liang and Kang. They appreciated that the Meiji emperor's public activities—his tours, encouragement of education and progressive ideals, and meetings with officials and commoners—had all contributed to a Japanese sense of identity and thus to national strength. Like Kang, Liang conceived politics to be the essence of national renewal and the emperor to be the core of politics. True, their search for an activist sage-king colored their understanding of the Meiji emperor, which was also influenced by Meiji's official account of events. Furthermore, if the Restoration formed any kind of blueprint for China's 1898 reforms, it was a fairly hazy blueprint.

Only after the defeat of the reform movement, when the reformers fled into exile in Japan, can they be said to have acquired solid knowledge of modern Japan—at which point they seem to have lost interest. In effect, the reformers of the 1890s constructed an imaginary Meiji: Chinese reformers were already predisposed to Meiji-type reforms, which we might sum up as administrative efficiency and constitutionalism, before they knew much about the Meiji. The failure of the reformers in 1898 was also the victory of the reactionaries, which helped lay the groundwork for the anti-foreign and anti-Christian Boxer Uprising. Though originating as a peasant uprising, it received some support from the Qing court and spread across northern China in 1899. Foreign forces led by the British and including the Japanese suppressed the uprising in 1900 and captured Beijing. The Qing royal house was in great danger. The foreign powers, however, fearing anarchy, came to terms with Cixi. The Qing was to pay an indemnity of 450 million taels of silver as well as submit to a larger foreign presence. It was a great blow to the prestige of the dynasty, but Cixi herself now turned to reform. Ironically, the New Policy reforms that began to be put into place in 1902 were remarkably like the 1898 proposals: modernizing schools and the examination system, streamlining the bureaucracy, and encouraging industry and trade. High officials now looked to the Meiji.[55] By 1905 the court had abolished the exam system and was promising a constitution and local self-government. We will return to those promises— which the Qing was exceedingly slow to carry out—in later chapters. At any rate, there were limits to official reformism: Cixi did not rescind the death sentences that the Qing had pronounced on Kang and Liang in 1898.

After he moved to Japan, Liang wrote extensively about Italy, Poland, even Athens and Sparta, as well as incessantly on China and increasingly on political theory, but not about Japan. The major exception to Liang's apparent lack of interest in Japan was several extensive analyses of Japan's colonization of Korea. This served, as far as Liang was concerned, as an object lesson for China. Liang, then, much as he admired the Meiji reforms, perhaps found contemporary Japanese policies too distasteful to take them as a model. Yet this explanation does not seem entirely sufficient: Liang did continue to admire Japan's constitutional monarchy. Perhaps he thought that after the Qing began to undertake the New Policy reforms in 1902, there was more to be learned from exploring theory than further exploring the Meiji.

It is worth noting that in 1902, Liang wrote a reply to an anti-democratic argument that cited Germany and Japan. According to this argument, the imperial governments of Germany and Japan were closest in form to China, and China could learn from them to suppress democracy.[56] Liang's essential response was to deny his interlocutor's premise that those governments were suppressing democracy. He believed that both were essentially constitutional monarchies. Germany furthermore, Liang noted, was a federal imperium, and sovereignty was situated in its various state nobilities. Indeed, local self-government was the very basis of German democracy (*minquan*).[57] The German emperor exercised some power due to Prussia's domination of the federation. But, Liang emphasized, there was no ancient theocratic basis for the imperial institution. Again, we see Liang's purely pragmatic approach to the monarchy.

As for Japan, Liang saw that power there too lay in the parliament, at least ultimately, not the monarchy.[58] Key to the Japanese system was the vulnerability of government ministers, for all their real powers, to the disapproval of the Diet. For if successive Diets refused to pass the government's proposals, even though the emperor disbanded the original Diet, the government's ministers must resign. Liang concluded that the Japanese people, being relatively backward, might worship their emperor (*junzhu*), but Japan was not an (absolutist) monarchy (*junquan*). He criticized observers of Japan who only focused on constitutional references to the emperor's privileges and "inviolability," for these did not capture the real spirit of Japan's laws. The Japanese reality had been shaped by popular movements that resulted in "shared powers" between the people and the monarchy.

Finally, Liang also refuted the premise that China had much in common with Germany and Japan in the first place. An examination of the "form of state" (*guoti*) of China, according to Liang, showed it to be distinct from both Germany's federal system and Japan's unbroken imperial line. Liang criticized opponents of democracy for not admitting that their real model was that of Russia, where the monarchy was absolute, but also barbaric and unstable. For his own part, Liang optimistically claimed that the "form of state" of China rather resembled the British state. This may seem far-fetched, but Liang was simply touting mixed constitutions, not doing comparative politics. He argued that while democracy limited monarchical powers, it could also stabilize them by sheltering them from political responsibilities.[59] What mattered to Liang was the "rule of law" regardless of the state's political form. Absolutist monarchs seldom if ever live up to their unique responsibilities, and their heirs never do so. Under systems of rule by law, however, all persons possess political rights (*quan*), which act to check one another, thus providing a firm basis for the state. The key lay in the construction of a constitutional system.

PUBLIC AND PRIVATE IN THE POLITICAL ORDER

As we have seen, the notion of *gong* (public, public-mindedness, impartiality, universalism) was critical to late Qing literati.[60] Many radicals looked to a (fantasized) West as the fulfillment of Chinese dreams of a universal commonwealth (*tianxia wei gong*) where democratic practices erased the gap between upper and lower, and society was unified. The "West" in this sense was a synonym for *gong* values. Even for scholars who abhorred or feared the West, the ancient Three Dynasties (*sandai*) offered institutions that could be called democratic, so that *sandai* became another synonym for *gong* values. At the same time, however, the application of principles of evolutionary history or linear time suggested that the *sandai* had to have been a primitive age. Such was the logical conclusion of Kang Youwei's notion of the Three Ages. In the mid-1890s, Liang interpreted social evolution in universal terms, and he thought the evolutionary stages of the Three Ages applied to the West as much as China. While ancient Greece and Rome may have practiced some "parliamentary" procedures, the vast majority of persons were disfranchised, making these societies essentially aristocratic.[61] This is why Liang thought that ancient Western societies, no less than pre-Qin China, remained in the historical Age of Disorder. Thus for Liang as well the point was not the origin of an idea—say, democracy—but its historical inevitability following the laws of progress. Liang's theory of *universal* stages of progress did not postulate that progress everywhere would be in lockstep. There were elements of democracy both in the ancient West and in ancient China, though these were developed further in the West. This approach was taken to its logical conclusion in 1903 by the radicals Liu Shipei (1884–1919) and Lin Xie (1874–1926). Their *Essence of the Social Contract in China* was a tour de force of antiquarian scholarship that took a loose interpretation of Rousseau's notion of the social contract and found it in numerous Chinese discourses on the duties of rulers and the mutual obligations of rulers and commoners across the ages.[62] Liu and Lin were not trying to argue that democracy originated in China, but that it was at least not foreign. And so, given the antiquity and ubiquity of democratic ideas, they could be recovered in the present day.

In the political realm, *si* (private, selfish) marked the opposite of *gong* (public). Liang Qichao was among the first to make this contrast explicit, although it was implicit in writings of the Self-strengthening Movement. Self-strengthening reformers as early as Feng Guifen (1809–1874) and certainly by the time of Wang Tao (1828–1897) and Zheng Guanying (1842–1923) had associated the parliamentary systems of the West with *gong*, and the autocracy of China with *si*. However, the explicit mapping of *gong* and *si* onto politics does not seem to have become a major trope until the 1890s. Liang Qichao developed this line of thought into a general condemnation of the imperial system. As we have seen, in his 1896 essay "China's Weaknesses Are Due to Preventing Problems," Liang had already linked selfishness (*si*) to the monarchy and the monarchy to China's current problems.[63] When Liang associated "the Former Kings" with public-minded (*gong*) rule and their descendants with selfishness (*si*), he was surely deliberately echoing Huang Zongxi. Liang traced a historical process that exalted imperial power, intensified oppression of the people, and isolated rulers from their own ministers. This was the essence of "privatizing" (*si*) the empire.[64] Liang suggested that the individual's rights to autonomy and benefits—as seen in Western theory of rights/power (*quan*)—belonged to the category of *gong*. In other words, Liang distinguished between public (democracy) and private (autocracy). Individuals could be associated with the private sphere, but *in their public capacity*, functioning as a community, they fulfilled *gong* values. In Liang's terminology, *gong* included individual rights as long as these remained within their proper bounds, while *si* essentially represented the same concept of "rights" but as practiced in an aggrandized, monopolistic, and predatory fashion.[65] At the same time, *si* is natural and perfectly acceptable within its proper sphere, just not in the political sphere.

Based on his sense of the political as normatively public, Liang Qichao developed a theory of civic nationalism between 1898 and 1902. This has been well explored in the scholarship on Liang.[66] Here, I simplify the chronology as follows:

1. Between 1896 and 1898, following Kang, Liang was simultaneously devoted to a vision of world historical progress, largely understood through Confucian New Text lenses, and to strengthening China; he was also, more than Kang and somewhat contradictorily, prone to anti-Manchuism and democratic ideas.

2. After the debacle of 1898, in exile in Japan, Liang's political ideas became both more radical and more sophisticated, as he learned more about European and Anglo-American political theory and history through Japanese sources. At least briefly, he became close to anti-Manchu revolutionaries, and drifted away from Kang's influence. However, he also began to develop a "greater Chinese" form of nationalism that was ethnically pluralistic and based on a political conception of citizen participation under constitutional monarchy. Liang thus rejected anti-Manchuism. Social Darwinism had become critical to Liang's thinking, and by the early 1900s he was taking the "nation-state" as the unit of the struggle for survival. The "nation-state" for Liang did not mean a state composed exclusively or even predominately of a single ethnic nation, but a state whose national identity was defined in patriotic and civic terms.

3. By 1903, Liang had come under the influence of the writings of Katō Hiroyuki (1836–1916), probably the most important Japanese political thinker of his day and a proponent of statism (which I discuss in Chapter 3). Reinforcing his opposition to the revolutionaries, statism gave Liang further arguments for the advantages of constitutional monarchism over republicanism. Yet Liang's monarchism, it should be remembered, was in no way based on any sense of the monarch's sacredness; rather, the monarch was to serve the state. Liang also attempted to mesh statism with a vision of civic republicanism based on individuals' participation in public affairs.

I use the term "civic nationalism" to distinguish Liang's views from the republican revolutionaries' anti-Manchu "ethnic nationalism." Liang reconceptualized the empire not as a nation-state but as a citizen-state. He was not only trying to think through the legitimacy of political authority in terms of a binary relationship between the individual (*si*) and the public (*gong*). He also sought to define the legitimate role of *si* as the basis of civic participation.

Perhaps Liang's first attempt to synthesize his new political knowledge after moving to his Japanese exile was an extended series of reflections on the "new citizen." Most of the *New Citizen* (Xinminshuo) was written over 1902 and 1903 as a series of loosely connected essays essentially calling for the Chinese to become more active, assertive, and responsible citizens, capable of contributing to a strong nation.[67] The *New Citizen* advocated a strong nationalist consciousness and the ideal of devotion to group. However, more was at work here than Liang's continuing concern with the Chinese nation. One of the longest essays dealt with the morality of *si*, or what may be best called "personal virtue" (or "private morality," *side*)—in contrast to civic virtue (public morality or "civic virtue," *gongde*). The essay, "On Personal Virtue," appeared late in the series and might in that sense appear to represent a rethinking of the problem. Another essay, "On Civic Virtue," published early in the series, had emphasized his central theme of the individual's duties to the political community.

"On Personal Virtue" did not retract these ideas, but it highlighted the moral responsibilities of the individual to the self, not to the community.[68] In this essay—one of the most sustained meditations on *si* in the late Qing—Liang demonstrated that the moral process he had in mind was essentially a private process. Essentially, Liang was engaged in a tirade against contemporary decadence (which is of course a classic conservative theme), as well as an attack on revolutionaries who favored more radical and disruptive change than he was willing to countenance. Yet he was also exploring the roots of morality in human nature with an emphasis on what we might call training for moral behavior—a training that ultimately depended on the individual's ability to introspect divorced from the concerns of the world and, ultimately, even the judgments of others.

Liang explicitly denied that he had anything to add to the "perfect" understanding of morality of the "earlier sages and worthies" but he seems to have felt that the difficult times needed a discussion that would relate timeless truths to contemporary events. He emphasized that he was not contrasting civic virtue to personal virtue as opposites (that is, in conflict with one another) but that they were complementary.[69] Liang began by claiming that the morality of the group was nothing more than the collective virtue of each member. Citing Herbert Spencer, Liang went on to claim that the basis of the group was the individual. Liang's point was not that the individual was more important than the group but that the group could only be as strong as its members. The properties that describe the group all stem from the individual, and whatever properties describe its individual members describe the group; conversely, the group could not make up for whatever properties its individual members lacked. At this point, what Liang meant by the abstraction "group" was the state. He was thus concerned less with "public morality" as a general proposition than specifically with civic virtue as the proper behavior of citizens. It is fair to conclude that his concern for civic virtue brought him to the problem of personal virtue—but he discovered that personal virtue was hardly a secondary issue. Rather, *side* was not merely the foundation of *gongde*: personal virtues, collectively speaking, *were* civic virtue.

Therefore, if the individuals [private persons, *siren*] lack their own individual moral natures [private moral nature, *siyou zhi dexing*], then even a group consisting of millions of individual members could not possibly possess a public moral nature. This is easy to understand. Blind individuals, if massed together, will not suddenly be able to see. Deaf individuals, if massed together, will not suddenly be able to hear. Cowards, if massed together, will not suddenly become brave. Thus if individuals possess no self-trust, how can they trust others? If individuals are faithless to themselves, how can they have loyalty to the group? This is also very clear.[70]

To bring the point home to the immediate political situation, Liang stressed that if the goal was to create citizens, the first requirement was to "nourish their personal virtue"—and this applied as much to those who would do the nourishing as to the citizens themselves. As Max Ko-wu Huang has pointed out, "for Liang, the mutual dependency of individual values and group values is very largely a question of individual morality."[71] Individuals were in one sense the only source of morality, and so ultimately stood at the base of Liang's political system. But individuals were always and everywhere members of a group.

Morality itself, for Liang, was relational: it arose through the inter-actions of individuals. What encouraged public peace and benefit was moral, and what hurt them was immoral. An individual isolated on an island inevitably lacked morality: moral questions simply did not apply to behavior in this context. Nonetheless, for Liang, the private individual remained the only source of moral behavior. Civic virtue is simply the extension of private morality. Indeed, thinking of the needs of the group, Liang concluded that a society might lack civic virtue, but if personal virtue could be found in abundance, then it would take very little effort to create civic virtue. Conversely, a society whose members lacked personal virtue could never become generally moral. And looking at China, Liang was very pessimistic.

Liang concluded that the Chinese people lacked personal virtue, a lack he attributed to five basic causes: traditional autocracy, modern despotism, repeated military defeats, a poor economy, and a lack of intellectual resources.[72] All five phenomena show Liang's concern with the problem of how individuals construct their own morality. Liang had various targets in mind here. One was the sad state of the backward Chinese people. Another was the virtually criminal state of the Confucian tradition as it was developed by the Qing. And a third was the revolutionaries of his day, whose actions would, he claimed, result in the final loss of China to the foreigners. The revolutionaries, in Liang's view, had gone overboard in adopting Western learning. Their theories of liberty, equality, and competition were destroying public order. They were negating the "national essence" (*guocui*), which Liang believed could temper the excesses of Western political theory. True, for Liang, the ultimate cause of all this awfulness was despotism, which was to say the imperial state of the day. All the same, Liang's new conservatism could not have been clearer. For all his contempt for the old society, he admired Confucian morality and could find no substitute for it. He said that advocates of Western theories—meaning his enemies in the revolutionary camp—were immoral even while they deluded themselves into thinking they were behaving honorably.

This theme of self-cultivation—and the substance of morality—formed the second half of Liang's essay.

Borrowing heavily from Wang Yangming, Liang emphasized that morality was a lonely pursuit of individuals. Yet it was not entirely subjective. He thus began this section by arguing that morality was an absolute necessity for everyone. The point here was that the revolutionaries were claiming (according to Liang) that although they were dedicated to eventual construction, their first task was destruction—for which morality was not necessary. Liang may, deliberately or not, have been misreading revolutionary attitudes, but with some psychological sophistication he pointed out that destruction and construction were in fact intimately related. He implied that even in the desire to overthrow the old system there exist the germs of constructive notions, while he granted that any destruction not simply for the sake of destruction is necessary for founding a new, better system. However, Liang specifically claimed that the revolutionary project needed its own unity and standards, another constructive notion. The greatest enemy came not from without but from within: the weaknesses of the Chinese themselves, which prevented them from unifying. For Liang this was an argument not merely that construction and destruction were interrelated but, as against the revolutionary position, that one must begin with construction (that is, reform). For although it is reasonable to want to destroy corrupt institutions, the slogan of "total destruction"—even if an angry expression not really meant—is dangerous. It becomes a kind of habit imprinted on the brain, and it thus weakens moral controls and ultimately threatens the whole of society.

In other words, revolutionary ideas were not themselves immoral, but the actual existing Chinese revolutionaries, being products of a sick society, were dangerously out of control. Liang thus brought the discussion back to private morality. He remarked that in the past he had not believed that "China's old morality" could encompass the consciousness (*renxin*) of contemporary people. He had hungered to create a new morality to supplement the old (for if revolutionary ideals were not totally wrong, total destruction was simply not necessary).[73] However, Liang emphasized that he had been overly idealistic. The tasks of unification and governing needed three qualities: morality, wisdom, and force. The latter two are easy enough, but morality is difficult. Ultimately, Liang seems to have thought it difficult because of what we might call a series of catch-22's. Given the corruption of the old society, how can proper moral education be instituted? Given the human capacity for self-deception, how can we know if we are really behaving morally? And given the ease with which evil habits can infiltrate themselves into our minds, how can we maintain moral purity in a corrupt world?

While the roots of morality were universal—the freedom of conscience that made morality possible was the same everywhere—Liang specially cautioned that moral *practice* was rooted in local customs.[74] More precisely, Liang believed that the ethics of human relations (*lunli*) were particularistic, encompassed in the larger, universalistic notion of morality. "Ethics" thus changes with the times—the ethics of concubinage, for example—but this does not mean the moral system is at fault.[75] But Liang's main point was that Western scholars offered the Chinese new moral theories but not a new *morality*. Liang emphasized that Western moral behavior was structured around religious teachings, legal institutions, and the notion of honor or reputation—none of which could be imported to China. Western theories could be used in moral education only after citizenship education was well underway. Since citizenship education was itself still far away, China's only option was to resuscitate the old morality. If "total destruction" included the old morality, then it could only lead to self-destruction as it would leave no foundation for future construction.

What the revolutionaries—and all Chinese—needed was a moral commitment to mutual self-improvement. Liang told the revolutionaries to look to the examples of Zeng Guofan, George Washington, and Yoshida Shōin (1830–1859, hero and martyr of the Meiji Restoration). These men accomplished great things while rooted in their moral traditions. Liang stressed that moral education was not a matter of academic schoolwork. Especially insofar as the "new morality" of European thinkers involved reading vast amounts of theory, it threatened to produce pedants who could speak of moral ideas but not behave morally. Moral *theory* could be studied like physics or other branches of knowledge, but morality itself could only be developed through practice. Ironically, according to Liang, Chinese were learning more now but their morality was still declining.

Westerners could use their moral theories to improve their morality, but Chinese still had to use traditional notions to provide a practical basis for actual behavior.[76] Liang mined the orthodox Cheng-Zhu school of Neo-Confucianism as well as the Wang Yangming school to get to his point, the importance of self-examination for every individual.

Liang said that the process of self-examination consists of three steps: "examining the origins" (zhengben), "caution when alone" (shendu), and "care in small matters" (jinxiao). The first, "examine the origins," referred to plumbing the depths of one's own nature and examining one's motives. Liang raised the example of patriotism: that patriotism is right and pure is beyond question, but people who act in the name of patriotism to fulfill their own selfish desires are worse than those who know nothing of patriotism in the first place.[77] In other words, Liang treated the question of motive or intention as the core moral question, explicitly noting that only the individual can truly know his or her motives. At the same time, the individual in question, even if originally acting out of pure motives, may gradually become corrupt and not even realize it. The second, "caution when alone," meant attentiveness to one's daily behavior. Above all, Liang advocated introspection not as passive reflection but as an active process of determining and eradicating one's faults. He said he meant to find a way to foster the individual's innate good knowledge (liangzhi) that Wang Yangming had spoken of.[78] But this was no path to unbridled self-confidence, and the third of Liang's steps, "care in small matters," deepened his theme of caution. It was not that small faults were important in themselves but that, if left unchecked, they would snowball into more general moral corruption.

Readers might have wondered to what degree Liang was transferring his own anxieties to the revolutionaries. Liang himself advertised his approach to morality as the old time religion, but by deriving so many of his views from Wang Yangming, he inevitably raised the problem of individual subjectivity. He had rooted morality in intensely private introspection and self-reform. On the one hand, innate good knowledge represents the worth of subjectivity, as well as the goal of a kind of technology of introspection. But on the other hand, by itself it can only represent the germ of moral praxis, which needs further efforts. Presumably moral theory, the admonishments of parents, teachers, and friends, as well as the "rules" could all help the individual achieve goodness. Yet Liang, although he was simultaneously writing an intensely political tract, emphasized only the individual's lonely pursuit of morality in mental isolation.

～～～

Not Kang Youwei, nor Liang Qichao, but Yan Fu (1854–1921) was arguably the first scholar to attack the monarchy as inherently despotic.[79] He did so on grounds that owed little to Confucianism. Yan was, compared to Kang, more cautious by nature and intellectual disposition: a less speculative thinker but a more rigorous one. He received a classical education in boyhood, but economic circumstances forced him to continue his schooling at the Fuzhou Shipyard's naval academy, where he studied naval science, and also English, mathematics, and the general sciences. In 1877 he was sent to England for further study, where he pursued his interest in political economy and sociology as well as naval studies. Returning to China in 1879, Yan joined Li Hongzhang's brain trust, but was never admitted into Li's inner circle. He failed to pass the civil service examinations, and found his career frustrated. Increasingly radicalized in his political views, Yan nonetheless kept his distance from the Kang-Liang axis, though he corresponded with Liang, as we have seen. Yan was working on his translation *On Evolution* (Tianyanlun), which turned a generation of Chinese intellectuals into social Darwinists. This work—as much commentary as translation—was based on T. H. Huxley's 1893 Romannes Lectures, but while Huxley was concerned to find a way to maintain a place for ethics in a world shaped primarily by purely natural evolution, Yan Fu followed the rigorous amoralism of Herbert Spencer. The survival of the fittest was a universal and impersonal code of Nature. Biological evolutionary theory did not, by and large, shock the Chinese as it had shocked nineteenth-century Westerners through its challenge to church doctrines.[80] That important questions about society were not to be based on morality was harder to digest. But was also instantly convincing.

Even before *On Evolution*, Yan had published a series of essays in 1895 urging fundamental institutional reforms. One of these was "Refutation of Han Yu."[81] The Tang dynasty scholar-official Han Yu was a direct precursor of the Song Neo-Confucians. He spoke out in favor of Confucian orthodoxy and against the Daoism and Buddhism that he saw dominating the Tang court. Why would Yan Fu suddenly go back a thousand years to make an inoffensive Confucian worthy his target? Yan's ire was provoked not by Han's career but by his essay "Yuandao." The title of this essay can be translated as "essentials of the moral Way," or "the origins of the Way," or perhaps even "recovering the Way."[82] For Han wanted to reclaim the Confucian "Way": to defend the sages from Daoist attacks and the ethical relationships (ruler-subject, father-son) from Buddhist attacks. Han argued: "Humankind would have died out long ago if there had been no sages in antiquity. Men have neither feathers nor fur, and neither scales nor shells to ward off heat and cold; neither talons nor fangs to fight for food. And so for this reason, the ruler is the one who issues commands." That is, the people needed to be forced to band together for survival. Han Yu said that the ruler commands the people through his ministers, and in return the people serve their superiors with grains and cloth and other commodities. Or at least that is how it is supposed to be; unfortunately, the social order is collapsing as rulers fail to rule and the people fail to serve.

Han believed that rulership is rooted in sagehood and sagehood in natural principles. This was the "Way" that the Daoists misunderstood. Perhaps Yan Fu was provoked by Han Yu's attacks on Daoism. In any case, Yan used Han Yu's "Yuandao" as a jumping-off point to embark on a bitter and startling assault on the monarchy. What Yan objected to was Han Yu's insistence that "sages" were rooted in the "Way" as a cosmological principle. Rather, according to Yan, sages or rulers and their ministers were simply useful. (Han considered them useful too, but not merely useful.) The first question Yan Fu tackled was Han's version of the origins of civilization. According to Han, before the sages arrived, people were naked, hungry, cold, homeless, threatened by animals, and generally suffering "harm." It was sages who created clothing and housing, tools, rituals and the social hierarchy, music, and trade, as well as government, punishments, and military measures—or in other words, the rulership that required people to work at given occupations for their own good. Here, Yan found several logical flaws in Han's notion of "sages." First, by Han's own logic, humankind should have become extinct before the sages arrived. And second, the sages could not have been human by Han's definition, for then they would have frozen to death or been eaten by wild animals before they had a chance to create their rituals. Furthermore, while Han Yu seemed to be saying that the sages' perfection would gradually permeate and reshape the entire world, only an imperfect world needed rulers at all. If the sages were all Han Yu cracked them up to be, then they would have put themselves out of business. Yan admitted the need for rulership of some kind, but he argued that rulership was not rooted in the Way. Rather, rulership was created by the people for their own convenience. Rulers were, in an imperfect world, indeed necessary, but they were natural only in the sense that they were a product of social evolution.

Really, according to Yan, it was the people themselves who first learned how to plant crops, make tools, and exchange goods. Then, however, they discovered that some people cheated and stole, so they realized the need for administrators. They taxed themselves in order to support a government. The "ruler" thus emerged out of a decision of the people, and when he did not fulfill his duties, they got rid of him. Yan concluded that rulership was a result of "necessity"—the people made rulers because they had to. But it was their rational and reasonable actions that created rulers. Yan implied that the exchange of goods for the ruler's policing and military expertise was at its core an egalitarian relationship. The ruler's sole duty was the protection of the people. As long as there were thieves and bullies, rulers would be needed. But, for Yan, since the Qin unification the monarchy itself rested on thievery and bullying. The state had been stolen from the people. And because the emperors were aware they had stolen the state, they were paranoid that the people would demand it back: hence all the machinery of despotism. And hence the destruction of the natural social bonds that should be uniting the people. The criminal monarchy, precisely by destroying social unity, left the country prey for stronger powers. Yan contrasted China to the Western countries, where he saw that states were the "common property" (*gongchan*) of their peoples and their rulers were merely their peoples' "public servants."

No doubt Han Yu would have replied that he perfectly well understood that rulers indeed had duties toward their people, albeit duties inscribed by Heaven, not stemming from some kind of social contract. But in Yan's view, Han not only failed to understand how rulers emerged from the people, he also assumed that rulers possessed some essential, inherent quality that marked them as such. For Han, it was part of the natural order that rulers give orders and people serve and obey. In Yan's estimation, then, Han could not distinguish between evil rulers and their saintly counterparts like Yao and Shun. Yan claimed that Han had even ignored the Mencian priorities: people first, state second, ruler last. But what really distinguished Yan's vision from Han's was what counted as "natural" (*ziran*). In Yan's usage, *ziran* implied that which was reasonable and logical: a despotic state, in creating artificial hindrances to natural human development, was an unreasonable institution. While obviously resting his argument on a vision of the social contract influenced by Rousseau, Yan here turned to early Daoist texts. He condemned Han's rejection of Laozi's understanding of *ziran*. He also cited the *Zhuangzi*: "He who steals a hook is put to death while he who steals a state is made a ruler." Han Yu had even failed to understand that "the Way ultimately originates in Heaven" (Yan was citing Dong Zhongshu, albeit out of context)—that is, that rulers were part of an integral system of mutual duties and not sacred in themselves. Han's absurd exaltation of the ruler is incompatible with any true conception of Heaven or of the Way. Rulership, in Yan's Daoist reading of the social contract, was "created out of necessity," meaning simply the community's need for protection. It is precisely in an imperfect world that rulers are necessary. Yet the true rulers are the people themselves and the state is their common property, Yan insisted.

This was tantamount to denying the legitimacy of the Qing, as Yan must have known. But Yan, like the 1898 reformers, supported the retention of China's monarchy, if it could be reformed, on grounds that actually shared much with the functionalist side of Han Yu's argument. Yan concluded that it was necessary to retain the monarchy, the bureaucracy, and the basic social order, for the time for fundamental change was not yet right, customs remained backward, and the people were simply not ready for self-government. Yan did not even dare to use the term "constitutional monarchy" to describe the direction that China should head in, though he implied it. He did sketch out the task facing a true ruler: to raise the level of the populace so that in time his job would be superfluous. A modern-day sage would return the people's liberty (*ziyou*) to them, which was after all bestowed by Heaven, allowing them to govern themselves (*zizhi*). The problem facing Yan as it had Kang Youwei was how to imagine a lever for reform. This was a much more difficult task for Yan, lacking Kang's New Text religiosity. It seems unlikely that Yan thought Guangxu could personally lead the armies of reform; Yan's modern-day sage was a rhetorical device.

In the wake of 1898 Yan retreated while Liang Qichao advanced. Essentially, Liang now worked out a bottom-up process of political change. He took elements of Confucian moral training—self-cultivation (*xiushen*) and a type of meditation called quiet-sitting (*jingzuo*)—and applied them not to sages but to citizens. As Chinese society experienced an explosion of study societies and political associations that broke free of traditional hierarchies, Liang anticipated the danger of excessive individualism. The individual naturally represented a private realm, which was thus not a residual category—left over after the public sphere is defined—but an essential part of the late Qing reconceptualization of the political. Nor was the private realm purely instrumental—designed to contribute to group survival and then to be discarded—but rather in Liang's moral vision an integral part of an ongoing political process.

Ultimately, as Mizoguchi Yūzō points out, in the broader political discourse it was *si* and not *gong* that became associated with government, rulership, and officialdom. *Gong* became associated with the people, equality, freedom, and non-official spheres.[83] In other words, the realm of the "public" shifted from the state to the nation, while in turn, late Qing thinkers in general came to associate the institution of the monarchy with *si*, condemning it as "selfish." Yet this move implied that the monarchy was *supposed* to be "public" and thus still rested on the ruins of the sage-king cosmology. The turn from monarchy (*junquan*) to democracy (*minquan*) was based on the concept of "grouping" (*qun*), the innate capacity of human beings to cooperate and forge a shared identity. In Kang Youwei's New Text reading of the Three Ages, a kind of automatic progress promised ever-expanding levels of grouping until the Datong was reached. In the wake of the debacle of 1898 and the unrelenting imperialist threats to

China, Liang could no longer believe this. Rather, he turned to the "nation" as the sole hope for China's survival, survival in a world of endless, brutal struggle. Units smaller than the nation were doomed to perish. Nations lacking internal coherence were doomed to perish. Entire races incapable of self-improvement were doomed to perish. For Liang, New Text Confucianism now described a fantasy, not the world he saw around him. Yet he was soon disenchanted with post-Confucian ethnic nationalism as well.

CHAPTER 3

"Sovereignty" and the Translated State

A FTER THE TURN of the twentieth century, three Western views of the state were particularly important among Qing intellectuals: social contract theory, the organic state, and the sovereign territorialized state as defined in international law. Perhaps none of these views was entirely new. But together they represented a new conception of the state. Late Qing intellectuals understood the state to be a secular human construct, to have in some sense its own goals and even personality, and to exist in a world of other states. The influence of contractarian theory on Kang Youwei, Yan Fu, and Tan Sitong cannot be overstated. Liang Qichao was able to combine contractarianism with social Darwinism's emphasis on competition.[1] In its Rousseau-inspired form initially popular in Japan and China, the social contract stood for the equality of citizens and the notion that the purpose of the state was strictly to serve its members. However, while the social contract describes the origins of the state in a compact made between people and ruler, it says little about how a state should develop. Discussions of what the state *was*, as opposed to how it originated, came to be dominated by political and legal theories of nineteenth-century Europe.

Qing officials by the 1860s had recognized the need for greater knowledge of the international system. This was provided in no small part through the work of an American, W. A. P. Martin, and his team of Chinese assistants, who carefully translated Henry Wheaton's *Elements of International Law* in 1863.[2] The Qing went on to hire Martin to head the Tongwenguan in 1869. Martin (1827–1916) had begun as a Presbyterian missionary but almost immediately after arriving in China sought to open Chinese eyes to all the glories of Western civilization—the sciences as well as the Calvinist God—on the grounds that the former would help lead to the latter.[3] Henry Wheaton (1785–1848) was an American lawyer and diplomat. His *Elements of International Law* was first published in 1836 to immense success, translated into many languages and issued in new editions over the next generation. It is not surprising that Martin would have thought it required reading for Chinese officials. Initial Chinese reception of *Elements of International Law* was skeptical, and its language, trying to convey alien concepts, was difficult. The translation was remarkably precise, but its large technical vocabulary and unfamiliar premises meant Chinese officials at the time relied on oral explanations of the text. But the text, one of the latest and most comprehensive of its day in any language, was eventually absorbed by China's growing corps of diplomats.

For our purposes, the importance of *Elements of International Law* lies in its discussions of the fundamental legal principles that formed the basis of the state. Wheaton did not explicitly follow the theory of the "social contract"; however, he cited a common definition of the state as "a body political, or society of men, united together for the purpose of promoting their mutual safety and advantage by their combined strength."[4] Although he noted several problems with this definition, Wheaton accepted it as a basis for a more precise view of the state. According to the Martin translation, "the original establishment of a state is necessarily derived from the people's obedience to their ruler."[5] At the very least, Wheaton took a secular view of the state: something made by humans for their own purposes. He went on to specify the constituent elements of the state—"habitual obedience" to authority, "fixed abode," and "definite territory"—all of which are necessary before a true state exists. In other words, the state is more than simply any kind of "body political." Wheaton gave four examples of non-states: first, civil associations whose powers are actually derived from the state, such as merchants' groups; second, criminal associations, which lie outside the state's laws; third, nomadic tribes, which obviously lack the criteria of fixed abodes and boundaries; and fourth, nations or peoples (*renmin*), since a state can be composed of many peoples (e.g., the Austrian, Prussian, and Ottoman empires) while a single people might be divided among several states (e.g., the Poles under the Austrian, Prussian, and Russian empires).

The state, for Wheaton, was a special kind of association marked by authority and cooperation, both taking place within precise geographical boundaries. For the purposes of statehood, any particular form of government—as long as there is *some* form of government—will do. Only in

the special case of "absolute or unlimited monarchical form of government" is the "person of the prince . . . necessarily identified with the State
(*guoti*) itself."[6] Whatever its source, whether monarchical or democratic,
rulership is critical. Wheaton defined "sovereignty" precisely in terms of
the rule of the state:

Sovereignty is the supreme power by which any State is governed. This supreme
power may be exercised either internally or externally. Internal sovereignty is
that which is inherent in the people of any State, or vested in its ruler, by its mu-
nicipal constitution or fundamental laws . . . [or] constitutional law. External
sovereignty consists in the independence of one political society, in respect to all
other political societies . . . [or] international law.[7]

The two aspects of internal sovereignty and external sovereignty are clearly
separated in this passage, but these two aspects stem from a single source:
supreme power. And how does sovereignty originate? "Sovereignty is acquired
by a State in cases when the people mutually agree to establish the State."[8]

The principle of independence (*zizhu*) was critical for Wheaton's definition of external sovereignty: "A sovereign State is generally defined to be
any nation or people, whatever may be the form of its internal constitution, which governs itself independently of foreign powers."[9] At the same
time, the concept self-governance (*zizhi*) speaks to the domestic political
situation as well. Although Wheaton denied the relevance of domestic
political forms to the status of the state in international law, a nation that
could not govern itself could not claim to be sovereign. Furthermore, to
return to Wheaton's definition of the state, it seems clear that his notion
of self-governance rested on there being a clear locus of authority or "supreme power." However, Wheaton acknowledged the reality of limited
and qualified sovereignty, and of semi-sovereignty. And he noted that even
among sovereign nations their true power differed. Weaker states were
still sovereign, until the point they weren't.

For Wheaton, this was a rules-based world. States and sovereignty existed only within a legal framework. And how did this legal framework
first arise? Wheaton cited the claim of E. de Vattel (1714–1767) and other
eighteenth-century jurists that international law is rooted in natural law.
While states certainly differ from individuals, "the precepts of the natural

law (*xingfa*) are equally binding upon States as upon individuals, since States are composed of men, and since the natural law binds all men, in whatever relationship they have with each other."[10] Wheaton thus implied that while the state is a human construction and is not rooted in any transcendental cosmological order, humans are themselves bound by natural law. The sovereign state, in other words, is secular but natural.

This chapter examines some of the ways that the Western concept of "state" was translated into Chinese, legal definitions of "sovereignty," and the development of statism in the late Qing. In the nineteenth century, the Qing was drawn into an international system of state relations that was not merely dominated by Western powers but defined by them. The treaty system of the modern world was based on the legal fiction of the sovereign state. In China, struggle was shaped by the logic of Western intramural competition whereby no one country could be allowed to establish colonies or other territorial claims to foreign territories without challenge.[11] By signing treaties, even at gunpoint, the "Great Qing" became a state in the international system.

THE SOVEREIGN STATE IN ACTION

In 1842, the Qing court signed the Treaty of Nanjing ending the Opium War with little idea what it signified to the Western powers. To the court, the treaty was a means of granting some privileges to foreign peoples in exchange for a return to peace, not unlike agreements reached with "rebels" in Turkestan in Central Asia—the last major sector of the Qing empire to be conquered. That is, treaties were a tactic of imperial policy, not an irrevocable promise.[12] It was the Second Opium War, or *Arrow War* (1856–1860), that really established the treaty system in China, and gave rise to Western enclaves, protected by extraterritoriality; open trade in opium; a single tariff tax on all Western imports; formal diplomatic recognition and representation; freedom for missionary activities; and so forth.[13] The Qing state gained a new kind of self-consciousness, or a consciousness of its place in the world. As Dong Wang points out, the lackadaisical attitude of the Qing toward treaty-making in the 1840s and 1850s had evolved into deadly seriousness by the time of new treaty negotiations in the wake of the Boxer Uprising at the turn of the twentieth century.[14]

Treaties constructed not merely a new framework of international relations into which the Qing was forcibly slotted, but a new language of sovereignty. In a sense, the treaties, in using European diplomatic language, created China as a modern state. That is, the "Great Qing" (*da Qing*) was treated as a member of an international order empowered to represent the interests and obligations of the millions of persons within its borders. The West made China sovereign, or at least the "Great Qing" sovereign, according to patterns of sovereignty developed in international treaty-making since the seventeenth century. Of course, there was little pretense that sovereignty meant equality. The Western powers in China usurped many of the functions usually associated with sovereignty, and "international law" tended to connote great power hegemony.[15] Zheng Guanying among others wrestled with the question of China's place in the world. Zheng, a successful comprador and one of the first generation of Chinese to have a real understanding of the West, highlighted the paradoxes of sovereignty.[16] In 1875 he promoted institutional reforms precisely so that China could join the international system, which would protect it.[17] Zheng implied that China's leaders had to better understand that China was but one country among many in the world. Twenty years later Zheng revised his essay. He still urged reform, and he critically noted that the traditional claims to universal rule expressed in the term "all under Heaven" (*Tianxia*) disguised the reality that the world was composed of many different states.[18] But now he also felt that international law disguised the reality that strong states dominated weak ones—he no longer looked to it for protection. Therefore, China needed to become strong; and this was why it needed a parliament to unite people and monarch. From the edges of the literati world, Zheng and a few others anticipated the radical Confucians of the 1890s.

Meanwhile, the fact remained that in international law, if the Great Qing was not sovereign, then it could not sign treaties. It was necessary for the Qing to understand this: the global imaginary of the nineteenth century depended on the mutual recognition of different political authorities, which required a certain common language of state norms or legal frameworks.[19] The concrete agents of the international system (via their delegates) were sovereigns who embodied their states. The Treaty of Nanjing created a formal equality of sovereigns, referring in the English-language version to "Her Majesty the Queen of the United Kingdom of Great Britain and Ireland" and to "His Majesty the Emperor of China." While the Chinese version refers to the "Great Qing Emperor" (*Da Qing huangdi*) rather than an "emperor of China" as its equivalent of the "British Monarch" (*Da Ying junzhu*), it does refer to "China" and the "Chinese" (*Zhongguo, Zhongguoren*) as well. The various Treaties of Tianjin (signed in 1858 in slightly different versions) display similar usages, though the U.S. version refers to the "Empire of China."

Western political language that revolved around the sovereign state was exported to China through imposed treaties, and had profound implications for the relationship between the dynasty and Chinese society. It conveyed a specific view of the state as an independent actor on the world stage. Such states had clear boundaries and continuing obligations. This was a view that seemed to disregard a state's internal politics. However, in both theory and practice, international law had much to say about the domestic aspects of the state. For example, Qing officials soon learned that they needed a foreign ministry and a system of embassies to deal with the foreigners. They also needed more fundamental reforms such as a cabinet system for Westerners to regard them as civilized.

"Translating" the Western notion of sovereignty, then, turned out to be fraught with unforeseen complexities. James Hevia has proposed that translation can be understood "as a special form of violence" or warfare, on the grounds British linguists in China and their political masters used their knowledge of Chinese to advance Britain's aggressive aims.[20] In this sense, Martin's motivations in translating Wheaton fit Hevia's framework of paternalistic and slightly sinister "pedagogy"—the effort to teach the Chinese how to behave properly in the international sphere.[21] But this misses half the story. There is no doubt that foreigners used their knowledge of Chinese to shore up their moral and political position. There is further no doubt that translation was part of a process that weakened the Qing by forcing China into the world of nation-states in ways designed to preserve its inferior status. But the Qing initially benefited from the discourse of international relations, for it ratified the court's sovereignty over China. The "emperor of China" was a new and distinguished position. The language of national sovereignty supplemented existing legitimation techniques among the target audience of officials and elites. The "translated state" was as much the result of Chinese pull as Western push.[22] As we have seen, by the 1860s a growing number of Chinese wished to learn more about how the West worked. By the 1880s, there was a great deal of interest indeed, even if "Western learning" was not quite mainstream. By the end of the century, some of the distinction between Western and Chinese learning had simply evaporated. The Chinese political vocabulary expanded dramatically not through mechanical translation but a process of adapting usage to conditions. The very term for the Western legal-political "*state*" (*guo, guojia*) is a case in point. "State" in modern Chinese was created by repacking an ancient term that meant something like "realm" or even "dynasty." This *guojia*, then, gradually became the primary focus of political concern and the locus of "sovereignty."[23]

However, Western theories of sovereignty ultimately proved incompatible with the traditional state. The Western discourses of diplomacy, international relations, trade, and colonialism were used by Chinese reformers to separate state from both rulers and subjects, or society. The West offered a theory of national representation to replace self-legitimation. "Representation" in this sense does not refer necessarily to democratic practices but to a new set of state claims. Late Qing intellectuals turned the state into an abstraction, reifying it and so distinguishing a transcendentally imagined Chinese state from any actual government.

THE FUNCTIONS OF THE STATE

In spite of abstraction, a state had to do and act as well as be and represent. Wheaton's sovereign state was master of its territory and member of the international system. In another translation, which appeared in 1885, the state was defined as beneficent and progressive. John Fryer and his team translated *Political Economy for Use in Schools and for Private Instruction* by the prolific Scottish brothers William and Robert Chambers.[24] Fryer (1839–1928), like Martin, had begun as a missionary but switched to translation work. While Fryer's own interests were largely scientific, his team's translation of this rather typical example of the new social sciences was republished often through the 1880s and '90s, and its influence can hardly be overestimated.[25]

The Chambers brothers' treatise fit the state into a framework of social progress and had already been well received in Japan.[26] The Chamberses wanted to explain the liberal distinction between the economic and political spheres. The "origins of government" lie in the moment when primitive societies attempt to even out natural inequalities.[27] Inequalities of strength are natural, and in primitive societies, the strong exploit the weak, while equality marks civilized states. Cooperation among people is based on the institution of law, "by which individual rights may be protected" (*geren jie neng zizhu*), including property rights. And "to frame and execute laws, as well as for other useful ends, a *government* becomes necessary; that is to say, a power concentrating the national will and calculated to give it force and direction."[28]

Clearly, *Political Economy* reflected Enlightenment values of rationality and progress. It did not hint at the crueler world of social Darwinism that was to shortly arrive. The Chambers brothers, too, sounded a contractarian note by attributing the origins of law to a combination of "the weak" unifying together to insist on laws. The essence of the primitive state (*yeren zhi guo*) is its relative lack of law.[29] People are left to settle grievances on their own, and the weak suffer. The progress of civilization consists of the progress of law. Civilized states (*wenjiao zhi bang*) have only recently emerged in a gradual process.[30] According to *Political Economy*, the state itself is universal. In the civilizing process, formal laws (*lüfa zhangcheng*) arise out of social customs (*fengsu guiju*).[31] States are thus ultimately based on the customs that regulate social interactions. Even the most primitive societies of today at least have chiefs. From such primitive conditions law and government gradually emerged due to "natural law" (*tianran zhi fa*).

How so? While not neglecting the theme of "conquest," again the Chambers brothers returned to a rough contractarian scheme, for they argued that amid the warfare of small states, the common people followed their best warriors and wisest elders for their own security. Leaders who did not abuse their authority attracted willing followers, and over time social regulations improved. Chiefdom gave rise to monarchism. Ultimately three basic forms of government emerged: monarchy (*junzhu guo*), government of the wisest (*xianzhu shanwei*), and democracy (*minzhu guo*).[32] These basic forms of government can be mixed. It is not so much the form of government that matters. As long as the government satisfies the people, they will follow it. How else will the state be stable? Monarchies can be tolerant if their rule is accepted, while democracies will fall if they lack popular trust. It is precisely a sign of civilization that some rules check despotic power.[33]

The "government" (*guozheng*) stabilizes the opinions of the masses and entrusts them to one person to carry them out. Thus the administration of the state, in addition to pursuing benefit and eliminating harm for the masses, cannot confuse their preferences and violate their wishes. Decision-making must be turned over to one person or a few persons, or otherwise political orders will end in confusion; if governance is chaotic, opinions will be in disarray, and nothing will get done. . . . [But], as long as the government rests on satisfying the people, the state's affairs will certainly benefit the people, and the people will then be happy to follow it, offering their own wealth for the state's use.[34]

In the final analysis, the functions of government are threefold: "to preserve the public peace, to secure the inviolability of the laws, and to conduct the intercourse of the state with foreign powers."[35] Governments should follow policies of light taxes, free contracts, and the protection of property.

The appeal of this book for Chinese readers was not its exact prescriptions for what governments should do but its basic premise: the key to good government was the support of the people. It followed that it was important that the quality of the people be high. Contrariwise, "a totally unenlightened community" will give rise to despotism.[36] And if the people are civilized and moral, then the rulers must be as well, in order to secure popular support. The image of perfect communion between rulers and people had deep resonances in the late Qing. The Chambers brothers then took the next step. They not only linked popular consent to the stability of the state, but also to the state's independence from outside pressures. What late Qing readers read was not the minimal state of nineteenth-century liberalism but a state-society team that would raise the level of the people and so strengthen the state. The greater the civilization of a country, the more its people will obey its laws and happily become dutiful subjects (*liangmin*). "Thus can the foundations of the state (*guoji*) be stabilized. The people of independent states like this will scrupulously follow their regulations, and if another country tries to invade, the people will never accept its rule."[37]

This work had a major effect on the younger generation of intellectuals such as Liang Qichao.[38] However, by the end of the century Chinese were turning to the more numerous Japanese translations of Western works and to the Japanese debates on questions of the state. Japanese scholars, sharing the Chinese ideographic script, had themselves adopted some, though by no means all, of the key neologisms invented by the missionaries.[39] For Chinese interested in political questions, both the Japanese written language (the most important style of which was essentially classical Chinese) and the Japanese experience seemed more accessible than those of the West. Furthermore, by the end of the nineteenth century, Japanese had been debating for thirty years issues that were still new to most Chinese.

In regard to statehood, the Japanese brought three terms into Chinese discourse. First, *shuken* (Ch. *zhuquan*) for "sovereignty" or supreme power.[40] Second, *kokutai* (Ch. *guoti*) to refer to the structure and institution of a state: the politic or, almost literally, "body politic."[41] And third, *seitai* (Ch. *zhengti*), which was originally used by Japanese thinkers like Katō Hiroyuki to signify the "forms of government."[42] Katō and other Japanese political writers recognized such basic *seitai* as absolute monarchies, constitutional monarchies, republics, aristocracies, and so forth. As we will see below, Chinese writers sometimes followed this use of *zhengti* and sometimes instead used *guoti* to delineate forms of government. In general usage, *guoti* referred to whether the fundamental form of the *state* was monarchic (including constitutional monarchies) or republican. *Zhengti* then referred to more substantial questions: whether the state tended to be more or less despotic or constitutional. In other words, the *guoti* might be monarchical while the *zhengti* was constitutional, as in the case of Britain. However the terms were used, they provided a language that was useful for the kinds of political distinctions Chinese intellectuals were making in the 1890s and early 1900s.

Other textual genres that discussed the state in the late Qing included law books. Writings on the law were used in new legal courses largely designed to produce the officials of the future.[43] Law books often began by introducing the topic of the state as the source of laws.[44] They defined the state in terms of people, territory, and sovereignty. The 1902 *General Discussion of Legal Learning* related sovereignty (or the state as "the sole subject of ruling powers," *weiyi zhi tongzhiquan zhi zhuti*) to a notion of the nation: people engaged in mutual cooperation on the basis of common language, customs, and ancestors.[45] The author did not call this condition a "nation," for which several terms might have been used, but rather a "society" (*shehui*—then still an unusual neologism). But the author's point was precisely that mere society (as we understand the concept today) is distinguished from a state by its lack of sovereignty, or a coercive force that requires obedience. Only states can guarantee unity.

States were (tautologically) seen as the "subject of states' rights" (*guoquan zhi zhuti*).[46] The notion of "states' rights" (J. *kokken*, Ch. *guoquan*) was critical to the political debates of Meiji Japan.[47] The notion was not as central to late Qing political discourse, but it did allow the *General Discussion of Legal Learning* to emphasize the distinction between the ruler and the state: rulers are merely persons representing (*daibiao*) the state's rights, and in international situations rulers do not seek their own benefit but work for all the citizens (*guoren*). First, according to the *General Discussion of Legal Learning*, independence refers primarily to the international sphere, but it also has domestic implications.[48] Since, to preserve its independence, the state has the right to a military, it must also have a right to tax its people. It also implies that domestic political change is protected: states should not interfere in each other's domestic affairs. Second, the right to equal treatment rests on the notion that regardless of their differences, all states are the same in their statehood.[49] And third, since both individuals and states are complementary to each other, they must meet and interact.[50]

But how does a society become a state? Here, the author adopted an organic view of the state, citing an entirely natural progression through four major stages.[51] First came an era of patriarchal clans independent of one another; and second, out of their struggles and as populations increased, a higher level of unity and cohesion was achieved in the form of tribes. Rulers and ruled were now separated (in other words, a kind of proto-state emerged). Third, the size and complexity of groups continued to increase, forcing chiefs to delegate authority to sub-chiefs: feudalism, or a kind of quasi-centralized authority. And finally, true unity emerged in the form of the state, out of the struggles that afflicted the feudal system as one leader was at last able to subjugate all the others. This legal text thus made use of a standard social Darwinist framework, which we will see more of below, to explain the emergence of states as hierarchically organized and coercive entities. Nor does social evolution stop with the emergence of the state. Early states had relatively simple institutions devoted to securing domestic order and defense.[52] Today's states, however, are devoted to the public good and are thus much more complex, with organs to encourage economic development, education, public health, and construction of the national infrastructure. They are also expansive, prone to enlarging themselves through colonialism, and ultimately no less coercive than emergent states had been.

It is clear that a nation, no matter how cohesive, does not of itself make a state. States are formed through coercion and obedience. Another legal writer, Wu Renda, simply defined sovereignty as power to rule over the group (*tongzhi tuanti de quanli*).[53] He emphasized that sovereignty is the highest inherent power (*zuigao guyou zhi quanli*), that is, power that is not delegated by another or, within the state's territory, affected by another's sovereignty. And finally, sovereignty for Wu is unitary and indivisible: it cannot be divided, as for example between the people and the ruler, nor is it divided among legislative, judicial, and executive branches, since these are only separate functions of a single sovereignty.[54]

The constitutional activist Yang Tingdong's law book of 1908–1909, *Study of Law*, also emphasized the inherent nature and indivisibility of sovereign power.[55] Yang (1861–1950), having achieved his *juren* degree in the traditional examination system, studied at Waseda University in Japan in the early 1900s and helped produce several translations, including Rousseau's *Social Contract*.[56] In 1906, having returned to Shanghai, he joined the Society for the Preparation of Constitutional Government (Yubei lixian gonghui). Yang was elected to the Jiangsu provincial assembly in 1909. For Yang, the notion of "sovereignty" (*zhuti*) or "supreme power" (*zuigao zhi quanli*) explains the independence of the state.[57] He thus linked the notions of domestic sovereignty and international sovereignty. Supreme power does not simply refer to omnipotence, but rather it is composed of three main elements. First, it is the only *indivisible* power; second, in the domestic realm, it is the *source* of all other powers; and third, in the international realm, it is equal to all other sovereignties: all sovereign states are "independent" (*duli*) and free from outside interference. Sovereign power is not the collection of various powers together; rather, its "supremacy" lies in its uniqueness. Yang attacked Montesquieu's "separation of powers" theory on the grounds of the indivisibility of power in the case of the state. What Montesquieu was referring to, said Yang, was merely the separate legislative, executive, and judicial functions in the hands of a single sovereignty. In other words, there should be no question of checking and balancing but only a single purpose.

But what is the state and where does it come from? Yang Tingdong's discussion of the origins of the state was less historicist than that of other authors. He highlighted two main schools of thought about the state: the concrete and the abstract. Concretely, a state is an "association formed by humans coming together" (*renlei jihe tuanti*). It possesses "a certain people," "a certain territory," and "inherent powers" (*guyou zhi quanli*) or sovereignty.[58] Not all human associations are states. Clans and corporations lack at least one of the three necessary features of the state. The requirement to have "a people" seems obvious: no people, no state. The concept of territory is a little more complex. Medieval and ancient states were not necessarily based on a particular territory; rulers were rulers of particular peoples. Yang dismisses the argument that power alone can constitute a state. Obedience to orders, he says, cannot constitute a state because this would make nomadic tribes and even pirate bands into "states." Rather, the state emerges as cooperation among humans begins to progress. So far, so familiar. What Yang stressed was the centrality of sovereignty as a unique kind of power.

The establishment of the state requires a certain order. If there is no order, then even with a certain people who live in a certain territory, no state is yet formed. But a certain order requires inherent powers before it can come into existence. The inherent powers domestically guarantee the peace of the populace and internationally protect from enemy invasion. This is generally called "sovereignty" (*zhuquan*). Without sovereignty, a state will disintegrate with no hope of recovery. Therefore, all states require inherent powers.[59]

What made Yang's views distinct was his insistence on the theoretical primacy of the state, regardless of its historical origins. Yang stressed that the state is prior to the laws. That is, the state creates the law and is not created by the law.[60] His point in this passage is that the state cannot be defined as a "legal person" (*faren*) parallel to the concept of the legal person in private law. However, it is acceptable to say that the state has a legal personality (*ren'ge*).[61] Both associations, whose powers are derived from the state, and the state itself have legal personality in public law (*gongfashang zhi ren'ge*). Yang thus stressed the complexity of the modern state, even while insisting that its sovereignty is indivisible.[62] States are assembled out of smaller associations (*tuanti*) but, we might say, the whole transcends its parts. Yang granted that associations—local governments, commercial organizations, charitable societies, and the like—are all "subjects of power" in their own right. But their status as "legal persons" is derived from the state and their powers limited and provisional. Ultimately their goal is not the private benefit of the group but the general interest of the state (*guojia zhi gongyi*).

How could the state have a legal personality but not be a legal person? The distinction is a fine one, but seems to stem from Yang's acknowledgment that the state is inseparable from the law, even while prior to it. Indeed, he defined law as precisely "regulations enforced by the state."[63] Yang's view of the state was thus derived from what he called the "abstract" school of thought. He maintained this view has much in common with the concrete view, but that it treats the state more as a legal concept. The reason why Yang denied that the state is a legal person, then, was because this would imply that the law created the state rather than the state the law.[64] Yang held that the state is distinct from both legal persons (local government bodies, voluntary associations, corporations) and individual persons, on the grounds the state does not have rights but possesses power. Indeed, states are virtually the opposite of persons. Persons are subjects of rights in civil law (*minfa*), but states are the subjects of inherent power in public law (*gongfa*). It follows that the legal meaning of the state never changes. Regardless of any particular state's form of government (*zhengti*)—monarchy, democracy, aristocracy, parliamentarian—its state-ness never changes. Essentially, Yang agreed with the view of the state as the "subject of power" (*quanli zhi zhuti*): it has agency just like legal persons. But only the state is the "subject of inherent ruling powers" (*guyou tongzhiquan zhi zhuquan*).[65]

If the state is the supreme "subject of power," what are the objects of power? They are that which obeys (*fucong*). In private law, the objects of *rights* are "property" (*wu*), and by analogy in public law the objects of *power* can also be called "property." However, in fact the objects of power are a little more complicated, and their nature depends on the particular subject of power. In the case of the state, the objects of its power are its territory and its people (*renmin*). The objects of local governments are similar to the objects of states: property rights and human rights. The objects of public associations are their own members.

Yang also dismissed the theory that the state is a kind of organism (*jiti*). The notion of the organic state has some metaphorical use, he said, but there are important differences between the state and an organism.[66] Yang attributed the organic theory of the state to the Swiss-German jurist Johann Kaspar Bluntschli (1808–1881).[67] Yang read Bluntschli to say that the different organs or institutions (*jiguan*) of the state have different functions, like the different organs of the body. Developing from individual cells, then, ears, eyes, and the various organs all contribute to the development of the whole organism. The advantage of the organic state metaphor, for Yang, was how it highlighted the common goal of different elements. Precisely because he insisted on the indivisibility of state power, he did not disagree with this aspect of the organic theory of the state. But he did not think it could explain the various historical shifts experienced by states, presumably referring to the dramatically different forms states developed over time. It is not clear whether Yang understood that the organic state for Bluntschli was a historical theory. Bluntschli thought the state's development and growth parallels that of an organic life form. Yang seemingly saw states as undergoing repeated vicissitudes rather than development.

In thinking about rights, Yang distinguished between public rights (*gongquan*) and private rights (*siquan*).[68] The latter refers to individual relations such as those regarding kinship and property, while "public rights" refers to the individual's relationship to the state. Public rights thus include "liberty rights" (*ziyou quanli*) such as freedoms of religion, speech, publication, assembly, and association, as well as rights to political participation through elections. Yang pointed out that the latter rights are sometimes termed "political rights" (*zhengquan*) and are limited to citizens. Private rights, however, can be held by foreigners in the form of "individual rights" (*geren quan*) as well as by citizens. Indeed, "as civilization has been advancing in recent times, transportation and communication improving, and different nationalities living together, the scope of citizenship rights is shrinking as that of individual rights expands."

All late Qing views of the state shared an emphasis on territoriality and sovereignty. And this approach formed the basis of Liang Qichao's reconsideration of the state. Liang's mature statism was probably, in spite of the growing clout of the revolutionaries, the most influential political theory in China in the years preceding the 1911 Revolution.

LIANG QICHAO: TOWARD STATISM

From the late 1890s through about 1902, Liang supported a Rousseauist view of the social contract that emphasized that a legitimate state must be essentially democratic. Then from about 1903, Liang turned to a "statism" that emphasized the authority of government.[69] As scholars have long pointed out, Liang wanted to promote nationalism and nation-building throughout both periods. But his goal was to create a people who would be worthy of citizenship. That is, in the final analysis he derived the people from the state rather than from nationhood defined as commonalities of blood, language, and culture. From the beginning of his journalistic career in 1896, Liang proclaimed that the Chinese state was weak because the Chinese people did not understand what constituted a state. This was not their fault. In an essay written in 1899 Liang contrasted the wars of monarchies, wherein kings forced their peoples to fight one another, with the wars of citizens (*guomin*), in which people understood they were members of a state fighting for their own lives and property.[70] In 1901, Liang argued that the root of the problem lay in China's long history of powerful dynastic states. Patriotism can only emerge out of struggle, but the Chinese disdained their weaker, or at least culturally backward, neighbors.[71] Liang was saying that by regarding their civilization in universal terms, the Chinese could not even understand statehood. Another problem, then, was that the monarchy's monopolization of the public sphere prevented the people from identifying with the state.

Liang presented a vision of the social contract gone wrong in the originary moment in which states arose out of clans. When clan leaders became kings, their relations with the people changed from that of putative
kinship to that of master-slave. As slaves, the people could not interfere
in matters of state and eventually did not even want to. Liang contrasted
China's decadence to the West, where the state is "shared" between ruler
and people.[72] Liang's binary approach to Chinese and Western political
forms may seem to be a form of self-Orientalizing today, but it provided
a powerful rhetoric of self-critique. At this point, he was essentially saying that only a democratic state counted as a true state. He began with a
standard view of the origins of the state—"when people come together
to form it" (*jimin er cheng ye*). But this is to say the people are managing
their own affairs, and state power (*guoquan*) rests directly on democracy
(*minquan*). And if democracy is destroyed, the state cannot survive.[73] So
in Europe, in Liang's view, an essential democracy was maintained even
in monarchies, since the state was not privatized but maintained as the
"public utility" (*gongqi*) of the people. This is not to deny the West suffered from tyrants, but Westerners (unlike Chinese, that is) have recognized
tyranny for what it is and fought for liberty.[74]

Writing in 1900, Liang defined statehood in the familiar terms of territory, population, and international standing.[75] He simply noted that three
forms of government (*zhengti*) dominated the world at the time: autocratic
monarchism, constitutional monarchism, and constitutional democracy.[76]
Of the major powers, only Russia was an autocratic monarchy, and only
the United States and France were constitutional democracies; the rest
were constitutional monarchies. In Liang's view, constitutional monarchism was the best form of government, because democracies tended to
be unstable while autocracies tended to be oppressive. A constitution is
the basic law (*xiandian*) that is never changed and is obeyed by all, including monarch, officials, and people; it is the source of all the laws and
institutions of the state; and all laws and orders must be in accordance
with constitutional principles. Constitutions serve to limit the powers of
all the organs of government, including the king, officials, and the people
themselves. Liang thus envisioned a political system of mutual checks but
also mutual support.

In 1901 Liang reiterated his despair over the lack of "national-ist"—or civic or "statist"—consciousness (*guojia sixiang*), analyzing in greater detail than previously the reasons for this deplorable situation.[77] Liang essentially traced the traditional universalism—or China's lack of rivals—to geographical and historical factors. And he again complained that emperors had "privatized" China and enslaved the Chinese people— to the point that they did not even have a name for their country (*wu guohao*)![78] Liang meant that China had always been called by the name of the reigning dynasty, which collapsed the state and the dynasty together. Historically, in spite of interruptions, long periods of political unity had given the Chinese a very weak sense of nation. Now, however, China was under threat. "The national consciousness of the people is an important element in the protection of the country (*guo*). The development of the state (*guojia*) and the perfection of its administrative organs both depend on it. Without nationalist consciousness, the state will decline and fall, even if its territories be large, its population great, its military strong, and its wealth great."[79]

At this time, Liang wrote brief critiques of Hobbes and Rousseau, which allow us to locate him on a map of Western views of the state. Overall, Liang was dismissive of Hobbes, seeing him as a spokesman for the kind of absolutism he thought was holding China back and seeing his ideas as overtaken by more recent trends in political theory.[80] (When Liang turned to statism in the following years, he found a guide in Bluntschli, not Hobbes.) Liang understood Hobbes's view of the social contract to be rooted in his strict materialism and belief in the human calculus of goodness/pleasure versus evil/pain. Hobbes thus equated natural morality with the pursuit of self-advantage, according to Liang. And so the social contract arose as a purely utilitarian or pragmatic step representing self-interest. Liang was not entirely convinced by either the social contract or such rigorous mate-rialism.[81] But he acknowledged that the state, whatever its origins, acted to tamp down the tendency of people to mistreat one another; the order that resulted from unity in this sense was a matter of need, not morality. Liang also noted critically that for Hobbes the social contract, once established, is irrevocable; the law thus becomes an instrument of coercion—and limits the rights of future generations.

Liang compared Hobbes's views on human selfishness and morality with those of Xunzi. Xunzi had also held that people needed strong kings, and that they needed rituals to restrain their selfishness. Liang found the biggest area of difference between Hobbes and Xunzi was in Hobbes's theory of the social contract, while Liang still preferred Xunzi's notion that the norms of state order were created by the sage-kings.[82] For Liang rejected Hobbes's thoroughgoing amoralism, and he found abhorrent a social contract that rested on reducing humans to their desires.[83] Furthermore, Liang held that Hobbes's belief that only despotism could maintain the political order ignored the reality that the despot's unchecked powers must lead to much evil. Rather, Liang said, even if we grant that people only pursue their own self-interest, it is still the case that only free institutions will create a system of mutual checks to preserve order.

Liang was much less critical of Rousseau.[84] Above all, he saw a positive progression from Hobbes through Locke to Rousseau. Liang did understand that Rousseau's version of the social contract was not meant to be history but rather a philosophical truth (liyi) or, as Kant had noted, a theory of the state. The state was not literally formed by free agreement among previously unattached individuals, for in reality persons had long had no choice but to live together. The roots of the social contract rather lay in the natural emotional ties among family members, which carried over into tribes and ultimately states. We might call this a Confucian view of cultural evolution. Liang found an element of liberty informing an implicit "contract" among people forming a state. He emphasized that for Rousseau the essence of the social contract lay in the equality of the members of the state. Unlike the Hobbesian social contract, which rests on individuals giving up their rights, Rousseau's social contract protects the liberties that make us human. At the same time—and this remained a notion dear to Liang's heart even after his conservative turn—people have the responsibility to protect their "liberty rights," which are the basis of all other rights. Furthermore, he noted, there can be no morality without liberty, since moral standards apply only to people who possess decision-making capacity. Yet Liang saw a contradiction at the heart of Rousseau's thesis. For Rousseau too says that while people cannot relinquish their rights to other people, they do relinquish them to the state. This is how the state becomes a "common political form" (*gongyou zhengti*), but in that case, whence liberty?[85] Nonetheless, Liang found much to admire in Rousseau, including his faith in equality, which does survive the social contract intact.

Liang's views of the state were in flux: was it servant or master? The notion of the organic state, greater than the sum of its parts as Rousseau already seemed to hint, was increasingly appealing to him. At this time, the greatest influence on Liang's thought was Katō Hiroyuki, translator and explicator of Bluntschli. In 1901 Liang offered a systematic comparison of Chinese and Western conceptions of the state.[86] He used an outline of the differences between modern and traditional Western concepts prepared by Bluntschli, adding China to the mix. Bluntschli's was a progressive view of Western history, from theocracy and feudalism to democracy and law. In Liang's view, if the traditional European view derived the state from God while modern Europeans thought that the people created their state, the Chinese state was established for the emperor. And if Europeans believed kings were God's representatives on earth but still subject to the law, Chinese believed the emperor is not the representative of Heaven but is given a trust by Heaven and stands above the law.[87] Borrowing Mencius's distinctions between people, ruler, and state, Liang concluded that eighteenth-century Europe had placed the ruler first, the state second, and the people third; the nineteenth century had placed the people first, the state second, and the ruler third, while the twentieth century was giving the state itself priority, followed by the people and the ruler.[88]

The contemporary Western state thus seemed the most "complete" or progressive form of the state. State-priority was also related to a shift Liang saw in the nature of nationalism: from ethnic nationalism (*minzu zhuyi*) in the nineteenth century to national-imperialism (*minzu diguozhuyi*) in the twentieth. He meant a kind of imperialism backed by popular mandate in the colonizing power, not simply the aggrandizing activities of a ruler. By the logic of social Darwinism, imperialism too was progress, though it was a threat to China. Nationalism itself was unproblematic. "Nationalism is the brightest, greatest, and most just 'ism' in the world," Liang declared.[89] Nationalism implied respect among nations that did not invade one another. It also implied democratic norms domestically. However, whereas old-fashioned nationalists thought the state served the people, imperialists wanted the people to serve the state: the group was more important than the individual. China's problem was not that it had failed to become an imperialist power but that it had not yet even gone through the stage of nationalism.

Liang then noted two opposing theories of the state.[90] The first, associated with Rousseau, emphasizes equal powers (*pingquan*): the social contract, human rights, individual autonomy, and limited state powers. On the positive side, this theory provides a motive force for nationalism, increasing the strength of individuals and thus helping the progress of the group; on the negative side, it tends toward anarchism and damages the social order. The second theory, associated with Herbert Spencer, emphasizes coercive powers (*qiangquan*): evolution through struggle, the rights of the powerful, natural inequality, state survival through struggle, and unlimited government. On the positive side, this theory helps establish state institutions and protects the group; on the negative side, it is the motive force of the new imperialism, disturbing world peace. Liang rejected this coercive statism, but he was unable to return to egalitarianism.

STATISM UNBOUND

In 1903 Liang published a brief translation of Bluntschli that marked his complete turn to statism.[91] Liang thenceforth preached the doctrines of the organic state, defined the essence of the state as coercion, and even saw a role for "despotism" in reforming China. He treated China's major problem not as tyranny but lack of unity. Liang's version of raison d'état clearly placed the collectivity above the individual. "Sovereignty" lay in the state itself, which thus possessed something like transcendental characteristics. Bluntschli's writings met his new need for a didactic state. Liang no longer believed democracy promised national unity and strength. So, channeling Bluntschli, Liang now argued that a social contract à la Rousseau suffered from three problems. First, it leaves citizens with the right to dissociate themselves from the state; but if people can leave it, it is a voluntary association and not a state. In other words, Rousseau fails to distinguish associations (*shehui*) from citizens (*guomin*).[92] Second, Rousseau called for equality; but in sheer practical fact, every state is ruled by a minority. And third, although Rousseau himself recognized that unanimity is impossible, the social contract does not allow for majority rule. Rousseau may have met Europe's needs, but China today needs organic unity and coercive order: liberty and equality are secondary.[93] The Chinese were still basically tribal and needed to become national (*guomin*).

By *guomin* Liang meant an identity defined by the state. He saw that Bluntschli's insistence on the distinction between the nation (*minzu*) and citizens gave him an argument against the ethnic nationalism of the revolutionaries. Citizenship is derived from the state. This holds whether the state is defined as a "personality" (*ren'ge*) in an organic sense or as a legal group (*fatuan*) determined by law.[94] Sovereignty lies only in the state, never in a nation. Neither can sovereignty reside in a monarch or any other head of state, nor yet society. Using the same language as Yang Tingdong albeit in a different context, Liang concluded that, as established constitutionally, sovereignty is completely public power (*gongquan*), never private (*siquan*).[95]

But most critical for Liang was the notion of the "organic state." That was to say the state is more than a chance assemblage of people, more even than simply a government: it is a human-constructed entity with its own will (*yizhi*) and praxis (*xingdong*). Like persons, states link spirit and form; the different parts of government function through limbs and organs, which combine to form a whole. What the state is not, then, is a machine. Neither its capacity for growth nor its response to outside stimulus is machine-line.[96] But as an organism, the state is only as strong as its weakest member. As a body needs strong limbs, organs, muscles, and blood, so too the state needs a people who are educated, progressive, and courageous.

As for the "goal of the state," Bluntschli noted two contrary views, both of which Liang thought were partially correct. If the state's goal resides in the state itself, then the state is the master of the people, who must sacrifice their interests for it. (Think Rome.) But on the other hand, if the goal of the state resides in its citizens (*guomin*), then it becomes a mere tool for furthering the interests of private persons. (Think modern Teutonic peoples.) Generally, there should be no conflict: the happiness of the people and the state go together: when the people are intelligent, the state is civilized; when the people are brave, the state is strong. However, sometimes the two goals of the state may come into conflict. In that case, ultimately the state is primary, and it can sacrifice people's property and lives to save itself. In this case, the state must act impartially: it may not abuse its powers, but if it does so, people have the right to oppose the state and protect their liberties.[97]

In his *New Citizen*, Liang returned to the emergence of the first state, suggesting that as tribal society developed and formed something like governments, it engendered consciousness of the state, which in turn led to the formation of full-fledged states.[98] He concluded with a rousing image derived from an ancient Chinese trope: the state is our parents—we depend on our fathers and mothers for our very survival.[99] "State consciousness" consisted of the state's relationship to the individual, to the imperial court, to foreigners, to the world. The first factor of state consciousness, the individual, depends on the capacity of humans to group together and cooperate in the division of labor. In a sense, humans had no real choice: the only way to survive was to devise institutions of mutual benefit. Recognizing that the individual depends on the group, the individual is prepared to benefit the group.[100] Second, according to Liang, the court is like a company's management: the management should not confuse itself with the company—as Louis XIV had proclaimed, "I am the state"—but the company still needs management. Cutting through Liang's metaphors, his point was simply that as long as the court was the legitimate representative of the state, patriotism encompassed the court.[101] But this was also to say that loyalty (*zhong*) was ultimately owed the state, not the ruler.[102] Third, the notion of foreigners was critically important to any concept of the state, since a sense of identity is only formed vis-à-vis others.[103] Fourth, and finally, Liang contrasted the reality of the state to the myth of world harmony. States exist precisely because the world consists of struggles between groups, which fosters progress. The state is simultaneously the largest form the group (*tuanti*) can take and the point of highest struggle. Utopian visions of world harmony simply weaken the state (here Liang was attacking both traditional Confucian universalism and the anarchist vision of voluntary cooperation).[104]

In his essay on "rights" (*quanli*), also a part of the *New Citizen* series, Liang was entirely unsentimental and had no truck with theories of naturally endowed rights; rather, he understood rights as inherently human and ethical, and thus playing out in the social sphere. The point is that rights are also inseparable from the state: "When partial rights are gathered together, they form the rights of the whole, and when the rights consciousness of individuals is amalgamated, it becomes the rights consciousness of the state. If we want to create this kind of consciousness, we must start with the individual."[105] Thus as the citizenry consists of individuals grouping together, so state authority (or state rights, *guoquan*) consists of the amalgamation of individuals' rights.[106] A state is only as strong as its people—and the rights of the people determine the rights of the state.

Liang's fear of Chinese "individualism" and clannishness on the one hand, and transnational cosmopolitanism on the other, were not new themes in 1903. Nor was his separation of the state and the ruler. In 1903, however, Liang looked a little harder at the Chinese intellectual tradition. Chinese had lived through something like Europe's national struggles— but in the Warring States period over two millennia earlier. Facing chaos, Confucius and Mencius had sought to return to one king, a world order, and the Great Peace. These beliefs were a kind of overcorrection in Liang's view. Later dynastic rulers had been able to use such "scholars' theories" to legitimate their rule. The people saw the emperor not as their representative but as the representative of Heaven.[107] And even at times of disunity, the Chinese had turned to their villages and families rather than the state: the result was 400 million little states today.[108] What was needed for China to survive today was nothing less than a change of consciousness.

"Liberty," for Liang, was a concept that could apply to both individual and collective bodies. As Wang Hui has pointed out, Liang's precise interpretation of liberty depended on his reading of the political situation, and Liang recognized that the differing situations of Europe and China meant that liberty would perform different historical tasks.[109] We might say Liang's liberty was defined by its functions. Liang did not disdain individual rights, but he emphasized the immediate importance of what are now called positive liberties, particularly the right of political participation, based on the equality of all citizens. The vessel for this was the state.

Overall, Liang favored a strong state but opposed autocratic rule. He did publish, in 1905, one essay promoting "enlightened despotism" that treated the essence of the state as coercive (*qiangzhi*).[110] Coercion is inherent in all rulership, regardless of institutional or legal framework, though from an equally realistic point of view all power is limited in practice.[111] Coercion is necessary because of the need to respond to two kinds of struggle—the struggle between states that Liang had previously emphasized and the struggle within states that he was now beginning to fear. Coercive rule maintains in-group unity; social harmony is not natural, *pace* Laozi, Zhuangzi, and Rousseau. In other words, society does not precede the state but is dependent on it. Echoing the Chambers brothers, Liang said that the state marks an inequality of rulers and ruled, but without the state, society would create even larger inequalities. The state functions to protect the weak and mediate conflicts. It can do this precisely because it stands above society.[112]

Liang's call for "despotism" can best be understood as part of his growing reaction to the spread of revolutionary thought, but it was also a result of his exploration of statehood as informed by social Darwinism. But Liang was not looking for a despot so much as noting the inherently despotic nature of the state. He stated that it is acceptable to speak of popular sovereignty in the case of republics, but the people are in fact exercising sovereignty on behalf of the state, and the "highest sovereignty" (*zuigao zhuquan*) remains in the state.[113] In other words, Liang recognized a real distinction in how despotic and non-despotic states were run.[114] But all states focus power.

At the same time, Liang claimed that as long as the state is a legal person, it should not be considered truly despotic.[115] As organic legal persons, then, like all groups (*tuanti*), states have their own natures and personalities (*ren'ge*). The state transcends both its ruler (*junzhu*) and the people as one body (*yiti*). It represents the highest achievement of humanity. Liang's point was that while the powers of the state are unlimited, the powers of its rulers—as natural persons—are still limited, limited by the state. Japan was Liang's example of a constitutional state where the "ruling powers of the state" (*guojia tongzhiquan*) itself were unlimited but the rulers, as private persons, had only limited powers. Despotic and non-despotic states alike participate in the same coercive essence of rule (*zhi*): "exercise of power in the formal restrictions of a part of people's liberties." The question is the harm done in a despotic state when the ruler completely monopolizes all the organs of state rule and completely distances himself from the people.[116] Or even when the ruler acts in arbitrary ways while lacking complete power. This was Liang's way of referring to Qing China's "incomplete despotism." This was to say, China had the worst of both worlds—a government with all the faults of despotism and none of the strength needed to accomplish anything.[117]

At this point in Liang's argument, readers might be nodding in support of democratic reforms that would help build both legitimacy and reform. But that was not where Liang was going, at least not immediately. Rather, China needed a strong government capable of unifying the people and compelling sacrifice. Granted, it should encourage moderate internal competition, but this too required a strong government to mediate among its citizens. What China needed, then, was nothing short of despotism. But it had to be a despotism entirely severed from the ruler's personal desires. Individual liberties were to be sacrificed, but only for the very survival of the state (*guojia zhi shengcun*).[118] The organs of the state, having been made effective, could act quickly to benefit the state and the people.[119] Liang's support for despotism was hardly unqualified; he saw its dangers. But given China's political realities, especially the outside threats it faced, he argued that good despotic government or "enlightened despotism" was needed to create a strong state that could adapt and survive.[120]

Liang argued that political power wanted to be unified (*zhengquan zhi yu quyu yi*). True, constitutional systems are inherently non-despotic, and were particularly designed to break up the power of traditional monarchs. But even in constitutional countries, power tends to concentrate in the hands of a few leaders in the executive or party leaders in the parliament.[121] Liang differentiated his theory of enlightened despotism from that of previous thinkers, both Chinese and Western.[122] Of ancient Chinese political thought, Legalism came closest to the Western notion of the sacrality of state power (*guoquan shensheng lun*). Liang found that the Legalists' emphasis on the importance of centralized control of a single ruler was like modern European theories of the state. When Liang turned to Western tradition, he found enlightened despotism from Aristotle to Machiavelli that, developed by Hobbes, became the basis of modern statism (*guojia zhuyi*).[123] The sixteenth-century French monarchist Jean Bodin, in Liang's words, taught that "the sovereign (*zhuquanzhe*) is the highest power of ruling over people, and cannot be restricted by law. This power is essential to an independent state; the existence of this power is precisely the symbol of the independence of the nation (*guomin zhi duli*)." Furthermore: Bodin's sovereignty lies in the ruler (*junzhu*) alone. Thus Bodin proclaimed that "the ruler is the master of the law" (*falü zhi zhuren ye*). Bodin's sole difference from Machiavelli, in Liang's view, was his insistence on retaining the ruler's moral responsibility. Liang then turned back to Hobbes, crediting him now with a formal logic that proved enlightened despots should have absolute power.[124] Liang now looked favorably on the Hobbesian social contract as a trade-off. Individuals sacrificed some of their own liberty, giving it to the ruler, who in return guaranteed order. But order was never Liang's ultimate goal, and his Confucian individualism reasserted itself in his praise for the German philosopher Christian Wolff (1679–1754), whose theory appeared even more advanced to Liang because it emphasized the state's role in promoting the development of the individual. Each individual has a duty to develop his or her own body and mind, and cannot interfere in others' development. For Liang, this brings liberties back into the equation, although in the sense of positive freedoms (self-development) as well as negative duties (against hindering the development of others).

It seems to me that Liang did not precisely see the state as a moral and political organization,[125] but rather as a form of "grouping"—to use his earlier New Text language—that transcended morality and even, in a sense, politics. Morality operated at a different level. In 1910, as the Qing was, however reluctantly, preparing for a constitutional transition with provincial and national assemblies, Liang again turned to a consideration of the state.[126] One cannot understand constitutional government without first understanding the state, Liang proclaimed. But the state is complex and cannot be reduced to territory, people, and ruler.[127] First, the state is not merely territory. The land has existed since the beginning of the world, but not so "China" (*Zhongguo*) or the state (*guojia*). Also, states change their territories. Second, the state is not merely its people. The older European notion of the state as "formed by amassing people" is false, because it turns the state into a mere collection of individuals. But just as piling objects together does not make a new whole object, amassing people is not enough. And third, an emperor does not make a state. If he did, then republics would not count as states, which is clearly absurd. Furthermore, it would imply that the state ceased to exist every time an emperor died, but this is also absurd. Liang further, and more radically, pointed out that the state, at least in the case of China, survived the fall of dynasties as well as the deaths of individual emperors. Without clearly defining the origins of China, he noted that there has been the "same state" for two thousand years. In sum, territory, people, and some highest organ are all necessary to a state but insufficient to make a state.

What, then, makes a state? It is "a grouping of the people (*renmin tuanti*) based on coercive organization in a certain territory."[128] So, first, territory is necessary: and it must be reasonably *stable* territory; pastoralist nomads are by definition not capable of making a state. Second, people too are necessary, but they do not need to be bound by ties of blood. As long as they dwell together in a territory, a naturally formed group in some sense sharing their fortunes then can be called a people (or *Volk, guomin*). Third, there must be coercive power (*quanli*)—this is what Liang took away from his earlier thinking about "despotism." Since conflicts among people are inevitable, there is a need for order that can only be provided through command and obedience. "Power" is defined by people having no choice but to obey; in the case of the state, power is called "dominion" (or sovereignty; lit. ruling power, *tongzhiquan*). Without such ruling power, there is no state; and conversely, only the state can possess that kind of ruling power. Individuals acting on their own behalf never possess it, but they may exercise coercive powers when they act as agents of state organs. And fourth, the state must possess unity-as-one-body (grouping, *tuanti*).[129] Liang was here reiterating the organic theory of the state.

This view of the state again brought Liang to the distinction between body politic (*guoti*) and government forms (*zhengti*). The *guoti*, according to Liang now, refers to the highest organ of the state, generally defined in terms of the political systems of monarchy, aristocracy, or democracy. Today, however, aristocracy has virtually disappeared, so only monarchy and democracy remain. Liang again stresses that merely knowing whether a country is a monarchy or a democracy tells you little about how power

actually operates there.[130] In this sense, a knowledge of the form of government tells you more: above all, whether the institutions of the state operate
in a despotic or a constitutional manner. The question is not whether there
exists a written constitution or even a parliament but whether in fact the
organs of state administration provide some kind of check on each other's
power. Liberal Liang was back. Or was he?

In the immediate wake of the disaster of 1898, Cai Yuanpei not only moved
in a democratic direction but completely secularized the state:

A state is like a company. The people are its shareholders while the emperor is its
manager. The lords and officials are all appointed by the manager to assist him.
The shareholders provide the capital to run the company, and the expenses and
salaries of the managers all come out of these funds. But since the Qin and the
Han, the managers daily steal the capital for themselves, trick the shareholders
into supporting them, and have completely seized the company for their own
purposes.[131]

Cai (1868–1940) was serving as a Hanlin Bachelor at the Qing court; he
was sympathetic to reform but he had kept his distance from the Kang-
Liang radicals. As Cai's biographer Chaohua Wang suggests, this view of
the state may have reflected Cai's merchant background.[132] Cai's strikingly
casual secular image of the state is certainly worth noting. As we have
seen above, Liang Qichao was also to compare the state to a company:
the imperial court was like the management, while the emperor served as
its director.[133] But Liang, though criticizing autocracy, did not pursue the
analogy from the point of view of the "shareholders"—he put the responsibility on the court to represent the nation. Cai was beginning to look to
the people while Liang looked to management. In sum, by the time of his
"conservative turn," Liang was skeptical of democracy, or at least of the
Chinese people's capacity to practice it at the moment. But more importantly, he combined social Darwinism and an organic theory of the state
to place the state clearly above society and individual. States have their
own purposes, and cannot be reduced to the private interests of anyone,
including the emperor. States are transcendent persons (not machines).

They are fragile. They must be protected from their own people as well as outside threats. States need a capable, competent citizenry. In return, states nourish and protect their citizens. The interests of a given citizen and the state largely correspond. Liang was skeptical of revolution, democracy, and the revolutionaries, whom he thought were immature and ignorant—yet the revolutionaries, while more optimistic about developing democracy in China, shared Liang's fundamental presumptions about the nature of the state.

The Revolution of 1911 was to usher in several stormy decades of attempts at state-building, all of which took for granted that the state was transcendent and irreducible to private interests. Praise for despotism no matter how "enlightened" was uncharacteristic of Liang and he was soon to make another one of his famous changes-of-mind and return to the camp of constitutionalism. He was even to support republicanism once the Revolution actually occurred. But the sort of transcendental state he described had wide appeal. Perhaps the revolutionaries took a different road to the same destination. Later chapters will describe the revolutionaries' visions of the state. First, however, the next chapter examines the enemies of constitutionalism and the basis for their fear of political change.

CHAPTER 4

Voices of Receding Reaction

"CHINESE LEARNING for the essence and Western learning for its utility" (*Zhongxue wei ti, Xixue wei yong*)—a famous prescription written by a famous statesman, Zhang Zhidong. Zhang wrote it in 1898 to simultaneously encourage reform and restrain it. Actually, his prescription had long become a fact: that is, to be considered educated, knowledge of the classics was necessary but no longer sufficient. The logical incoherence of Zhang's formula has also long been obvious; perhaps less obvious is that it was not a bad description of a lived historical process. By 1898, however, the two spheres could no longer be kept separate.[1] Zhang's language of essence or substance (*ti*, lit. body) and utility or function (*yong*) drew on a millennium of philosophical discussions. But in the traditional view, *ti* and *yong* were different aspects of one thing, not distinct things themselves. Indeed, relentlessly rejecting Zhang's formula, Yan Fu pointed out the problem in so many words. He insisted:

Essence and utility refer to a single object. The body [essence] of an ox is the utility of carrying burdens, while the body of a horse has the utility of traveling far. I have never heard of using the body of an ox with the utility of a horse. The difference in Chinese learning and Western learning is like the difference in the appearances of Chinese and Westerners: one cannot arbitrarily call them the same. Thus Chinese learning has its own essence and utility, and Western learning has its own essence and utility. While they are separate, they can coexist, but if they are combined then neither will survive.[2]

Even more boldly, Yan made a double claim: that science is universally true, and that Western governance is based on science. However, neither of Yan's claims was widely accepted. Western learning, including political concepts, was gradually accepted piecemeal. Western claims to universal validity were particularly subject to challenge. Late Qing conservatives responded to Kang-Liang radicalism with a major pushback in the late 1890s.

This chapter examines their defense of orthodox Confucian morality. In the end they were defeated more by circumstances than radical arguments, but Confucian morality was able to evolve into the twentieth century.

CONFUCIAN REFORMISM

First understudy to Li Hongzhang, then rival, then in effect Li's replacement as the most powerful voice for reform in the Qing court (Li died in 1901), Zhang Zhidong was a true scholar. In this, he was more like Zeng Guofan than Li Hongzhang. As governor-general of Hubei and Hunan, Zhang built new schools and infrastructure, encouraging the development of a relatively isolated region. But he was always concerned with the moral basis of the polity he wished to reform, and he opposed any reform that might challenge the social or political hierarchies. When Yan Fu's refutation of Han Yu was published in a journal that Zhang personally sponsored—and that his enemies might use to attack him—Zhang's first response was pure horror.[3] Zhang, whom Yan had once looked to as more committed to reform than Li Hongzhang, ordered the editor to apologize, and he organized a rebuttal to be written by the censor Tu Renshou. Tu's rebuttal granted that there were imperfections in Chinese culture and some things might be learned from the West.[4] Nonetheless, the reformers were going much, much too far. As for Yan Fu's criticism of "Yuandao," Tu also granted that Han Yu's essay was not perfect, as Cheng Yi and Zhu Xi had noted long ago.[5] But it was, as Zhu Xi said, essentially correct. This meant that Yan Fu's views completely twisted right and wrong. In particular, for Tu the ruler-subject relation was rooted in the cosmos (Heaven), as was the entire hierarchy that it stood at the top of.[6] To speak, as did Yan, of the differences between honorable and base as "arising out of necessity" was perverse. Tu claimed that the Son of Heaven became ruler by possessing the empire and all his subjects, just as the feudal lords became the rulers of their individual kingdoms, within which all were their subjects, and the great ministers, whose family members were their subjects, and so on down to the scholars and commoners, who were "masters" in their own, smaller spheres. Tu had a top-down vision that encompassed the world in nested hierarchies, while he said Yan Fu pictured the cosmic order from the bottom up. But if the people regarded their superiors as merely fulfilling the functions of protecting their lives and property, then they would regard Heaven in a similarly utilitarian fashion. They would even think they had created Heaven instead of being Heaven's creation. This, of course, seemed utterly absurd to Tu. For Tu, the nested relationships of the natural hierarchy were by definition ethical. So Yan Fu, in reversing the order of these relationships, was condemning humanity to immorality. In Tu's reading, Yan believed superiors must respect their inferiors, who would then condescend to their masters. Yan thought that officials were selected from the elders, lords from officials, and the emperor from the lords. Yan's immorality stemmed from his denial that human relationships were rooted in the cosmic order.

Tu Renshou believed that Heaven and the emperor did function to love and protect the people, but this was due to their very nature, not because the people selected them to carry out these tasks. Heaven is the source of humanity, not merely a guardian deity. According to Tu, Confucius had already understood the basic importance of "wealth and power," but unlike the Westerners he also understood their moral basis.[7] Yan is drawing the wrong lesson from Japan's defeat of the Qing. The Japanese are not successful because of any democratic ways they might possess but because of their good leaders. In fact, while the Japanese are basing reforms on the (Chinese) classics and official dynastic histories, too many Chinese are degrading their own sages.[8] If, instead, China followed the kingly way (*wangdao*), both "wealth and power" and humanity and righteousness (*renyi*) would follow.

Yan Fu never replied directly, but at the beginning of 1898 he wrote another essay in the guise of advice to the emperor. It can be seen as his rebuttal of Tu's points. Yan made the by-now-familiar case for institutional reforms, though without any New Text dressing.[9] Yan looked to the emperor to rally the forces of reform, and suggested that the essence of rulership lay in the ruler's resolution and bravery. He urged Guangxu to tour the West, in order to improve relations with the Powers; to gain popular support and shrink the gap between ruler and ruled; and to deal harshly with official stagnation, incompetence, and obstructionism. Yet Yan still attacked the notion of "sage-emperor." He said that while the Way never changes, institutions (*fa*) constantly do.[10] This Way, however, is not a matter of Heaven or emperor but rather the survival of the group (*qun*). The constant virtues—benevolence, loyalty, fairness, shame, and so forth—have a purpose. Yan was perfectly happy to sound Confucian: if the emperor was to learn the will of Heaven (*Tianyi*), he had to look to the people. But it was not difficult to discern Yan's radical utilitarianism behind this classical trope.

Finally, Zhang Zhidong himself took to the field. He wrote *Exhortation to Learning* in 1898 to steer a middle course between reactionaries and progressives.[11] This work was disseminated widely by government offices and private publishers all around the country. Notwithstanding Zhang's genuine commitment to reform, his loyalty to the imperial state was absolute. He supported the emperorship and its role in the polity, society, and the cosmos; he opposed "democracy" and "equality" utterly. It does not require a teleological theory to conclude that Zhang was both a reformer and a reactionary in the heated political conditions of the late Qing. This was also true for many others of the scholars considered in this chapter, who were literally reactionary in the sense they sought to maintain traditional ways in the face of threats, as they saw it, to the social order, yet supported certain sets of reforms. It was not that Zhang never regarded the state itself as the highest good. Rather, the preservation of the state (or dynasty, *bao guojia*) was justified because it encompassed the two other critical goals of preserving Confucianism and the Chinese race.[12] The distinction between Zhang and the Kang-Liang school, which Yan Fu had brought into the open, was that Zhang believed the imperial state was the bulwark of the social system, and that both were rooted in the cosmic order that the classics had described for all time.

Zhang used chain logic: the race depended on wisdom—that is, the correct Teaching (Confucianism)—while the Teaching in turn depended on the state. His counter-examples included a strong state maintaining an unreasonable Teaching (the Ottoman empire's support of Islam) and a reasonable Teaching declining without state support (a weak India unable to support Buddhism). In this sense, strengthening the Qing was not Zhang's ultimate goal, but it was inseparable from preservation of the Chinese people and Confucianism. In fact, Zhang claimed the foundations of the Qing were deep and stable, protected by Heaven.[13] He praised the Qing's benevolence and accomplishments—for example, its low taxes and judicial mercy proved its superiority to previous dynasties and, for that matter, the West.[14] The Qing was precisely heir to a tradition whose strength lay in combining the "Teaching" and politics.[15] For thousands of years, Zhang said, the sacred Teaching had flourished without change, resting on the unity of kings and teachers (*yi jun jian shi*) and guiding governance (*yi jiao wei zheng*). The Qing, with its special efforts to support Cheng-Zhu orthodoxy, edit the classics, and purge heresies, represented a kind of acme of the unity of the Teaching and governance (*zhengjiao xiang wei*).

And what, at root, was the Teaching? For Zhang, it lay in the ethics of the Three Bonds: ruler-subject, father-son, husband-wife. The Three Bonds were simultaneously a political, a social, and a moral prescription. In a flurry of classical quotations, Zhang concluded that it was the Three Bonds that defined both the sage and China.[16] People respected those whom they should respect and were filial to those whom they owed filial piety.[17] From Zhang's point of view, the Kang-Liang camp worshipped the West and denigrated China, wanting to abolish Confucianism and the government. He had even heard that in the treaty ports some people openly advocated abolition of the Three Bonds. Actually, such persons had not only turned their backs on morality, they failed to understand the West.[18] In the political realm, the West was not egalitarian but recognized natural hierarchies.[19] For example, even in parliamentary systems, some kind of supreme figure (king or president) represented the ruler-subject bond. And in nonpolitical realms, the Ten Commandments marked Westerners' respect for filial piety, as did their mourning rituals (even if they lacked ancestral halls and tablets), and thus they recognized the parent-child bond. And since Western women could not be found in public office, parliament, the military, or the labor force, Zhang concluded Westerners had some conception of the distinction between men and women. This was tantamount to recognition of the husband-wife bond.

Though Zhang favored strong government, his political philosophy was nothing like the statism being developed by Liang Qichao and Yan Fu. Ironically, it was perhaps closer to Kang Youwei's Confucius-as-reformer that Zhang so despised as uncanonical. But Kang could imagine a world of equality and liberty that he thought Confucius had prophesied. For Zhang, only loyalty and righteousness could unify the empire (*zhongyi haozhao he tianxia zhi xin*). And the strength of the Chinese could only be unified under the court's awesome power (*weiling*). "This is the unchanging and eternal

Way, the principle universal in the past and today, in China and abroad," he noted.[20] "Therefore, knowing the ruler-subject bond means that democracy cannot be exercised; knowing the father-son bond means that equal punishments, the abolition of mourning, or the elimination of sacrifices cannot be undertaken; and knowing the husband-wife bond means that the equality of men and women cannot be effected."[21] The pursuit of democracy would lead directly to social disorder and chaos.[22] The common people, doing fairly well under the Qing, would be the first to suffer; ultimately, the foreign powers would take advantage of China's domestic disturbances to take over the country. And precisely because the Qing practiced benevolent government, Zhang triumphantly concluded, "democracy" and the violence associated with revolution were simply not needed.

In any case, according to Zhang, the true meaning of "democracy" only encompassed parliaments as an expression of public *opinion*, not a means of exercising power. Similarly, Western theories of "autonomous rights" (*renren geyou qi zizhu zhi quan*) properly referred only to the religious notion that God gives every individual some intelligence and knowledge. While the West had not benefited from the wisdom of Confucius, neither had it been so crazy as to really pursue egalitarian and democratic social doctrines. Rather, in the West, as in China, there were clear distinctions between ruler and ruled. Indeed, even thieves had their chiefs. If "autonomy" were practiced in the social realm, selfishness would rule. People would favor their own families and villages, the strong oppress the weak, merchants exploit the poor, the poor rob the righteous, inferiors disobey their superiors, students disrespect their teachers, and so on. Particularly worth noting, I believe, is Zhang's prediction that sons would not obey their fathers or wives their husbands. We will see more of this in the pages below. Through the Three Bonds, the patriarchal family remained inextricably tied to the state formation.

Zhang's opposition to democracy was less about specific political institutions and more about his fear of egalitarianism. Granted, Zhang did not merely attack the immorality of democratic and egalitarian ideas. He also made the case that institutional reforms were unnecessary. The Qing government already had the advantages that the reformers attributed to democratic institutions with none of the disadvantages.[23] Merchants did not need democracy to establish companies and factories, but excessive freedom for merchants would produce corruption. It was the present system whereby officials regulated merchant activities that kept the economy functioning. Similarly, new schools could be established under the present system, while democracy threatened the official powers to award the ranks and stipends that kept the educational system functioning. Officialdom was also necessary to military reforms, which, Zhang implied, excessive liberties would threaten.[24] And he claimed that parliaments were not necessary to convey public opinion (their only conceivable justification), because petitions and memorials already performed this function, while parliaments threatened to usurp the throne's legitimate powers.[25]

Democracy and egalitarianism: disunity, factionalism, and chaos. Such views were not new in 1898. One of the first firsthand accounts of a democratic movement was penned in the late 1880s by Huang Zunxian in his treatise on Japan.[26] We have already met Huang as a proponent of the view that the origins of Christianity and Western politics—equality and democracy—were derived from pre-Qin philosophers such as Mozi. For all his respect for the achievements of the Western powers, like Zhang Zhidong, Huang believed that the ethics of equality was rotten to the core. It leveled the king and the people, parents and children, and lumped everyone together. If the promise is to turn strangers into kin, the reality is to turn kin into strangers. "It is natural Heavenly Principle and the highest principle of human feeling that there must be noble and inferior, kin and non-kin, upper and lower." The emperor was chosen by Heaven, not the people, precisely to control chaos. True order and unity follow from the hierarchical order created by the sages, which rests on natural distinctions among people. The Western powers, Huang thought, were currently vigorous but would face problems in the future. If ever they should begin to falter, they would fall apart. He seems to have been thinking of Europe's socialist movements. Their egalitarianism, according to Huang, would lead to the struggle of all against all; their fear of the laws of Heaven would disappear. In a hundred years, they would collapse amid war and bloodshed, abandoning their kings and ignoring their kin.

Huang admitted he had no firsthand knowledge of Europe, but as a diplomat stationed in Tokyo in the early 1880s he had witnessed Japan's

People's Rights Movement and seen the danger posed by democratic ideas.[27] The great changes of the Meiji Restoration, Huang attributed to both Han (Chinese) learning and to Western learning. The Restoration of 1868 itself, Huang attributed to the Chinese classical injunctions to "revere the emperor" and "expel the barbarians" (J. *sonnō jōi*, Ch. *zunhuang rangyi*).[28] The rise of Western learning had then been tempered by the court's desire to maintain Chinese learning in order to regulate popular moral standards. But the popularity of Western learning was equally a result of Meiji policies, especially by the 1880s, by which time schools, universities, museums, and newspapers had done their work. Shockingly, shallow Japanese scholars, according to Huang, justified Christianity in Confucian terms and argued for a morality in which each person possesses liberty and autonomy (*ge you ziyou zizhu zhi dao*). In Huang's reading, these shallow scholars believed that since all persons receive their lives from Heaven, all possess equal rights (*quanli*). The ruler and the people, the father and his son, women and men: all have the same rights.[29] Huang was less alarmist in his descriptions of the Meiji's administrative reforms, but remained skeptical of the use of elections and assemblies.[30] While the objective of expanding the "public" (*gong*) was irreproachable, such institutions were vulnerable to capture by private interests. The sage, after all, operates for the sake of the public good, but not necessarily in the public eye. "The people may be made to follow it [a path of action], but they may not be made to understand it."[31] Huang's fear was that democracy was merely a cover for "hegemons" to pursue their private interests. This was a fear he saw confirmed after his appointment as consul in San Francisco in 1882. He was horrified by the city's machine politics and the anti-Chinese labor movement. Still, Huang turned to the West for technology and economic reforms. This was the means whereby the morality of the Former Kings could be instilled in the people today. And whereby China would resume its rightful place in the world.[32]

These were precisely the views Zhang Zhidong would propagate in 1898, but Huang's opinions were not set in stone. Let us turn the clock ahead. Huang returned to China in 1894 to accept a position in the Hunan provincial government, making him a member of Zhang Zhidong's political machine. From this posting at one of the strongholds of the reform movement, his views grew more radical. In the wake of the 1898 debacle he was dismissed but not otherwise punished. In a letter to Liang Qichao in 1902, written from retirement, Huang spoke of his personal journey toward democratic ideals.[33] While in Japan, he said, he was startled by the rise of "people's rights." They made more sense after he was able to read Rousseau and Montesquieu, which Huang describes as almost a conversion experience: he then thought that a just world would be created by democratization. However, he found no one with whom he could discuss his new ideas. And then, stationed in San Francisco, he witnessed the world of official corruption, political tricks, and the labor movement's success in keeping out Chinese workers. This experience left Huang confused and intellectually lost. If the great civilized nations could not handle democracy, what hope was there for peoples who were still backward? Thus Huang turned to Mozi (critically, as we have seen).

However, Huang experienced yet another change of heart after he was briefly posted to Britain in 1890. There he saw a political form (*zhengti*) that China could follow. Primarily, he now favored decentralizing Qing rule by turning it into a constitutional monarchy. He proposed abolishing China's provinces, replacing them with five large states, each under a governor-general system like Australia or Canada. Huang proposed a clearer distinction between legislative and administrative functions. Legislative decisions should be made by popularly elected local assemblies, which would determine fiscal and legal policies, while schools, the military, and infrastructure should be managed by the central government. Something like a federal system would stabilize the economy by limiting official malfeasance and strengthening the nation. This kind of constitutional monarchy would also muffle calls for more revolutionary change. Huang sought to preserve the kingship in a form of "equality" with popular power. Huang had not abandoned the Three Bonds, but he was stretching them.

The tensions between radical reformism and a more deliberately Confucian reformism can be seen both in the split between Kang-Liang and Zhang Zhidong, and in the evolving views of the diplomat-scholar Huang Zunxian. These tensions also played out in the new educational system. In 1902, the Qing committed itself to building a state school system. It is not surprising that on paper its values reflected those of Zhang Zhidong. Zhang was, among his other duties, ultimately in charge of this new project, which built on his experience in Hunan and Hubei.[34] By the time a new Ministry of Education was put on a sound footing in 1906, it was able to set out the general goals of state education. The original vision of gradually building a system that would provide primary schooling for all boys was expanded to include girls, though in fact only a very small percentage of boys and an even smaller percentage of girls actually enrolled. For our purposes, the question is how the ministry's goals reflected elite and official views, and Zhang Zhidong's views in particular. The ministry's regulations promoted reform on the one hand but criticized reformist extremism on the other. It was the latter problem that seems to have struck the ministry as especially worrisome. Echoing Zhang's *Exhortation to Learning*, it did not claim that the West set a bad example but that some Chinese did not properly understand the West. The ministry frankly declared that education was ultimately a means to inculcate loyalty and inoculate the population against revolutionary "heresies"; it was also a means to strengthen the state by mobilizing the people.[35]

More specifically, the ministry claimed that proper policies could only be established on the basis of *China's* circumstances and popular customs. Above all, the traditional ideas of the state and scholarship (*zhengjiao*) rested on loyalty to the emperor (*zhongjun*) and reverence for Confucius (*zun Kong*). Esteem for three forms of learning—public-mindedness (*shanggong*), the military arts (*shangwu*), and the practical arts (*shangshi*)—was needed in order to maintain these foundational principles.[36] Although the Eastern and Western countries had different political forms, all based their politics on reverence for the king (*guozhu*). For example, the recent rise of Germany could be traced to its schools' emphasis on preserving the unity of the empire, while Japan's rise had much to do with its schools' emphasis on the unbroken imperial line. The Qing, in its great beneficence and care of the people, could, according to the ministry, shape its educational system similarly.

In the ministry's view, public-mindedness, the military arts, and the practical arts would strengthen the state within a framework of Confucianism and loyalism. Nonetheless, in terms of curriculum and class time, the ministry offered a more immediate set of purposes to school builders. Public-mindedness referred to creating a unified populace that was determined and unconquerable.[37] (The ministry could have been quoting Liang Qichao here, though this was in fact language Zhang Zhidong found acceptable.) The role of schooling was essential, the ministry declared, in creating trust and friendship through lessons in self-cultivation, ethical relations, history, geography, and the like: all such courses encouraged the sentiment of cooperation. Patriotic unity, the ministry explicitly noted, should be rooted in childhood, just as Confucius taught that universal benevolence was the extension of particularistic filiality. Central to this process would be the revival of a "national learning" (*guoxue*) that was in decline. Zhang Zhidong's strong reaction against the radical reformers' talk of democracy and equality was by no means obscurantist, but by planting his flag on the Three Bonds he tried to block any fundamental change to the social order.

Nonetheless, what actually went on in classrooms could be another matter. A degree of egalitarianism, at least, can be discerned in some of those most orthodox of pedagogical tools, textbooks. Nothing too radical—for textbooks to be used in the state schools were vetted and censored by the ministry. Still, in addition to emphasizing filiality, friendship, justice, diligence, hygiene, and so forth and so on, ethics textbooks (*xiushen jiaokeshu*) began to discuss the role of citizens. Overall, children were expected to learn that they had duties to the state. At the same time, they were taught that the state would protect the people. In a sense, then, the state had duties to the people. At a deeper level, several morality textbooks emphasized the strong links between the state and its people—even their virtual unity. According to the *Common Citizen's Required Reader*:

You need to know that the term for "citizen" (*guomin*) originally referred to the inseparability of the people (*renmin*) and the state (*guojia*). The reputation of the state is the reputation of the people; the glory of the state is the glory of the people. . . . The survival of the state is the survival of the people.[38]

This notion could be taken in either a radical or conservative direction. Conservative textbooks emphasized harmony: "The family is the basis of the state, and the relationship between husband and wife is the basis of the family."[39] And so, "if there is harmony between husband and wife, then the country will be at peace." Yet even a relatively conservative emphasis on the duties of the people also spoke of their duty to become involved in affairs of state, a notable break with the tradition of restricting state affairs to high officials. The *Primary School Textbook on Self-Cultivation* began with the common observation that if citizens took it as their personal responsibility to be strong and civilized, then the state would be strong and civilized as well.[40] This is precisely why citizens needed self-cultivation. This textbook nicely combined traditional Confucian self-cultivation with modern purposes: self-cultivation not to produce sages (*shengren*) but a stronger state. Zhang Zhidong would probably have had no problem with this formulation, but the textbook went on to observe that people are prior to the state. It concluded:

The empire is not the private property of a few individuals but rather the public property of the billions of people. As well, the state is not the property of one or two individuals but rather the public property of the billions of people. Since it is public property, nothing at all in this empire and state is not public property. Therefore, anyone who tries to take this public property as his own is the public enemy of the empire and the state.[41]

The *Introductory Textbook on Self-Cultivation* also treated the people as prior. "The state is established by the people, while the people are maintained by the state."[42] And coming close to a republican stance, it stated: "There are no states without governance, but governance that is not in accord with reason (*gongli*) is no different from lacking governance."[43] Morality textbooks also discussed, at least briefly, the old trope of the state as extended family. The more radical view used the contrast between private/selfish (*si*) and public good (*gong*) to emphasize that just as a family could not be "privatized," so the state should not be "privatized."[44] The state is the common property of its people just as a family is the common property of its members. This did not settle questions of *guoti* or *zhengti*, but Liang Qichao would have been proud.

HUNANESE REACTION: LIVING THE THREE BONDS

Zhang Zhidong engaged in a rational—largely unemotional—style of argumentation. A sharper reaction against the Kang-Liang reform movement arose in Hunan in 1897 and 1898. This was the center of the reform movement, with Liang Qichao, Tan Sitong, and other Confucian radicals teaching at the Academy of Current Affairs in Changsha, the provincial capital. The Hunanese conservatives used a much more violent rhetoric, accusing the Kang-Liang reformers of leading their children astray, of "heresy" (*xieshuo*), of betraying the dynasty and deserving execution. Their anti-egalitarianism was far more moralistic and displayed a paranoiac vision that they were the only good men fighting evil conspiracies. The Hunanese gentry, and especially Changsha's elites, had become notorious in the 1870s and 1880s for their opposition to missionaries and any project tainted by Westernization. But by the mid-1890s reform had come to Changsha.[45] The Hunanese reactionaries were not unalterably opposed to reforms of the kind backed by Zhang, but they had come believe there was only one real crisis facing China. This was not that democracy would wreck the political order in the future but that egalitarian notions were already destroying the social order. The conservatives were happy to count Zhang as one of them, and republished some of his writings (but not the reformist bits) in their *Compendium to Protect the Teaching*. Nonetheless, they did not think Zhang had gone far enough.[46] First published in 1898, the *Compendium to Protect the Teaching* included the conservatives' memorials, essays, and letters, including letters to Kang, of the preceding few years. It was frequently republished in the years of reaction immediately following the defeat of the reformers.

Who were these conservatives and why did they want the Qing to execute Kang Youwei? Why did Kang deserve death for writing a couple of virtually unreadable if erudite books? The conservatives were sophisticated and cosmopolitan members of the gentry elite of Changsha: officials, teachers, classicists, and poets.[47] Su Yu (1872–1914), the main compiler of the *Compendium*, was a student of Wang Xianqian (1842–1917), particularly admired the writings of Dong Zhongshu, and later traveled to Japan. Su's compendium included the writings of Wang and Zhu Yixin (1846–1894) of the older generation, and Ye Dehui (1864–1927) of the younger, among others. Wang had become a *jinshi* at the age of twenty-four and a Hanlin Bachelor, but soon returned to teach in Changsha, supporting the Self-strengthening reforms. Ye Dehui (*jinshi* 1892) began as a supporter of Kang's reform ideas but soon turned against his views on Confucius. Su was himself the same age as Liang Qichao. This was not a generational split but a difference of opinion. Partly, it was also a division between Changsha natives and outsiders.[48] A redistribution of political power under a reforming administration threatened local interests, and the Changsha natives fought back with ideological appeals to higher authorities. As well, I think the vehemence of the Hunanese reaction shows that something highly personal was at stake.

The conservative reaction against talk of equality rested on a unitary vision of family and state as rooted in the nature of the cosmos. This kind of conservative vision did not preclude moderate reform; as noted above, many of the leading conservatives of the late 1890s supported some specific reforms. But these were largely limited to the spheres of technology and infrastructure. Education, for one, was trickier. By the late 1890s, whatever disagreements they may have had among themselves on other issues, the conservatives were unified in their opposition to any fundamental political reform and especially to anything that seemed a threat to the social order. Conservatism, at least of this sophisticated variety, was not mere unthinking traditionalism but a line carefully drawn in the sand, although shifting sands as it turned out. From Zhang Zhidong to the Hunanese reaction, modern Chinese conservatism was built around efforts to limit and manage change in such a way as to preserve the Qing's existing cosmological, moral, and institutional foundations. And in some cases, the conservatives did turn against any kind of reform whatsoever.

But to put it this way is to present only half the story. Beyond a reasoned defense of the political status quo lay a deeply reactionary and fearful response to what the conservatives perceived as threats to their way of life. In other words, the arrival in Changsha of young, radical teachers spreading talk of democracy and equality in 1896–1897 brought home to leading Hunanese gentry a sense that their children might be in danger. And if the morality of their children was in danger, their own lifestyles were in danger. Their response was thus literally "reactionary": a highly critical, even perhaps hysterical response to the threat of change. Kang Youwei in particular was demonized, but so too were his younger followers Liang Qichao, Tan Sitong, Tang Caichang, Fan Zhui, Pi Jiayou, and others. Ironically, it may be that the vehement defense of the Three Bonds suggested some inherent weakness in the traditional doctrine more than the scattered criticisms being made by a radical fringe. If radicals at this time occasionally attacked the inequality between ruler and subject and between father and son—and even sometimes between husband and wife—they tended to concentrate on broader political theory.[49] What the conservatives did, was to reemphasize the links between the political and the personal. If the position of monarch was rejected, then the position of father could not survive. In many ways, the demise of the patriarchal family seemed a worse fate than the collapse of the monarchical state. Equality might be bad for the state, but it was a calamity for the family.

The full psychological aspects of the Hunan reactionary movement of the late 1890s may remain closed to us, but we can examine how the rhetoric of anti-egalitarianism worked. The reactionaries built arguments that followed particular patterns. While each spoke in an individual voice, collectively they argued that radical reform would simply produce disaster. In Albert O. Hirschman's terms, their rhetoric largely followed the "jeopardy thesis," which proposes that the cost of change is too high, even putting previous reforms in jeopardy.[50] We can also find strains of the "perversity thesis," which argues that reform will actually result in worsening the very condition to be reformed, and of the "futility thesis," which holds that reforms will simply fail to do anything. Above all, the Hunanese reactionaries spoke in tones of moral outrage, predicting disaster and chaos if reforms were pursued. Their loyalism was totalistic, that is, loyalty to dynasty, Teaching (Confucianism), patriarchy, and social hierarchy constituted a unitary formation.

Many of Zhang Zhidong's arguments were based on the perversity and jeopardy theses: that radical reforms would produce results opposite to the intentions of the reformers and that radical reforms threatened existing accomplishments. Such a position was perfectly compatible with Zhang's support for moderate, or conservative, reform. The Hunanese reactionaries differed from Zhang, however, in their sudden distrust of reform itself. They were not merely loyalists to the Qing, since their vision encompassed the entire social order and even the cosmic order. Nor can they be defined simply as conservatives—trying to conserve—because this misses a key ingredient of their rhetorical passion: their paranoia. They not only feared change; they saw a conspiracy of enemies, including even officials, who were in effect absolutely evil.[51] How else but through a conspiracy could Kang and Liang have made their way into positions of responsibility, "agitated" the populace, and led Changsha's youth into perdition? The conservatives sensed that something in the trends of the time had turned against them; if they did not take immediate action, the situation could well be lost. Given the heretical nature of their enemies, conservatives wanted them exterminated: there was no room for discussion or compromise (though ironically the result was to produce a debate). In fact, the activities of Kang and his disciples and associates were neither, for the most part, secret nor vast, and the approbation of officials was strictly conditional. But none of that assuaged reactionary paranoia.

At the same time, the Hunanese reactionaries were also committed to positive virtues. In other words, they were *for* things as well as *against* things. They were in general committed to the patriarchal family, to the high traditional culture of art and poetry, and to Cheng-Zhu morality. They were explicit in their loyalty to the Qing. This was not loyalty for the sake of loyalty or a generalized loyalty to monarchism but quite specific loyalty to the ruling dynasty. Thus, in his preface to the *Compendium*, Su Yu began by praising the virtue of the emperor and the long era of peace that the Qing had secured.[52] The imperial spirit was "luminous" and the Sagely Learning (*shengxue*) supreme. Scholars were loyal, according to Su, rebellions suppressed, and heterodoxy nonexistent (until the present moment, presumably). Similarly, Ye Dehui claimed that the Qing treated the people like its own children, and did not raise taxes even when faced with an empty treasury.[53]

All this might be dismissed as rhetorical boilerplate. And indeed, conservatives did not take loyalty to the Qing as a supreme moral virtue in a hierarchy of virtues; rather, loyalty was inseparable from a set of integrated virtues. Thus the Hunanese reactionaries viewed the Three Bonds as an indissoluble whole. For example, Zhu Yixin rooted the social order in the cosmos, linking ritual (*li*), as that which gives pattern, to its substance, righteousness (*yi*). Furthermore, given the goodness of human nature, sages were able to create order: that is, "from matter stems laws (*ze*), from character (*qizhi*) stems righteousness and principle (*yili*), from the father-son relationship stems caring love, and from the ruler-subject relationship stems ordered hierarchy."[54] Putting aside questions of Neo-

Confucian metaphysics, it seems clear that for Zhu this described a universal state of humanity that by no means made evil impossible, but precisely defined certain actions as evil.[55]

Ye Dehui not only expressed faith in Confucian moralism, but predicted its worldwide victory. Even (or especially) without special efforts to preserve it, Confucianism would prevail; "trustworthiness and reliability will spread across the world, and evils disappear in the daylight."[56] He concluded, with a paradoxical note: "Attempts to reform institutions will fail to reform; it is by *not* promoting democracy that [we] will move [in a progression] from the Age of Disorder to the Emerging Peace and to the Great Peace." This seems a fine example of Hirschman's perversity thesis, squared. Ironically, Ye was accepting a progressive vision of history, echoing Kang's New Text interpretation of the Three Ages and a future of Datong democracy.[57] However, the point here is that Ye attacked reformism (and efforts to promote democracy) as futile and dangerous. That is to say, the reformers were not only doing damage such as agitating the masses, but, even more tellingly, their efforts were simply in vain. Ye thus adopted the persona of a realist: he admitted the good points of the West without idealizing it, and he admitted China had long had problems, but monarchism nonetheless represented the best option available.[58] Ye was committed to Confucianism precisely because it supported monarchism; ultimately, the two were indivisible. Contesting Zhang Zhidong's views, he noted in a private letter that Confucianism was not a bulwark of *China* alone, but rather marked monarchism everywhere. This is in contrast to Christianity's links to democracy; according to Ye, the Mosaic laws originally omitted loyalty to monarch and state (*zhongjun aiguo*), which Western priests had added only after acquaintance with Confucian writings.[59] Confucianism may spread across the world, then, when the West returns to the righteousness of the ruler-subject relationship.

Su Yu began by accusing Kang Youwei of "using institutional reform (*gaizhi*) to throw the country's basic institutions (*chengxian*) into confusion, proclaiming equality to destroy human relations (*gangchang*), promoting democracy to abolish the ruler (*shen minquan wu junshang ye*), and marking time from Confucius so that the people would forget the present dynasty."[60] Furthermore, Kang's New Text scholarship amounted to destroying the sacred classics. Indeed, for Su Yu and the other Hunanese reactionaries, questions of classical scholarship were central to the political debates of the day (as for Kang Youwei but not, perhaps, in the same way for Zhang Zhidong). Zhu Yixin, for one, offered a straightforward defense of Old Text readings, but, above all, stressed that the real issue was not textual minutiae but establishing righteousness and principle (*yili*).[61] Indeed, while Zhu attacked Kang Youwei harshly and by name, he also criticized academic trends of the Qing such as the Han Learning evidential studies movement for ignoring matters of principle.[62] For Hong Liangpin (1827–1897) the main issue was simply that the differences between the New and Old Text traditions were not all that great.[63] The Hunanese reactionaries were academically eclectic.

Zhu Yixin also referred to the pivotal role of the classics in an argument that essentially admitted reforms were needed, but concluded they could only be carried out on the basis of the existing system.

From ancient times, no institutions (*fa*) have been perfect, but when kings are active, small faults are rectified with small reforms and major problems with major changes—institutions can be changed but the meaning of institutions cannot. Therefore, as long as the ruler exists, then governance is practiced, but lacking a ruler, governance ceases. The evils of governance are the faults of those who administer the institutions, not the fault of established institutions.[64]

Zhu's point was that Kang's justifications of reform were based on a false reading of the classics. There was no textual foundation for reform "in the name of the 'uncrowned king.'" So it was too for Ye Dehui, who went on to point out that Confucius never saw himself as either a reformer or an "uncrowned king." The latter term was only used by his disciples.[65] The entire *Gongyang* school was but a pretext for agitating the populace, according to Ye. The theory of the Three Ages was not reliable, while the notion of Confucius as any kind of reformer had only the most indirect classical foundation.[66] Ye determined that the *Gongyang* reference to "institutions" (*zhi*) that Kang had cited actually referred to putting down rebellions and restoring order. For Ye, as for Zhu, the point of classical scholarship was to illuminate the Great Way through traditional commentaries, not provide obscure textual sources for arbitrary hermeneutics in the style of Kang Youwei.

The case for morality and hierarchical human relations was persua-
sively argued by Wang Renjun (1866–1913), a follower of Zhang Zhidong.
Wang began by granting the Three Bonds the status of cosmological truth,
then pointing out that the ruler-subject bond precluded the possibility of
democracy—which, in any case, would simply lead to the factional fighting
of ancient Rome or contemporary South America.[67] Even more pointedly,
Wang claimed that promoting the equality of father and son would destroy
all ethical relations (*lunli*) and reduce the Chinese to the level of beasts.
Similarly, the granting of autonomy to women, as in the West, would lead
both to the reversal of yin and yang and to the loss of proper feminine behavior. Like many others at the time, Wang believed that democracy was
a Western practice originally derived from China.[68] But in China, Mozi's
democratic theories had been refuted by Mencius, who dismissed Mozi's
notion of "universal love" (*jian'ai*) as "denial of the father."[69]

Wang's real concern, of course, was not with the origins of democracy in the West but with China's pressing need to maintain the rites and
music—the righteous spirit that could be traced back to the sage-kings
and the classics—and the suppression of heresy. For when the king is not
reverenced, the people become haughty and restless.[70] Only the rule of a
loving king can maintain moral governance. Still, turning back to Western history, Wang claimed that four historical conditions had given rise
to democracy: military coups; heterodox popular uprisings; revolts of
colonized or oppressed peoples; and finally, rebellions caused by anger at
the emperor's mistakes.[71] However, none of these conditions was found
in China. According to Wang, the view that history or the "trends of the
times" were leading the world toward democracy was simply wrong, and
many democratic experiments, such as the French Revolution, had proven
disastrous. Wang granted a point to democrats who opposed the selfishness inherent in the transfer of the state to the king's heirs. "However,
to disperse the charisma of the kingship among all the people is a great
mistake." Democracy has no way to assure the rise of the meritorious.
Wang's point was that in practice in democracies the political class simply
reproduces itself. American elections are decided by bribes and factions,
for example, not any true popular will.[72] Nor is democracy a recipe for
achieving wealth and power. Successful modernization has occurred with-

out democracy, as in Peter the Great's Russia, while democracy has led to collapse of the state, as Wang demonstrated in examples ranging from the Roman Republic to France in the 1830s.[73] Political leaders, fearing popular opinion, refuse to deal with tough questions—for example, the American politicians catering to anti-Chinese prejudice even if they are not prejudiced themselves.

Lying behind Wang's wide reading in Western history and arguments about the practicalities of different political systems were two great fears: first, that the demise of the Three Bonds would lead to moral chaos and the breakdown of the family; second, that the demise of the Three Bonds would lead to social chaos and the collapse of the state. These two concerns were rhetorically and logically related, but they were psychologically distinct. The latter fear was about status and stability, but not direct assaults on the self. The former fear was more personal, about relations within the family. The Three Bonds in this sense constituted a highly particularized sense of ethics. The horrific image of sons disobeying their fathers or wives talking back to their husbands fueled reactionary angst. Wang mentioned how deeply wrong it would be—indeed, against the order of nature—if fathers were given the same punishment for hitting their sons as sons for hitting their fathers.[74]

POLITICS AS PERSONAL

On a philosophical level, the father-son bond and the emperor-subject bond were one: both rested on filial piety and both were rooted in Heavenly principle (*tianli*). But on the psychological level, one was literally closer to home. The notion that democracy might define political institutions in ways that need not be leveling seems not to have occurred to late Qing conservatives. The fear of egalitarianism lay at the root of their attacks on democracy. In a memorial attacking Kang Youwei, Wen Ti (Zhonggong) emphasized that Kang's egalitarianism would lead to disorder and chaos. According to Wen Ti, the reformers were so extreme that they would make ruler and subject equal and blur the distinction between male and female.[75] China was becoming a Western nation in its politics and customs in the quest to gain wealth and power. Yet not wealth but endless struggles among the Chinese, each seeking self-advantage, would ensue from democracy. Wen said he told Kang to his face that patriotism (*aiguo*) was not enough: loyalty to the monarch (*zhongjun*) and to the Qing was also necessary. Similarly, Ye Dehui simply argued that given China's vast size and its many bandits—its long history of mostly chaos rather than order—democracy would only convince the people that they could rule themselves. The result would be factionalism and division and end up harming the people.[76] This was a feeble defense of monarchism, since even if Ye's interpretation of democracy was correct, he was well acquainted with the history of court factionalism.

The Hunanese reactionaries attacked "equality" on the grounds that it denied the distinction between superior and inferior, and thus denied rulership—and by the same token denied the bonds of kinship, in which case there could be no "fathers."[77] Nothing was worse than the destruction of ethical relationships. In Ye Dehui's view, democracy, at least as practiced in Western republics, precisely expressed the betrayal of ethical relationships: republicanism denied the ruler-subject relationship, in addition to simply lacking the father-son relationship. Like Wang, Ye believed that excessive respect for women's rights symbolized the reversal of yin and yang and the overturning of natural human sentiment. Zhu Yixin's faith in the goodness of original human nature, which we have noted above, led him to conclude that the ruler-subject relationship and the father-son relationship are not so much analogous but equally rooted in cosmic patterns. The former is marked by the principle of ranked hierarchy and the latter by the principle of loving affect.[78] For Zhu, these were universal norms that applied to all societies, indeed the very stuff of humanity. Nor were ethical relations voluntary norms. It was by institutionalizing ritual that the Former Kings perfected order, though this also meant that people had the opportunity to betray that order.[79] Order was thus based on original good human nature; yet at the same time, if ritual failed to restrain desires, evil could result.

Similarly, Ye Dehui argued that attempts to base a Chinese version of democracy on the abdications of Yao and Shun confused decision-making that came from the top with that from the bottom.[80] Ye's point was that the hierarchy was maintained in China's historical vision of public-mindedness (*gong*), which was not the latent democratic notion that the reformers talked of. As for the Mencian emphasis on valuing the people, here Ye found the point in the king's cherishing of his people, not their cherishing of themselves.

As for their understanding of the West, conservatives essentially made three arguments about barbarians: first, that based on their common humanity, even barbarians recognized some form of the Three Bonds, and so radical reform in the name of emulating the West was simply based on a false premise; second, that barbarians were indeed different, but, while their system worked for them, it was inappropriate for China, either because the Chinese way was vastly superior or because China was not yet ready for changes that would come eventually; and third, that barbarians were thoroughly inferior, their system offering nothing useful to the Chinese. These arguments, while in theory mutually exclusive, could in practice be combined in rhetorically effective ways. Zhang Zhidong basically argued the first line, while the Hunanese conservatives emphasized the second and third lines. Several, including Ye Dehui, at least implicitly hinted that democratization of some sort might occur without deliberate effort—someday, in ways and forms yet to be determined. There was a mystical tinge to Ye's argument, suggesting that reform might result without deliberately pursuing it. But Ye, at least, had no use for barbarian theories at all, believing in the universal truth of Confucian metaphysics. His faith that one day Confucianism would spread to the West was, at least implicitly, based on the notion that democracy and equality were inherently destructive and immoral, not simply inappropriate for China at the time.[81] Zhu Yixin pointed out that if the purpose of reform was to follow sages and return to the sage-king system of the Three Dynasties, there was no need to use the barbarians' systems.[82] He, too, granted that in spite of the barbarians' lack of the relationships of ruler-subject, father-son, younger-elder brother, and husband-wife, they nonetheless maintained a kind of variant of righteousness and principle.[83] That is to say, righteousness and principle were antecedent to institutions and customs, which are systematically related. But this thought led Zhu to the conclusion that even if barbarian morality was acceptable, if Chinese institutions were changed, the *Chinese* righteousness and principle would be directly threatened. And given China's particular moral system, even "mere" technology threatened to overwhelm it with utilitarianism and selfishness. Indeed, already people are turning to evil, according to Zhu, and to create new laws would merely be to add new sources of evil. Rather, "rulership lies in giving priority to the rectification of morality and customs"; institutions were secondary.

Personally threatened, as they saw it, the Hunanese reactionaries got personal in their turn. For Su Yu, the issue was not so much the ignorance of Kang Youwei and his ilk but that they took advantage of the ignorance of ordinary people.[84] Kang was trying to form a traitorous faction.[85] Repeatedly, the Hunanese conservatives accused Kang of promoting heresy, betraying the sagely Teaching, destroying ethical relationships, and agitating the population.[86] Another member of the Changsha conservative circle, Bin Fengyang, claimed Kang and Liang desired "the death of the Chinese humaneness" (yu si Zhongguo zhi renxin).[87] Liang Dingfen (Jie'an, 1859–1920), a Cantonese follower of Zhang Zhidong and a stalwart moderate reformer, found the activities of Kang and Liang equivalent to criminal bands (huifei). A certain Wang Choujun dismissed them as rebels who would not stop until rulers and fathers were all regarded as garbage.[88] An Xiaofeng (Weijun) claimed that in calling himself Changsu, or the "eternal uncrowned king," Kang was pretending to the sagely status of Confucius.[89] Nor did Ye Dehui refrain from pointing out his enemies' hypocrisy. If Kang and Liang so despised the eight-legged examination essays, he asked, why did they travel to Beijing to take the exams?[90] If they were obeying the wishes of their parents, it was unfilial to criticize the exams and a pretense to purity to take them.

Ye Dehui traced the origins of Kang-style heresy to the excessive criticism of imperial power in Huang Zongxi's Plan for the Prince (Mingyi daifanglu), which he condemned out of hand.[91] Ye and others also associated their theory of equality with Buddhism as well as Mohism.[92] Ye specifically accused Liang Qichao of "confusing" Chinese and Western teachings by mixing Confucianism and Christianity; confusing the foreign and the native by finding Datong in China and the West alike; confusing past and present by dating from Confucius; and confusing social inferiors and superiors by equalizing the monarch and the people.[93] Liang used the theory of democracy to throw the empire into chaos, while Kang's theory of Datong functioned to destroy Confucianism.[94] Kang and Liang, by denying fathers and rulers, became enemies of Confucius, reduced to their own animal natures. Denying the classical canon, they encouraged people's desire for power. All this amounted to treason.

Such views were not limited to major intellectuals like Ye Dehui. We can see similar fears, for example, in the writings of Liu Dapeng (1857–1942). Liu was a fairly poor schoolteacher from peripheral Shanxi province. Liu nonetheless struggled through the exams to finally win his *juren* degree in 1894. In his diary, Liu noted his resentment of foreign expertise as he faced the prospect of the abolition of the examination system for which he had spent decades preparing.[95] For Liu Dapeng, loyalty to the Qing was literally unquestionable. It was part of an indivisible system of political, social, and moral values, for throughout the ages, "emperors have upheld the Way through their reverence for Confucian [scholars]."[96] Conversely, "when learning is muddied, then the people's hearts will not be upright, customs will decline, and the empire will fall into total chaos."

This is exactly what Liu saw happening. Perhaps most telling of Liu's attitudes, though, is his account from 1904 of a story of a high official's son who, returning from study abroad, demanded the termination of their father-son relationship. In this story, the father was forced to agree, and Liu concluded that, "if this is so, then the way of ethical relationships has become rotten, and the empire is falling into chaos."[97] Liu recorded a similar story in 1906, while in the following year he observed that 80 to 90 percent of students had become revolutionaries, even thinking it natural to deny their fathers along with their ruler (*wufu wujun, jie xi wei guran*).[98] Liu frequently paired and condemned the denial of fathers and rulers—which he seemed to see all around him, albeit at secondhand. Not only students but scholars were turning to equality and freedom. For Liu, this all represented a disastrous betrayal of China's one true strength as a nation of rites and righteousness that reverenced filiality and loyalty.[99] The fate of the family was linked to the fate of the state.

That was certainly the opinion of Enguang (1852–?), a minor official and probably a Manchu who lived in Beijing and kept a meticulous diary for most of his life. As the 1911 Revolution unfolded to the south, he recorded his despair.[100] Enguang did not express fear for his life, but he noted—repeatedly—his contempt for "immoral rebels and traitors" and "agitators" who were destroying thousands of years of Chinese morality, ritual, and politics, and turning China into a barbarian country.[101] They were ingrates and knaves, deluding the ignorant. Enguang also blamed foreign plots for the crisis facing the Qing. "From the beginning of civilization, the rulers of China never asked what was a monarchy and what was a republic. This came from the new and preposterous theories of the barbarians, which the traitors now use to promote their rebellion."[102] For Enguang, perhaps above all the attack on the Qing was simultaneously an attack on the patriarchal order. He implied some of the fault lay with the Qing's New Policy reforms, which attempted to "utilize Western methods to improve education and strengthen the military [but only ended up by] squeezing the empire's wealth."[103] In Enguang's cri de coeur, China now faced a world of "no rulers and no fathers" (wujun wufu).

None of these views were like the conservative turn that Liang Qichao took in about 1903. Liang's conservatism reflected a disillusionment with "democracy," but Liang was doubling down on his commitment to reform. Liang maintained his teleological faith in progress. True conservatives were more skeptical and fearful. But radicals as well as conservatives distanced themselves from populism. Like Huang Zunxian, Kang Youwei had cited Confucius, saying, "Restrain the people with rites, pacify the people with music," making them good and joyful without their even knowing how this came to pass. "Thus it is said, 'The people can be made to follow it [the Way] but not to understand it.'"[104] This common trope was even taken up by Yan Fu in the wake of the 1911 Revolution. Let us look ahead to the first years of the Republic. Yan had never been tempted by the myth of popular sovereignty, so he could not have been speaking out of disillusionment. Rather, in a public lecture, Yan tried to suggest how Confucian principles of governance could aid the new Republic.[105] On the surface, Yan was arguing that Confucianism was compatible with republicanism. He took the same phrase for his text: "The people can be made to follow it but not to understand it." According to Yan, this phrase had been seized on by critics of Confucianism, who used it to condemn Confucius as an apologist for despotism. But they were misinterpreting the phrase. For Yan, it was an appeal to educate the people.

In his analysis of the passage, Yan stated that Confucius was not referring to "the people" in general but only to those who were completely
ignorant and blind. Regardless of how civilized and developed a country
became, there would always be some people simply incapable of compre-
hension. Second, the phrase "may not be" was never meant to be a blanket
prohibition. But, third, Yan's argument really rested on his interpretation
of the inherently ambiguous "it." What was it that Confucius thought the
people could be made to follow but not to understand? Yan suggested three
possibilities, the point being that whatever "it" meant precisely, it referred
to the people's natural tendencies—they did not need to understand "it"
in the first place, because they already knew how to do it. In a sense, they
already instinctively understood it. The first meaning of "it" might be
morality. Borrowing from evolutionary theory, Yan insisted that morality
belonged to the first stage of social development. Citing John Stuart Mill,
Yan determined that morality was a kind of technology of group living,
and not a science, and therefore it simply did not require knowledge or
reason. Indeed, morality would probably collapse if it relied on analysis:
morality lay in following, not understanding.

The second possibility Yan canvassed was that "it" might refer to religion.
Now, religion referred precisely to the unknowable, or, following Herbert
Spencer, what science could not explain. Religion was inherently outside
the intellect, and so had to be a matter of following rather than understanding. And third, "it" might refer to the law. Yan pointed out that laws were
indeed artificial instruments designed to help the group function, implying
that law was not natural in the same sense as morality and religion. And
the more civilized and developed the country, the more numerous and complex its laws. Citing Jeremy Bentham and Henry Sidgwick, Yan concluded
in effect that since laws were based on fundamental principles of morality,
it was sufficient for ordinary people to follow their consciences. People already knew what was basically right and wrong, and if they did what was
right, they could not violate any basic laws. Any ambiguous cases could
be decided by state experts through legal actions. Given the complexity of
the law, if perfect understanding was necessary, then the laws would never
be obeyed. Conversely, Yan revealingly commented, if ordinary people really understood the laws, they would find loopholes. When life was simple,

people did not know the laws (but still obeyed them), but when people become too shrewd, governance breaks down.[106] So Yan decided not so much that people could not be made to know, but that they already knew what they needed to know. Perhaps this Daoist-tinged cynicism was not the most rousing endorsement of republicanism, but the fading of outright reaction had left the way clear for conservative as well as radical constitutionalism.

Confucian reactionaries won the battle of 1898 but lost the war. Reaction contributed to the Boxer Uprising, which led to the invasion of Beijing in 1900 and the humiliation of the court, as we have seen. In 1905, when the Qing court proclaimed its intention to write a constitution, it invited officials and even non-officials to submit their opinions on the matter.[107] The "road of speech" was open once again. And the court received innumerable memorials. These ranged from horror at the very idea to rapturous faith that a constitution would solve all the government's problems.[108] The court's conservative approach to constitution-making can be seen in many areas. After three years of preparation, it was announced in 1908 that, yes, a constitution would be promulgated. But not till 1916. Sovereignty was to remain solely in the emperor's hands; the franchise would be strictly limited to educated and prosperous men; elected bodies were to be strictly advisory, able to do no more than "propose" suggestions. As expressed by the Qing court: "The Way of constitutionalism lies solely in the total agreement between ruler and ruled and their complete identity, the abolition of selfishness and promotion of the public good, and mutually setting about governance."[109] But the effects of official constitutionalism were nonetheless radicalizing. Many powerful men had clearly been reading the proscribed writings of Liang Qichao carefully, and they were prepared to push the Qing toward constitutional government. Gentry pressure in fact forced the Qing to move up the schedule for elections to provincial assemblies and a national parliament, and these bodies began operating after elections in 1909 and 1910, respectively. Suffrage was highly restricted, but many elites took an interest in the elections. The assemblies became sites where gentry could criticize Qing policies of which they disapproved and debate reform proposals.

In his diaries for the summer of 1906, Sun Baoxuan (1874–1924), a reform-minded official and well-known scholar, claimed that top officials all opposed the constitution. However, according to Sun, the high official and Cixi confidant Yuan Shikai said, "The man who dared to oppose the constitution was Wu Yue, and this Wu Yue . . . was a revolutionary!"[110] And so no one dared to say anything against constitutionalism.

Qing constitutionalism was partly a response to international pressures and trends that had essentially created the need for modern state-building. The competitive nature of the international state system reinforced the circulation of global ideologies of state authority, which were best expressed in constitutions. Chinese elites hoped that a Qing constitution would gain approbation from the Western powers.[111] The early twentieth century was an era of international constitution-making, as modernizing elites from Iran, Portugal, and Mexico to the Ottoman and Russian empires sought to provide clear foundations for the political order. Constitutions were therefore aimed at an international audience, but they also were attempts to claim domestic legitimacy through a global ideology.[112] The court's promise to turn the Qing into a constitutional monarchy was also an attempt to combine the graded hierarchies of the Confucian social order, with their unequal but mutual responsibilities, with something of the egalitarianism of the nation-state. It forced officials to think furiously about how to discipline the populace: about schools, censuses, armies, and other technologies of the modern state.[113] This differed from the traditional goal of the civilizing process (*jiaohua*) in its universality, in its desires to penetrate down to local society, and its claims to be seeking a uniquely Chinese version of political modernity. Confucian imperial subjects had been expected to absorb as much moral education as possible, but state instruction was very limited and the subject's main duty was to obey. Modern citizen-subjects were expected to see themselves as units in the political system, to participate and understand, as well as to obey.

CHAPTER 5

Identity, History, and Revolution

THE IDENTIFIER "Han" had long been a legal category of persons within the Qing empire.[1] Late Qing intellectuals used it to build the equation that linked the Han to nationhood and state sovereignty to the exclusion of other peoples. This involved a logic of revolution. On one level, this logic was simple, and devastating. If the Chinese nation was tantamount to the Han people, then there could be no justification for a Manchu ruling caste or a Manchu emperor. Once peoples are regarded as nations and a link made between the nation and the state, then the idea of "foreign" control becomes abhorrent. This was one way to read the international nation-state system that culminated in the support of Woodrow Wilson for "national self-determination" in 1918.[2] Of course, there were other ways to read the international state system: international law in the hands of the likes of Vattel and Wheaton, as we have seen, recognized all forms of state, from empire to city, as equal in their sovereignty, resting on the somewhat circular logic of the premise that they could in fact maintain their claims to sovereignty. No particular legitimacy attached to the state aspirations of nations or "peoples." That did not stop nationalist movements from forming around the ideas of eighteenth-century romantic nationalists such as Herder and nineteenth-century liberal nationalists such as Mazzini. This chapter and the next will examine how ideas about identity, history, and the state came together to justify revolution in China.

Tan Sitong was the first of the late Qing scholars to reject both the traditional cosmology and the monarchy. As Hao Chang points out, Tan not only criticized the "ruler-subject relationship" but attacked the Three Bonds in toto.[3] And he singled out the Manchus for the special cruelty of their rule. Tan's sense of ethnic oppression fell short of full-fledged nationalism, but he derived anti-Manchuism from his quest for a new political order. Just as the one-sided obedience of subjects to their king was wrong,

Tan said, so too the authoritarianism of filial piety and the subjugation of women were wrong. All these forms of inequality perverted the natural egalitarianism that Tan considered permeated the universe as the morality of *ren*. "*Ren*" (cosmic benevolence, humanity) was a traditional Confucian value associated with human relationships that Tan reinterpreted in radically egalitarian fashion. By 1896, Tan's earlier, rather conservative anti-foreignism had been replaced with a universalistic vision indirectly based on Christian, Confucian, and Buddhist sources.[4] In *On Cosmic Benevolence* (Renxue), Tan created a new metaphysics that rooted *ren* in the scientifically interconnected nature of the cosmos. Tan followed Kang Youwei in treating Confucius as a far-sighted "reformer" who, in Tan's view, was dedicated to the promotion of democracy (*minzhu*) and equality (*pingdeng*).[5] Buddha, Mozi, Jesus, and other spiritual leaders had equally understood the nature of *ren*.

In Tan's historical reading, the true teachings of Confucius were lost after Mencius and were perverted by the likes of Xunzi, whose ideas became the basis of the imperial system. "When the teaching of Xunzi is practiced by the ruler, then he utilizes it as a means of making himself superior to his subjects, of keeping the people in ignorance, and of ruining the minds of the people through his self-indulgence and violence."[6] Politically, the imperial institution is nothing less than a perverse form of oppression using the "three bonds and five relationships" to "steal" the state.[7] In the famous opening paragraph of the second part of *Renxue*, Tan states:

Once monarchical rule (*juntong*) flourished, no regime after the days of Yao and Shun bears examination. Once the Confucian teaching perished, no books since the Three Dynasties have been worth reading. . . . When human beings emerged, there were no distinctions such as that between ruler and subject; all persons were simply known as the people. As the people could not govern themselves and did not have time to do so; they therefore collectively raised one from the multitude to be their ruler. As the ruler was said to be "collectively raised," it was not he who chose the people but the people who chose him. As the ruler was said to be "collectively raised," then his position was neither above nor below the people. And as the ruler was said to be "collectively raised," then the people existed before the ruler, and thus the ruler was the branch and the people the root. . . . The ruler is he who works for the people; subjects are those who help in this work for the people. The purpose of collecting taxes from the people is to have the necessary resources to work for the people.[8]

In even stronger tones than Yan Fu's "Refutation of Han Yu," Tan focused on the criminality of the Chinese monarchy and its roots in a perverse culture. Tan noted the "slavery" of the Han under Manchu dominion, and he associated the monarchy itself with death and sacrifice.[9] That is, Tan asked how it was that the people "obediently accepted" all the punishments handed out to them by oppressive rulers and gladly wished to "die out of loyalty" when a ruler lost his throne. Given that it was natural to change leaders who did not do their jobs properly, this was indeed a puzzle. One problem was that the Chinese misunderstood the true meaning of "loyalty." Confucius meant, according to Tan, to refer to reciprocity, impartiality, and equality, and not to blind obedience and bending to force.

Tan had a touch of paranoia. How had the egalitarian teachings of Confucius and Jesus been rendered moot if not by their crafty misappropriation by evil monarchists and popes? For the people, though naturally intelligent, had become ignorant. "When the evils of the ruler-subject relationship reach an extreme, father and son, husband and wife naturally follow suit and each will use these status positions to control the other. All these evils stem from how the Three Bonds determine status."[10] Tan insisted that the father-son relationship was as artificial as the ruler-subject relationship, so if an analogy was to be made, it had to be based on the understanding that fathers and sons were equal as offspring of Heaven. The Three Bonds were made for tyrants (minzei).

Tan Sitong had already worked out most of the revolutionary package: republicanism, egalitarianism, repudiation of the Confucian cosmic-social hierarchy, and anti-Manchuism. All that remained was to define the Han-Manchu distinction more precisely and construct the "Han nation." His work done, Tan was ready to become a martyr and a symbol of national aspiration in 1898. Liang Qichao burned the image of Tan's sacrificial death onto a generation of young intellectuals. Liang's first writings from his exile in Japan broadcast Tan's story, and Liang published Tan's Renxue.

THE SCIENCE OF RACE

During the last years of the Qing, from the late 1890s, "race" (*zhongzu*) became a keyword in political discourse, centrally related to discussions of nationalism, evolution, and society among other topics, yet it remained ambiguous and multivalent.[11] Racial discourse in the late Qing could claim the imprimatur of Western science. Ethnography out of biology seemed to offer proof of the link between race and culture. Social Darwinism applied the principles of "struggle for survival" and "survival of the fittest" to human groups, and Chinese intellectuals found the results terrifying but convincing.[12] The science of race had spread around the world by the late nineteenth century, though its application could take many forms. On the one hand, racial knowledge was a critical element of colonial hegemony. Yet on the other hand, the dominant interpretation of modern racial knowledge was also open to contestation. Late Qing intellectuals used this knowledge to challenge Western justifications of imperialism. One side effect of racial knowledge was to marginalize the traditional Confucian emphasis on the distinction between civilized and uncivilized. It is not that something like racial categories were unknown in premodern China, but they were not central to political legitimacy.[13] The Manchus could claim to be a distinct people and also to be so highly civilized that Heaven had mandated them to rule over China as well as other places. The empire was multinational from the beginning, and from the eighteenth century self-consciously so.[14] It may be that from the point of view of officials in the late Qing, "China" (Zhongguo) was already a multiethnic state, naturalizing and essentializing what were in fact historically contingent and shifting borders and populations.[15] But intellectuals were engaged in a slightly different project: not trying to define an imperial state but trying to create a nation-state. Han identity was essential to this project.[16]

The Western taxonomic approach to race reached China through a variety of sources, including missionary schools and nineteenth-century travelers to the West.[17] Japanese translations of works dealing with Western racial knowledge began to be published in the early 1870s.[18] In 1892, the widely read *Gezhi huibian* (Scientific miscellany) published an article on the "five races" that constituted humankind.[19] History and geography textbooks that proliferated in the first decades of the twentieth century also followed this scheme. Skin color, hair type, nose shape, head shape, mental capacity, and culture were correlated. Yellows and Whites were more civilized; Browns, Blacks, and Reds less so.[20] This view of the racial equality of Yellow and White may not have been widely shared among Western scientists, but it became an operating premise in Asia. It accepted the premise of racial hierarchy and set up the basis for the Yellow-White struggle for supremacy.

Sub-races were also important: while all recognized that Han and Manchu both counted as Yellow, the trend was to emphasize their differences. At the same time, late Qing intellectuals tended to conflate the Yellow race with the Chinese, its largest and allegedly most industrious representative. Yan Fu, writing in the dark hours of China's defeat at the hands of the Japanese in 1895, pointed out that although China had been "conquered" by outsiders in the past, these outsiders had all been members of the same race. Such was not the case any more, as China was threatened by the Western powers.[21] Since today's Manchus, Mongols, and Han were all members of the "Yellow race," China had never fallen to a truly *alien* race. Furthermore, Yan maintained, all conquests of China to date had come at the hands of peoples who were militarily strong but weak in the arts of civilization; China could be conquered because the civilized were peaceful, and in turn it would conquer its conquerors (that is, through Sinifying them). The point about the Westerners or Whites, however, was that they also represented a high level of civilization. They were learned, progressive, prosperous, stable, unified, and very strong. Not incidentally, Yan's essay introduced social Darwinism via Herbert Spencer's "sociology" (*qunxue*), taking races as an important unit in the struggle for survival.

Liang Qichao played a major role in popularizing these ideas, while refusing to essentialize racial difference.[22] Liang largely accepted Western racial science, but he emphasized the mutability of races. Like other late Qing scholars, he also emphasized the superior qualities of the Yellow race. As we have seen, in the final analysis Liang treated nationality as essentially a matter of citizenship, and thus defined nation in terms of the state rather than ethnicity. Nonetheless, it remains true that Liang worked out his definition of China within a larger framework of racial knowledge that had largely been imported from the West. Indeed, in spite of moments of anti-Manchuism in the late 1890s, Liang justified Han-Manchu unity on the grounds these two groups were the natural leaders of the Yellow race. This amounted to a critique of both anti-Manchuism and of the Qing's ethnic policies that favored Manchus. Even before Liang specifically became an anti-anti-Manchu in about 1903, he had laid out the basis for this position, which relied on a New Text interpretation of the growth of the civilizational core of China in antiquity.[23] As for Kang Youwei, miscegenation seemed a route to equalizing the races or dissolving the "boundary" separating them. Yet Kang's desire to create a single human race also seemed to assume that this race would be more White.[24]

Liang was not so teleological. His first sustained consideration of "race" was written on the eve of the 1898 debacle. It was a direct product of his concern over the Han-Manchu division in the face of White imperialism.[25] His argument rested on the premise that although history—indeed, biology—was marked by "racial competition," this led to a tendency for races to merge. On the one hand, the essay displayed a social Darwinian vision of survival through struggle, continuing endlessly, beyond the power of even the "sages" to change. On the other hand, it argued that struggle leads to the domination of just a few races, and that as a race takes control of a particular place, peace breaks out and civilization progresses. Originally, numerous races all struggled with each other. Gradually some progressed and were able to defeat their inferior counterparts. These inferior races disappeared either through extinction or absorption. Liang treated races as bio-historically dynamic.

In Liang's view, the differences between the Manchus and Han may have had some of kind of biological root, but they were not biologically separate for all eternity, nor did their racial differences determine their political fate. In his early writings Liang seems to have accepted the theory of a single origin of humanity but emphasized its rapid division into "smaller groups" (*xiao tuanti*).[26] Liang pointed out that under primitive conditions these small groups would have been separated geographically. Without contacts between them, such groups would develop into separate "races" (*zhongzu*), each with its own small state (*guo*). Originally, these states—really, clans and tribes—were very numerous, but through conflict and conquests, fewer but larger groups emerged. The "struggle

for survival" amalgamated races while "racial competition" led to an evolution of state forms. We might also call this a process of *forgetting*: the
distinct biological or ancestral origins of different groups are no longer
considered in terms of their distinctiveness. In this sense, Liang did not
regard perceptions as arbitrary: the perception of kinship followed from
the reality of intermarriage. Owing to intermarriage, the original racial
boundaries (*zhongjie*) cannot be maintained.[27] But historical continuities
meant that, for example, we might say that today's "Han" people were
not entirely of the same "blood" as the Han people of the Spring and Autumn period—but we can still call them "Han." In the final analysis race
was not a thing but a relationship. "We," Liang proclaimed, are Yellow
in relation to the White, Brown, Red, and Black races, but "we" are also
"Han" in relation to the other races of Miao, Mongol, Xiongnu, and other
neighboring groups.[28]

Explicitly, Liang warned the Manchus that they must assimilate to the
superior Han or eventually face extinction.[29] This is because Manchus were
the "inferior race" (*liezhong*). Liang's emotive language was soon to be
picked up by the revolutionaries. But Liang merely meant to refer to the
triumphant standard of social Darwinism: the ability to survive. He argued that both Manchus and Han faced a threat from the outside that was
greater than any threat they posed to each other, and explained this threat
in racial terms: the White race was trying to dominate the entire Yellow
race. Liang claimed that final victory would depend on general racial improvement—and unity. In other words, if Han and Manchu were distinct
races that had struggled against each other in the past, today they needed
to band together. Indeed, this was the Manchus' only hope; the Han, as a
numerous, intelligent, and productive people, would survive foreign oc-
cupation and even the dismemberment of China—but the Manchus, who
were few, stupid, weak, and ignorant of work, would not. The coming
racial conflict would be at the highest level (White/Yellow), and therefore
racial unity (*hezhong*) at the next level (Manchu/Han) would be needed.[30]

As he learned more about social Darwinism and statism during his
exile in Japan, Liang was increasingly drawn to a vision of global racial
struggle and the concept of "historical races" (*lishi de renzhong*).[31] He
posited that Whites were now the strongest race, within which Teutons

constituted the strongest sub-race, and Anglo-Saxons the strongest sub-sub-race.[32] In his *New Citizen* essays, Liang outlined the sources of racial success in order to urge the Chinese to "renew the people." Logically, if the Chinese could do this, race was not destiny, but races were historical subjects: they made history. At the same time, Liang's descriptions of what he labeled as racial characteristics were in fact almost entirely social and cultural. For example, he believed that the "Teutons" had founded the European states, because their political abilities and political thought were superior to those of other White races such as the Slavs and the Latins. In other words, Liang's real interest was in the evolution of political institutions, not races. The lesson he drew from evolution was that humans made history, not history humans, though they did so in groups.

RACIAL CONSCIOUSNESS AND REVOLUTION

Until about 1900, the distinction between radical Confucianism and revolutionism was ambiguous. In the wake of 1898, the Qing treated both reformers and revolutionaries as equally traitorous. Sun Yat-sen (1866–1925) had attempted to organize an armed uprising against the Qing in Guangzhou in 1895. The tiny effort naturally failed. So, too, Kang You-wei's Society to Protect the Emperor (Baohuanghui) attempted an armed uprising in 1900. This effort was in the name of the Guangxu emperor, anti-Cixi but not anti-Qing. It too failed. One can see why the Qing made no distinction between reformers and revolutionaries as long as both were both mounting armed attacks against the government. But equally, the Qing court's failure to reform discriminatory laws contributed incalculably to the birth of the revolutionary movement.[33]

In the first years of the twentieth century, revolutionism distinguished itself from the Kang-Liang constitutional reform movement by its extreme anti-Manchuism, not by its political theory. The notion of replacing the imperial bureaucracy with a republican government was much more amorphous than calls to expel and exterminate the Manchus. The revolutionaries' numbers were steadily growing from about 1900, particularly among the younger generation of students provoked by the Qing's failures to reform. Their logic was simple. They saw that the most effective way to construct a popular national identity was on the basis of racial unity. This was to construct a pure nation-state based on Han identity. This project rested on memories of anti-Han oppression stemming from the Manchu conquest of the seventeenth century combined with nineteenth-century racial knowledge.[34] The younger generation of Han Chinese scholars concluded that the Manchus were a vile and worthless race. The new schools that emerged across China in the first years of the twentieth century saw extensive revolutionary agitation. Overseas Chinese communities from Singapore to Vancouver also provided revolutionary sympathizers. And Tokyo became a center of the Chinese revolution, since it was both a home for exiles and a center for education.[35]

A tract entitled *Revolutionary Army*, published in 1903 in Shanghai by the eighteen-year-old Zou Rong, may be taken as typical of a growing genre. Perhaps a million copies were published in the ensuing years.[36] The Qing did much to help the revolutionary case by trying but failing to bring sedition charges against the men associated with the journal that first published Zou's tract in Shanghai. Two of the men, Zhang Binglin (1868–1936) and Zou Rong (1885–1905), deliberately gave themselves up, albeit to the foreign authorities of Shanghai's International Settlement. Those authorities refused to cooperate with the Qing's manifest desire to execute Zhang and Zou but rather agreed to prosecute them for the relatively minor crime of lèse-majesté, for which they received three and two years' imprisonment, respectively. Zou died in prison, a martyr, and Zhang was released in 1906, a hero. The Qing court had managed to make itself look vindictive and impotent at the same time. The case did much to clarify the objectives of the revolutionaries. At about the same time, the court looked equally vindictive and impotent in its response to the anti-Russian student campaign of 1903. These were protests against Russia's stationing of troops in Manchuria. The Qing responded not by talking tough to Russia, nor even by pretending sympathy with the students, but by suppressing their activities, which it judged to be diplomatically disruptive.

If the anti-Russian campaign began as a movement that a more farsighted government might have tried to turn to its advantage, the *Revolutionary Army* was indeed simple sedition. Zou Rong called for the violent overthrow of the inferior and barbarian Manchu overlords. Zou's invective, based on his belief in a pure-blooded Han race, was combined with a belief in republicanism. It is important to note that Zou's argument was also thoroughly imbued with the rhetoric of rights. The purpose of revolution for Zou was to destroy the Qing and restore Han self-rule, and also to provide all the rights (*quanli*) of freedom, equality, independence, and autonomy for the citizenry.[37] Revolution, for Zou, was the duty of all citizens since their natural rights (*tianfu quanli*) were being suppressed by the Manchus.

Everyone should know the principles of equality and freedom. At birth, there are none who are not free and equal. In the beginning there were neither rulers nor subjects. . . . Later generations were ignorant of this principle. As soon as they achieved power, countless traitors, despots, and thieves monopolized what belonged to the common people and made it the private property of their families and clans. They called themselves rulers and emperors, so that nobody in the empire was equal and free. . . . So today the revolution of our compatriots should drive out the foreign races ruling us and exterminate the autocratic monarchs to restore our natural rights.[38]

Zou's debt to Huang Zongxi's vision of an egalitarian originary moment in human civilization is as clear as his debt to Rousseau's social contract. His prose goes one step further than Tan Sitong's. Zou combined republicanism and anti-Manchuism into a smooth mixture. He envisioned a kind of virtuous cycle based on rights and duties. The citizens Zou wanted to create through "revolutionary education" needed such qualities as self-respect, independence, boldness, and civic virtue in order to rule themselves; at the same time, precisely by claiming their natural rights, people would cultivate their independent personalities. In this respect, there was little that Liang Qichao would have disagreed with, particularly the link between individual autonomy and collective dynamism.

What made Zou's pamphlet popular was neither its originality nor its intellectual coherence but its sweeping language and emotional condemnation of all Manchus, as Manchus: "the furry and horned Manchu race," and "the wolfish ambitions of this inferior race of nomads, the bandit Manchus."[39] Zou classified the Manchus with other northern barbarians, racially distinct from the Han, nomadic, a "goat race" with "beasts' hearts."[40] Zou's essay was consumed with the traumatic history of Chinese "slavery." The Chinese were but "slaves of slaves"—the Han slaves of the

Manchus, who were slaves of the foreign powers. His preface was dated "the 260th year after the fall of the state of the great Han race"—that is, the fall of the Ming dynasty.[41] But what exactly made Manchus Manchu and Han Han? For Zou, as for many others at the time, the Han people were literally descended from the Yellow Emperor (Huangdi), a founder of Chinese civilization in the fourth century BC, according to ancient myth. Other peoples were not so descended, which made them foreigners.[42]

Anti-Manchuism was more than a passing prejudice or mere revolutionary rhetoric.[43] Although it disappeared quickly after the 1911 Revolution finally erupted, it was integral to the revolutionary movement and so to the founding of the Republic. To the extent revolutions are about purification, anti-Manchuism promised to expunge pollution from the body politic. A sense of racial taintedness, supported by science, was ubiquitous in revolutionary publications. The Tongmenghui was founded as an umbrella organization bringing together small revolutionary groups in 1905. As Zhu Hongyuan has noted, its organ, *The People's Journal* (Minbao), repeatedly made two points: that the Manchus and Han had different origins and that the Manchus had not assimilated.[44] It does not follow that 1911 is best conceived as a "racial revolution" (*zhongzu geming*),[45] because it was much more than that. Anti-Manchuism was a form of resistance.[46] This is precisely why, after 1912, what had been useful for nation-building proved useless for state-building.

Nonetheless, the debates between revolutionaries and reformers did much to clarify issues surrounding the state.[47] Revolutionaries and reformers shared much. And as Rebecca Karl shows, from about 1907 late Qing intellectuals conceived nationalism at least partly in terms of multiethnic anti-imperialism rather than a more narrowly conceived ethnicity.[48] But many still excluded the Manchus from "the nation" (*minzu*), now on the grounds they were colonizers, like the Americans in the Philippines or the British in South Africa. This, too, was essentially an ideological move that was still based, in my view, on the scientific racism of the day, which equated a people with the ruling elite. It was a political theory based on prepolitical categories.

One consequence of thinking in terms of the "Han nation" was to reconceptualize the state as the "property of the people," namely the Han.

To many revolutionaries, though not all, only a true nation-state was compatible with democracy and equality. At the very least, Han nationalism inevitably fostered a vision of horizontal ties among the people and taught the importance of a civilized (and homogenized) people. "Nationalism" in this sense was the natural heir of the imperial emphasis on unity (*dayitong*) and civility (*jiaohua*), although such universal values were in tension with its ethnic particularism. In the end, anti-Manchuism played a critical role in smashing the imperial state. The anti-Manchu ideologues were perhaps incoherent, basing their arguments, as we can now see, on pseudo-scientific ethnography, forced readings of history, and the strange teleology of the nation-state. But these were not visible problems in the late Qing.

What was visible, at least to a critic like Liang Qichao, was that anti-Manchuism was "narrow nationalism" (*xiaominzu zhuyi*) opposed to "great nationalism" (*daminzu zhuyi*), which he defined as "the unity of all groups belonging to the national territory to resist all foreign groups." Liang's emphasis on civic unity led him to conceive the new China as an "empire" (*diguo*).[49] Ultimately, the groups that counted for Liang were not really races—it was states that made history.[50] Liang also argued that the Manchus *were* becoming assimilated (*tonghua*).[51] This was not a matter of miscegenation, nor cultural adaptation, but of *both* groups becoming citizens. But in the end he too insisted that the Han would form the core of the future Chinese state, and predicted that under the right circumstances "Han will certainly be the rulers of China."

If Liang Qichao saw the Manchus assimilating, Yang Du (1874–1931) combined a rigorous contempt for the Manchus with a belief in constitutional reform under the Qing. Yang saw the strength of the republicans' arguments but eventually rejected them.[52] He was a classically educated Hunanese who had passed the lowest level of the examination system and also studied at the Academy of Current Affairs under Liang Qichao and other reformers in Changsha. In 1902 Yang made his way to Japan, where he studied law, and by 1907 he returned to China as a leader of the constitutionalist movement. He wrote several technical articles on railroads and fiscal policy as well as political essays. He firmly believed that of the five major races in China, only the Han had the qualifications to be citizens of a constitutional order.[53] The Manchus, Mongols, Hui, and Tibetans were all backward people, living in tribal, clan, or pastoral societies. He also argued that the Chinese (Han) people, though relatively advanced, suffered from an inability or unwillingness to take responsibility. China's basic problem was not one of despotic government but a failure of the state to be more proactive.

Yang was gratified that the Chinese lacked nationalism, while he found hope in traditions of statism (*guojia zhuyi*). Yang's views clearly differed from those of Liang, who despaired of the lack of nationalist sentiment, but they both prescribed the same medicine: given the civilizational level of the Chinese people, and given the need for active government, China must pursue constitutional forms. In theory, for Yang, constitutional monarchies and constitutional republics were equally advanced forms of polity.[54] However, in practice, given China's current political conditions, a constitutional monarchy was more appropriate—it was considerably easier to say how China was to get from here to there, than if "there" was a republic. In the language of the day, Yang argued that it was more practical to change the form of government (*zhengti*) than the fundamental state form (*guoti*).[55] If the Chinese were to preserve the existing territory and peoples, then the existing sovereignty (*tongzhiquan*) had to be preserved, although political power for all practical purposes could be transferred to an elected parliament. Another fatal weakness of republicanism for Yang was that it would require immediate equality between the Han and the other races. The "nationalism" (*minzu zhuyi*) of the Manchus, Mongols, Hui, and Tibetans would threaten the more advanced statism of the Han. Given foreign interference, it would even lead to the breakup of China. Only under a constitutional monarch could these groups be assimilated and unity maintained. Yang's vision of parliamentary supremacy kept the monarch as a bulwark of the multinational state.

It should be noted that the ethnographic approach—casual references to tribes and races—was by no means limited to scholars and pamphleteers. With the establishment of the new school system in about 1904, history texts sometimes and geography texts always included an overview of the populations of China and the world. A geography text published by the Commercial Press, China's largest publishing house, described the overarching Mongolian race or Yellow race that dominated Asia.[56] Historical China, it said, was founded by the Han race, a race that early became civilized and was characterized by its devotion to morality and political principle. A geography text by Tu Ji (1856–1921), a prominent geographer and historian associated with Zhang Zhidong, was more encompassing. Tu listed seven races of China based on linguistic differentiation: the Han of China proper; the Mongols and Tungusics (i.e., Manchus) of the north; the Turks of the northwest; the Tibetans of the west; and two somewhat scattered races in the southwest.[57] Each group had its own distinct history. This matter-of-fact science tended to lend credence to the revolutionaries' arguments once people were ready to accept the logic of the nation-state.

TRAUMA AND VENGEANCE

Anti-Manchuism was as much an emotion as an ideology. Neither the peace of the eighteenth century nor the efficient Qing censorship entirely erased memories of the horrors of the civil wars and the conquest of the seventeenth century. Whole cities had been razed when they did not submit to the conquering Qing. Men were killed, women raped, and children enslaved. As a final symbol of their subjugation, Chinese men were ordered to cut their hair and grow a queue in the Manchu style; some committed suicide rather than do so. Firsthand accounts of the violence survived.[58] These accounts were rediscovered in the late nineteenth century and helped fuel anti-Manchuism. They did so by creating a traumatized memory of the seventeenth century that enabled the construction of a discourse centered around the victimization—enslavement—of the Han Chinese. Of course, no one literally remembered the terrors of the seventeenth century; they had to learn about them. And the learning involved considerable "forgetting." That Han Chinese armies and bandits had massacred thousands did not become part of the late Qing historical memory.

Revolutionaries claimed that the Manchus' incorrigibly "bestial" nature was proved by their evil history. The revolutionaries, mostly students in their teens and twenties, relived the conquest of the seventeenth century, experiencing the old trauma vicariously. Repeated references to the bloody events of the conquest were designed to arouse popular anger, but they were not merely instrumental or cynical: they were themselves signs of uncontrolled anger and hurt, incessant picking at old wounds, and an

inability to forget. This is seen in the emotionality of so much revolutionary rhetoric. A particular version of victimization in the seventeenth century was reimagined in the late Qing, and graphic details of massacres
and rapes functioned to bring this past alive.[59]

The experience of trauma that certain young men and women felt in
the late Qing was no doubt partly existential—that is, inherent to the lives
of the period. They displayed a sense of acute loss. This was perhaps, at
root, a mythical loss of the perfect China. At the very least, the pervasive
fear for the "lost country" (wangguo) also marked a fear of the loss of the
self. Such a loss was bound to be traumatic. Yet while the trope of "lost
country" referred to the Manchu conquest, like the trope of "slavery" it
hinted at deeper problems. The revolutionaries knew perfectly well there
had never been a perfect China, though scapegoating Manchus was a way
to displace anxieties that were really about the future.

Constructing identity through the racial categories discussed above
was critical to the process of traumatization. That is, the slaughters of the
seventeenth century did not just happen to some people but to "us"—to
the Han, our ancestors, our family. Psychological definitions of trauma
emphasize its subjective nature—what one person finds traumatic another person might take in stride. The revolutionaries displayed a kind of
"secondary trauma" in the sense that they themselves did not, of course,
experience firsthand the traumas they described, but rather internalized
them through readings and repetitions.[60] In this way the "Yangzhou massacre" entered national consciousness. In May 1645, Qing forces had conquered the wealthy city of Yangzhou. Since it refused to surrender, Qing
commanders authorized their troops to loot and kill at will for five days.
A survivor recorded his experience:

Several dozen people were herded like cattle or goats. Any who lagged were
flogged or killed outright. The women were bound together at their necks with
a heavy rope—strung to one another like pearls. Stumbling with each step, they
were covered with mud. Babies lay everywhere on the ground. The organs of
those trampled like turf under horses' hooves or people's feet were smeared in the
dirt, and the crying of those still alive filled the whole outdoors. . . . It goes without saying that there were droves of orphaned children and widowed women,

crying in hundred-voice choruses, their lamentations verily shaking the earth. By afternoon the stacks of corpses had grown mountainous, but the killing and pillaging just grew more intense. . . . [A soldier] had already taken a young woman, her daughter, and little boy captive. When the boy cried to his mother for something to eat, the soldier grew angry and bashed in the child's skull with one blow. Then he carried the mother and daughter away. . . . Several soldiers had captured four or five women, the older two of whom were crying dolefully while two of the younger ones were smiling, laughing and enjoying themselves. . . . Then the two other younger women were sullied while the two older ones wailed and begged to be spared. The three younger ones shamelessly thought nothing of it when about a dozen men took turns raping them before handing them over to the two soldiers who'd run up later. By that time one of the younger women couldn't even get up to walk.[61]

The survivor, Wang Xiuchu, describes his efforts to keep his family alive by hiding from the soldiers and, when caught, by bribing them. His *Account of Ten Days at Yangzhou* was understandably suppressed by the Qing government, but it is not particularly anti-Manchu. Wang's account makes clear that the Qing's soldiers included Chinese and the pillagers of Yangzhou included local bandits. Indeed, Wang described how Manchu officers imposed what little discipline there was, and finally brought the entire massacre to a halt.

By the late 1890s, both the *Account of Ten Days at Yangzhou* and a similar *Account of the Jiading Massacre* were being reprinted in great numbers—both by the Revive China Society (Xing Zhong hui) under Sun Yat-sen in Hong Kong and by Liang Qichao and the reformers in Hunan, and subsequently by many others in many other places.[62] To turn the *Account* and other descriptions of the Qing conquest into a nationalist manifesto required that they be read in a new way. They were read through traumatized memory. The perpetrators all became foreigners while the victims all became Han Chinese. Late Qing readers of the *Account* experienced not merely empathy with Wang Xiuchu but a transferential relationship imagined in terms of the rape and murder of an entire nation—"my ancestors," "my nation," "myself." In this way, the Manchus were turned into a completely "alien race" (*yizhong*), and revenge was called for. Zou

Rong, for one, brought the memory of the fall of the Ming alive in his *Revolutionary Army*:

When I read *Account of Ten Days at Yangzhou* and *Account of the Jiading Massacre*, I began weeping before I finished reading them. I speak out to proclaim to my fellow countrymen: Were not the ten days at Yangzhou and the three massacres at Jiading typical of the slaughter of Han that the Manchus perpetrated in every single district? These two books merely describe one or two cases treated very briefly. But at that time when troops were let loose burning and plundering, when strict orders were issued to shave heads, and when the cavalry of the Manchu scoundrels murdered and pillaged wherever they reached—what really took place must have amounted to ten times more than these two cases. For these two incidents, which are known to everyone, there are a hundred thousand other Yangzhous and Jiadings. When I recall them, I am in anguish. . . . When the Manchu scoundrels entered China, were not those butchered by them the great-great-grandfathers of your great-great-grandfathers? . . . Were not those raped by the Manchu scoundrels the wives, daughters, or sisters of the great-great-grandfathers of your great-great-grandfathers? . . . The *Book of Rites* says: "A filial son cannot live under the same sky with the murderer of his father and elder uncles." Even a child understands this.[63]

It is worth noting that much late Qing writing, including that of Yan Fu and Liang Qichao, includes references to weeping and sighing and a kind of "alas alack" rhetoric. But it is the ancestral connection that turns Zou (and his audience) into secondary witnesses of the earlier massacres. We can see here both identification with people defined as victims by the crime committed against them and with people defined more ambiguously by the humiliations and shame they endured—humiliations seen now as lasting 260 years. For Zou, the transferential relationship is completed by the appeal to filial piety, which demands immediate revenge no matter how distant the crime. In the new political context, revenge demanded revolution, which was Zou's most immediate goal.

Sun Yat-sen was at least as fiery as Zou Rong. Sun used a rhetoric of racial invective playing on the themes of barbarism and slavery.[64] Sun's vocabulary featured degrading epithets (such as barbarians, slaves, caitiffs, thieves, inferior race), as well as calls for "Han revenge" (*xing-Han fuchou*) and "restoration" (*guangfu*).[65] "*Think back* to when we lost the nation," he told an audience in 1906, "*our ancestors* were not willing to submit to the Manchus. Close your eyes and *recall* the history of our ancestors' blood flowing in rivers and their corpses lying everywhere."[66] In a speech given in the United States in 1904 Sun had explained: "The Manchu's object was to stamp out the patriotic spirit of the Chinese, so that in the course of time they might forget that they were subject to a foreign rule."[67]

One student wrote that he understood the history of his ancestors (that is, the Han Chinese people) and remembered (recorded, *ji*) their shame—it was impressed on his brain and would never be forgotten.[68] The barbarian Mongols had killed 19 million Chinese (in the thirteenth century) but the slaughters of the Manchu beasts were far worse. The ten days of Yangzhou and the myriad families of Jiading represented the ratios of dead in every county. The unprecedented cruelties included cannibalism in Shanxi and the sale of human heads in Henan. "Whenever I think of these things, my blood boils and I want to exterminate this bastard race and eat them for breakfast." A natural act of sympathetic imagination was turned into traumatized memory: "The cruelties of the ten days at Yangzhou and the three massacres of Jiading were utterly inhuman. I still wonder about what happened. It is as if my spirit is still fighting for them and my heart still afraid for them, and so the events of those days can be known."[69] The time for revenge had finally arrived.

HISTORICIZING IDENTITY, CREATING NATIONAL ESSENCE (I)

One group of revolutionaries often spoke of "national essence," borrowing the term *guocui* from the Japanese *kokusui*.[70] The scholars of the National Essence school regarded the classics and other ancient texts, art, history, literature, and language as China's repository of culture. They conceived of the Han people not merely as a victimized ethnic group, but also as bearers and developers of a great civilization that had originated in the Yellow River valley several millennia before. The "essence" of greatness was always present, right from the originary moment of civilization founding. And the germs of republicanism could be found in the enfeoffment system (*fengjian*) of the Zhou. This is another way revolution was conceived as "restoration" (*guangfu*)—restoring the Han, restoring *fengjian* updated as republicanism, and, not least, restoring national learning from the depredations of the Qing autocracy. Founded in 1905, the *National Essence Journal* (Guocui xuebao) was equally devoted to anti-Manchu revolution and to traditional scholarship. From the start, the National Essence scholars adopted a defensive tone, fearful that Chinese learning was on the verge of being completely eclipsed by Western learning.[71] The National Essence reformulation of Chinese culture and history expelled the Manchus, so to speak, and formed one of the pillars of revolutionary reimagination of China. National Essence scholars sought to critically rethink Confucianism, and they unearthed long-buried non-Confucian aspects of Chinese culture precisely in order to foster China's rebirth. Like the students, they wanted to create a modern nation-state based on the principles of equality and liberty, but still rooted in the Chinese past.

Zhang Binglin and Liu Shipei (1884–1919), pillars of the National Essence school, were adherents of Old Text scholarship. They thought ludicrous the New Text school's belief in apocrypha, prophecy, and "Confucius as a reformer." They denied that Confucius "invented" the classics.[72] Both men were from prosperous regions of the Yangzi River valley, long centers of scholarship and somewhat remote, at least through the nineteenth century, from Western contacts. Both men were centrally concerned with rescuing Chinese history, as recorded in the classics, as distinctively national history.[73] In his early writings Zhang criticized Confucius and virulently attacked the establishment of a Confucian religion that Kang Youwei was edging toward. In the hands of Zhang and Liu, the Old Text scholarship of Han Learning became a means to desacralize the classics while turning them into a reservoir of historical data. The classics became one source, along with the "hundred schools" of the Eastern Zhou—the non-Confucian writings of antiquity—that could nourish the "national essence" and trace the ancient roots of Han identity. For Liu, Western Zhou institutions of about the eleventh century BC offered a model of political order. The historicism of National Essence scholars allowed them to abandon both Confucian universalism and the teleology of political modernity. In other words, they were not interested in the Datong, nor, though they were interested in Western political institutions, did they think a republican China would become an Asian United States.

Zhang had originally supported reform along the lines of Kang Youwei's 1898 program. His 1900 collection of erudite essays, *Qiushu* (Words of urgency), was an effort to rethink the cultural tradition and enrich Confucianism with the non-canonical schools of thought, modern science, and Darwinism.[74] Supporting reform, Zhang argued for the legitimacy of "guest"—that is, foreign—emperors.[75] Just as a country could use foreigners as officials, so, as long as the "rulers" did their job, there was no problem in their outsider status. Zhang was well aware of all the criticisms of the Manchus as cruel usurpers, but he argued that their rule was really a kind of practical administration, while the "emperorship" actually remained in the hands of Confucius and his descendants. Borrowing, for the moment, from Kang Youwei's idea of the "uncrowned king" and probably influenced by Meiji propaganda about the "imperial line unbroken," Zhang contended that the true rulership of China always lay in the hands of Confucius, comparable to Christ in the West and Buddha in Tibet. Others merely "called themselves emperors" but were ultimately doing the will of Confucius and preserving the Mandate of Heaven (and protecting China from foreign invasion). However, immediately after the publication of *Qiushu*, Zhang converted to revolution. He repudiated his essay, condemned the Manchus for abandoning China to the predators from the West, and called on the Han to "rule themselves" (*zizhu*).[76]

Many of Zhang's subsequent writings demonstrated the traumatized mode of thinking described above. Zhang often spoke of his childhood memories of his grandfather teaching him about the Ming loyalists such as Wang Fuzhi. On the grounds of the justice of vengeance, Zhang argued that it was just for Han to kill Manchu but not for Manchu to kill Han.[77] Perhaps more than any other thinker, Zhang defined the tropes of "revenge" (*fuchou*) and "restoration" (*guangfu*). These were moral imperatives for Zhang. He argued, first, that the Manchus perpetrated racial crimes against the Han (group against group); and second, that these crimes persisted till the present day. But Zhang's greatest contribution to late Qing political discourse was to rest these arguments on a historical narrative that traced the various populations of China back to ancient times. In his statement for a planned meeting to commemorate the 242nd anniversary of the loss of China (*Zhina wangguo*) in 1902 in Tokyo, Zhang claimed a quasi-racial, clan-based continuity of the Chinese for over four thousand years.[78] Zhang frankly reveled in the past, tracing the territorial claims of ancient tribes and clans, but also noted that remembrance is pain, invoking the martyrs of resistance to the Manchu invasions.[79] Heroic martyrs—from the last Ming emperor, who hanged himself, to Tan Sitong, who let himself be executed—were symbols of national unity and of crimes crying out for vengeance.

Zhang's Han nationalism depended on rereading the classics and the official dynastic histories through the lenses of Western racial science and social Darwinism. In an open letter to Kang Youwei published in mid-1903, Zhang relentlessly attacked Kang's thesis that Han and Manchus were essentially the same people.[80] Zhang's letter began with a world-class series of insults (Kang was engaged in lying and trickery and "buttering up" the Manchus, seeking office with them, the very model of the corrupt Confucian). The emperor Guangxu, whom Kang supported, was, in Zhang's opinion, completely hopeless—talk of his sageliness was pure nonsense. "The little clown Zaitian couldn't even distinguish between beans and wheat."[81] Zhang condemned the Manchus for their "abuse of the ancestral lands" and their treatment of the Han as their enemies. He argued in detail that the Manchus had failed to assimilate to Han ways and were precisely alien conquerors. And this is why revenge against the Manchus was justified. Kang had suggested that present-day descendants of ancient Zhao did not blame the descendants of Qin general Bai Qi, though he buried Zhao troops alive; nor did Qin posterity hate the descendants of Xiang Yu for burying Qin troops alive.[82] Zhang, however, objected that these historical cases of forgiveness involved, first, men of the same race, and second, actions that should be attributed to individual leaders, not entire groups. But in the case of the Manchus, that race as a whole agreed on its hateful purpose—to slaughter the Han race. Finally, Zhang added, we do not really know who the descendants of Bai and Xiang are, but the Manchus are still a privileged group living in their conquered land. That was to say that their refusal to assimilate was itself a kind of crime.

"Today five million Manchus rule over 400 million-plus Han only through rotten traditions, making them stupid and keeping them ignorant," Zhang said. "As soon as the Han wake up, the Manchus will be unable to rest peacefully within the Great Wall."[83] That was to say, the Han race of China proper, south of the Great Wall, would expel the Manchus to their original homeland to the north. (However, in reality, millions of Han Chinese had settled in Manchuria in the nineteenth century, outnumbering native Manchus.) In any case, Zhang insisted that Manchus were "as stupid as deer and pigs" and the emperor, the "little clown," was the "public enemy of the Han race." Zhang repeatedly linked revenge to the execution of justice. As a son has a right to avenge a father wrongly killed, so the Han had the right to avenge their ancestors.[84] This was not a matter of killing innocent later generations but active participants in an ongoing crime.

No wonder Zhang was convicted of lèse majesté along with his young friend Zou Rong. "Little clown" indeed (worst of all, Zaitian was the personal name of the Guangxu emperor and taboo). Above all, more clearly than any previous scholar, Zhang constructed a Han Chinese nation on the grounds of its historical development racially, culturally, and politically.[85] But especially politically, it was not very clear what Zhang proposed should take the place of the Qing. Unlike most revolutionaries, Zhang exhibited considerable skepticism about republicanism, which he was afraid would lead to new problems, such as power grabs by local strongmen. Nor could he support the anarchism of his friend Liu Shipei. Yet neither was he tempted to support the imperial institutions that his own desacralization of the classics weakened (and that the despised Kang Youwei supported). Furthermore, Zhang's opaque prose concealed his scholarship from all but a few adepts. His historical and religio-philosophical writings made no concessions to the reader, though he aimed some anti-Manchu writings at the student generation. The question was, what else were the Han, aside from being a race? Zhang's answer was, carriers of a great cultural tradition, albeit one deformed by the imperial state and foreign rule.

Where could true political institutions be found? Certainly, in part, late Qing intellectuals looked to the West and Japan. But if the ancient

Chinese sage-kings could be resuscitated, they would provide both political and ethnic sustenance. In the traditional view, the sage-kings were
quasi-divine yet historical figures. Politically, they had naturalized and legitimated the institution of the monarchy, as seen in Han Yu. This is why
Yan Fu's attack on Han Yu was a truly radical step. However, for most
late Qing intellectuals, both reformers and revolutionaries, it was important not to junk the sage-kings but to rethink their role in China's history.
The sage-kings provided a way to think about modern Chinese identity
and—to some extent—political institutions. They exemplified the origins
and early development of the nation. Since the sage-kings were so prominent in popular collective memory, they also provided a link between late
Qing elites and the masses.

History was a weapon in the debates between reformers and revolutionaries. But they held much in common as well. Liang Qichao tried to
understand the history of China as a story of the progress of the nation-
state. In 1902, he called for a "new historiography" that would fit the
dominant form of historical writing of the day: the narrative of national
becoming, the story of the nation.[86] Historiographically, Liang called for
a complete break with the past. He condemned traditional historiography as the mere records of the doings of a few families—the dynastic
rulers. It supported the notion of "orthodox succession" (*zhengtong*),
while the new history would find the Chinese people. For Liang, then,
nationalist history was democratic; traditional historiography was monarchist and obscurantist. However, he still wrestled with the problem that
the sage-kings represented an originary moment after which something
went wrong, at least politically. Liang's attempts to apply the principles
of linear progress and social Darwinism to Chinese history resulted in a
paradoxical picture.

By imposing an evolutionary scheme onto the sage-kings, Liang made
them into primitives. They might have been people who accomplished
great things, but they were just people, not gods. Yet they were also ex-
emplars of the universal laws of evolution. Essentially Liang argued that
the sage-kings represented stages of Chinese civilization that followed universal patterns of development such as tribal society, feudal-aristocratic
rule, and monarchical unity. The long-accepted line of the mythical sage-

kings went something like this: Fu Xi, inventor of hunting and trapping; Shennong, inventor of agriculture; the Yellow Emperor, inventor of the state (more on whom below); Yao and Shun, paragons of good government; Yu, founder of the Xia dynasty, which brings us out of the realm of mythology into history and the Three Dynasties (Xia-Shang-Zhou).

It was quite possible to map these myths onto the development of early Chinese civilization. If an earlier generation of Self-strengtheners had associated Yao and Shun with "democracy," Liang saw their so-called abdications as simply marking the transfer of power within aristocratic clans.[87] There was an ancient age of "barbarian freedom" that was dominated by small groups, all free and lacking classes and ranks. Then the second stage of China's development saw increased competition between these groups, which therefore needed leaders, who, in turn, gradually emerged as a nobility. This was the age of "aristocratic monarchy," which lasted from the Yellow Emperor to the Qin unification. In the third stage, increasing struggles gave rise to greater centralization, and diffuse aristocratic systems were replaced by strong centralized ones: the "age of flourishing monarchical power." Liang found this stage lasted all the way from the Qin to the eighteenth century—the reign of the Qing's Qianlong emperor. This led to the fourth stage, wherein sovereignty was established, populations were orderly, and monarchical powers became more and more absolutist—all of which "developed" the people to the point they could claim their collective powers. Now China was beginning to experience the "age of civilized freedom."[88]

According to Liang's historical logic, the centralized monarchy was a progressive step. But according to Liang's moral logic, the Qin unification was an autocratic disaster leading to centuries of stagnation.[89] At the time of the 1898 reform movement, Liang had lamented a historical process that exalted imperial power, intensified oppression of the people, and isolated rulers from their own ministers.[90] Later in Japan, he seemed to accept a somewhat different logic: combining his belief in linear progress with social Darwinism, it appeared that autocracy was the necessary stage between barbarian freedom and civilized freedom.

The trick that remained was to find the Chinese nation amid the historical documentation that focused on emperors and generals. Liang's attempts to turn the Chinese nation into the subject of history brought him back to the Yellow Emperor:

This was the age when China became China, as the Chinese nation (*Zhongguo minzu*) developed itself, struggled among itself, and unified itself. Most significantly, the barbarian tribes were defeated as the powerful [rulers] and their worthy ministers and kinsmen divided up the important territories, so tribal chieftainship became an enfeoffment system. More and more lands were annexed and conquest was unceasing. . . . Finally, with unification, the Han nation was truly managing its own internal affairs. At this time there only remained intercourse with the Miao tribes.[91]

In his history writing, Liang seems to have taken the "Han people" as a kind of historical given, but the Chinese nation had to be created through struggle. Liang strongly implied that the Chinese nation was created out of various peoples or nations. This was the achievement of the ancient period from the various sage-kings to the Qin. Liang's efforts to provide a historical judgment of the Chinese monarchy were fraught with ambivalence. When he was feeling optimistic, Liang could not help noticing that the unitary monarchy had saved the Chinese much suffering.[92] Monarchism was not only an objectively necessary stage, but it was a real blessing—a "Lesser Peace"—in its own right. And even now, precisely because it was facing unprecedented outside challenges, China could expect rapid progress. This optimism, though tinged with trepidation that the Chinese might not in fact rise to the challenge, was framed in terms of Liang's view of the historical subject, namely human collectivities.[93] Nations and races evolved through competition. Some unified themselves and survived. Others did not. This was a universal process of struggle and domination that gave rise to the familiar stages of clans, villages, tribes, and finally the nations of the present age.[94] In Liang's hands, this process treated the "national essence," if at all, as a by-product of universal evolutionary progress.

And yet, it was not clear if progress was in fact universal. Hence Liang suggested that perhaps monarchical rule had suppressed the natural development of the state, by which Liang seems to have meant a state committed to public-mindedness (*gong*). China was called a state (*guo*), yet it did not achieve a true state form (*guo zhi xing*).[95] Rather, the state had always belonged to clans, tribal chiefs, feudal lords, or the emperor. As we have seen, Liang repeatedly bemoaned China's isolation, lack of competition, and stagnation. It was also oppressive and decadent.[96] And worse: China seemed stuck in old ways just as modern Europe was leaping ahead.[97] Liang's efforts to convey optimism seem a bit forced. In "Ode to Young China" of 1900 Liang suggested that the country might be on the verge of vigorous youth.[98] After all, true nation-states had but recently emerged even in the West, so how far behind could China be? But for the most part it seemed very far behind.

HISTORICIZING IDENTITY, CREATING NATIONAL ESSENCE (2)

The approach of revolutionary intellectuals to the questions of origins, development, and essence can be represented by Liu Shipei. In 1903 Liu published his first article, a plea for the Chinese to use a calendar dating from Huangdi, the Yellow Emperor.[99] This was in effect an attack on the legitimacy of the Qing, which claimed the right to determine the calendar. Liu positioned the Yellow Emperor as the creator of civilization, the man who civilized the Chinese people. Liu noted that dating from the Yellow Emperor would bring China in line with the Western and Islamic nations, which dated from Christ and Mohammed. Although Kang Youwei's notion of dating from Confucius would have similar advantages, Liu argued that the Yellow Emperor better represented "preservation of the race" (baozhong), and not merely the "preservation of the Teaching" (baojiao). Liu also argued that dating from the Yellow Emperor would make China's dating system analogous to that of the Japanese, who dated from their founding emperor Jimmu. Significantly, Liu claimed that even though China historically had different dynasties, all the Han rulers were descended from the Yellow Emperor. Equally significantly, Liu suggested that as the current system of dating according to imperial reign period faded away, China's autocracy would be weakened.

That the Yellow Emperor carried special significance was not new in the late Qing. He was an ancient cultural symbol that was reworked to meet the new need to represent national identity.[100] In fact, Manchu Qing as well as Han Ming emperors had honored him. If the Yellow Emperor was to be an ancestor, he could be claimed by several Asian groups, not just the Han. However, in the hands of late Qing intellectuals, the Yellow Emperor became purely a symbol of Han identity. Liu dated the birth of the Yellow Emperor to 4,614 years previously, or 2711 BC, not incidentally giving China an impressive claim to continuous development. Under the Yellow Emperor arose embryonic forms of civilized institutions. The Yellow Emperor had previously been just one of several sage-kings; now he became the founder of the nation politically, culturally, and biologically.

Like Liang Qichao, Liu in effect historicized the traditional mythology, but Liu did so in order to claim a kind of racial essentialism. He emphasized that a nation (*minzu*) needed to know its origins. He stopped short of specifically claiming that the Yellow Emperor was literally the ancestor of all (Han) Chinese, though this would soon become a revolutionary cliché that has continued to reverberate to the present day. But in any case, in Liu's scheme, Chinese history acquired meaning from its relation to this originary moment. Nationhood, political institutions, and culture all stemmed from the Yellow Emperor, and developments were plotted on a continuum of temporality that flowed from him. At the same time, much of the mythological ethos surrounding the sage-kings was being dissolved. There was no sense that the Yellow Emperor was anything more than a good leader. Liu cited no aid from Heaven, no prophecy, and no supernatural elements. Liu's anti-monarchism was already evident.[101]

Liu's political views were embedded in a larger world-historical framework. In the late nineteenth century, Terrien de Lacouperie, a Frenchman brought up in Hong Kong, developed a theory of the origins of the Chinese, later called the "Western origins theory."[102] He said that the "Baks" were a tribe that originated in Mesopotamia, wandered around Central Asia, and then entered China under their leader, the Yellow Emperor, in the third millennium BC. The Baks defeated the native aborigines, some of whom moved south, becoming the Miao, while some remained as a labor caste under the Baks. This rather bizarre theory intrigued many late Qing intellectuals.[103] Insofar as the theory highlighted the immigrant status of the Yellow Emperor and his followers, it might not seem well adapted to the needs of Han nationalism. However, it perhaps had the advantage of emphasizing the monogenesis of humankind: since humanity shared a single origin, Chinese and Europeans were alike in having branched off from a Near Eastern core. As well, the revolutionaries may have enjoyed presenting the Han as conquerors in their own right, as we will see.

Liu believed that a process of segmentation and differentiation gave rise to racial groups that competed against one another for resources. The Han nation had differentiated itself from other groups early on and settled in China proper. These groups included Tibetans, Indo-Chinese, Tungusics, and Turks, though the Han was dominant and these other groups backward and literally peripheral. Liu outlined these views as early as his *Book of Expulsion* (1904).[104] These ideas would provide the basis of his more historical and scholarly investigations for the next several years. In sum, Liu believed that the Baks *were* the Han—or had somehow turned into the Han, through a process not very well explained.[105] The Yellow Emperor led the Han conquest of the Miao, and this conquest marked the creation of China as a sociopolitical entity out of the original Western-derived tribes. But this was just the beginning of the story. Liu regarded history as revealing a long struggle between the populace and those who would rule them. Sprouts of democratic thinking and even institutions had emerged in antiquity, although growth was stunted. In his co-authored *Essence of the Social Contract in China* of 1903, Liu highlighted the struggle between rulers and ruled.[106] Judged by the standard of public-mindedness, Liu found devolution rather than progress since antiquity.

The period of the Three Dynasties was an era when the ruler and the people shared power, and so it was recorded in the *Book of Documents* that the people were the hosts of the country and the rulers the guests. The establishment of a state (*guojia*) comes about when the people of the nation (*guomin*) coalesce. . . . In high antiquity the government of the country was in the hands of the people, and so the theory of the people as the basis of the state was recorded in the Teachings of Yu. [Then] with the Xia and the Shang, power was divided between the ruler and the people. . . . At the beginning of the Zhou, popular power was increasingly weakened. To strengthen it, it was necessary to use the theory that Heaven commands the ruler (*Tian tong jun*), [which gave rise to the saying that] "Heaven sees as the people see, Heaven hears as the people hear." Thus if we look at the classic *Book of Documents*, we can see the development of monarchical autocracy, and as monarchical powers increased, popular power yielded.[107]

In *The Origins of Ancient Learning,* which Liu began serializing in 1905, he remarked that theocratic government emerged when strong-minded leaders took advantage of the superstitions of the people to cement their own authority to that of the gods.[108] Theocracy was one face of autocracy.[109] Rulers also used sheer coercion to force the people to submit to them.[110] Liu clearly linked the development of a full-fledged class system (that is, inheritable rank and position) with the development of rulership.[111] Even into the Zhou dynasty, however, Liu found relatively few distinctions between the ruler and the people. He outlined a vision of primitive communism that did not dismiss it as simply backward but one in which, even with the evolution of rulership, checks were maintained on autocratic excesses. Liu seemed to imply that the historical task of the philosophers of the late Zhou was to contrive a means to check autocratic power. For he specifically criticized the Confucians for failing to do this. The Confucians understood part of the problem, but their emphasis on morality and rites at the expense of the law was inadequate. Liu said that Mohism, with its doctrine of striking fear into the heart of the ruler, was superior, while he praised Daoism's egalitarianism but not its doctrine of "non-action" (*wuwei*). Legalism had originally seemed capable of combining morality with the rule of law—laws that would apply to the ruler and thereby limit autocratic tendencies—and emphasized that both ruler and people had duties to the state. However, the Qin conquest created a system that shackled the people and limited freedom of speech. The implication was that China had never recovered.

In another series of essays published in 1905, Liu outlined why he thought it important to understand the origins of the state.[112] He presented a somewhat more complex picture here, though it still culminated in the Yellow Emperor.[113] The Baks were a nomadic people under the sage-kings Fu Xi and Shennong. It was Shennong who began to mark out a smaller, bordered territory. The Yellow Emperor, spreading his conquests from the Kunlun Mountains, conquered Chi You. Shun expelled the Miao peoples and began to spread civilization (*lijiao*) south into the Yangzi regions. Then Yu continued the expansion to the southeast. This is the order in which the ancient sages expanded the borders.[114] It was a process that Liu frankly called colonization and subjugation of native peoples. He also mapped this process onto socioeconomic stages. The period before Shennong marked pastoral nomadism, while the period from Shennong to Shun marked a slow and partial transition from nomadism to settled agriculture and urbanization.[115] Politically, China's borders and capitals changed with each sage-king, but the enfeoffment system (*fengjian*) that defined the Chinese polity stemmed from the moment territory began to be demarcated (from Shennong). This also marked a transition from a matrilineal to a patrilineal society, according to Liu.[116]

The Yellow Emperor's great accomplishment, Liu said, was the creation of the bureaucracy, the official system that established basic patterns of rule followed through the ages.[117] Imperial power was augmented by officials who kept track of the feudal lords. This was an effective means that the Former Kings used to position themselves at the center to rule the peripheries.[118] Liu also credited the Yellow Emperor with the creation of education.[119] "Education" here referred to a larger set of ritual behaviors and civilizing influences within an essentially theocratic framework. Not until the Zhou, Liu said, was a more complete system of education and scholarship developed, and the pure theocracy modified.[120]

Liu traced the origins of the emperorship back to the most primitive times, when it emerged out of shamanism.[121] Liu essentially argued that the sage-kings' use of supernatural forces demonstrated the theocratic nature of this primitive age. Fu Xi invented the eight trigrams and used secret spells to dazzle the people; Shennong discovered useful drugs, at a time when medicine was a shamanic field; the Yellow Emperor conquered Chi You with supernatural techniques. Furthermore, the early rulers monopolized the right to conduct sacrifices. According to Liu's philological analysis, as Chinese ideas of rulership became invested in the *jun*, this represented a concentration of authority in the administrative, legislative, and judicial spheres. Liu defined the *jun* as he who drew the world to him, and hence cognate with "grouping" (*qun*).

Therefore, when the Way of the ruler was established, benefits were derived from grouping. . . . In the very earliest period, the ruler was set up by the people, and the hereditary monarchy was not yet established. Thus the realm was managed by the Five Emperors differently from the way it was treated as private property (*jia tianxia*) by the Three Kings.[122]

This is reminiscent of the language of Huang Zongxi and the early Liang Qichao. But Liu was not particularly trying to contrast ancient virtues with present-day corruption, still less trying to establish ancient China's democratic credentials. Rather, he was mapping a naturalistic evolution from the relative equality of primitive society to a more organized polity, and on to what he regarded as recorded Chinese history (that is, the classics, which needed careful decipherment in order to grasp the true conditions of past eras).

Liu also felt the emperorship was historically rooted in the family system. The emperor-subject relationship was not analogous to the family but derived from it.[123] Patriarchal authority and the father-son relationship emerged in the transition from matrilineal and polyandrous society to patrilineal and polygynous society. Again, Liu used philological arguments to show that the terms for "father" (*fu*) and "ruler" (*jun*) originated in similar symbols for power. In this sense the state (based on the emperor-subject relationship) emerged out of the earlier family-clan structure. Liu argued that later clan laws were fundamentally based on the father-son relationship. In the ancient period, sacrifices were made both to local gods and to common ancestors. The emperor, then, as the head of a sort of clan of clans, was the chief officiate of the sacrifices of the nation.

The wise kings of old had united the people by demanding respect for the ancestors and the clan, in Liu's view.[124] People worked hard to avoid humiliating their ancestors and breaking the rules. In effect, the system worked like local self-government; ultimately, it united the people and established the ruler.[125] The clan laws and the class system that emerged were the logical products of an agrarian society.[126] Although farming had existed since the time of Shennong, only after the floods that Great Yu quelled did the emperor lay claim to all the fields. Liu thus traced the "well-field" (*jingtian*) arrangement back to the Xia's system for collecting taxes.[127] "Well-field" referred to an ancient land system described in the classics whereby nine fields were framed in a square three-by-three (as delineated by the character for "well"); the harvest of the central field belonged to the lord while the other eight fields belonged to individual families. Although Liu noted that the effects of the well-field system were egalitarian (at least among the commoners themselves), he emphasized the inevitability of its transition to a more productive system of private ownership. The well-field system was thus part of the development of class structure.[128] In the end Liu was to conclude that the only way out was through a revolution—a forward-looking mass political movement—based on the principle of equality.[129] In the name of egalitarianism, in 1907 Liu abandoned Han nationalism and became an anarchist.

The political discourse of late Qing intellectuals—revolutionaries, reformers, and undecideds alike—revolved around history and identity, public-mindedness and democracy, and constitutionalism and republicanism. Origin stories seem to hold a peculiar grip on the imaginaries of most human societies. Myth or history, they answer the critical question, "Where did we come from?" The question is critical because its answer at least partly defines identity—who we are—in a logic parallel to the seed somehow containing the tree. Old myths assumed new significance in the political context of the late Qing. They now spoke not merely to flexible ways of distinguishing "us" from "them" through ethnicity and culture but also to the early growth of a specific "Chinese" nation that—by implication—grew like the tree from the seed into today's Chinese nation. The late Qing's unprecedented need for national identity, so to speak, led to the recasting of ancient myths and histories into coherent narratives in which contemporary Chinese could find themselves, or at least find their ancestors.

If we try to determine less politicized, more mainstream views of educated persons in the late Qing, we might turn to the textbooks being written for the new state schools. These reflected a synthesis of the theories of the intellectuals and the needs of officials. On balance, history textbooks, for example, legitimated the imperial state by naturalizing it. But by naturalizing it, they also secularized it, removing one of its claims to legitimacy. Naturally, school materials were never going to explicitly challenge the Qing state.[130] In their dry and matter-of-fact way, following the chronology of the different dynasties, textbooks effectively naturalized the dynastic cycle. Without offering any explicit guidelines to determining the legitimacy of a regime or the means by which it came to power, histories of China followed the long-accepted story of "orthodox succession" (*zhengtong*). Political success—that is, conquest, unity, and defense—was its own justification. The foreignness of the Mongol Yuan and the Manchu Qing was frankly noted, but after all, *all* dynasties were conquest dynasties. Thus the Qing was judged by the same standards that applied to the Ming or the Han or any other "Chinese" dynasty.

Two implicit challenges to the imperial state emerged in historical study. First and most obviously, the logic of the dynastic cycle suggested that the Qing was coming to an end. Claims to legitimacy in the historical view came not from abstract appeals to Heaven but the practical ability to preserve domestic peace and protect the borders. No textbook, however loyalist its author, pretended the Qing had been able to do this over the preceding hundred years. And second, it was seen that the monarchy was not eternal—there was a time, in many ways superior, before the hereditary dynastic system was established, and there was now another time of fundamental change. Discussions of the sage-kings and the Three Dynasties spoke of more democratic-ish institutions, intellectual freedom and vitality, and the rapid development of civilization. Such Golden Age nostalgia was mixed in some textbooks, however awkwardly, with progressive stages of history. There was often an implication—a hint in the dry textbookish air—that as the dynastic cycle might be bringing the Qing to its end, so larger progressive forces were bringing the monarchy itself to an end. Whether the result was a constitutional monarchy or a republic scarcely mattered in terms of the fundamental political transformation being hinted at.

In its origins, "China" in the sage-king stories represented a nation that preexisted, and in some sense transcended, the later dynastic states. Most textbooks followed the Western origins theory and reflected the centrality of the Yellow Emperor stories to the identity of the Han people. For example, the *Illustrated Vernacular History of China* stated that the Yellow Emperor amalgamated the Chinese tribes to establish a kingdom that stretched from north of the Yellow River to south of the Yangzi.[131]

The Yellow Emperor thus became the "first ancestor of us, the Chinese people." A highly successful history textbook put out by the Commercial Press in 1904 began with the cosmogony of Pan Gu but observed that the ancient world consisted merely of tribes or villages. After it evolved into a unified state, this "China" essentially remained unified through fourteen historical dynasties.[132] In this account, the Yellow Emperor was not only a conqueror but also a progenitor who institutionalized the bureaucratic system and "improved the lives of the people through civil rule."[133] The history text by the reformist educator Ding Baoshu had little good to say about hereditary rule, but Ding praised those emperors who protected the Chinese race from foreign incursions.[134] The theme of racial struggle was never far from intellectuals' minds.

CHAPTER 6

Restoration and Revolution

A NTI-MANCHU REVOLUTIONARIES became increasingly committed to democracy-now in the first years of the twentieth century.
Although republican ideas remained secondary to anti-Manchuism as
a rallying cry and were less thought out, the revolution was clearly not
going to attempt to establish a new dynasty.[1] Committed revolutionaries
remained a small minority of students and an even smaller minority of
gentry. The number of full-time conspirators was miniscule—perhaps a
few hundred. Still, young, educated elites could not but feel the importance of national identity and the urgency of state-building. Their views
gradually influenced more and more persons in China. Their fathers and
uncles might not approve of their activities, but would still try to protect
them from the Qing's wrath. And fathers and uncles might not agree with
revolution but still find much sense in what the revolutionaries had to say.

Propaganda could be churned out by exiled intellectuals and students
abroad. Their journals made their way into China's coastal cities and eventually into the hinterlands, still being passed hand to hand years after initial
publication. And radical students usually returned to China, sometimes
even taking official posts (where they might act as a force for change), or
more typically becoming teachers sympathetic to the radical tendencies
of the *next* generation of students. Some joined the New Army, which
turned out to be key to the revolution.[2] The New Army had its roots in
Japan's defeat of Qing forces in 1895. Yuan Shikai and Zhang Zhidong
were entrusted with the development of new battalions that would receive
modern training and weapons and were organized on the model of the
German military. New Army troops tended to be better educated, especially the noncommissioned officers, than regular army troops, and higher
social elites began to join the officer corps. Many proved to be amenable
to nationalist and revolutionary ideas.

The height of revolutionary enthusiasm probably came in the period from about 1905 to 1907. "The revolutionaries" were in fact a disparate group, prone, as revolutionaries are, to internecine quarrels, and prone, as students and intellectuals are, to changing their minds. Revolutionary organizations fused and fissioned rapidly.[3] Revolutionaries feared that the Qing reforms would enable the dynasty to survive, and this fear created new strains among the revolutionaries. They continued their efforts, however, and by 1905 or so the *reformers'* pressures on the Qing to pursue constitutionalism were equally unremitting.

REPUBLICANISM, LIBERTY, AUTONOMY

In his 1903 open letter to Kang Youwei, Zhang Binglin argued that the key to revolution was not violence but the determination of the people.[4] This was the age of nationalism, and revolution was necessary to create a self-governing Chinese nation. Zhang argued that if the Chinese people were ready for a constitutional polity as Kang proposed, then they were ready to carry out a revolution. While Zhang was still in prison, revolutionary ideas continued to spread among students and Overseas Chinese. The Tongmenghui (Revolutionary Alliance), founded in Tokyo in 1905, brought disparate revolutionary groups together and gave them new national reach.[5] The Tongmenghui's official organ, the *People's Journal* (Minbao) propagated revolutionary ideas, above all anti-Manchuism, and engaged Liang Qichao in direct debate. The Tongmenghui was also supported by a mix of Japanese sympathizers—ranging from liberals to ultranationalists—who shared distaste for the Qing. Sun Yat-sen emerged as the logical leader of such a group due to his long history as a revolutionary, his foreign contacts, and his support among Overseas Chinese. Sun was a son of farmers near Guangzhou; his successful older brother helped him continue his schooling in Hawaii and then in Hong Kong. Sun lacked a literati background, but he was able to use his secret society contacts in south China to organize uprisings against the Qing. He was also a master at raising money from Overseas Chinese—both his revolutionary forces and Kang Youwei's Protect the Emperor Society raised most of their money from traders and coolies in Southeast Asia, Australia, and the Americas. Sun gradually developed a reputation among literati-minded students after the turn of the century, and Sun was chosen to head the Tongmenghui.

Revolutionary unity was not maintained for long, but the Tongmenghui achieved a rough ideological consensus based on Sun Yat-sen's notion that the revolution should encompass anti-Manchuism, republicanism, and "equalization of land rights." This was an embryonic version of the "Three People's Principles" that received their final form in his speeches of 1924: nationalism, democracy, and people's livelihood (socialism). Sun's outline of a common program for the Tongmenghui was elaborated by others, especially Wang Jingwei (1883–1944) and Hu Hanmin (1879–1936), both fellow Cantonese close to Sun. Other leading revolutionaries tended to go their own ideological ways. Most critically, in the summer of 1906 Zhang Binglin, freed from his Shanghai jail cell, arrived in Tokyo. Zhang was greeted as a revolutionary hero and made editor of the *People's Journal*. This gave the revolutionaries new intellectual firepower.

Soon after his arrival in Japan, Zhang wrote an elegant gloss on the term for "China," *Zhonghua*. Zhang insisted on the historical coherence of a distinct Chinese identity, associated with the name *Hua*, in distinction to outlying barbarian ethnic groups.[6] This was not a matter of absolute purity of bloodline but a more or less self-conscious cultural-ethnic continuity. Ultimately, the problem with the Manchus was not their inability to assimilate or their tribal qualities but their political claims to rule over China in spite of their status as a minority caste. The central task of the revolutionaries lay in reclaiming sovereignty (*zhuquan*) for the Chinese.

Zhang had less to say about the concept of "republic." Sometimes, he spoke favorably about republicanism, but he was more comfortable promoting a more abstract form of egalitarianism. He accepted the basic premises of democracy (*minquan*), demanding the right of political participation on the part of the poor (at least assuming they had been educated, as was their right).[7] But, as in his speech to revolutionaries and students when he arrived in Tokyo, Zhang's main interest lay in promoting nationalism through two principles: the national essence and Buddhism. The first provided a general pride in past achievements. While revolution would destroy much, Chinese could still build on the heroes, ideas, and institutions of the past.[8] For example, traditional practices of land equalization minimized the gaps between rich and poor. The second, Buddhism, encouraged egalitarianism and would help unite Chinese of different classes. Properly understood, at least, Buddhism creates a capacity for action and even justifies rebellion.[9] Zhang rejected Christianity as suitable only for barbarians, while he rejected Confucianism (*Kongjiao*) as too imbued with the values of aristocrats and officials to be of use to the populace.[10]

Insofar as Zhang thought well of democracy, it was as a form of egalitarianism. But Zhang sharply expressed his skepticism toward republican institutions. He derided the very notion of representation and was more attracted to something like Rousseau's "general will." He attacked parliaments on the grounds that elections would merely confirm the present-day corruption of local power-holders.[11] Furthermore, for any kind of democracy to work, property had to be equalized. Socialism was thus a necessary condition for the kind of democracy Zhang could support. Zhang seems to have regarded socialist egalitarianism and state ownership of resources and industry as the sole guarantee that democratic institutions would not increase the gaps between rich and poor, rulers and ruled.

If this can be called an ideology, it was ultimately subversive of the state itself. Zhang's 1907 essay on the "Five Negations" began by calling for the abolition of government. Zhang went on to call for the dissolution of communities, humankind, living creatures, and the world.[12] The logic here might be called Buddhist nihilism. Governments, Zhang declared, were inherently oppressive. They lacked any nature of their own (in today's terminology, this might be to say they were socially constructed). But even if governments were abolished, natural human communities would still give rise to struggle and to new authority. So communities needed to be abolished. But even if communities were abolished, humankind was violent and would reestablish communities. So biological life must be abolished, lest humankind evolve again. And so on. Coming back to our world in an essay on the "state," Zhang argued that states were contingent, formed out of necessity but in no sense natural phenomena. The *nation* was also "imagined"—but still Zhang seemed to think it was more real than the state. Indeed, no one worked harder than Zhang to make it real: ethnic and cultural commonalities surging through history formed the basis of the national community. In this world, at least, Zhang justified nationalism and even the state. He argued that since nation-states in fact did exist, all peoples should defend themselves from outside oppression. He thus condemned anarchism as shallow, a recipe for ongoing oppression, even if his own thought sometimes led in an anarchist direction.[13]

Constitutionalism, Zhang distrusted: both because it seemed a way to maintain the Manchu sovereignty over China, and because republican institutions were a means by which vested, private interests entrench themselves. Constitutionalism was little more than a disguise for "feudalism" (*fengjian*)—but China had abandoned the *fengjian* system two thousand years earlier.[14] Under these circumstances, constitutionalism would simply augment the powers already held by local power-holders, especially without top-down measures to ensure that property was held equally. As for the success of Meiji Japan, this was due not to its constitution but to its militarism, which was a reflection of the strength of Japanese feudalism.[15] Zhang's distrust of constitutionalism and the principle of local self-government was echoed in much discussion in China.[16] But even Zhang could not suggest an alternative to constitutionalism, at least in the present age. His fears were to prove prescient, however.

Most revolutionaries waved aside Zhang's doubts about constitutional order and representative institutions. Ironically enough, only the anarchists Zhang so despised were also engaged in unmasking republicanism as a trick to preserve authoritarian rule. But overall, revolutionaries adamantly supported "democracy." The revolutionaries' critique of monarchism differed little from that already laid out by Liang Qichao. But when Liang attacked the idea of revolution and the moral character of the revolutionaries, and when he came out in support of "enlightened despotism," the revolutionaries were ready to defend a revolution designed to bring about a republic. They pointed out that if Liang feared a republican revolution might be violent, well, so might attempts to found a constitutional monarchy in the teeth of an intractable court.[17] The real danger was that without a revolution, China's slide into decrepitude would continue. It was a people awakened through overthrowing their despotic overlords who could protect the country.

Revolutionaries offered little detail on how they would create republican institutions. Rather, they engaged in a kind of poetics of democracy.

Hu Hanmin explained the Tongmenghui's principle of "republicanism" (*gonghe zhengti*) as a "democratic-constitutional polity" (*minquan lixian zhengti*).[18] Constitutional democracy, Hu contended, could be based on China's historical lack of class distinctions. The nobility had been abolished by the time of the Han dynasty, and so establishing democracy would be an easy task. All it would take now would be to get rid of the Manchus. Hu looked to the United States as model and as warning, for there the path to democracy had been eased by the absence of a nobility, but the United States now suffered from the divisions of economic classes. Curiously, Hu denied that China even had economic classes. Presumably, he was thinking of China's lack of Rockefellers and Carnegies and their ilk. He did recognize the danger of growing landlordism, since he spoke of the need to nationalize the land. Other revolutionaries tended to agree that China was a classless society. Zhang Binglin, for example, made the same point in highlighting how China's early abandonment of the feudal system had erased the distinction between noble and base.[19] At any rate, for Hu Hanmin, the point was that China was ready for republicanism. The very existence of Han nationalist consciousness and democratic thought showed this readiness. If, as Liang Qichao had argued, it was necessary that popular standards be raised through a period of enlightened despotism, this had already occurred in the Han and Tang dynasties (why China had not become democratic a thousand years previously, Hu did not explain).

Hu's optimism also rested on a kind of teleology that stipulated that the time for monarchism was simply over. Hu contrasted his "democratic constitutional polity" to aristocratic forms and to popular democracy. Conflating aristocracy with constitutional monarchism, Hu criticized its built-in gap between ruler and ruled. But on the other hand, he rejected popular democracy (*minquan zhengti*) or pure democracy on the grounds it really amounted to "popular despotism"—with the same faults as autocracy.[20] Hu also distinguished republicanism from the anarchists' proposals. Anarchists were simply interested in destruction, he implied, while republican ideas represented wise planning for the future construction that would be needed after the revolution.[21] Nor were the Chinese people ready for anarchism, Hu felt, though he did not follow up this teleological hint that anarchism might supersede democracy one day.

A more substantial defense of republicanism or a "democratic consti-tution" was mounted by Wang Jingwei, writing in 1906 in direct rebut-tal to Liang Qichao's promotion of enlightened despotism.[22] Expanding on Hu Hanmin's arguments, much of Wang's essay consisted of showing that revolution was a realistic means of bringing about a republican pol-ity: revolution need not lead to a new form of tyranny.[23] In fact, according to Wang, only a revolution—and a "racial revolution" specifically—could bring about any kind of constitutional order.[24] In suggesting that this ra-cial revolution was also a republican revolution, Wang, too, asserted the readiness of the Chinese people to adopt democratic practices. First, he insisted that democracy—liberty, equality, and fraternity—was part of humanity's universal nature.[25] This was a "spirit" shared by Chinese as much as by Westerners. Nations differed in many particular respects, and Chinese democracy need not be precisely modeled on the constitutional forms of Western nations, but it would resemble them in its essential spirit. And second, Wang emphasized that the Chinese political tradition had treated the people as the basis of the state "since the times of Yao and Shun." Wang did not mean that ancient China had seen democracy. Rather, he thought that traditional Chinese political theology, in equat-ing the will of Heaven with securing the security of the people, was like Western insistence on the ruler's responsibility to God. Both, in other words, were transitional stages to democracy. Wang, like other intellec-tuals of the day, saw a trend toward greater absolutism since the period of the Three Dynasties. Yet precisely because the ruling house changed in the dynastic cycle, he argued, the Chinese people had learned not to confuse the monarchy with the state.[26] And today, finally, they were fully cognizant of their national rights.

More specifically, Wang objected to any theory of the state that treated the monarch as its owner. He criticized Liang's notion of enlightened des-potism because it would leave the Manchus in control: and they simply lacked the ability to rule well.[27] As well, Wang implied, any kind of au-tocracy, no matter how supposedly enlightened, infantilized the people, who needed to be taking responsibility.[28] More broadly, Wang argued that the state is neither an instrument created by an individual nor an organ-ism rooted in nature. Rather, the state expresses the collective will, which is formed by individual wills but, once formed, exists independently of them.[29] In a word, the state possesses its own "personality" (ren'ge) and general will (zongyi). If "state" is an abstraction, it is an abstraction that refers to a territory and people that cannot not be reduced to their ruler. Nor can the state, in the case of a democracy, be equated even to its parliament: it is larger than representation. Sovereignty lies in the state (guoquan) as a matter of legal principle. It is in this sense that the state is a legal personality.[30]

Wang could only locate sovereignty in the state because even the people conceived collectively were still natural persons, as limited as a monarch. Still, the people were not the objects of rule but rather the "subjects of rights and duties."[31] In a democratic state, "the people as a whole" do constitute the highest organ of governance, so the question of sovereignty is an abstract one. Wang found that parliament, in representing the people, stands above any single element of society and pursues the interests of the whole. Contrary to the fears of Liang, following a point made by the German monarchist Conrad Bornhak (1861–1944), Wang claimed that representative organs are fully as capable of resolving conflicts among the citizens as is a monarchy. The representative nature of the parliament is assured by elections. If electoral systems in the past had produced representatives of private or local interests rather than the public interest, Wang flatly claimed, such was no longer the case today.[32] His point seems to have been that the modern parliament is by its nature a national organ. Wang also noted that while truly popular assemblies of all the people might work in a small country, China (like the United States) was simply too big to avoid a representative system.[33] Wang insisted that representative institutions, as for example in the American system, were based on a theory of individual rights distinct from Rousseau's theory of the general will (contrary to Liang Qichao's conflation of the two). This was not, Wang thought, to disown Rousseau completely but to insist that the "social contract," once it was agreed to and the state already founded, necessitated representation as a practical matter.[34]

Wang stressed (contrary to his comrade Zhang Binglin) that only a democratic polity could maintain an egalitarian social order. At the very least, Wang stressed, any theory that posited sovereignty in the state itself was incompatible with absolute monarchism. For if the state was sovereign, the monarch could be at most an organ of the state.[35] There was some mystification of the state in Wang's views. Insofar as he attributed personality to the state, this was much like the organic view of the state. We might say that Wang's state was simply a democratic organism with a parliament rather than a monarch forming its head. We might also say that Wang's faith in an electoral system that would transcend private interests was naïve. However, Wang was in fact aware of the problems of unfair and manipulated elections, although the best he could propose was the careful application of laws to prevent cheating. For Wang, sovereignty was derived from the will of the people as a whole, concretized in a parliament, and located in the state itself. At the same time, Wang argued that the separation of powers would prevent any single organ of the state from becoming dictatorial.[36]

Rather than Bluntschli or Bornhak, the German legal scholar whom Wang turned to was Georg Jellinek (1851–1911).[37] Not the least of what Wang got from Jellinek, rightly or wrongly, was a notion of the need to place limitations on the state in the name of human rights. In his essays of 1906 and 1907, Wang deemphasized the teleological thrust of much of the writing of the period. He spoke of "institutions" (zhidu)—meaning elections and parliaments—and of "spirit" (jingshen)—meaning an almost innate popular feeling for liberty, equality, and fraternity. These views actually had much in common with those of Liang Qichao before his conservative turn and were probably as much directly influenced by Liang as by Wang's reading of Western political theory. Wang was essentially using democratic Liang to attack despotic Liang. Wang himself complained it was difficult to rebut Liang's arguments, not only because Liang's opinions shifted (as Liang himself admitted), but also because Liang did not consistently adhere to any particular school of thought.[38] What Wang did not consider was that both he and Liang were using a vocabulary and adopting intellectual schemes so utterly foreign to the Chinese political tradition that conceptual slippages were unavoidable. The basic notions of elections and parliaments were clear enough, but to speak of "legal persons" and the "personality of the state" was to traverse new lands with only the sketchiest of maps. Another of these explorers was Song Jiaoren.

THE POLITICAL AS THE PERSONAL

Song Jiaoren (1882–1913) grew up in Hunan, where he received a traditional education. He fled to Japan after a failed revolutionary plot in 1904, and in 1905 he became a founder of the Tongmenghui. He had moved from being a local student activist to a committed revolutionary with contacts in various provinces. In many ways he can be seen as representative of his generation, both in this transition and in the stress he experienced in his personal life. His unusual diary, though, allows us to explore the links between the political and the personal in ways not possible with other student revolutionaries.[39]

The pressures experienced by intellectuals of the last years of the Qing were incalculable. The regime was collapsing before their eyes. Self-avowed patriots were constantly frustrated that the Qing gave no support to their anti-foreign protests—such as against the Russian refusal to leave Manchuria in 1903 or the racist American immigration laws in 1906. Yet the dynasty proved remarkably durable, surviving blow after blow. Among revolutionary students, despair mixed with resentment and fury. There were suicides. For example, the student revolutionary Chen Tianhua jumped into the sea in 1905, for reasons not entirely clear but connected with his call for students to exhibit greater patriotism. There were suicide attempts, such as that of the older radical Wu Zhihui when he was deported from Tokyo in 1902. There were assassinations and attempted assassinations of Qing officials, designed to jump-start rebellion. Revolutionaries sometimes blew themselves up preparing bombs. There was the memory of Tan Sitong's martyrdom. At the same time, many students faced financial pressures and an uncertain future. Those studying abroad needed to learn a foreign language, were made fun of by local children, and lived with culture shock.

It is not my intention to pathologize revolution or revolutionaries, but to suggest that, just as with the reformers, psychological factors and intellectual work cannot be separated. Among Chinese intellectuals, as Jing Tsu suggests, a sense of defeat or generalized "failure" became a key element of identity formation.[40] The nation thus became an object of desire for intellectuals. Even while their sense of humiliation gave them a new capacity for self-criticism and agency, it perhaps trapped them in a need for failure as well. Defeat gave rise to utopian hopes; hope gave rise to the capacity for resistance. Anxiety was a natural result of these intellectual twinnings. More generally, as Haiyan Lee has pointed out, the extreme sentimentality of so much of the literature of the last decade of the Qing reflected a new interpenetration of the private and public spheres.[41] Readers of such fiction, along with its authors, formed a kind of community in which emotional expression became foundational to the individual's identity as well as the bonds among individuals. As we noted above, a rhetoric of "alas, alack" cries of pain permeated both radical and conservative political literature.

When young, educated Chinese assumed a modern national identity, they literally felt that humiliations inflicted upon China were inflicted upon themselves. And as John Fitzgerald has recently pointed out, the quest for national dignity was simultaneously a quest for personal dignity.[42] The "politics of recognition" applied to individuals and nations alike. We may go further: the motivating force creating this link operated at that level of individual psychology. Certainly, Chinese students in the last years of the Qing often (not always) experienced the stress of a sense of degradation. The trope "slaves of slaves" was taken personally, acting as an incitement to rebellion but also describing a deeply depressing condition. Students experienced two sets of juxtapositions: China (backward, slavish, oppressed) versus the West (modern, free, and oppressive), and Chinese realities versus utopian visions. It was easy enough to imagine a future without "boundaries," where all were equal and free and even labor was largely abolished, but harder to determine the correct course of action.

Song Jiaoren, for one, felt keenly the distance of the exile. After he had been in Japan for almost a year, Song received a letter from his family telling him of his grandmother's death, three months after the event. Song records that his unfilial behavior reached to Heaven.[43] In the spring of 1906 another family letter to Song spoke of his mother's love and longing for him, and he was reminded of his love for his mother.[44] But he also replied that his family needed to remember why he had to go into exile in the first place. By the summer, he had admitted himself to a hospital for depression (and a kind of nervous breakdown we will return to below), when his wife wrote urging him to return.[45] Displaying no affection for his wife, Song was resolved to get cured first. But when his older brother wrote to ask him to send money or return home, noting that the family had sold land and pawned their clothes and that his mother missed him, Song reports how sad he felt.[46] He wished he could rush home, wished he had money to send, wept with frustration. But he actually did nothing. Not until late 1906 did Song promise to return home, though only for a visit. He wrote a lengthy letter to his mother emphasizing the need to finish his education—that is, to remain in Japan.[47] The letter implied that his family was facing various problems in which they were trying to involve Song. He urged his mother to correct his brother through shame rather than scolding, that his youngest sister should unbind her feet and continue her studies, and that she be married to an educated man but not necessarily to a rich one.

In all, it is not clear that Song was especially close to his family, even his mother. He did not keep his promise to visit them early in 1907 but left for Manchuria in an attempt to foment rebellion there. He was the younger son, but his older brother seems to have been feckless, and it could be said Song did not fulfill his filial responsibilities very well. Song expressed strong filial feelings through guilt. Yet ultimately Song's loyalty was to China, not his family. During his hospital stay he wrote poetry of exile. "Within the four walls, the insects urgently chirp / Alone by the lamp, the cold night rain / I myself, in melancholy / my native country, seen in a dream."[48]

Song was not one of the Tongmenghui's great propagandists, but he was one of the most sober and skilled activists in Tokyo, an alliance-builder in the highly factionalized world of Chinese revolutionaries. He was also a romantic who took his pen name from the *Shuihu zhuan*,[49] who compared himself to the ancients who sacrificed themselves for the benefit of humanity, who wept easily, and who worked at his own moral self-improvement and the cause of revolution to the point of breakdown.[50] Yet it is also worth noting that Song was an indefatigable tourist, ever ready to enjoy the sights even while fleeing for his life.[51] If not a traveler in Kang Youwei's league, Song still enjoyed puppet shows, bookstores, the hurly-burly of town life, and once safely in Japan continued to note occasional outings. Song did not pretend to his diary that he was a single-minded hero lacking all self-doubt. On the contrary, he admitted to home-sickness and, especially, full-fledged depression. He stayed in hospital from

August 19 to November 4, 1906, for his "nervous disorder." He aspired to the revolutionary comradeship for which historical knights-errant and the *Shuihu zhuan* provided models.[52] Song also engaged in a strenuous program of self-education—reading widely in history and philosophy, political theory (socialism), psychology, and military affairs, and studying Japanese. (In the hospital, he also read *Dream of the Red Chamber* and detective stories.) Song was able to witness the Japanese patriotism of the Russo-Japanese War firsthand, noting how it was fostered by public ceremonies and even popular entertainment such as puppet plays.[53] He also noted the Russian Revolution of 1905, lamenting that the Chinese lacked the popular spirit of the Russian people.[54] He recorded enormous respect for the Japanese—even its jailers seemed highly moral.[55]

Like Liang Qichao, Song believed that moral self-cultivation, not merely scholarly or political accomplishments, was important. And like Liang, Song found the mutual criticism of friends to be key to self-cultivation. Following the example of Xue Jingxuan as recorded in the *Mingru xue'an*, Song resolved to keep a record of his reading and thenceforth used his diary as a commonplace book.[56] He believed that to follow the Way, one needed self-control (*keji*) and empathy for others. One's actions needed to be based on humanity, righteousness, propriety, and wisdom. "When one acts completely according to Heaven's laws (*Tianze*), then the Way is present." At the beginning of 1906, Song was reading Wang Yangming's *Chuanxilu*, which he saw as a guide to "entering the Way."[57] Song was particularly interested in "establishing the will" (*lizhi*), which was a critical notion for justifying revolutionary action and which Song based on Wang Yangming's theory of innate good learning (*liangzhi*). Song told his friends that if they knew their own will, then all else would follow.[58] There is also a sense in Song's diary that he was modeling himself on Wang Yangming, who was, after all, a man of action as well as a philosopher. At the very least, Wang's model of sagehood, so influential in creating the revolutionary thrust that would lead to Japan's Meiji Restoration in the 1860s, aided Song in the creation of his own revolutionary personality.

As he worked out his ideas in his diary, Song followed Wang closely.[59] It is not our concern here to judge whether Song understood Wang correctly, nor to turn a few random diary jottings into a philosophy on its own account. Nonetheless, we can see what ideas Song found exciting and useful. Song thought he was following the mature Wang in basing the Way of the Sage on the active pursuit of moral knowledge (*gewu zhizhi*), which was based on one's own sufficient nature (in contrast to the younger Wang's attempt to investigate the patterns of affairs and things in the external world). However, Song wanted a unitary vision encompassing both the mind-heart—and therefore the Way of the sage—and a form of the investigation of things that was all-encompassing. He seems to have felt Wang did not precisely provide this. In any case, within his own version of the all-encompassing, Song found two constituent parts: the mind-heart and objects. The mind-heart referred to the learning of the spiritual. Objects referred to the learning of material things. Investigation lay in investigating objects while reaching lay in reaching objects. These references to objects might seem to suggest that Song was returning to the philosopher Zhu Xi, but Song accused Zhu of excessively dividing the mind-heart from principle. Neither Zhu Xi nor Wang Yangming had understood how to plumb principle as well as had Confucius, in Song's view, and he was not content to say that mind was simply principle.[60] In the end, it is not clear to me (or perhaps to Song either) exactly what Song's metaphysics was or how he derived it from the Cheng-Zhu and Wang Yangming traditions. It is clear that Song concluded that the moral evolution of humanity had thus far failed to reach its highest point, and that at least one of the reasons for this was a failure to apprehend the importance of both the mind-heart and objects. This failure, Song said, was manifested in the entire history of Chinese thought since the age of the Three Dynasties. Since Truth and Humanity remain partial, we are like the world before Columbus discovered a new continent.

For Song, Wang Yangming offered the best entry to true understanding through his conception of the mind-heart. Though he does not spell it out, I suspect Song found Wang useful in solving a particular moral problem facing the revolutionaries. That is, what justified their violent actions and how did they know they were right? Song would certainly have been familiar with Liang Qichao's criticisms of the revolutionaries as immature and hypocritical. For Song, the epistemological aspect of this problem was subsumed in the morality of praxis. This is because through (Confucian) self-cultivation—particularly caution-when-alone (*shendu*) and self-control (*keji*)—one can learn to trust the righteousness of one's will.[61] In Song's highly traditional terminology, through introspection and self-control one could learn to distinguish what is Heavenly pattern (*tianli*) and what is mere selfish desire (*renyu*).[62] Revolutionaries needed to make sure they were not confusing the public good with their private desires. In a letter to a friend, Song had previously defined the nation as composed of individuals. There-fore, individuals needed to have the qualifications to make the nation, or in other words, to be citizens. The core notion here, for Sung, was that this in turn required complete possession of the Way of being human, which included patriotism but also thought, morality, knowledge, and ability.[63]

Self-cultivation did not solve all of Song's conflicts. Possibly, his ef-forts at self-cultivation even heightened them, for the very process of self-cultivation must produce daily dissatisfaction with the self, except for the most smug and oblivious of persons.[64] Like Liang Qichao, Song gave up the love of a foreign woman to pursue his political career.[65] Song's love affair was intensely debated with his friends, who disapproved, and in the end prompted the thought that as one could become a sage with a moment's thought, so one could become a moral criminal. Song emerged from hospitalization to carry on revolutionary work.

RIGHTS, CITIZENSHIP, SOCIALISM

The revolutionary understanding of citizenship pushed the reformist view to its logical political conclusion. "Rights" (*quanli*), "natural rights" (*tianfu renquan*), and "human rights" (*renquan*) were not trump values as in late twentieth-century liberal discourse. But they were integral to late Qing thinking about the relationship between the citizen and the state.[66] The ubiquitous trope of slavery was based on the difference between the rights-bearing citizen and the "slave," which was to say the subject of a monarch. Human rights were central to the revolutionary righteousness of the likes of Zou Rong. Indeed, they were almost foundational:

Everyone should know the principles of equality and freedom. At birth, there are none who are not free and equal. In the beginning there were neither rulers nor subjects. . . . Later generations were ignorant of this principle. As soon as they achieved power, countless traitors, despots, and thieves monopolized what belonged to the common people and made it the private property of their families and clans. They called themselves rulers and emperors, so that nobody in the empire was equal and free. . . . So today the revolution of our compatriots should drive out the foreign races ruling us and exterminate the autocratic monarchs to restore our natural rights (*tianfu renquan*).[67]

For the most part, however, "human rights" referred to the rights of citizens, not humanity in the abstract. The concept of human rights thus functioned to naturalize citizenship as political participation. Revolutionaries spoke of "individual rights," "natural rights," and "political rights" in indiscriminate opposition to despotic monarchy. As early as 1901 an anonymous article on "Citizens," published in a short-lived radical journal in Tokyo, defined republicanism not in terms of processual institutions but of rights.[68] Since states rest on their people, kings are not necessary. But to form a state, people must be citizens and not slaves. Slaves care only for themselves and their families. But citizens possess rights, responsibilities, freedom, equality, and independence. Rights are natural, and include personal freedom and political participation. But in particular, it is the "true rights" of *citizens* that "cannot be suppressed by tyrants, cannot be infringed on by cruel officials, cannot be denied by parents, and cannot be presumed on."[69] The state depends on rights-bearing citizens, but citizens must be prepared to assert their rights—even, so the author implied, against the state. It is the ability to assert rights that makes citizens. Further, the author defined liberty as freedom from oppression, which occurs in two forms, monarchism and imperialism. France represented the break from monarchical oppression while the United States represented the break from colonialism. Only with their revolutionary breaks did the French and the Americans become citizens. So what do the Chinese need to do to become citizens?

We must first break away from the oppression of thousands of years of tyrannical customs, thought, moral education, and learning. The "form of freedom" lies in breaking away from monarchism and imperialism, while the "spirit of freedom" lies in escaping from ancient customs, thought, moral education, and learning.[70]

As for equality, this can be seen in original Nature (*Tian*), which completely lacks hierarchies. The author contended that inequality only came about through violence. Equality and rights were inseparable. Citizens recognized no distinction between rulers and ruled. Women and workers were specifically included in this embrace of citizenship, and the author attacked contemporary society for depriving peasants of their rights: oppressed by officials, exploited by landlords, and abused by criminals. A key role of the state was to support rights with law. "In sum, the rights of the citizens must be established through constitutional provisions; only then can they be called rights."[71]

In this view, the claim to rights was first made through revolution, then maintained by legal habit. A key figure in this "revolutionary rights" thinking was Liu Shipei, though he was not exactly a republican.[72] In his 1905 textbook on ethics, Liu spoke of rights as a form of legitimate individual interests that should not threaten social solidarity.[73] Liu attacked the Three Bonds on the grounds they restricted individual freedom, but while "rights" were rooted in natural desires, humans were ultimately social beings and rights were intimately linked to duties. Using Confucian language, Liu posited that, "If one can extend one's self-interest to others [empathy], then the boundaries between the social whole (*gong*) and the individual (*si*) will disappear."[74] In spite of his Confucian language, Liu cited Rousseau's notion of the general will to describe his meaning. Both rights and duties stemmed from the social nature of human beings, yet it was important to find a precise balance: the "liberties of one cannot transgress the liberties of another."[75]

Liu turned to anarcho-communism in 1907 for reasons that are not entirely clear. One reason may have been that he saw in anarchism a way to reconcile tensions between individual rights and social equality. A purely national or racial revolution threatened to establish new hierarchies, or as Kang Youwei would have said, "boundaries." Liu sought to embed the individual in the community through rights conceived as equality. Liu derived equality logically from his belief that rights and individual autonomy could only operate mutually. He understood individuals always to be in relationship to one another: there was no such thing as absolute autonomy. Rather, when autonomy was applied to humanity as a whole, it led to equality.

Humankind has three basic rights: equality, independence, and liberty. Equality consists of everyone having the same rights and duties; independence consists of neither enslaving others nor depending on others; and liberty consists of neither being controlled by nor enslaved by others. We consider these three rights to be natural (*tianfu*). Independence and liberty treat the individual as the basic unit; equality must be considered in terms of humankind as a whole. . . . Independence is what maintains equality. However, since the excessive exercise of the liberties of one conflicts with the liberties of another, and since the liberties of one tend to conflict with the overall goal of equality, individual liberties must be limited.[76]

What we might call the social consciousness of the late Qing anarchist movement had much in common with the republican revolutionaries' national consciousness (which had of course been vehemently promoted by Liang Qichao). That is, for Liu at least, liberty was only one of the three basic human rights. These three rights were not only in tension with one another but mutually supporting. Equality guaranteed liberty and independence by ending all forms of human oppression. Liu's vision of a future anarchist utopia thus began with duties rather than rights—the duty to contribute to society through production, to which all persons would contribute equally.[77] Such a society would have no such categories as capitalists and workers, much less rulers and commoners, and hence there would be no oppression. For all persons, "rights and duties will both be equal."[78] Liu's utopian demand that all persons should labor was combined with his technological faith that machinery would make the burden light and the produce plentiful. But duties were inseparable from rights in anarchist imagination as well as in republican definition.

An anonymous essay from 1903 on "Rights" began with an attack on the seizure and privatization of "the powers common to all" by evil despots.[79] With this familiar trope of despotism as privatization, the author attacked Confucian ritual propriety as the basis of despotism. And the rites—that is, the hierarchies of rulers and subjects, superior and base, parents and children, and the like—were the fundamental cause of China's weakness. It is, however, "rights consciousness" (*quanli sixiang*) that can rescue the nation as its people learn to defend their rights. Rights are natural and their violation is illegitimate. Rights complete human nature. The repression of rights, the author cannot help admitting, has been a fact of life, though one that seems to require constant work. So, too, laying claim to rights requires struggle—here the author's social Darwinism linked the struggle for rights with the struggle for national survival and a kind of natural, never-ending competition. In the consciousness of rights lies the human predilection for autonomy and equality, the very basis of integration: the creation of family, society, and the state. True cooperation among humans can only occur on the basis of their equality, which allows for the full and enthusiastic participation of citizens; at the same time, citizens recognize the legitimacy of their duties, including the duty of political participation.

In spite of the power of such revolutionary rhetoric, the notion that rights were entirely natural and somehow self-legitimating proved difficult to sustain. Yet even in the debilitated form of legal positivism, rights implied a dramatic reconceptualization of the state. In his *Study of Law*, for example, Yang Tingdong seemed torn between a definition of rights as stemming from law and a definition that was somehow rooted in the natural order of things.[80] Similarly, as early as 1902, Liang Qichao had rejected his earlier naïve belief in natural rights and now believed in a more complex concept. First, rights stemmed from the state (they were not natural, or cosmically endowed properties attached to individuals). But, second, the *consciousness* of rights *was* natural to humankind.[81] Liang argued that Nature (*Tian*) gives birth to our innate abilities to defend and preserve ourselves, abilities that constitute a kind of rights. Rights in this sense are connected to a natural desire for power, and humans must preserve their rights or become slaves. The desire for rights, or rights consciousness, is thus entirely natural. Liang thus never *reduced* rights to law or physical force. Rights for Liang still possessed an ethical dimension revolving around the development of the whole person, as Stephen Angle has pointed out.[82] Yet Liang taught that no one should expect rights to be freely granted to them; people had to fight for their rights. Indeed, given Liang's social Darwinist premises, there was normative value attached to fighting for one's rights: this was how progress was made. Liang then had to explain the failure of rights consciousness to make much actual progress in the world.

If one observes the histories of nations that have been destroyed—whether Eastern or Western, ancient or modern—one sees that in the beginning, there have always been a few people resisting despotism and seeking freedom. Again and again the government seeks to destroy them, and gradually they become weaker and weaker, until eventually their original passion for rights consciousness comes increasingly under the control of the government and weakens to the point that hope for recovery is lost and people simply take the government's controls for granted. After a few decades and a few centuries of this worsening situation, all rights consciousness has completely disappeared. This is certainly due to the weaknesses of the people: so how could the government's crimes be avoided? . . . A citizenry is made up of an assemblage of individuals; and the right of the state (*guoquan*) is made up of the grouping of the rights of individuals.[83]

Liang did not hold despotism to be immoral because it concentrates power but because it suppresses struggle and therefore retards progress. Through their struggle for their rights, the people strengthen themselves and thus create a strong nation. Liang's increasing statism did not mark any belief in the goodness of governments.

From thinking about rights of the individual, community, society, nation, and state to thinking about socialism was not a big step in the late Qing. Socialism, too, was an intrinsic part of the package that described the modern nation-state. As we have seen, Zhang Binglin treated socialism as necessary to the egalitarian nation and Liu Shipei believed in a communist form of anarchism, while the Tongmenghui supported land equalization. Still, most late Qing intellectuals did not believe "socialism" meant the abolition of all private property. Rather, socialist thought included a general concern with economic equality and state development of resources and industry.

Like the other "isms" discussed in this book, socialism came to China through translation. The earliest descriptions of socialism in the West were penned by missionaries who wanted to introduce Western political conditions.[84] Starting in the 1870s, they conveyed a sense of the variety of social reform proposals being propagated in Europe at the time, including Christian socialism. But these descriptions of the West tended to be sketchy and had little interest for Chinese reformers in the Self-strengthening Movement. More important in the long run was Japan, where Chinese students and political exiles found a vibrant and intellectually powerful socialist movement. By 1903 a number of Japanese books on socialism had been translated.[85] The very term "socialism" (J. *shakai shugi*, Ch. *shehui zhuyi*) was a Japanese neologism based on the translation *shakai* for "society." Indeed, one concrete result of discussions of "socialism" was to popularize the concept of "society" (*shehui*). Yan Fu had used the term *qun* (group, masses) to translate the English "society," and Liang Qichao's early writings followed Yan. However, while the Western notion of "society" referred to the totality of human relations, institutions, and cultures that were held together in a structured way, in the late 1890s Chinese intellectuals regarded *qun* more as a dynamic process closely tied to notions of solidarity—a goal that was both natural and in need of cultivation.[86] The timing of the adoption of the language of *shehui* gave it a distinctly organic and analytical flavor. The organism, composed of distinct but integrated parts, had to be strong to survive in a Darwinist world. In this context, one of the appeals of socialism was its promise to strengthen the people. Outside of anarchist circles, "society" generally referred to the nation-state and socialism often seemed its natural accompaniment.

Scholars have pointed out that socialism was introduced to China as a mode of development.[87] However, the egalitarian thrust of socialism was also a moral value in its own right. Intellectuals naturally approached socialism in terms of classical and premodern Chinese thought—the critical concepts from Confucianism and Buddhism were Great Harmony (*datong*), the well-field system (*jingtian*), secular equality (*jun*), and spiritual equality (*pingdeng*). "Pingdeng" was originally a Buddhist concept and operated something like a neologism in late Qing political discourse. Three conceptions of socialism quickly emerged around the turn of the century: as a means of preventing Western-style dislocation and class struggle; as a means of national economic development; and as a moral force for equality. By the early 1900s few intellectuals remained unaware of the immense social conflicts of the West. The huge gap between rich and poor that had arisen was not only morally disturbing, but also seemed to give rise to social unrest. Yan Fu, for one, authoritatively described not just the growing gap between rich and poor in the West, but its political consequences. This included attacks on the monarchy and a general spirit of anxiety and protest, he warned.[88] Chinese intellectuals were not merely observing the fruits of industrial capitalism, they were also becoming acquainted with the West's own social critiques. But attention to society and socialism was not merely instrumental. At a deeper level, it reflected the logic of political modernity. Late Qing intellectuals understood that some degree of equality was necessary for a sense of shared group life in modern states.

Socialism was part of late Qing attacks on traditional hierarchies to create a new Chinese subjectivity. The "social revolution" (shehui geming), however, was not necessarily all that revolutionary. It was, for Sun Yat-sen, for example, the third and definitely last of his three major principles. This was made clear in the wake of the 1911 Revolution, as the revolutionaries sought merchant and gentry support. Political revolution was by definition violent, but most revolutionaries seem to have assumed that with the founding of a new state, "social revolution" would be gradual, tied into the process of building new economic institutions. Socialism would inoculate China from the social disorders afflicting the advanced Western nations. While Hu Hanmin spoke of state ownership of the land (tudi guoyou), he had less to say about how this would be effected.[89] Over the years, Sun Yat-sen and his supporters would vary in their commitment to full land nationalization. They accepted the American socialist Henry George's analysis of land as a natural resource that should not be controlled by individuals. According to George, the landowner's profits were illegitimate because they did not stem from the landowner's efforts but rather from public investment. George was particularly thinking of the remarkable increases in the value of land around America's cities, which he proposed to tax. Sometimes, Sun Yat-sen spoke of George's "single tax" as if that were the sole key to his own notion of "people's livelihood." Nonetheless, with the founding of the Tongmenghui in 1905 and at times in later years, the revolutionaries advocated full nationalization of the land. They did so both on grounds that this was necessary for national development and on grounds of social justice.

It may be that the term "people's livelihood" (*minsheng*), with its classical overtones of paternalistic policies directed at inferior persons, was chosen to sound more acceptable than "socialism." Yet the concept of *minsheng* was widely equated with socialism in the late Qing.[90] The revolutionaries also spoke of "equalizing rich and poor" (*jun pinfu*). As we have seen, few revolutionaries thought that China at that time suffered from class divisions, which they concluded had largely disappeared with the collapse of the feudal order some two millennia earlier. But they were sharply aware of the *potential* of class conflict for damaging national unity. For Hu Hanmin, socialism was the future: it was being developed now in the advanced countries where economic classes had become a major problem. The advanced democratic states were able to implement socialist measures for the benefit of their people as a whole. China was not so advanced, but it was still ready to put one form of socialism into practice, namely land nationalization. Hu argued that land nationalization was particularly appropriate for China because of China's long experience with the well-field system. With these precedents, then, Chinese socialist development could begin with the land. Without nationalization, Hu said, landlords would accumulate simply too much political and economic power.[91]

But how was socialism to be achieved? Like Wang Jingwei, Zhu Zhixin (1885–1920, also a Cantonese revolutionary close to Sun Yat-sen) was inspired to write a rebuttal to the anti-revolutionism of Liang Qichao in 1906. Unlike Wang, Zhu frankly called for "social revolution."[92] What exactly did Zhu object to in Liang? Liang had said the revolutionaries failed to consider the applicability of socialism to China in practical terms, and roughly sketched out his own vision for China's economic future.[93] The result amounted to what would later be called a mixed economy, something like a social democratic polity. Nonetheless, immediately after his exile to Japan, in 1899 Liang had predicted the eventual success of socialism.[94] Both laissez faire capitalism and socialism (or state controls, *ganshe*) possessed historical roots, Liang saw. However, the contemporary age was one of growing state involvement in the economy. Politically, imperialism depended on it. And economically, socialism was in the ascendant because it could deal with the excesses of laissez faire. Capitalism distributed power down to individuals, while "free competition" expanded the gap between rich and poor. Thus socialism, which represents the "concentration of powers at the center," performs a necessary corrective function. Socialism produces social unity and equality. In terms of China's specific needs, Liang gave about a 70 percent role to the state and a 30 percent role to laissez faire.

Several points about this brief early article are worth noting. Liang did not endorse socialism as intrinsically superior to capitalism. Rather, socialism simply represented a set of policies appropriate for the present moment. Historically, the two economic modes alternate with each other, almost beyond human control. Nonetheless, Liang offered a striking image of socialism: as a kind of machine that powers the nation, its different parts working together. Socialism was obviously compatible with Liang's statism. Yet over the ensuing years, Liang decided that what China needed most was capital investment. Most of this should be in private hands, though he thought workers' cooperatives were also acceptable. What China needed was not more equitable distribution, but more wealth production. Liang feared excessive state ownership, on the grounds it could lead to despotism. He thought that historically in the West the exploitation of the peasantry by aristocrats had led to a particularly exploitative form of industrialization. Like the revolutionaries, Liang believed China had lacked a true aristocracy and landownership was relatively egalitarian. But whereas revolutionaries concluded that this made the tasks of social revolution easier, Liang held that since most owners acquired their land through hard work, it would be unjust to deprive them of it.

Liang was consistent on the one point that a revolution of any kind was dangerous: and this included social revolution. Nonetheless, Liang supported protections for labor, national ownership of utilities, and regulation of monopolies. He favored a progressive income tax and an inheritance tax. He did not abjure the label of "socialist" as long as socialism was understood in moderate and gradualist terms. For Liang, the problem with the Tongmenghui's proposal of land nationalization was not that it was inappropriate for China, but that it was not even sufficiently socialist. True socialism had to consider industry, which was where China's future lay, and not merely deal with farmland.

Zhu Zhixin's response, in spite of his rhetoric of "social revolution," actually conceded some ground to Liang. Or, at least we can say Zhu's vision of "revolution" was relatively non-violent and non-disruptive. Zhu broadly defined social revolution as a "radical change in social organization" but also claimed that the revolutionaries were merely seeking a limited set of economic changes for the time being.[95] Zhu conceded that "pure communism" was not practical. One of the few Chinese of the late Qing who read Marx, Zhu claimed to be following "scientific socialism," which he held in China's case amounted to "state socialism" (*guojia shehui zhuyi*).[96] He further claimed, contra Liang, that the revolutionaries' strategy of combining political revolution with social revolution would actually *avoid* social disruption. This was to look forward to the economic-developmental policies of the postrevolutionary period. The point of social revolution, Zhu said, lay in the fact that the main force of the anti-Manchu revolution could not come from the rich, nor even from the traditional secret societies. Rather, the revolution would be made by commoners (*ximin*).[97] The social revolution would be for their sake. At the same time, however, Zhu also believed that the gap between rich and poor was relatively small; moreover, once the Manchus were overthrown, policies to equalize the poor and the rich could be moderate and gradual, and carried out democratically.

Zhu claimed that the revolutionaries would not simply expropriate land but planned to pay landlords for it. This was an important clarification that again moderated the idea of social revolution.[98] As well, based at least partly on his reading of Marx, Zhu had developed a notion of how social forces determine historical change. Nonetheless, he did not advocate class struggle; rather, he proposed that social "revolution" should come about only through democratic means. More radical visions were limited to utopian and Buddhist strains of late Qing thought, and to the anarchists. Kang Youwei's *Datong shu* spoke of abolishing class distinctions and advocated public nurseries and public ownership of all the means of production. But this work remained unpublished and represented a future vision, not a policy. There can be no doubt of Zhang Binglin's commitment to equality as an ideal, even a religious ideal. But although Zhang supported revolution, he had little to say about concrete steps to achieve equality except perhaps for noting China's historical propensity to socialism via land equalization programs.[99]

The most resolute supporters of the "social revolution" were the anarchists. For other late Qing activists, the anarchists represented extreme or "pure" communism. This was a fair reading.[100] They were not utopians in the sense of Kang Youwei, who worked out his vision in shining detail. The anarchists spoke of the need to reach out to peasants and workers as part of a revolutionary project. They advocated a revolution of the "whole people" (*quanti zhi min*), that is, excluding only the tiny minority of rulers and capitalists. They also spoke extensively of the need for cultural revolution, particularly the destruction of Confucian ethical norms. Zhu Zhixin wanted to combine the political and social revolutions, but he still distinguished between them—a distinction that the anarchists regarded as inherently false. For the anarchists, revolution was a single, total process. In 1907 Liu Shipei and his wife He Zhen predicted that, "Those who in the past had obeyed their superiors will now resist their superiors. Farmers will resist their landlords; workers will resist the factory owners; the people will resist the officials; the soldiers will resist their officers."[101] Any true revolution would overthrow the government and not replace it, creating purely voluntary forms of economic and social cooperation. Radical changes in culture were necessary to prepare for such a revolution and would continue to follow from it.

In many respects, the revolutionaries were backward-looking, speaking of "recovery" (*huifu*) and "restoration" (*guangfu*)—that is, expulsion of the Manchus in order to recover China for the Chinese (Han). But as Sun Yat-sen himself noted, if the revolution was to begin with a nationalistic expulsion of the Manchus, it could only be completed with the establishment of a democratic republic. In 1905 Sun lamented, a bit anachronistically, that Ming Taizu had succeeded in expelling the Mongols but failed to lead a political revolution, and the Ming fell to a second foreign invasion.[102] A Han emperor would be no better than a Manchu emperor: republicanism was necessary.

The "debate" between the revolutionaries and reformers was largely over by 1907. Everything that could be said had been said. (This is not to deny that the debate in fact continued right through the 1911 Revolution and its echoes are still heard today.) There was agreement on many issues. Still, anti-Manchu republicanism confronted constitutional monarchism. Even more starkly, those who sought to violently overthrow the political system—a significant segment of the student population and a few older intellectuals—confronted those who sought to change the political system from within—mostly men whose educations had been conducted within the framework of the traditional examination system.

In their attempts to mobilize support among the Chinese population, revolutionaries and reformers alike made the Qing government more transparent. Mainstream newspapers and magazines not only discussed theoretical issues but also published official memorials and edicts as well as independent reporting on the activities of local and national officials. They publicized and condemned instances of corruption. They often encouraged quasi-popular movements such as the anti-American boycott of 1905 and publicized the activities of pro-constitutional groups. Revolutionary journals, from the safety of foreign shores, talked about uprisings and assassinations. And Shanghai's tabloid press, from the safety of the foreign concessions, criticized and ridiculed local and national officials.[103] Even the court's activities were not immune. While tabloids focused on entertainment and scandal, their default mode was political attack and sarcasm. Overall, the tabloids were arguably "conservative" and certainly anti-revolutionary, yet their debunking and jokey approach to political gossip helped to delegitimize the government. The tabloids had little to say about political systems, but much to say about the ignorance and hypocrisy of specific officials. Much the same was true of popular fiction.[104] Aggrandizing and corrupt officials and military officers made good targets, and so did reformers, who were portrayed as doing well by doing good. Even the emperor was parodied, as in one story where the winner of a popularity contest among Shanghai courtesans was announced by imperial edict.[105] Cixi was a natural target. As Juan Wang points out, criticism of the court and officials on moral grounds was particularly devastating in terms of the traditional Mandate of Heaven theory.[106]

The emperorship, with its private rituals and high walls, was hesitantly moving into the open. By 1904, photographs of Cixi were on sale in Shanghai bookstores.[107] Advertisements also offered them for sale by mail. According to these advertisements, one could buy photos of Cixi alone or with other members of the imperial family, or dressed up as the goddess Guanyin, with a favorite eunuch, Li Lianying, dressed as Guanyin's acolyte Wei Tuo. Cixi was carrying on a venerable portraiture tradition of linking the imperial body with Buddhist gods. According to the art historian Cheng-hua Wang, Cixi seems to have personally enjoyed being photographed and understood well how to portray herself to particular audiences. Some of her photos were displayed in the Qing's palaces and some were exchanged with foreign heads of state. But the Qing did not keep control of its photos, which slipped into general circulation. This put the imperial family in the same company as high officials, famous foreigners, notorious rebels, and even courtesans, whose pictures adorned many tabloids and photo albums.

The revolution finally came at the hands of mutinous New Army troops in Wuchang on October 10, 1911. No one had predicted it, and in fact no one could have predicted it. The New Army troops in Hunan and Hubei had long been infiltrated by revolutionaries, including returned students from Japan. Song Jiaoren was one of a number of Tongmenghui members who had long been interested in the possibility of a revolutionary uprising in central China. They had become dubious of Sun Yat-sen's efforts to instigate rebellion with secret societies in the south. But the uprising that provoked what would turn out to be the revolution came about as a result of sheer chance. When an accidental munitions explosion led to the exposure of a small revolutionary cell, the revolutionary soldiers fought to take over the garrison. Needing an officer to head up the rebellion, the soldiers found their colonel hiding under his wife's bed. So goes a good story, anyway; wherever he was found, it took two days to convert the colonel to republicanism. Colonel Li Yuanhong (1864–1928) went on to lead the New Army rebellion, and the mutineers reached the governor's palaces. The Manchu governor fled. The revolutionaries took the city of Wuchang. They proclaimed their republic. Then—this was the key—other provinces followed. Sun Yat-sen continued his trip from America to Europe, announcing he would try to raise money and gain foreign recognition for the revolution (and waiting to see if this was the one). But the Hunanese revolutionaries Huang Xing and Song Jiaoren reached Wuchang by the end of October. Huang Xing (1874–1916) played a major role in the fighting that ensued.

By November, some six provinces had seceded from the Qing: the dynasty was looking at the loss of central and southern China. Revolutionary leaders came from the ranks of long-time revolutionaries, from New Army soldiers, and—most critically—from provincial gentry. The Qing had alienated its natural supporters. Committed to constitutionalism, they could support republicanism if the monarchy refused to compromise. In 1909 the Qing had allowed elections for provincial assemblies and had created a National Assembly (half of whose members were chosen by the court, half elected by provincial assemblies). Though suffrage was extremely limited and the assemblies were not to have legislative powers, they became sites of gentry protest against Qing policies. They played no direct role in creating the revolution, but once the Wuchang Uprising broke out, they dominated provincial politics. Liang Qichao—finally allowed to return to China by act of the newly assertive National Assembly—arrived in mid-November. He pronounced the Qing already dead. While he could not predict the future of the revolution, Liang said, he could see that the dynasty was collapsing.[108]

The decade or more of fundamental shifts in China's political culture had prepared the elites for revolution. The Qing's response to the Wuchang Uprising was not as feeble as the preceding paragraphs might indicate. It sent troops to central China, won several victories, and by November had brought Yuan Shikai back into the government and made him commander-in-chief. Yuan was a Han Chinese who had originally taken charge of the New Army military reforms. After Cixi's death in November 1908, an extraordinarily shortsighted cabal of imperial clansmen came to power. They dismissed Yuan from all his posts in January 1909, but he remained in touch with military leaders who owed their careers to him. He was suddenly the indispensable man in the wake of the Wuchang Uprising. But returned to power, Yuan was not necessarily eager to deal a deathblow to the revolutionaries who had been so inadvertently helpful to him. In any case, it was probably already too late to stop the revolution.

The revolution was not a popular revolt or mass uprising, but it did rest on an unprecedented set of social mobilizations in central China.[109] Key segments of local elites had turned completely against the Qing while others were no longer willing to defend it. Revolutionaries were able to make common cause with gentry and other social groups, in particular merchants and secret societies, which brought in some peasant support.

Yuan sought to negotiate with the revolutionaries. By the time a truce was declared in early December, central and southern China along with Shanxi and Shaanxi in the north were in revolutionary hands. The revolutionaries could claim fourteen provinces by the end of the month. The Qing, under Yuan Shikai's prodding, promised to turn itself into a true constitutional monarchy. Understandably, this was not acceptable to the revolutionaries. However, most revolutionaries were willing to promise good treatment if the imperial house abdicated. Many, probably most, revolutionaries were willing for Yuan, strongman of the north, to become president. Yuan was also the most acceptable leader to the foreign powers, whose attitudes were a real concern to the revolutionaries. Yuan's chief negotiator was Tang Shaoyi (1862–1938), a Western-educated fellow-townsman of Sun Yat-sen. The ingredients for a deal were in place.

In the course of the 1911 Revolution, anti-Manchu violence engulfed Wuchang, Xi'an, Taiyuan, Zhenjiang, Fuzhou, and Nanjing.[110] Manchu quarters in these cities were torched. The slaughtered included women and children. It is difficult to assess the role of anti-Manchuism in the specific events of the revolution; in any case, such a task would need to take into account local conditions. But the language of "revenge" that accompanied that of "extermination" and "expulsion" demonstrates, at the least, how anti-Manchu ideology was used to legitimate the slaughters when they did occur.[111] "Racial memory" played a double role in revolutionary rhetoric. The Han could be blamed for forgetting but could be awoken to their national destiny through recollection. And memories could be created and incorporated into the self, which resulted in essentializing populations or the "races" of Han and Manchu. Scapegoating Manchus was not only a matter of displacing anger at an uncontainable Western imperialism onto a minority, but also a way to define the national body. Adopting Zhang Binglin's term *Zhonghua* for this body—the Zhonghua minguo or Republic of China—the new Han leaders faced a political vacuum in 1912. The Qing was gone and the task of state-building was at hand.

CHAPTER 7

Founding the Republic of China

T HE GOVERNMENT of the Republic of China was weak, its fiscal house disordered, and its politics convoluted. Regional and local power-holders gained ever greater freedom of action. While he lived, Yuan Shikai was able to hold China together through his command of a military that remained more or less unified. Warlordism emerged after his death in 1916, and the central government in Beijing became a shadow. Sun Yat-sen organized a new Guomindang (Nationalist Party) in 1919 and, with the help of the Communist International, in 1928 it unified most of China proper under Sun's political heir, Chiang Kai-shek. Chiang proclaimed Sun the Father of the Country and made the Three People's Principles into the state's official ideology.

But this is getting ahead of the story. In February 1912, Yuan gave the Qing court a choice: abdicate or be destroyed. The true father of the Republic of China, which he treated more as a bastard child than his acknowledged offspring, Yuan went on to try to found his own dynasty. In truth, the revolution had many fathers, and not a few mothers, who were later written out of the story. Perhaps this entire parental metaphor should be abandoned. What Yuan, and equally Sun Yat-sen and other revolutionary leaders, were doing in 1912 was attempting to rule without reference to a paterfamilias role. In some ways, the political struggles of the Republic can be seen as a continuation of the reformer-revolutionary struggles of the late Qing. The reformers envisioned a measured, controlled, top-down reconstruction of the Chinese polity. Yuan Shikai can be put in this camp, and it is not surprising that Liang Qichao thought he could work with Yuan after the revolution. Chiang Kai-shek was in this sense Yuan's heir as much as he was Sun's. But the revolutionaries did not disappear with the revolution, and they continued to promote a bottom-up vision of more totalistic change. It is not surprising that Yuan assassinated Song

Jiaoren, put Zhang Binglin under house arrest, and forced the Sunists to flee into exile again.

Symbolically, the Republic of China was founded several times. Self-chosen provincial representatives met in Nanjing and proclaimed the Republic on January 1, 1912. They wrote a provisional constitution and elected a provisional president, namely Sun Yat-sen. Having been away from China for so long, Sun was in effect a safe compromise choice while negotiations with Yuan continued. As Sun insisted, the delegates adopted the solar calendar, marked at Year One of the Republic. The southern revolutionaries, Yuan's northern army, and the Qing court came to agreement in February on the "Articles of Favorable Treatment" for the imperial house. This finally cleared the way for the Qing's abdication. The Qing court's formal abdication edict was issued on February 12. By this edict sovereignty (*tongzhiquan*) was transferred to the people and a republican constitutional form of government (*gonghe lixian guoti*) established. If anyone was paying attention, the Qing's edict not only purported to establish the Republic, but rooted it in the Mandate of Heaven, as seen in the will of the people (*renxin*). It further claimed to be fulfilling the intention of the "ancient sages" who thought the empire should be held in common (*tianxia wei gong*), and not incidentally conferred authority on Yuan Shikai to take the needed practical steps. A few days later, the Nanjing delegates elected Yuan to be the new provincial president, and he was sworn in on March 10. Yuan kept the government at his power base in Beijing, and elections for a new parliament began.

October 10, 1911? January 1, 1912? February 12, 1912? March 10, 1912? When was the Republic of China founded? Did a revolutionary act create a new state de novo, a form of self-legitimating violence as the people through its representatives formed a new state? Or did the Qing create the new state through its generous abdication? At any rate, China now had a constitution and a president and was soon to have national elections for a parliament. This chapter and the next focus on the attempts of elites and intellectuals to grapple with a political world that lacked imperial institutions. This chapter examines the political rituals that emerged in the wake of the revolution, while the next discusses how ideas about democracy and autocracy played out in the initial years of the Republic.

In the wake of the abdication, anti-Manchuism did not completely disappear, but it did dissipate. The Republic of China officially and often invoked the "harmony of the five [Chinese] races." Taking his oath of office on January 1, 1912, President Sun Yat-sen spoke of the Han, Manchu, Mongol, Hui, and Tibetan as one people (*minzu*). The notion of "five races" unity was repeatedly invoked in official speeches on national holidays and in the symbolism of the new state: especially in the five-color national flag, but also in national songs. The rituals of republicanism the new state pursued were designed to convey its new definition of citizenship. Above all, commemoration of the Wuchang Uprising—the tenth day of the tenth month (of the solar calendar), or "Double Ten"—came to represent the essence of the Republic.

Let us begin with three stories of the first national day of October 10, 1912. First, the sacrifices to martyrs of the revolution in Beijing. The sacrifices were led by a representative of the president and included top officials, former Qing Manchu princes and generals, lamas from Mongolia and Tibet, foreign dignitaries, and (at the rear) Western and Chinese women.[1] Originally scheduled to take place at the old Qing's Altar of Heaven, the sacrifices had to be moved to Liulichang when the altar could not be made ready in time. The Republic Commemoration Society (Gonghe jinianhui) offered a prayer to the martyrs, announcing the success of the revolution. This prayer informed the martyrs' spirits that their blood sacrifices over ten years had finally ended the despotism of five thousand years and the Qing's rule. When the revolution began a year ago, the whole nation responded, resulting in a new form of government, or so the martyrs were informed. Now the people were important and the ruler insignificant.

Sacrifices to the martyrs of the revolution linked the living to the dead and the new state to a more or less specific revolutionary vision. With the martyrs safely dead, their memory could be invoked by any who would claim their mantle. The gravitas surrounding these sacred rituals was meant to infuse the Republic with purpose. The rituals also fostered a new sense of national identity. The martyrs joined the Yellow Emperor and ancient heroes to become the collective ancestors of the Chinese people. Furthermore, although the new state's new rituals were not held there, it de-imperialized the Altar of Heaven by opening it to the public.

Second, in Nanjing, requests from female students to hold a lantern procession were turned down by the Bureau of Education, and a request from prostitutes to do the same was rejected by the police. The prostitutes' request had originally been approved by the local head of the Bureau of Commerce before the police stepped in.[2] Other groups, including soldiers, schools, and an orphanage, proceeded with their lantern processions over the nights of October 9, 10, and 11. Women, students from an art school, did participate in ceremonies honoring revolutionary martyrs by placing flowers in front of their spirit tablets in the Memorial Hall.[3] The place of women in the political imaginary of the Republic was ambiguous but they had a public role.[4]

And third, one young man simply found the day represented excitement, like a temple fair. A dozen years later a certain "Mouzi" published a few of his recollections, based on his diaries, of bygone Double Tens.[5] Thinking back to the first national day, he noted that the events in Beijing had been minimally organized and the term "Double Ten" did not yet exist. Nonetheless, young Mouzi and his brother found the Changdian marketplace bustling with commemoration activities. Inside were pictures of revolutionary martyrs next to souvenirs. There was an area set aside for speakers—a vigorous Song Jiaoren spoke of the hardships the revolutionaries had overcome and praised the great achievements of Sun Yat-sen, other revolutionary leaders, and even Yuan Shikai. Mouzi and his brother wandered about the dining hall, the sports stadium, and the martyrs' temple. They saw magicians, fund-raisers, and the theater where new and old operas were being performed. Then, walking over to Liulichang, they enjoyed the sight of people cutting the queues off passers-by.

Such rituals of republicanism linked the individual and the individual's social community (family, school, employment) to the political community. The modern state requires special rituals for two reasons: to mark the putative involvement of citizens in the political sphere, and to mark the double claim of the nation to both an ancient past and an essential newness.[6] State rituals include the quotidian, such as students saluting the flag or bowing to pictures of national leaders. And they include the sacred, such as remembering war dead or national martyrs or celebrating the birth of the nation. Political rituals are also designed to shore up the rulers' own sense of legitimacy and potency. Of course, they can be arenas of struggle, expressing and shaping political power.[7] But also, while the Qing's state rituals were mostly closed and private, the Republic's were gloriously open and public.

In the first years of the Republic of China, political rituals worked to create citizens.[8] Elites, at least, and the urban classes more generally were drawn into political rituals as participants and spectators. As Henrietta Harrison argues, the rituals also created standards of Chinese-ness (or ethnic identity) and standards of modernity, including cosmopolitan habits: short hair instead of the queue for men, handshaking and bowing instead of the kowtow, unbound feet for women. Moreover, over the first years of the Republic, political rituals that focused on the theme of commemoration linked the collective memory with the future. Commemoration defined moments designed to transcend the present by forcing a concurrent looking back and looking forward. The meanings of the national flag, the music and lyrics of the national anthem, and sacrifices to the martyrs came together on national days in the early Republic. Yet what was to be remembered and what this was to mean for the future differed remarkably from year to year. The popularity of Double Ten waned over the first few years of the Republic. This reflected disillusionment with the political failures of the Republic.

Republican rituals of state were subject to enormous debate and conflict as political forces contended. Whose republic was it? Who would decide the national day, compose the national anthem, design the national flag? Differentiated civic roles determined who had the right to appear and to speak publicly—who marched, who stood on the dais, who listened in the hall, who snacked on the streets, who banqueted with officials. As Harrison points out, one's role was based on membership in particular groups such as political bodies, schools, commercial organizations, and the military. Yet citizenship implied the subordination, at least under certain circumstances, of other identities such as family, religion, ethnicity, or even nationality. It should not be surprising, then, that the civic rituals promoted by political elites in 1912 revolved around citizenship. Their exact meaning was open to interpretation, but participation did indicate a common identity of some sort.

The basic forms of the new civic rituals, particularly Double Ten, were determined by the National Assembly and the president, as a matter of law and executive orders. At the same time, local officials, merchants, and educators determined exactly what ritual forms to use, who would be invited to speak, and how banquets would be arranged. On the surface, civic rituals were basically the same in all of China's cities, based on a cultural repertoire that owed much to traditional festival activities—lantern processions, sacrifices to the spirits—and to cosmopolitan forms of the nation-state's expression of itself: military marches, the virtual worship of the flag, and the like. In particular, Double Ten rituals and symbols encouraged remembering; that is, they commemorated the founding events of the Republic.[9]

Exactly what was to be remembered, however, and how, was subject to much debate. The triumph of October 10 over rival dates was by no means assured. Different patriotic songs emphasized different themes of republicanism and history. And competing flags offered directly opposed views of this "precious" symbol of state. The first problem was to choose the right founding date. But before picking a date, it was necessary to agree on using the solar calendar. Some groups assumed that the anniversary would be marked according to the lunar calendar, in the tradition of popular festivals.[10] As well, some observance of the lunar calendar anniversary (the 19th day of the 8th month) of the Wuchang Uprising, which fell on September 29 of the solar calendar in 1912, was apparently encouraged.[11] In Wuchang itself, major ceremonies were held according to the lunar anniversary under the direction of Li Yuanhong, now serving as Hubei's governor and vice-president of the Republic. Numerous localities followed suit.[12]

The decision officially to mark the national day (guoqingri) on October 10 (in the official solar calendar) emerged out of a debate that suddenly erupted in September. It was partly a matter of local pride. Hubei natives in Beijing proposed that the anniversary of the Wuchang Uprising mark the origins of the Republic, arguing its equivalence to the uprising of Parisians on July 14, 1789, which became the French national day, and the signing of the Declaration of Independence on July 4, which became the American.[13] Their original petition called for October 10 to be the "Day of National Sacrifices [to the martyrs]" (*guojiri*) while January 1, marking the creation of the Nanjing government, and February 12, marking the proclamation of the Republic in Beijing, both be declared "Commemoration Days" (*jinianri*). They proposed that October 10 be celebrated by closing businesses, offices, and schools, hanging flags, holding military parades, making sacrifices to the martyrs, bestowing rewards and amnesties, granting alms, and hosting banquets, while the two commemoration days would also be holidays, though on a smaller scale.

By early October, the Shanghai County Assembly began to plan for commemoration of Shanghai's own revolt against the Qing on November 3 (solar).[14] It held that Shanghai should participate in a national October 10 commemoration but also supplement it with a local holiday. The city government planned smaller-scale ceremonies including military music, sacrifices to the martyrs, speeches, and teas.[15] Groups like the fire brigades planned lantern processions. In Guangdong, a provincial assembly-man suggested that the Huanghuagang Uprising of April 1911, which in revolutionary eyes produced "72 martyrs" in the lead-up to the Wuchang Uprising, and the later expulsion of the Qing garrison from Guangdong should both be made holidays, and similar sentiments were reported from Ningbo and Anqing.[16] Hu Hanmin, now governor of Guangzhou, stressed that "the achievement of the revolution did not depend on arms but on the popular will."[17]

The National Assembly began discussions on September 12 in response to a telegram from Li Yuanhong asking that Beijing send representatives to participate in Wuchang's own (lunar calendar) commemoration ceremonies.[18] At the same time, a Revolution Commemoration Association had been formed and was calling for the nation to remember the revolution.[19] Chen Hanyuan (1876–1928), a Hunanese follower of Sun Yat-sen, insisted that since the people tended to be confused and forgetful, they needed historical and artistic objects to serve as daily reminders of the difficulties and sacrifices that had led to the creation of the new nation. Otherwise, corruption would spread and the very foundation of the nation would be threatened. Above all, it was still necessary to encourage a revolutionary spirit. Chen saw this as key to raising the moral standards of the Chinese people and gaining the respect of foreigners.

Perhaps most influential were the views of the old anarchist revolutionary Wu Zhihui. Wu calmly dealt with the issues one by one.[20] First, since the Republic had decided to use the solar calendar, all commemorations of past events should follow it. Since the Wuchang Uprising fell on October 10, the holiday could be called "Double Ten" (Wu appears to have been the first to use this phrase, citing the traditional "double nine" festival as his precedent). Second, there were no other good candidates for the paramount national day. The problem with February 12, marking the abdication of the Qing and the final "national unity" of northern and southern forces, was, according to Wu, that it did not mark a true national unity since the Mongols had not yet submitted. Furthermore, the day of the loss of the Qing was not an appropriate day for celebration. Wu's arguments here seem forced. The real issue was that making February 12 the national day would be to ratify a founding myth of the Republic in Yuan Shikai's image. That is to say, since Yuan engineered the abdication of the Qing and the establishment of the Republic nationwide, February celebrations downplayed the role of the revolutionaries. Commemorating the Wuchang Uprising, on the other hand, highlighted the actions of the revolutionaries while marginalizing Yuan. In this vein, Wu acknowledged the importance of the Huanghuagang Uprising as a forerunner of Wuchang. But there could only be one national day, and there were, Wu implied, two problems with Huanghuagang. First, it was more of a defeat than a victory, and second, if one started to trace all the significant steps on the march to final victory, where would one stop? Wu correctly noted that no single event could symbolize the entire revolutionary process. France's July 14 and America's July 4 marked specific events that only later came to represent their revolutions. Second, Wu said Huanghuagang was specifically tied to the Tongmenghui, while Wuchang seemed to capture a broader range of revolutionary forces.

Wu Zhihui's conception of the national day was completely integrative. In his irrepressible optimism he thought Double Ten would overtake the traditional holidays. Merchants would use it to pay their debts, which was traditionally done just before the lunar New Year's festival. It would combine old festivities such as song, dance, juggling, and lantern displays with "new operas" (featuring revolutionary and republican themes) and displays of new products. It would serve to enlighten the people, discourage traditional superstitions, and foster general social improvement. These goals had long been central to Wu's political vision of economic progress. Like world fairs and industrial exhibitions, Double Ten would have an educational function. Wu wanted all the people to be actively involved, not merely enjoy a few lantern processions and banquets. He called for Double Ten festivities to be carried out in each county seat. By the end of September, the cabinet drew up plans along these lines and the National Assembly approved them.

In the end, Double Ten became a three-day holiday in the major cities.[21] Houses and storefronts were covered with decorations in five colors; colored lanterns were hung; five-color flags were flown; and ceremonial arches, again decorated in five colors or else with the memorial evergreens (ilex, pine, and cypress), were erected.[22] In the morning, groups paraded along the streets: officials, the military, police, merchants, and students (and sometimes "gentry" and members of political parties). The military (and sometimes students) performed rifle and sword drills for the public. Students or the military held sports competitions and flag exercises. There were also flag-raising and -saluting ceremonies at specified locations. Parades culminated at an assembly hall (or tent). Military music was played. There were formal speeches; opera performances, usually of "new operas"; and even films. At various points, groups sang national songs that they had rehearsed. Officials gave a little money or food to the poor and also to soldiers and police. At the sacrifices to the martyrs, officiates were led by officials and military officers, who doffed their hats and bowed three times.[23] Or instead of bowing, soldiers saluted the martyrs with their rifles and swords. Offerings of incense, flowers, fruit, and wine were made to the martyrs' spirit tablets.[24] Prayers were read and music played. Sometimes specific groups (merchant guilds, schools, general bystanders) were allowed in as a kind of audience. Finally a banquet was set out. Sometimes different groups held separate sacrifices over the three days. In the evening, lantern processions and assemblies were held by groups in neighborhoods or the whole city. There were displays of firecrackers and fireworks.

Double Ten festivities were inclusive. In Shanghai "workers' circles" participated.[25] One large company invited all its workers to a banquet, and promised them one day's vacation with two days' pay. And foreigners, too, were participants, at least insofar as they were specially invited to banquets. Each group made meticulous plans for its participation, including rehearsals for events such as performing flag drills and patriotic songs. As well, crowds participated in a less organized way. Operas, souvenir stands, and food stalls were all designed to bring in the crowds. Newspapers printed detailed schedules of activities so readers could plan what events they might care to see. And the people did pour in, as frequent journalistic accounts of huge crowds suggest. Some observers made a distinction between the public and the private. Parades, sacrifices, honors lists, official banquets, and alms belonged to the "government's sphere," while individuals participated by taking the day off, hanging flags and decorations, setting off firecrackers, and feasting with family and friends.[26] Everywhere factories, offices, and businesses closed; even foreign consulates closed at least on Double Ten itself. The holiday, though, was good for some businesses, especially wine shops, butchers, and flag-sellers. Souvenirs such as commemorative badges and postcards also sold well.

In the following years, Double Ten became increasingly subdued as officials sought to limit any potential for popular disturbances. The holiday disappeared in 1915 as Yuan Shikai made clear he was going to declare himself emperor. It did not really revive until 1916, after Yuan's death. In Beijing that year, the presidential review of troops was restored and the "rebels" who had opposed Yuan were specially honored.[27] That Li Yuanhong was now president gave the government a new stake in reviving the Wuchang myth. It spent over two million yuan on Double Ten in 1916.[28] Numerous towns reported a full-blown return to the earlier modes of celebration: flags, lantern processions, assemblies and lectures, and singing (in one case by prostitutes for guests of the city council).[29] Shanghai again saw officials and merchants cooperating to put on a big show.[30] Major events were planned in Hangzhou, Suzhou, and Nanjing, as well as Beijing and

Shanghai. As Henrietta Harrison observes, Double Ten became a genuinely popular holiday, at least in cities.[31]

RITUALS OF REPUBLICANISM: FLAG AND ANTHEM

One way to celebrate the nation was, of course, in song. The need for a national anthem was already felt in the late Qing, if only to play along with those of Western nations on state occasions. Like previous dynasties, the Qing had always sponsored performances of ceremonial music on ritual occasions, but there was no national anthem.[32] Schools in the late Qing used various patriotic songs, but these were not standardized.[33] According to orthodox Confucian theory, the purpose of music was to educate, and the political stability of a dynasty depended directly on the health of its music. In early 1911 officials began studying European national anthems to find more suitable music for the immediate purpose. The Qing promulgated the new national anthem on—ironically enough— October 5, 1911. The lyrics of *Gong jin ou*, or "Strengthening Our Hold on the Golden Cup"—the golden cup being a ritual vessel associated with imperial rule—referred to the Mandate of Heaven and to the peace and prosperity of the empire. There was no problem with the lyrics; however, the music left traditionalists aghast. They said the composition was extremely inauspicious and they predicted the end of the dynasty.[34] The traditional musicians seem to have had a point.

Many patriotic songs were written over the decade following the Revolution. These show something of ideas about how the spirit appropriate to republican government should be cultivated. As early as February 1912, the Ministry of Education (of the provisional Nanjing government) issued a call for musicians to send in songs that would represent the nation's character and raise the people's spirit.[35] The ministry soon published an example of what it had in mind.[36] These lyrics described a new Asia developing, a new nation forming, the five-color flag flying, glory filling the country, and the people welcoming a civilized age of peace. While the main idea of this song seems clear enough, it seems, a bit ambiguously, also to acknowledge China's backwardness and the need to catch up with the West.[37]

Shen Xingong (1870–1947), a prominent musician and educator with radical leanings, wrote the lyrics for the "Song in Commemoration of the Founding of the Republic of China."[38] This was a celebratory paean to the revolution. The nation (*minzu*) has come together to achieve independence *and* self-respect; it has sacrificed its blood to abolish over four thousand years of autocratic poisons. All the people will be like kin working together in a "democratic republic" to improve education and armaments. Shen's lyrics captured many of the main points the revolutionaries had been making for a decade, including a certain militant spirit. Other songs emphasized China's age and size, its natural resources and fertility, and its high degree of civilization. One song that achieved some popularity was a simple hymn for Double Ten:

Think! Everybody think!
What is today's excitement about?
Hang high the red lanterns,
And raise up the national flag
To blow in the wind.
For this is the anniversary of raising the flag of revolutionary righteousness
    in Wuchang,
Overthrowing the autocracy
And establishing the Republic.
The people's spirits are raised,
May the Republic be forever wealthy and powerful![39]

And in October the Wenming Bookstore of Shanghai published a somewhat more complex song, complete with references to the glories of the Yellow Emperor and Zhou civilization, but:

For four thousand years
Autocratic government was binding,
The people were kept unfree.
From ancient times
Only heroes achieved great deeds.[40]

The song implies that the revolution was accomplished by heroes but now all people can now contribute to their nation. Furthermore, China is both ancient and new, now "the Republic's five peoples sharing a boat."

In September 1912, the Ministry of Education offered an open competition for writing a national anthem, offering 500 yuan to the winner to be selected by the National Assembly.[41] In the end, some three hundred songs were received, but none was in fact chosen.[42] In 1913 the ministry asked for submissions from specific scholars including Zhang Binglin, Yan Fu, Liang Qichao, Zhang Jian, Cai Yuanpei, and Gu Hongming. This list ran a certain political gamut. Like Zhang Binglin, Cai Yuanpei had been a revolutionary, though he studied mostly in Europe before returning to China to work as an educator in 1912. Like Liang, Zhang Jian (1853–1926) had been a prominent proponent of constitutional monarchism, having been the top *jinshi* candidate of his year but deciding to become an entrepreneur, industrialist, educator, and politician. Gu Hongming (1857–1928) was entirely different: born in Malaya and educated in Britain, Germany, and France, he worked many years for Zhang Zhidong, and proclaimed his loyalty to the Qing until his death.

Zhang Jian submitted three songs. These were perhaps more like erudite poems than songs and certainly featured classical allusions. Zhang particularly appealed to the myth of the Golden Age, using stories of ancient imperial abdications as symbols of the Republic:

[China] was civilized before modern times,
Fu Xi, the Yellow Emperor, and Shennong,
Lofty! lofty! Yao and Shun,
The empire was held in common.
The emperorship was held by noble offspring
Who abdicated as the people wished.

. . .

Yao sought only Shun
And Shun sought only Yu;
None was compelled,
And none used evil [methods].
Confucius recorded these ancestral [stories],
And Mencius well explained:
"Respect the people and humble the ruler."[43]

And thus democracy was finally reached and the five peoples were united.

Zhang Jian depicted the people as passive, enlightened by the sage-kings, Confucius, and Mencius. The people, in Zhang's lyrics, are virtuous, but he rooted the Republic in ancient culture rather than modern revolution.

For his part, Zhang Binglin treated the revolution as a restoration and celebrated the Wuchang Uprising.[44] His lyrics implied that the Republic represented the culmination of all of Chinese history. The barbarians have been transformed and the imperial system abolished in accordance with the popular will. All this, without any real violence: "No dust of battles raging / but still we recovered our land and our traditions." And with the old barriers between them destroyed, the five peoples would now be in harmony.

Liang Qichao's approach avoided Zhang Jian's classicism and Zhang Binglin's focus on contemporary events to speak generally of China's greatness.[45] He sang of China's great size, fertile land, large population, and long, refined history. Liang did refer to ethnicity in the common descent of the Chinese from the Yellow Emperor, and he concluded: "It has been thousands of years since the Han explorers / The time has come for heroes to emerge again."

National anthems are generally meant to be politically neutral. That is, they foster a general, shared patriotism and try not to divide people. In fact, many of these would-be anthems insisted on the harmony of the five peoples. The Yellow Emperor was less a sign of ethnicity than one of a group of culture heroes such as Fu Xi and Shennong symbolizing Chinese origins. As for Yao and Shun, they became ancestors of republicanism itself, echoing the traditional claim of the ancient Chinese origins of democracy. The Republic failed to establish a new official national anthem until Yuan Shikai finally chose "China Stands Boldly in the Cosmos" in May 1915.

China stands boldly in the cosmos,
Spreading in all directions,
The Chinese descendants from the Kunlun peaks,
The rivers vast and restless and the mountains never-ending.
The five peoples of the Republic will recover Yao's heaven,
Forever and ever.[46]

The Republic's first national anthem neglected the revolution and celebrated the existence of a China beyond space and time. However, critics detected an imperial tendency in the lyrics. Xu Shichang (1855–1939), Yuan's premier, justified the anthem on the grounds of the links between music and government that had long been recognized by the ancients.[47] However, Yuan's own minister of education, Tang Hualong (1874–1918), excoriated the lyrics.[48] Tang ridiculed the image of "standing in the cosmos" as opposed to resting on solid land. He found a contradiction between the unity of the "five peoples" and the image of Yao, a Han ancestor. Furthermore, "Yao's heaven" implied an imperial mindset. Without reference to Shun, according to Tang, the symbolism of abdication was lost. In the event, the anthem was soon made unambiguous. Once Yuan's monarchy was announced, the fifth line was changed to: "The five peoples of the empire (*diguo wuzu*) will recover Yao's heaven," with the suggestion that eternity applies not to the Republic but to the emperor Yao-Yuan. Finally, the line was changed again to: "Meritorious China makes way (*xun Hua yirang*) for constructing Yao's heaven," with an even clearer implication of the "abdication" of the Republic itself. Various versions of the song were sung by elementary school students in 1915 and 1916.[49] But not until 1920 did the Beijing government again formally adopt a new anthem.

Even more contentious were debates over the flag. As for the flags themselves, suffice it to say that the five-color flag quickly won out over several competitors.[50] One of these alternative flags was the blue sky/white sun banner strongly favored by Sun Yat-sen, dating back to the 1895 uprising. Later a red "earth" background was added to it, and it eventually became the basis for the Guomindang and Nanjing government flags, surviving on Taiwan to this day. Other flags originally favored in the Tongmenghui included ancient weapons or the character *jing*, to represent the well-field (*jingtian*) system and hence socialism. A flag of eighteen stars was used by revolutionary forces in much of the fighting over 1911 and 1912, each star representing a province. The five-color flag was used by several revolutionary militarists, most importantly Jiangsu's Cheng Dequan (1860–1930) and Shanghai's Chen Qimei (1878–1916). Cheng had been a high official under the Qing, while Chen was a revolutionary. What was the appeal of the five-color flag to such disparate men?

Perhaps one factor was the ability of its symbolism to capture the territories of the Qing empire for the Republic. Although there were various interpretations of the five colors, by far the most prevalent was that they represented the five peoples—red for Han, yellow for Manchus, blue for Mongols, white for Hui, and black for Tibetans. Since these peoples held more or less distinct regions, the flag symbolized the Republic's territory. But could it symbolize territorial integration? The flag symbolized both difference and identity: five peoples but a single Chinese-Republican people. In spite of the claims of their supporters, the other flags seemed excessively partisan or partial. The eighteen stars offered a representation of China as a whole, based on its provinces. This was rather like the American use of stars to represent states, and struck some as tainted by federalism. Critics complained that imagining China as provinces was divisive.[51] Another complaint about the eighteen-star flag was that it did not include Manchuria, Mongolia, or Xinjiang, which were not then part of the provincial administrative system.

The Provisional National Assembly, in spite of the lobbying of Sun Yat-sen, voted on January 10, 1912, to adopt the five-color flag as the national flag, while the eighteen-star flag would represent the army and Sun's sky-sun flag the navy. The National Assembly in Beijing opened the issue again in May, but Yang Tingdong among others pointed out that by now the five-color flag was recognized by most Chinese and foreigners.[52] This was probably the key argument that carried the day, along with Yuan Shikai's desire to avoid a flag that would remind people of the revolutionary myth.

For all his political flexibility in other spheres, Sun Yat-sen never accepted the five-color flag, criticizing it through the 1910s. To the provisional National Assembly he had argued that the five-color flag was fatally flawed. Adopted from a Qing banner for naval officers, it betrayed the revolution, he said, and by linking Manchus to imperial yellow it betrayed republicanism as well. And finally, even in terms of its own symbolism, its hierarchy of colors from top to bottom betrayed the notion of the equality of the five peoples.[53] As well, obviously it neglected the smaller minorities.[54] For Sun, the sky-sun flag was made legitimate by its history—no other flag was used as long or in so many uprisings—and he emphasized that the sun represented a great nation rising in Asia. (Its critics said it resembled the Japanese flag, and also that Sun was suspiciously close to the Japanese.) Within a few months, Sun was offering a new explanation of the sky-sun flag's own color symbolism. The red background symbolized the blood of martyrs and their sacrifices in the revolution, and thus represented liberty. The white sun symbolized purity and fraternal love, while the blue sky symbolized righteousness.[55] For his part, Cai Yuanpei criticized the five-color flag on the grounds that the use of these colors was not scientific (he said there should be seven colors).[56] More importantly, the flag should represent the whole nation.

Nonetheless, the five-color flag had its own revolutionary credentials, and its symbolism was more straightforwardly nationalist. The National Assembly voted to adopt it in June.[57] The resolution noted that five colors had long been accepted by the Chinese people. It also noted traditions of using five distinctions in various spheres of rank, sound, smell, and so forth. And there were Confucianism's five constant virtues: benevolence, righteousness, propriety, wisdom, and trust. What was not explicitly stated was any appeal that might have stemmed from remnant notions of the correlative cosmology of the "five phases" (*wuxing*), which were also associated with the dynastic cycle. With the Qing reaching the end of its reign, this seems a plausible interpretation. But the main point was that the flag was supposed to symbolize the elimination of the "boundaries" between the peoples of China.

From one point of view, the exact nature of the flag did not matter— what mattered was having a flag, any flag. A "History of the Chinese Republican Flag," published in 1912, recounted the story of one revolutionary battle.[58] The revolutionary armies were forced to retreat. The dispirited revolutionary troops left behind their flag on a battlement. Suddenly, a 13-year-old boy rushes out to bring it back. The Qing forces concentrate their fire on the flag, and revolutionary soldiers try to hold the boy back. But he cries, "The flag is the soul of the army. How can we let the enemy have it?!" And he manages to run out for it and make his way back to the revolutionaries' lines through a hail of bullets.

A few years later a newspaper editorial commented on the profusion of national flags that appeared on Double Ten—hanging outside of offices and businesses, carried by students, attached to carts and automobiles, and worn on clothes.[59] Students, who had been prohibited from marching, nonetheless brought out their flags and paraded. There is a hint here of using the legitimacy of the flag as a cover for protest. Nonetheless, the author's concern was the state of the people as seen in their attitudes toward the flag. The flag here becomes something more than a mere symbol but a kind of essence of the state itself:

It used to be that when the Chinese people's heads were in the imperial era, they only had room for the emperor and the great officials, and never thought of the flag. Recently we've changed our name to a "republic," and what everybody thinks about now is only the president, the premier, the soldiers, and the assemblymen, and again the national flag is superfluous. But if the Chinese would look at the advanced civilized nations, they fight not for their king nor for their president but for their flag; they protect not their king nor their president but their flag; . . . every method of conducting domestic policies and foreign affairs is based on the flag.

Naturally, Yuan's monarchical movement brought about official reconsideration of the flag in 1915. One possibility floated was a flag with two golden dragons embracing the sun against a white background with a red border. Officials favoring change argued that the five-color flag represented an egalitarianism at odds with the monarchism they were restoring. Others, however, argued that the five-color flag was already recognized domestically and internationally, and also that its symbolism of the unity of five peoples was equally applicable to the monarchy. In the end, a compromise was planned to keep the basic five-color flag but add a new symbol in the upper corner.[60]

In the wake of the defeat of the monarchical movement, the five-color flag reemerged, though not untarnished. The sense of the importance of the flag was captured in an opera, *The Double Ten of the Ghosts*, produced in 1924.[61] Speaking from the dead, the hero Cai E (1882–1916)—who had fought against Yuan from his redoubt in Yunnan—raises the flag for all to see and demands: "Everyone! What is this? Is this not our lovely national flag? Look how beautiful are its colors of red, yellow, blue, white, and black!" But the flag has exacted a heavy price: "Is not this red dyed by our blood? Is not this yellow our flesh? Is not this blue created by the grasses growing on our graves? Is not this white the white of our bones? And is not this black from our bullets?" Cai says that the flag has been shamed and tarnished; the Republic has been stolen by militarists and politicians. The Double Ten ghost suggests that the five-color flag has come to represent more than the unity of the five peoples: it stands in some sense for the ideal of the Chinese Republic itself. But this was an ideal that may have been rapidly fading.

YUAN SHIKAI AND REPUBLICAN STATE RITUAL

When Yuan Shikai was converted to republicanism in 1912, it was for all to see. He turned the 1912 Double Ten commemorations in Beijing into a display of power. The ceremony started at 6 AM at a ceremonial arch built at the Zhonghuamen ("China gate"). Beijing's public space was being reconstructed. The walls within walls within walls that sheltered the hidden empire began to come down. Military parades followed what is now Chang'an Avenue, with dignitaries seated at Tiananmen. The gates blocking this route were permanently opened by 1914; the walls of the imperial city (though not the Forbidden City within it) and the offices lining the road leading north to Tiananmen were torn down shortly afterward.[62] The Zhonghuamen was simply the renamed Da-Qingmen (Great Qing Gate), which had previously granted entrance to the corridor leading up to the Tiananmen and the Forbidden City beyond. In 1912 the Qing's abdication edict was written at the top of its arch. Using Zhonghuamen as the starting point for Double Ten celebrations reminded the nation that the Wuchang Uprising had led to the Republic only by way of the abdication Yuan had arranged.[63]

Yuan himself presided at Tiananmen in uniform over a military parade of some 13,000 men while martial music played.[64] Yuan was said to have appeared strong, confident, serious, and alert—the virtues of a ruler. The military review was followed by a reception for parliamentarians, civil officials, foreign ambassadors and their staffs, reporters, and living buddhas from Manchuria, Mongolia, and Tibet. Yuan awarded medals to particularly meritorious heroes such as Li Yuanhong, as well as his own generals, Duan Qirui and Feng Guozhang. Sun Yat-sen and Huang Xing, however, turned their honors down on the grounds they were only working for the people, and in a republic such honors could mark invidious distinctions.[65]

In other words, it did not take long for republican inclusiveness to collapse. The electoral success of the Guomindang, organized by Song Jiaoren with Sun Yat-sen's backing, was a thorn in Yuan's side. On the verge of becoming prime minister in the new parliament, Song was assassinated in March 1913. Yuan was moving to dominate parliament by any means necessary. The "second revolution," a short-lived uprising, broke out in the south in July 1913 in response to Yuan's repressive measures. The uprising was defeated within a matter of months, and its leaders, such as Sun Yat-sen and Cai Yuanpei, fled abroad. Facing no further opposition, Yuan was elected president in October by the remaining members of the National Assembly.

Yuan took the oath of office on October 10, 1913. At 9:30 AM Yuan arrived at the Tiananmen in a ceremonial carriage and, accompanied by a military band, entered the imperial city.[66] At 10, officers, guards, officials, and other spectators were led into the Hall of Great Harmony (Taihedian) in the Outer Court area of the Forbidden City, where the oath-taking would occur. Foreigners were led to a viewing area in the northeast corner. During this time "national music" was played and a 101-gun salute fired. Yuan then ascended the platform at the north end of the hall, facing south with officials on either side of him. When the music stopped, Yuan took the oath; the audience bowed to him once and he bowed back. Then Yuan read his declaration; the audience bowed to him three times and he bowed back three times. Finally, music was played as Yuan and the audience left.

Yuan's inauguration departed from the enthronement rituals of emperors in many ways, but in facing south he emulated the single most critical feature that had marked kingship since the most ancient times. Since the early eighteenth century, this critical moment of the ascension rituals of the Qing emperors had taken place in the Hall of Great Harmony. Once all the ceremonies were over, the foreign ambassadors, top officials, representatives of the Qing house, and Yuan Shikai himself viewed a military procession.[67] For almost four hours, six military units marched in front of the viewing stands. Yuan wore an army uniform with a long sword. His blue cap displayed a five-color five-pointed star, its sides were of gold chrysanthemum, and it featured a white plume. His uniform was of blue wool, with gold braid and gold decorative motifs. His boots were black leather. His trousers had three red stripes and his sleeve-ends were red.

Yuan's generalissimo drag was designed to symbolize something about the political structure of the young republic.[68] But equally significant was the opening of the Outer Court to the public. When the inauguration ceremonies were all over, ordinary citizens could obtain free tickets to visit the old imperial halls where Yuan had taken the oath of office.[69] In terms of the traditional sanctity and taboos surrounding this place, Yuan was acting to secularize rulership. But in terms of his own power, his ritual performances were part of a process of personifying the new state. Yuan's militarized body continued to dominate Double Ten in 1914. Again, in 1914 the parades were followed by Yuan's formally opening a museum to display art and relics from the old Qing palaces at Rehe and Mukden (Shenyang).[70]

So far, Yuan's presidential rituals can be seen as in accord with a certain view of republican values. In assuming the right to conduct sacrifices to the spirits of revolutionary martyrs, or at least to authorize such sacrifices in the name of the government, Yuan was treating them as his ancestors. He thus appealed to common cultural norms not only by displaying a kind of extended filial piety but also taking their charismatic strength into himself. Yuan's use of military symbols also appealed to what had become a widespread value. Militarization had been a radical demand since the turn of the century. At the same time, the Qing house was deliberately re-duced to museum status. The Gate of Heavenly Peace (Tiananmen), which used to mark the entrance to the imperial city, became a republican civic monument, dominating instead of protecting the old palaces.

Yuan also showed he was building a modern state in a variety of legal gestures. By mid-1914, regulations were proposed to prohibit queues for government workers, rickshaw pullers, and merchants. (Similarly, a cen-sor's request to revive the kowtow was summarily refused.[71]) Government offices were closed on the solar New Year's Day, while attempts were made to curtail the traditional lunar New Year's holiday of early spring. Follow-ing international custom, Yuan held formal receptions to meet foreigners and Chinese. The military parades conducted before Yuan and invited guests—and also before officials in other cities—represented order, disci-pline, and the citizenship of members of a state. At the same time, mass participation in national-day festivities represented a sense of the nation as defined by solidarity and commonality.

To some extent, the museumification of the Qing was the symbolic equivalent of guillotining the king. By the Articles of Favorable Treatment, the imperial family—the boy emperor and the empress dowagers and an uncountable number of eunuchs—remained alive and reasonably well, living in seclusion in the northern quarters of the Forbidden City. But the general public was invited to peruse both the magnificent architecture of the Outer Court and the new Institute for Exhibiting Antiquities (Guwu chenliesuo). The institute's displays, though limited to a small portion of the vast imperial art collection, came to be viewed as the core of China's "national essence."[72] Scholars labeled many of the objects "national treasures" and took pride in them. The legal status of the imperial art works was not entirely clear, but in the popular imagination they instantly became part of the national heritage. Possession of some of the works, such as ancient bronzes, had long represented dynastic legitimacy. Their public display now spoke to the legitimacy of the Republic.

The symbolic scaffolding of Yuan's presidency was not entirely republican, however. His quarters and offices were located in the Zhongnanhai—the park-like grounds just to the west of the Forbidden City originally reserved for imperial use. The American ambassador, Paul Reinsch, recounted the presentation of his credentials to Yuan there as a kind of fairy-tale journey.[73] Yuan sent an ornate carriage "enameled in blue with gold decorations" and drawn by eight horses for Reinsch. He was accompanied by Yuan's cavalry escort, as well as his own American marines and the legation staff, since, after all, ceremonial forms had to be upheld by the American side as well. They arrived at the Zhongnanhai and were taken to Yuan's home, which Reinsch believed had been the palace Cixi had used to hold Guangxu prisoner. Reinsch was moved.

We alighted at the monumental gate of an enclosure that surrounds the lovely South Lake in the western part of the Imperial City. . . . The remote origin of its buildings, their exquisite forms and brilliant colouring, as contrasted with the sombreness of the lake at that season, and the stirring events of which they have been the scene, cannot fail to impress the visitor as he slowly glides across the Imperial lake in the old-fashioned boat, with its formal little cabin, curtained and upholstered, and with its lateral planks, up and down which pass the men who propel the boat with long poles.[74]

Unlike many other Western visitors, Reinsch quite liked the architecture of the imperial city, which he found pleasant, spacious, and even reserved.

Conducted through various rooms into Yuan's presence, Reinsch was led through files of extremely large guardsmen, which reminded him of Frederick the Great's preference for tall men. Finally, the formal introduction of ambassador to president was made. Reinsch concluded, "This rather naïve emphasis on externals and on display is born of the old imperialism, a more significant feature of Chinese political life than it may seem. . . . The rustle of heavy silks, the play of iridescent colour, the echoes of song and lute form the theatre—all that exquisite oriental refinement still seems to linger."[75] Preferring his Orientalism neat, Reinsch did criticize the audience room where he formally met Yuan as a "pretentious modern structure erected by the Empress Dowager." He also used the ceremonies to read Yuan's character: "Republican in title he was, but an autocrat at heart. All the old glittering trappings of the empire he had preserved."[76] It is, of course, not literally true that Yuan preserved the Qing's trappings in their entirety, but it is true that the question of state rituals was carefully considered and many of the features of the past were deliberately perpetuated.

As early as the winter of 1913–1914 Yuan floated plans to revive one imperial ceremony, the worship of Heaven at the winter solstice. He also displayed interest in the summer sacrifices to Earth and the spring and autumn sacrifices to Confucius. Yuan strenuously denied that these gestures represented imperial ambitions. The case for his conducting the old imperial sacrifices was utilitarian. It held that the moral standards of the people had been declining since the revolution while the "rites and music" (*liyue*), or Confucianism, were ignored. The point was not that sacrifices mobilized spiritual powers but that Heaven and Confucius represented virtue in the popular imagination.[77] If the government neglected the worship of Heaven, the people would blame the government in the event of crop failure. "Although the president is different from the emperors, he is still in the end the leader of the state, representing the nation in modifying and performing the grand sacrifice."[78]

Yuan proposed a deliberate mixture of traditional and updated rituals. There would be a bullock sacrificed, silk and wine offered, bowls, a gold incense burner, one jade cup, and so forth. The kowtow would be performed and ancient music resuscitated. The worship of Heaven would take place before dawn, as during the Qing, but the Temple and Altar of Heaven would be festooned with electric light bulbs to illuminate the ceremony.[79] Yuan would wear neither modern clothes nor the imperial dress of the Qing, but the coats of the high dukes of the ancient Zhou dynasty.[80] There was much research for the antiquarians to do, such research itself having long been part of the ritualization of power. Yuan proclaimed that the ancient sacrifices had originated to honor Heaven as the source of all things, and that to eliminate them would be tantamount to abandoning the creation of the commonwealth (*tianxia wei gong*) and the linkage of humankind to Heaven.[81] The ancient rulers understood that Tian was a barometer of the people's will and so protected the people impartially—Yuan suggested that all this was perfectly compatible with republican principles.

Yuan's greatest break with the past was his decision to allow the private sacrifices to Heaven (*shuren siji*) and to mandate local government participation. No longer would Heaven signify the unique essence of the emperor. The president would merely serve as the exemplary and "chief officiate."[82] In February 1914 Yuan ordered that the worship of Heaven be made general (*tong*), and that citizens might conduct the appropriate rituals in their homes.[83] Yuan said that he would be representing the citizenry (*guomin*) while local officials represented the people of their locality (*difang renmin*). In the event, few if any private households sacrificed to Heaven, though local officials, following orders, did so. In Shanghai, special platforms were built as a temporary Altar of Heaven at the Industrial Training Depot outside the South Gate. Local education officials were in charge of the ceremony.[84] Beijing enjoined them to follow the ritual procedures established by the central government, while in the capital all government offices were expected to dispatch a representative to participate in the main ceremony.[85] A proposal to personify Heaven in the form of the Yellow Emperor was rejected on the grounds the Yellow Emperor represented the Han race while the Republic encompassed the five races.[86]

It may be that the Temple and Altar of Heaven had already been desacralized by repeated secular use. Foreign troops had deliberately desecrated the precincts in the wake of the Boxer Uprising, and in the first years of his administration Yuan had complained about American soldiers playing football there. Nonetheless, the Qing architecture remained. Yuan's sacrifices occurred, then, on the winter solstice, December 23, 1914, at the old altar. For the first time, Heaven was worshipped by the president and by local officials throughout the realm.[87]

We can now put the incident described at the beginning of the Introduction to this book in historical perspective. That Yuan claimed to have fasted for three days beforehand signified his personal ritual purity, even as he proclaimed that he was merely a representative of the nation. His power was symbolized by both soldiers and his appropriation of the imperial yellow. Yuan prayed:

Heaven, Thou dost look down on us and givest us the nation. All-seeing and all-hearing, everywhere, yet how near and how close: We come before Thee on this winter solstice day when the air assumes a new life; in spirit devout, and with ceremony old, we offer to Thee jade, silk, and meat. May our prayer and our offerings rise unto Thee together with sweet incense. We sanctify ourselves, and we pray that Thou will accept our offerings.[88]

The 1914 sacrifices to Heaven turned out to be a unique event in the history of the Republic. Besieged the following year by opposition to his monarchical plans, Yuan let the sacrifices fall into abeyance, and in time the grounds of the Temple of Heaven became a park and museum.

Somewhat more successful were the spring and fall sacrifices to Confucius, especially in the school system. These had been abolished by Cai Yuanpei, first minister of education, at the beginning of the Republic, but were revived under Yuan. Essentially, Yuan tried to find a middle way that gave some official recognition to Confucius—a nice symbol of continuity across the boundary of revolution—while refusing pleas to make Confucianism China's official religion. On the one hand, Yuan noted that the Chinese Republic's constitution specifically recognized religious freedom, and desperate to hold on to the vast frontier regions, he had to think of more than traditional Han culture.[89] On the other, Yuan defended Confucius from the charges he had promoted autocracy. Born in an aristocratic and despotic age, Confucius had tried to ameliorate those conditions, Yuan said; Confucianism was a protean system that had evolved with the ages. Yuan adopted some of Kang Youwei's Confucian progressivism, claiming that Confucius promoted the Emerging Peace and foresaw the Great Peace or Datong. Heaven had given birth to Confucius as the teacher of the ages. Yuan thus thought it appropriate for schools to continue sacrifices to Confucius.

The Confucian sacrifices in the fall of 1913 in Beijing were held in the old Imperial Academy (Guozijian) with Finance Minister Liang Shiyi (1869–1933) representing the president.[90] Before the ceremonies, the offerings were viewed by Beijing's elites, including foreign reporters, educators, and diplomats. The ritual itself seems to have been conducted with considerable formality, although it was reported that some felt the ceremonies had deteriorated. The next year, Yuan personally led the sacrifices acting as chief priest, proceeding to the Wenmiao (or "Confucius Temple") in his armored car through crowds of soldiers. Four ritual kowtows were followed by offerings of wine, animals, and paper money, which were followed by another four kowtows.[91]

Confucius had only become so central to state ritual in the very last years of the Qing. In 1906 worship of Confucius was promoted from a middle-ranking sacrifice to a grand sacrifice.[92] As Ya-pei Kuo has shown, this had been a long-cherished dream of Kang-style reformers who saw in Confucius a symbol of the Chinese nation, and in Confucianism the essence of Chinese culture. The Qing hoped Confucius could help hold the realm together after the abolition of the examination system. Yet while the grand sacrifices to Heaven highlighted his son the emperor's unique role in the cosmos, in sacrificing to Confucius, the emperor became just one of a mass of humanity. Unlike the traditional objects of grand sacrifice—Heaven, Earth, Land and Grain, and the imperial ancestors—Confucius had long been worshipped by gentry and literati commoners. The Qing's new promotion of Confucius was an attempt to strengthen national identity and the ties between the people and the monarchy at the expense of the emperor's transcendence.

In the event, little transcendence from either Heaven or Confucius rubbed off on Yuan. Suitably enough, the generalissimo-president also gave attention to the Wumiao (Martial Temple), the military twin of the Wenmiao. The Qing had long honored the martial hero and god Guandi at the Wumiao, but in 1914 Yuan ordered that Yue Fei be given equal status and that sacrifices to both of them should be conducted along with ceremonies for the martyrs of the Republic.[93] Like the revolutionary martyrs, they might be transmuted into symbols of modern patriotism. Guandi represented virtues such as loyalty and righteousness. Yue Fei (1103–1142) had been a Han Chinese general who had resisted northern invaders who were predecessors of the Manchus. Late Qing revolutionaries had venerated Yue Fei, and Yuan may have been trying to remind people of his own Han identity without offending China's other nationalities. As he began his campaign to become emperor, there was a report that Yuan was even trying to have one of his ancestors be canonized in the Wumiao.[94]

Yuan's "superstitions" were ridiculed by some,[95] but Yuan may have had a better grasp of popular sentiment than the revolutionaries. It was reported that revolutionaries' attempts to limit public observations of Confucianism in Guangzhou in 1912, for example, met with hostility.[96] The revolutionaries seemed to envision Double Ten as a celebration of nation and state, and to dismiss Confucius and Heaven as irredeemably tainted with monarchy and empire. In the immediate wake of the revolution, military and civil officials led a new ritualization of the new Republic in China's major cities. Bowing replaced the three kneelings and nine prostrations of the full kowtow, but the basic meaning of sacrifices to the spirits was maintained. These official rituals offered the Chinese a shared experience while carefully differentiating selected groups in a hierarchy that privileged official and male. For Yuan Shikai, the task was to link his rule to ultimate sources of authority, or at least to sources of authority that transcended his person. He was basically able to remodel symbols of state in his image. But as we will see in the next chapter, even his monarchy accepted new norms of the nation.

The dual nature of the founding of the Republic of China—starting with revolution and ending with constitutional succession through abdication—was reflected even in that modern symbol of national sovereignty, the postage stamp. The government announced in September 1912 that it was issuing two stamps: one of Sun Yat-sen against a background of rice plants, and one of Yuan Shikai against a background of wheat.[97] Nicely combining north-south ecological motifs, then, the mails reflected the Republic's tenuous political unity. The Tongmenghui restorationist mythology, which was later promoted by the Guomindang government of the 1930s, was displaced in the first years of the Republic by a story about the peaceful resolution of the "chaos" by the capable Yuan. Still, in the first years of the Republic, Double Ten sanctioned a set of performances that moved bodies from the periphery to the center. Exemplary bodies—those of officials, soldiers, and students—were on special display. It was also an occasion for the mingling of bodies; in the excitement, public and private experiences were mixed. One example of the modern idiom of the body was the extensive use of bowing in various rituals, and handshaking on formal occasions as well. The new body of the citizen was also marked by short hair, at least for men. Campaigns to cut men's queues were fairly successful.[98] As for women, the equivalent remaking of the body was unbinding their feet. And just as men were discouraged from growing their hair long, so women were prohibited from cutting their hair short.[99] Citizenship remained gendered in law and practice. Clothing of course was changing as well. Again, officials, students, and soldiers led the way in male sartorial reform—the Beijing government took care to detail the proper attire for formal occasions. Girl students' uniforms, however, were fairly close to those of boy students.

In the first years of the Republic, memory of the revolution was embodied in ritual forms sanctioned by the state. This did not just happen but came about through a combination of habit and consideration, debate and contestation. Debated rituals and ritualized debates: both reflected the complex political culture of the first years of the Republic of China. The republican state claimed a fundamentally different basis of legitimacy from the Qing or any other previous Chinese state. It sought more intimate ties with the nation and also sought to control its citizens more closely. In the late imperial era, community-wide celebrations such as the Lantern Festival and the Dragon Boat Festival offered subversive potential and moments of transgression of social boundaries, carnivalesque celebrations not unlike those of late medieval Europe.[100] They celebrated the complex cosmic hierarchy and ultimately reaffirmed the social order with the emperor at its apex. Double Ten, on the contrary, while involving many of the same physical actions such as parades, lanterns, and banquets, emphasized common identity. It did not promise complete equality, but its participatory forms suggested that the individual was importantly a member of an appropriate segment of the citizenry: soldier, student, official, merchant, and so on. Through that group identity, emotionally weaker than familial ties but operating at a higher political level, the new state laid claim to the individual. Double Ten was a political ritual, not a cosmic ritual. Insofar as it embodied memory, it was a memory of the revolution. In 1916 in the wake of Yuan's death and the complete rout of his monarchy, the newspaper *Shengjing shibao* reminded its readers of the blood sacrifices that had been made for freedom, both in 1911 and again in 1915.[101]

But what was that revolution? What had it accomplished? Within a few years, intellectuals had become disillusioned and cynical. A newspaper article published on October 10, 1924, compared each of the thirteen years of the Republic to a disease.[102] In this sense the body politic was in constant crisis. The revolt of 1913 was like an infection of the diaphragm, while Yuan's monarchy was like the brain filling with blood. The Qing restoration of 1917—a military coup that restored Puyi to the throne for two weeks—was a "fake death." The betrayal of the nation in 1919—the Versailles Treaty, which turned the German concessions in Shandong over to Japan—was smallpox. The incessant civil wars of the 1920s represented various disorders. Such a cynicism was inherited from the beginning of Yuan Shikai's dictatorship. On October 11, 1913, *Shenbao* had commented:

If we ask our countrymen what all the fuss was about yesterday, all the clapping and yelling, they will reply, "It was to commemorate the Republic, to celebrate the president." If we ask why commemorate and celebrate, they will reply, "We are hoping for the progress of the Republic of China." But we've still got the same old president, the same old administration, the same old legislature, the same old judiciary, the same old citizenry, and now that it's the same old day after the fuss, the people are calm and forgetful, but it's still the same old China. Where is the progress? I thus hope that everyone from the president on down will reject all the same-olds and raise their spirits to construct a new nation on this Asian continent so we can be worthy of the true meaning of the words "Republic of China."[103]

For the writer Lu Xun (1881–1936), reflecting on the 1911 Revolution in 1925, the fundamental issue was the failure of memory and the tendency of the Chinese to forget.[104] What happened to all that revolutionary vengefulness? Lu noted that the accounts of the massacres at Yangzhou and Jiading, like the writings of Ming loyalists, were published to revive forgotten hatreds. But this desire for revenge dissipated with the coming of the revolution. Lu suggested this was because of both revolutionary optimism and the desire to appear "civilized." Lu noted that the Man-chu quarters in Nanjing had been destroyed, but he denied this resulted from Han desire for revenge. Rather—or so he heard (or claimed to have heard)—most of the damage was caused by the Manchus themselves. In any case, "even if you hung the *Account of Ten Days at Yangzhou* in front of your eyes, you couldn't maintain your anger." Lu complained that with the supposed success of the 1911 Revolution, conditions soon regressed to the point monarchism reemerged. Revenge itself, Lu neither glorified nor denigrated. Or rather he thought it both normal and dangerous. But his real point seems to have been that the anger of the Chinese people was too often misdirected and intermittent.

Yet, in spite of the understandable doubts of Republican intellectu-als, the failure of monarchical movements in the wake of the Revolution shows that something had fundamentally changed. The new state was certainly not a democracy; it was not perhaps even a state in much more than form.[105] The imperialist powers continued to severely limit the range of action available to any Beijing government, while the revolution enabled local and regional power-holders to operate with increasing independence. Nonetheless, socially disenfranchised groups such as women, workers, students, and to some extent peasants and minorities, were claiming citi-zenship. Citizenship implies a status of commonality with other citizens vis-à-vis the state, and in this limited sense need not entail democratic rights (voting, office holding, and so forth) but simply entitlement to the protection of the state. Citizenship was unstable in discourse and prac-tice, but still the marks of citizenship spread rapidly from virtually none to virtually all of the various symbols, ceremonies, festivals, rituals, and commemorations of the early Republic.

CHAPTER 8

The Last Emperors

FROM THE 1911 Revolution to 1924, the Forbidden City, with the rump Qing court ensconced there in decayed splendor, was a center of fruitless but persistent plotting against the Republic. During the Euro-American War of 1914–1918, quaintly known as World War I, the Japanese government dramatically increased its mercantile and military presence in China. Yuan Shikai spent most of 1915 fending off Japanese efforts to take over his government and trying to cement his powers in China. A diplomatic crisis between China and Japan in 1915 formed the background to Yuan's efforts to found a new dynasty. In historical hindsight, Yuan's plan looks futile and farcical.[1] Unfortunately for Yuan, in the end even supporters of his autocratic presidency did not want to see the monarchy restored. The true monarchists, so to speak, were still looking forward to the restoration of the Qing. Their moment came in the summer of 1917 when the Beijing government, cobbled together after Yuan's death, collapsed. A monarchist general was able to put the boy emperor Puyi back on his throne, where Puyi stayed for two weeks before the status quo ante was restored. It was finally in 1924, in another shift of the military balance of north China, that Puyi and the court were expelled from the Forbidden City. Puyi had just turned six when he abdicated the throne, and he was eighteen when he left the Forbidden City and Beijing.

If the Qing had not quite ended in 1912, it was certainly gone in 1924. (The enthronement of Puyi in 1934 as emperor of Manchukuo thrilled some old Qing loyalists, but it was not a continuation of the Qing dynasty.) The dozen years between 1912 and 1924 saw momentous social change and political turmoil. New ideologies sprang up on Chinese soil, including eclectic forms of anarchism, socialism, communism, liberalism, and Confucianism.[2] This chapter examines some of the competing conceptions of the state in the first dozen years of the Republic.

THE CONSTITUTIONAL DYNASTY

Perhaps Yuan Shikai could imagine no other path for China's future than the constitutional monarchy he had long favored.[3] Perhaps he thought he could garner popular support. He should have known many people would disapprove—Liang Qichao told him as much to his face in June 1915. But Yuan proceeded with his plans to become emperor over the summer. He would, he stressed, be a constitutional emperor, and he would be elected to the post. Yuan inaugurated the Great Constitutional (*Hongxian*) era on January 1, 1916 (or, as he insisted, Hongxian year 1). However, enthronement ceremonies were delayed and in the end never took place.

Yang Du wrote an eloquent defense of constitutional monarchy in April 1915. Frank Goodnow (1859–1939), Yuan's American adviser for constitutional affairs, wrote a critique of the Republic in August. Ariga Nagao (1860–1921), Yuan's Japanese adviser for legal affairs, had already determined that Yuan's presidency stemmed from a "transfer of sovereignty" (*tongzhiquan*) from the Qing by its abdication.[4] In other words, the Republic was not established by revolution or by popular will; therefore, one could conclude, to restore the monarchical system was within the scope of Yuan's powers. These men essentially argued that republicanism had failed in China because it was not suitable to Chinese conditions. Given China's tradition of autocratic rule and the ignorance of her masses, they said, monarchy could prepare China for a republican future. But the time for republicanism had not arrived yet.

Yang Du founded the Peace Planning Society (Chouanhui) to promote Yuan's monarchy in August. Cofounders included Liu Shipei (who had betrayed the revolutionary cause in 1908, floundered in the first years of the Republic, and was appointed to a teaching position at Peking University in 1917) and Yan Fu.[5] The society organized a petition drive urging Yuan to become emperor while Yuan pretended to stand above events. In September a so-called National Congress of Representatives—all 1,993 members of unanimous accord—voted for Yuan to become emperor of a new dynasty. Over the winter more petitions and memorials flooded into Beijing. On December 12 the Council of State voted for Yuan to become emperor. Yuan refused three times. Then he graciously said yes.

In an essay, "A Constitutional Monarchy Will Save the Nation," written in April 1915, Yang Du declared: "We need a constitutional system to save the nation and we need a monarchy to establish a constitutional system."[6] Wealth and power depended on constitutional government, but constitutionalism could only come from a monarchical form of government, not unworkable republican institutions. Yang argued that republicanism was not suitable for a weak nation. The Chinese military in particular had been hurt by notions of freedom and equality. Strong nations like Japan and Germany had avoided republicanism, while only wealthy nations like France and the United States could afford it. China, a poor country situated between the two strong monarchies of Japan and Germany, needed all the strength it could find. Furthermore, republicanism hindered China's path to wealth. Entrepreneurs needed freedom from foreign intervention and domestic disorder, which elections only fomented. Yang argued that the "second revolution" of 1913 was proof of China's unreadiness. In a republic,

the majority of the people must possess a common morality and a level of knowledge about republican politics. Then the people become the main element, and the president and officials are entrusted with the organs of governmental affairs by them. . . . How can we say that the Chinese are up to this standard? The majority of people do not know what a republic is and do not know what laws or the various theories of liberty and equality are. They precipitously abandoned an autocratic monarchy and instituted a republic, and now they think no one can restrict them and they can do whatever they want. . . . Moreover, since the emperor was so abruptly deposed, the prestige of the center has become insubstantial, like scattered sand, impossible to reassemble. No matter who is in charge, he will find no other policies to unify administration or pacify the country than a monopoly of power (zhuanzheng).[7]

Yang insisted that in spirit, China remained autocratic. He also insisted that he supported constitutionalism, but constitutional institutions had to evolve out of autocracy. Autocracy was necessary to foster education, industry, and the military. Citing Mencius, Yang claimed that only a single ruler could create unity.[8] Once the state was pacified, constitutional order could emerge. A constitutional monarchy, Yang granted, should not be a pure autocracy. Rather, the monarch would depend on popular support, which would in turn exert pressure for continuous progress. In 1907 Yang had remarked that China's territorial integrity can never be diminished, nor can the national polity (*guoti*) ever change, but its political institutions (*zhengti*) might be adjusted.[9] Now he emphasized the consistency of his support for constitutional monarchism from the late Qing.[10] In Yang's own view, he was not seeking to return China to the traditional dynastic system but to foster a strong nation-state.

Liu Shipei expressed his support for Yuan in a highly abstruse and allusive essay, "Imperial Government and the Restoration of Antiquity."[11] Liu did not mention Yuan by name, but he argued that a nation needed wise and strong leadership. Using quasi-transcendental language, anticipating a more traditionalistic rhetoric used to support Yuan specifically, Liu stated, "Heaven gives birth to the common people and they will be afflicted with chaos if there is no ruler."[12] Liu reinserted the emperor into the cosmic order and linked kingly "virtue" to broad powers.[13] He granted that if the Republic worked properly, then a "restoration of antiquity" might not be necessary. But as it is, "the throne should not be abolished even for a single day."[14] And so, "the time to renew the national mandate is now."[15] That task required an enormously creative person, who would be thrown up by a time of crisis and who would restore the political system.[16]

The argument *against* Yuan's monarchy was led by Liang Qichao, though many figures—even Yuan's former aide Tang Shaoyi—spoke out. Liang would have found Yang Du's arguments familiar, since he had recently been making those same arguments. But that was before the revolution. Liang now charged that changing the constitution was inherently destabilizing.[17] Having just undergone the 1911 Revolution, Chinese should now act within the parameters of the Republic's laws. Bravely resisting the temptation to say "I told you so," Liang did add that just as he had opposed the republican revolution on the grounds that reform within the existing monarchical system was preferable, so he now opposed monarchism on the grounds that reform of republican institutions was preferable to another radical change. In other words, the Republic was far from perfect, but it would be worse to change the "national polity" yet again.

The months that Yuan needed to prepare for his move allowed the anti-Yuan conspirators to set their counter-plots in motion. Liang was still serving as a member of Yuan's cabinet as the monarchical movement got underway, and he prepared a bolt-hole for himself in the foreign concession in Tianjin. In December he went on to Shanghai, where he was better protected than in Tianjin and where he could use Shanghai's media to thunder his disapproval. At the end of December, Cai E led a military rebellion against Yuan out of Yunnan, and Cai quickly claimed several victories over Yuan's larger forces. Cai was a former student of Liang's from the Academy of Current Affairs in the late 1890s and had followed Liang to Tokyo.[18] Cai studied military science in Japan and became a professional soldier. Their National Protection (*huguo*) Movement was joined by militarists in Guizhou, Guangxi, and other southern provinces. Former Tongmenghui leaders also took part, but the role of the constitutionalists was critical, not least because they had a kind of respectability the revolutionaries lacked. Their influence in provincial military units was much stronger.

"How Strange! The So-Called Question of the National Polity" was Liang Qichao's riposte to monarchism, published in August 1915 and reprinted widely.[19] Liang's essay veered between icy logic, unrestrained sarcasm, emotional pleading, and clever tropes. In a nutshell: the revolution was irrevocable because it had destroyed the myth of monarchism. Monarchies depended on a sense of magic, Liang argued. A decade of republican slander had damaged the charisma of the emperor, and the revolution had destroyed it. Once an idol has been pulled off its altar, its efficacy is forever weakened. Liang granted that the Republic was chaotic and inefficient, but he thought the solution was a strong presidency. He would gladly give the president the power to disband parliament and call for new elections, for example. Liang had fun accusing Yang Du of being a revolutionary. He also detailed the means by which Yuan Shikai manufactured the appearance of political support out of whole cloth, or at least out of his provincial goons. Finally, Liang accused the monarchists of favoring an absolute monarchy, rather than a constitutional one.

If Yang Du supported constitutional monarchy as a modernizing step and Liang Qichao supported the Republic in the name of stability, there was also a traditionalist case for Yuan's monarchy. Petitioners and memorialists praised his sacred and sagely qualities, his meritorious deeds and his virtue, and his transformative powers. Historical analogies were an important means of promoting Yuan's cause. As the modern case used elections and popular will, so the traditionalist case claimed that the people were demanding that Yuan become emperor: but their will was the will of Heaven. "The masses unanimously and respectfully hope for order," wrote one memorialist.[20] "Your majesty knows only to take the nation as his premise and the will of the people as his goal," wrote another.[21] "The people" appeared in the form of chambers of commerce, Overseas Chinese, provincial representatives, and representatives of minorities.[22] They agreed that in order to plan for the benefits of long-lasting and stable rule, as well as new national institutions, China needed to be an empire. And an empire needed a sage to rule it.

In December 1915 Yang Du and Sun Yuyun (1869–1924), co-directors of the Peace Planning Society, memorialized Yuan to assume the emperorship.[23] Their memorial may be taken as a model of the publicity campaign. Yuan's becoming emperor would assuage the hopes of the people, they said, for only an outstanding sage could "continue Heaven's mandate and become emperor" (*jitian liji*).[24] Yuan should "stand correct" and "establish his orders" (*zhengwei dingming*).[25] His wisdom was a gift from Heaven and his understanding was limitless; he embraced the vastness of Heaven and Earth. "Your military prowess is miraculous and your civil abilities sagely. Your thought has long been linked to the minds-and-hearts of the people." As if events were out of his individual control, Yuan's duty was to "submit to" Heaven's will and "follow" the "clear orders" of the people. "The beautiful sounds are surging harmoniously." Heaven had given Yuan the "sage's throne" and the people could see the flourishing rituals of Han officials. As emperor, Yuan would execute Heaven's mercy and accept the power of Heaven (*Tianwei*).[26] By "fixing duties" and "rectifying names" (*dingfen zhengming*) Yuan would exemplify the "love of the mind of Heaven" (*Tianxin zhi juan*).[27]

The notion of effortless or truly charismatic rule was a prominent motif in traditional political discourse that Yuan's supporters could not ignore, however badly it fit the circumstances. Updating old texts, Yang and Sun proclaimed that Yuan's great virtue swept over the five races of the Chinese while his awesome prestige brought him the trust of even the imperialist powers. If he refused the emperorship, the world would be unsettled and the people distrustful and rebellious. The whole nation wished to approach the sun and the clouds, and to become the mass of stars circling the pole star (an ancient trope of emperorship).

Your majesty has displayed the virtues of divine intelligence and penetrated the very sources of energy itself. You have molded the six directions as metal and cast that which exists as pottery. You have again suspended the sun and the moon and recombined the starts and constellations. Your majesty has created the three powers [Heaven, Earth, and Humanity]. Your awesome power is like the summer sun whose bright rays reach the whole world. Your benevolence is like the spring. . . .[28]

Such rhetoric blurred the lines between effortless charisma and actual abilities and accomplishments. "Your merit is so bountiful and your deeds so great that the people cannot find words to describe them," proclaimed Yang and Sun. Yuan's "benevolent heart" (*renxin*) inspired him to "enrich the people and benefit the nation" (*fumin liguo*). While seeming to combine a classical virtue with a modern concern for state-building, this piece of rhetoric was also a homage to Mencius, who had already linked princely benevolence to a range of ancient, effectively law-based actions.[29] Yuan himself put the situation with disarming simplicity:

In my original capacity [as president] I had the duty to maintain the national polity (*guoti*). I have repeatedly explained this, but the people will not accept this view. . . . Since national sovereignty resides in the whole people, how can I dare to maintain my own opinion in contravention of the people's will? "Heaven sees as the people see; Heaven hears as the people hear." Heaven inevitably follows what the people want. According to historical texts, whether one follows or contravenes Heaven is extremely serious. One cannot see Heaven, but one can see the people's will.[30]

But Heaven never organized elections, and Yuan's monarchy sank beneath the waves of foggy rhetoric. If Yuan was Heaven's charismatic choice, why bother with the modern rituals of representation? Nor were they of concern to most peasants, though they shut out the very people—the political activists—who knew they were being shut out. Yuan had in fact accepted the basic premises of political modernity. He assumed that the most suitable and effective way to replace the emperor was with a dictator, but he had difficulty ruling without parliament altogether. His only model was the imperial state. The failure of Yuan's monarchy scarcely made the Republic a success. But it suggested that the 1911 Revolution was irreversible.

CONFUCIANISM AND REPUBLICANISM

Confucians greeted the Revolution of 1911 with mixed emotions. They feared the collapse of social and moral order and, indeed, found signs of such a collapse all around them. They believed Confucianism would play a role in regenerating the nation. Such beliefs may seem a fairly typical conservative reaction to revolutionary change, not unlike Catholic support for monarchism in nineteenth-century France. But Chinese Confucians in the 1910s often welcomed the new Republic with enthusiasm. Many associated the revolution with the arrival of the Datong utopia that they took to mark the culmination of Confucianism. For them, the physical survival of the nation and the national culture were intimately linked in a single fate that seemed simultaneously precarious and millennial. As Liu Xiaofeng has pointed out, New Text Confucian thinkers in the 1910s drew parallels between the ancient *geming* (Mandate change) and the modern *geming* (revolution).[31] If the notion of Datong was associated with historical progress by way of Kang Youwei and the New Text tradition, the Old Text and Song-Ming traditions also contributed to Confucian optimism in the early Republic. Confucians such as Xiong Shili (1885–1968) criticized the revolution for its failure to bring about democracy and equality, not for its goals. Like the reformers of the late nineteenth century, Xiong believed the ultimate aim of Confucius was democracy. Xiong linked the Confucian notion of Heaven to the people, so that the Mandate of Heaven (*Tianming*) represented the reordering of the world through sagely morality. In Liu Xiaofeng's reading, Xiong's vision had utopian elements. That Heaven was found in the human mind and nature and could be developed by individuals perhaps even to the point of sagehood was a strand of Neo-Confucian thought particularly prominent in the Wang Yangming school.[32] In this view, the Mandate was (at least potentially) found in or available to every human. But that it could be a lever to pry open social reform was a discovery of the twentieth century.

Popular Confucianism naturally persisted across the political watershed of 1911, not only within the family setting but also in public expression. The solemn sacrifices offered to Confucius within temple and school walls two or three times a year in most towns and cities were sometimes accompanied by vibrant street festivals. In urban areas, the ceremonies associated with sacrificing to Confucius underwent self-conscious modernization, largely at the hands of local elites. Confucianism had a powerful advocate in the Confucian Association (Kongjiaohui), which was headed by Kang Youwei and the scholar Chen Huanzhang.[33] Chen (1881–1933) was the only person ever to possess both the *jinshi* degree and a Ph.D., which he earned at Columbia University with a long dissertation on Confucian economic thought. The association preached a doctrine that was both universal and particular. It believed Confucianism offered the best future to humankind. And it believed Confucianism was a marker of Chinese identity. It did much to shape Chinese schools in Southeast Asia. In China, it preached the need for a moral revival in the wake of the revolution.[34]

Confucians did not want to link their teaching too closely to that other quintessentially Chinese institution, the monarchy. So they argued that Confucianism had been misunderstood and misappropriated in the service of private interests, while it had still served as the foundation of morality and culture.[35] The emperors selfishly monopolized the worship of Heaven and often dominated scholars who themselves did not understand the original truths Confucius had propagated. Yet, for the modern Confucians, if imperial despots had repressed the people, it had to be remembered that they did so in an earlier stage of political evolution. Confucian morality had at least checked the worst excesses of the monarchy. Above all, it maintained national unity and Chinese culture (*jiaohua*): it belonged to the people. This is why, according to the Confucians of the early Republic, popular culture revered Confucius above all others. And because of the pervading influence of Confucius, the people respected morality and despised private advantage. In this view, the great historical role Confucianism had played in China was due to its moderation. It exerted beneficent influence while letting the people get on with their lives. In other words, Confucian norms were natural, already rooted in society, and ultimately stemmed from human nature.

And they were suited to the republican age. This was not to abandon all status distinctions and gradations based on virtue, birth, family relationships, education, and so forth. But it was to lessen the barriers dividing humanity. To these republican Confucians, the old emperors had illicitly monopolized the worship of Heaven and insinuated their own ancestors into the rituals, thus "familizing" the empire (*jiatianxia*). In today's Republic, however, the state was to be shared as common property (*gong tianxia*), and its citizens (*guomin*) were the people of Heaven (*Tianmin*). They should participate in Confucian rituals of state. Indeed, if Confucius and Mencius came back to life, it was claimed, they would certainly approve of republicanism.

This utopian thrust was perhaps short-lived, but it showed that the Confucianism of the early Republic had something in common with the other "isms" of the day. For Kang Youwei, Confucianism was no less essential to the Republic than it had been to the empire. He feared "if we abolish Confucianism, we will become a nation without a Teaching (*jiao*) and the nation simply will not survive."[36] Why? Because filiality and loyalty, rooted in self-cultivation, are the basis of the state. Kang insisted that the ancient sage-kings had wanted to regulate the monarchy precisely to discourage autocracy.[37] Yet as we will see, Kang's republicanism was lukewarm at best.

Short of making Confucianism China's official religion (*guojiao*), Yuan Shikai supported the Confucian Association.[38] Yuan emphasized that Confucianism was a protean system that had evolved with the ages.[39] So far, so historically accurate. Yuan also found Confucianism and republicanism to be perfectly compatible. This justified his desire for public schools to continue sacrifices to Confucius. Since, according to Yuan, Confucianism was not a religion, state sacrifices in no way violated the principle of freedom of religion.[40] Yuan emphasized the functional or moral aspects of Confucianism, not its spiritual ones. Proper learning was the basis for political progress, on which the survival of the nation depended. The following year, the Ministry of Education ordered middle and elementary schools to emphasize self-cultivation and morality using Confucian textbooks.[41] The Provisional Constitution of 1912 had not mentioned Confucianism. The draft constitution of 1913 made elementary schooling compulsory and proclaimed that "in the education of citizens, Confucianism (*Kongzi zhi dadao*) is the basis of moral training."[42]

Chen Huanzhang was the most tireless supporter of Confucianism in the first years of the Republic. Contrary to Yuan, Chen argued that Confucianism—encompassing as it did not just humanism (*rendao*) but also the spirit world (*shendao*)—*was* a "religion."[43] To some extent, this was an argument about semantics and translation—how to understand the Western (English) term "religion" and whether it was a category that Confucianism might fit. And to some extent this was an argument about Confucianism's place in the world—how it ranked as a spiritual system on a par with Christianity and other world religions.[44] But the political point was that Chen thought the Confucian religion should be institutionalized as China's established faith, supported by the government. Chen and other Confucians argued that Confucian rituals and teachings would settle the people and restore order. Alluding to Confucius's own words, they pointed out that the reach of politics ("laws and punishments") was always limited, while morality had infinite power. If the government had the popular trust, then the rich would support it, the poor work for it, the wise give it advice, and the brave fight for it, all in a spirit of unity and solidarity. To save the Republic, it was necessary to regenerate national morality; to improve morality, it was necessary to promote national culture and discipline (*jiaohua*). In another formula, the "rectification of character" (*zhengxin*) would save the nation. "Correct learning" provided the path to the rectification of character. In turn, the essence of correct learning lay in knowledge of one's responsibilities, placing what was right above profit, exalting the public (*gong*) and controlling the self (*keji*), and knowing one's place. In 1912 an editorial in the *Shibao* held that the reason for China's long existence as a nation lay in Confucianism: no matter how many times foreigners had invaded,

China always revived. And the heart of Confucianism, what made intangible beliefs and values tangible, was the rites. It was precisely the rites that shaped the ordinary people, who were all, in their way, Confucians.[45]

Chen Huanzhang was not content with utilitarian arguments. He insisted that the classics had not only taught ethics but also spoke of spirits and the ultimate nature of the cosmos—that is to say, of religion. Confucianism taught that the rectification of behavior is to follow the Way, which in turn is in accord with human nature as granted us by Heaven. Chen further argued that religion was essential to life. Both logically and in the actual evolution of human culture, religious life preceded political forms. The Confucian teaching, according to Chen, particularly emphasized the importance of religion and morality to good government while relegating administrative techniques ("laws and punishments") to second place. Therefore, religion is not mere superstition but the very basis of both individual and social life. Another view in the Confucian Association simply held that Confucianism was a religion because Tian was the equivalent of the Western "God."[46] Religions differed in their rites but were one in their regard for Heaven.[47] Still, according this view, Confucianism was unique in the way it combined morality and politics.

For Chen Huanzhang, the task was to bring back rituals, or to ritualize Confucianism so that it could demonstrate the sacrality of moral behavior and republican citizenship. In the *Journal of the Confucian Association*, Chen argued that sacrifices to Confucius should accompany the sacrifices to Heaven, thus in a sense giving Confucius a standing similar to that of Heaven.[48] Like the Qing promotion of Confucian sacrifices to the level of grand sacrifices, this would have marked a break with traditional cosmology. After all, Confucius was merely a human being. Chen acknowledged that Heaven created the world, but if humans can form one body with Heaven, it is the sages who show humanity how this is possible. Similarly, for the classical scholar and Qing official Zhang Ertian (1869–1945), Confucius deserved worship because, like Heaven, he was ultimately a life-giving force (as well as ancestor of the Chinese people).[49] The Confucians, Zhang said, identified national culture with the sage-kings: Yao, Shun, the Yellow Emperor, and so on—a line culminating in Confucius. Even the sage-kings were inferior to Confucius, though. For it was Confucius who single-handedly recovered their forgotten legacy after centuries of turmoil and moral degeneration.

Confucians of the early 1900s argued that the worship of Heaven had been monopolized by emperors, while Confucius was a popular culture-hero and hence an appropriate symbol for a democratic age. But they deplored the moral degeneracy they saw around them, and condemned radical republicans for selfishly grabbing for power. The sense of moral degeneracy was so common that few wrote to prove that the problem existed or detail its exact shape; rather, it was simply noted in passing.[50] Disunity and strife were leading to the rise of evil people unchecked by any punishment. Customs were declining. The "family revolution" was turning children into strangers; the "marriage revolution" was leading to divorce; and militarization was leading to violence in all spheres of life. No one was supporting widows, the elderly, and the weak. Magistrates were taking bribes; soldiers had turned into gangs. Benevolence and righteousness had disappeared. People were no longer capable of guilt or shame but wantonly committed evil acts.

Liang Qichao, in his speech at the autumn 1913 sacrifices to Confucius, traced moral decline to the actions of officials.[51] In other words, he did not blame the people or backward popular customs. Yet, the solution still had to lie in the people. For Liang, then, the main point of Confucianism was to develop character with the goal of creating upstanding people (*junzi*). It might not be expected that all people could become *junzi*, but Liang argued in familiar terms that the influence of the virtuous (wind) always persuades those of lesser virtue (grass). It is not surprising that Liang signed the Confucian Association's 1913 "Petition" to establish Confucianism as the national religion.[52]

Disputes over some kind of establishment clause raged throughout the 1910s. It should be noted that discussion of the question was by no means limited to Confucians, intellectuals, and politicians. In 1913 the Shanghai Chamber of Commerce voted after a heated debate in favor of establishmentarianism.[53] In that debate, an ultraconservative faction argued that Confucianism could not be considered a religion since it was far greater than any religion; at the same time, since Confucianism was so essential, they opposed freedom of religion. According to a *Shibao* analysis of 1916, the various sides of the debate were not related to political factions—individual parliamentarians had strong views of their own on the question.[54] In this analysis, one group favored establishing Confucianism while maintaining religious freedom. A second group felt that Confucianism was not a religion in the first place; and if it were established as such, it would also irritate China's minorities. And a third group favored a compromise: while establishing Confucianism would be too difficult, it should play an official role in education. It is interesting to note that this analysis does not even mention the radical view that Confucianism was itself a source of evil; even those who opposed establishmentarianism were themselves largely Confucian.

NEW CULTURE INTERLUDE

It was no coincidence that the self-proclaimed New Culture Movement got underway in 1915: it started as a reaction to the Yuan monarchy. In Jerome Grieder's words, New Culture intellectuals thought that republicanism was meeting "systemic resistance . . . a cultural rejection of the political remedies that had been attempted, a cultural rejection of the political innovations ushered in by the revolution." Many intellectuals thus "sought to establish cultural and social conditions to nourish the qualities of individual and collective character which might, in time, mend the disease."[55] Operating in the name of "science and democracy," such progressive intellectuals sought to invigorate China's youth. In essence, they blamed old habits of thought, or the shackles of Confucianism, for Yuan Shikai's autocratic tendencies. Their turn to cultural concerns was partly a temporary retreat from politics—but only partly and very temporarily. It was really an attempt to influence politics by nonpolitical means, and progressive intellectuals soon discovered that cultural questions were inherently political. New Culture intellectuals could be as condescending toward their countrymen—or more so—than conservatives, but they persistently sought to enlarge the political sphere. In September 1915, Chen Duxiu (1879–1942) founded *Youth Magazine*, soon to be called *New Youth*. Chen had been a revolutionary since the turn of the century (though he never joined the Tongmenghui) and worked as a teacher and journalist. In 1917, Cai Yuanpei appointed him to be dean at Peking University. Cai had himself accepted appointment as chancellor of the university after Yuan Shikai's death in 1916. Cai had promptly augmented the old faculty with a range of liberal and conservative scholars, the latter including, for example, Liu Shipei and Gu Hongming.

New Youth signaled the rise of a radical but cosmopolitan sensibility, as many scholars have pointed out. The immediate spurs to the movement, however, were fear and disgust provoked by the specter of restorationism.[56] Chen Duxiu was moved to total condemnation of Confucianism primarily because he saw Yuan's monarchical movement as founded on it. Chen argued that Confucianism was essentially an ethics of hierarchy, incompatible with modern, republican ethics. He tried to reconcile the need for China to adapt to a social Darwinian world of ruthless competition with his faith that civilization was progressing through universal stages. His solution: humankind was advancing from autocratic and hierarchical societies to a democratic and egalitarian order marked by respect for science, human rights, and individual autonomy. Chen defined the legitimate state as one that defended the individual and collective rights of the people. The state was the arena in which struggles for rights inevitably occurred; a progressive nation would produce a stable and democratic government. For Chen, rights were neither "natural" (prior to society) nor granted by the state; rather, they were part of the evolution of civilization. Individuals possessed consciousness, which allowed them to break with the past and become the subjects of their own decision-making. Chen denied that such individualism conflicted with society or the state, which instead properly served to put individualism on a sound basis. Individuals who possessed rights, and were thus autonomous and independent, were necessary to the establishment of a strong state. In this way Chen minimized conflicts between collectivity and individual.

For Chen, Confucianism was the exact opposite of everything he believed in. Confucianism was the old social hierarchy, loyalty to the emperor, and patriarchal authority; it offered no grounds for building democracy, freedom, egalitarianism, and human rights. Chen's "Call to Youth" in the inaugural issue of *New Youth* was designed to arouse China's youth to struggle against the "old and rotten" society by becoming independent, progressive, daring, cosmopolitan, pragmatic, and scientific.[57] This famous essay contrasted the values of independence (*zizhu*), equality (*pingdeng*), and rights (*renquan*) to slavery, a familiar trope. Most striking was Chen's optimism. Historical progress was leading humanity toward "liberations" of the weak from their oppressors—liberations political, religious, economic, and sexual. Chen defined liberation as the attainment of a completely autonomous and free personality, but only within a context of equality among all persons. Chen did not claim that Confucius himself personified evil or backwardness, granting at times that Confucius might even have played a historically progressive role. But Chen did argue that precisely because Confucius was a man of his times, thoroughly steeped in "feudal" values, his ideas could not be applicable to the present age.[58]

"Confucianism and the Chinese monarchical system possess an inextricable relationship."[59] Chen not only criticized Confucian morality, but attacked its cosmology for ascribing rulership to the generative forces of the universe.[60] In mid-1917, Chen noted that the future of the Republic looked grim,

only because at this time, although the majority of the Chinese people say they are not opposed to the Republic, their minds are in fact stuffed full of the old thought of the imperial age. There is not even a shadow of the civilized systems of Western societies and nations, so as soon as people open their mouths or extend their hands, they are unconsciously carrying the stench of monarchical absolutism. . . . To firmly secure the Republic today, we must totally wash the old thought of anti-republicanism clean away from the minds of the Chinese people.[61]

Chen seems to have regarded popular struggle for rights as something like the motor of history. It explained how the survival of the fittest led to progress of humanity as a whole. Seizing their rights, the people had created democracy in the recent past and were in the process of creating socialism in the present. Chen also used the concept of democracy to tame nationalism. Chen was critical of nationalism because it tended toward excesses that injured the rights of the people.[62] But the collective consciousness of nationalism was necessary for democracy to function. Historically, under feudalism and despotism the people lacked any sense of collective consciousness, and such "loose sand" was useless in the struggle for survival among nations.[63] Nationalism was a necessary stage along the road of progress.

I do not exalt nationalism (*guojia zhuyi*) and think it an absolute good; indeed, today the evils of nationalism are appearing in Europe and it should self-destruct soon. But looking at conditions in China, our people are still in the age of scattered sand. We have to follow the times, and nationalism has truly become the best means by which the Chinese can save themselves. To use this doctrine, the Chinese must first understand what it means. What does it mean? Scholars of politics in the West have defined the characteristics of all modern states as follows: "The state (*guojia*) is a group of people gathering together, domestically unified, and guarding against the outside to preserve the benefit of the whole group. It is not the private property of rulers." In other words, contemporary nationalism refers to democratic nations, not nations of enslaved people. Democratic nations are true nations, the common property of their citizens, making the people the masters and the government their servant. Nations of enslaved people are false nations, the private property of the rulers, treating the rulers as the masters and the people as their slaves. True nations sacrifice a portion of the rights belonging to individuals in order to preserve the rights of the whole citizenry. False nations sacrifice the rights of the whole citizenry in order to exalt one man.[64]

It could have been Liang Qichao speaking. True, Chen did not valorize the state to the same degree as Liang; he understood a democratic state to be a force for liberation. But like Liang, Chen thought the "people" (*renmin*) was a politically defined entity, not a group defined by ethnicity, blood, culture, language, and the like ("nation"). He spoke of the "self-awareness" (*zijue*) not of the individual but of the people in this sense.[65] The people came together to form the nation in order to protect their rights and plan for the common good. The advanced European pattern was to provide for the rights of the people through constitutional provisions. Chinese rulers, however, had always built the state on thoroughly selfish principles. Even so-called "sagely rulers and worthy ministers" kept their own interests uppermost. China was therefore not yet able, Chen concluded, to produce a patriotism that was not distorted. Patriotism was an emotion, while "self-consciousness" was an intellectual understanding— self-consciousness would lead to the nation understanding that its purpose lay in realizing the interests of its members. When people were dependent on others, they became "unconscious" (*wuyishi*)—by which Chen seems to have meant they lost their capacity to act as subjects making decisions for themselves.[66] China had not yet undergone a true national movement, like the French and American Revolutions and the Meiji Restoration, when people united to overthrow a common enemy. Rather, Chen complained, recent Chinese experience, including even the 1911 Revolution, was merely of small groups fighting over power and, without the support of the majority of the people, unable to effect basic progress.

As for the Chinese people, Chen frankly found them backward, in desperate need of "self-consciousness." This created a dilemma. The goal was to create a modern state, but this was precisely what the Chinese were not ready to do. A backward people, Chen feared, would produce an oppressive state. Yet unlike Liang Qichao, Chen did not believe that autocracy, however enlightened, could strengthen the state. Whatever the problems of the Republic, autocracy had been worse and, if reestablished, would be worse again. "If the intelligence of a people is insufficient to establish a republic, it is not necessarily enough even for a constitutional monarchy, which is the same as a representative system. If we fail to establish representative politics, even the most unassailable of autocratic rulers cannot preserve the nation in today's world as long as the people lack the intelligence to establish the nation."[67] To deal with dictatorship, corruption, poverty, immorality, and natural disasters, Chen called on patriots to be diligent, frugal, honest, clean, sincere, and trustworthy. These were Boy Scout virtues, it may be noted, either taken directly from Confucian texts or compatible with them.[68] Nonetheless, Chen was not simply trying to foster private morality as a basis for the public good in the style of Liang Qichao. He insisted the individual was logically and legally prior to the collective, but it would be meaningless to imagine the individual outside of collective social existence. The question was, what kind of collectivity?

One possible approach was to rethink the question. If the nation could only be built by a free people, then neither intellectuals nor political elites could prescribe what the people should create. As Leigh Jenco shows, Zhang Shizhao (1881–1973) constructed a notion of the political community on the basis of individuals who would come together to work out their differences—but not reach a single consensus—with mutual respect.[69] Zhang had been an early supporter of revolution but in the 1910s was trying to promote a difficult cause: building democratic institutions within the law, which in effect meant the acceptance of the legitimacy of Yuan Shikai's rule. He did not assume the existence of a bourgeois liberal order that already assured a degree of toleration, but rather argued that the Chinese could construct their own order, linking individual moral transformation to the shared public life of ongoing engagement. Zhang valorized the potential contributions of individual talent, not limited to the elite. However, another kind of democratic populism (*pingmin zhuyi*), not precisely prescriptive but much more radical, came to dominate political discourse by the end of the decade.[70] One of its most prominent and optimistic proponents was Li Dazhao (1888–1927), the Japanese-educated librarian of Peking University. For Li, the spirit of democracy lay in enabling workers, peasants, and women to "develop their individual natures and enjoy their rights."[71] Writing at the end of the Great War in 1919, Li proclaimed:

Every aspect of contemporary life is colored by democracy and follows democracy's route. This is true of education and of religion; and in terms of literature and art, everything that occupies a place in human life is dominated by democracy. To put it in a word, democracy is the only power operating in the world today, and the present era is the era of democracy.[72]

Li saw the Allies' victory as a victory for mutual aid, equality, liberty, and labor. In time, he predicted, everyone would become a commoner, that is, a worker. In Li's anarchist reading of the Russian Revolution, Bolshevism spelled the end of the capitalist nation-state and the replacement of government by workers' unions. The 1911 Revolution represented the victory of democracy in China, and its enemies were doomed to destruction like Yuan Shikai.[73] In time, traditional government would be replaced by "management" under "workers' government." Like Liu Shipei and Zhang Binglin before him, Li noted that bourgeois democracy was flawed, but he tended to regard it as insufficient rather than false democracy. The very nature of the modern state seemed to him to imply the existence of strong democratic forces. The liberation movements of the day—anticolonial, nationalist, peasants', workers', and women's movements—were all democratic by their nature.[74] The "dictatorship of the proletariat" in Russia, Li promised, was but a transitional period during which the bourgeoisie would be eliminated. Once society was made up of only workers, Li implied, its structure would necessarily be democratic. He also treated democracy, or democratic ideas, as a historical force in their own right.

Democracy is a kind of temperament, the habituation of a kind of spirit, a worldview. It is not merely a concrete political system but in fact an abstract philosophy of life, not merely a product of pure understanding but in fact a sought-after resplendence deeply imbued with emotion and excitement.[75]

Everything from the transformation of despotism to republicanism and from the conversion of centralized power to federalism—everything is the manifestation of freedom for individual development. In the past monarchism meant the oppression of the masses by one individual, and the masses lacked the freedom to develop their individuality. Only with the advent of democratic systems could everyone freely develop their individuality. . . .

The term "democracy" . . . refers to the "rule of the people." Today, however, the connotations of "democracy" no longer include "rule" in its original sense. The term "rule" refers to a person or a group of rulers who rule over other people. One rules, the other is ruled; one orders, the other obeys. This kind of relationship is not the relationship of pure democracy. Today the meaning of democracy lies not in rule over people but in the management of affairs. If we want to practice democracy, we need to study techniques of administration rather than how to get power.[76]

NATIONALIZING THE FORBIDDEN CITY

Notwithstanding Li's optimism, the struggle for power continued. The prize of Beijing attracted hungry militarists. Meanwhile, a rump Qing court continued to function deep within the Forbidden City as the emperor Puyi grew up. The Articles of Favorable Treatment—the deal for the Qing's abdication in 1912—specified that the royal house and all Manchus would remain unharmed. The emperor was permitted to retain his title and was even to be treated by the Republic "with the courtesies which it is customary to accord to foreign monarchs"—as if, then, the Qing retained sovereign status.[77] The Republic was to grant the emperor an allowance, protect the imperial temples and mausoleums, complete the mausoleum of the Guangxu emperor, and safeguard the emperor's private property. The court was to move to the Summer Palace, it was not to accept the service of new eunuchs, and its imperial guards (except for the emperor's personal bodyguards) were to be placed under the government's control. In fact, neither side abided by the Articles: the government paid but a small fraction of the allowance due the court, while the court showed no signs of ever moving to the Summer Palace. Court officials never used the republican calendar and were certainly involved in restorationist plots against the Republic. Beyond the court, a certain segment of elite opinion, by no means solely Manchu, remained "loyal" to the Qing to one degree or another.[78] Much of the Beijing political elite—warlord cabinets, bankers, and military officers—remained close to their friends in the little court. So did a segment of the scholarly and cultural elite.

In 1917 the single most powerful of the northern militarists, Duan Qirui (1865–1936), quarreled with most of his colleagues and the regime split. On July 1 the Xuzhou-based general Zhang Xun (1854–1923) marched north and staged a restoration of the Qing.[79] Zhang had famously never cut his queue nor allowed his soldiers to cut theirs. In the wake of Yuan Shikai's death, amid political instability, Zhang was able to expel the hapless Li Yuanhong from Beijing and soon had the city festooned with yellow dragon flags. It was said people descended on pawn shops to find suitable Qing gowns and fake queues that were suddenly de rigueur. Kang Youwei was welcomed by the court, though Zhang ignored all his suggestions to modify traditional rituals. But powerful northern generals soon fought back. By July 12, Zhang was sent running and the Republic was soon back in business, albeit in warlord hands. Interestingly, after fleeing to foreign legations, the leaders of the restoration, including Zhang and Kang, were not charged with treason but allowed to go home. Granted the farcical elements of the 1917 restoration, Zhang Xun's declaration (possibly drafted by Kang Youwei) nonetheless made some telling points:

Ever since the uprising at Wuchang and the establishment of the Republic, peace and order have been cast to the winds and good, reliable people have vanished. Anarchists are holding sway, and unscrupulous people are monopolizing power.

Robber chiefs are called heroes and dead convicts are worshipped as martyrs.
. . . In name we are a republic but nothing is known of the citizens. People are
called citizens but they know nothing about their country. . . . Compare this with
the continuous reign of the monarchy, wherefrom the people may enjoy peace
for tens or hundreds of years; the difference is at once seen to be as great as the
distance between heaven and earth.[80]

Kang Youwei had opposed Yuan's monarchy, largely out of his emotional commitment to the Qing.[81] But he welcomed the 1917 restoration,
at least initially. In an edict he drafted for the restoration (though Zhang
Xun disallowed its promulgation), Kang returned to the themes of the late
Qing reform movement: unity of monarch and people, abolition of racial
and ethnic divisions, search for new knowledge and talents, enrichment of
the people, improvement of customs and education, and so forth.[82] Unlike
Zhang Xun, Kang did not want to call the new state the "Great Qing"
but rather the "Chinese Empire" (*Zhonghua diguo*). In the first years of
the Republic Kang had worked out a theory of a titular monarchy—of a
powerless, or least actionless (*wuwei*) figurehead who would nonetheless
inspire awe and foster stability.[83] Such an empire would be a commonwealth, not a land held privately.[84] How Kang Youwei deluded himself
into thinking Zhang Xun and Puyi might make such a commonwealth
must remain a historical mystery.

For his part, Yang Du had been initially sympathetic to the Puyi restoration of 1917. But he too soon discovered Zhang Xun's goals were not
what he considered to be constitutional monarchism. Yang then announced
his retirement from politics, following three defeated efforts to turn China
into a constitutional monarchy.[85] He was to conclude that the "times" were
more suitable to republicanism after all. He later joined the Guomindang
and finally the Communist Party. In general, progressive intellectuals were
horrified by the restoration. As Timothy Weston has described, Peking University professors were shocked by the sight of dragon banners and false
queues suddenly appearing in their city.[86] Cai Yuanpei briefly resigned as
head of the university. Yet the rapid defeat of Zhang Xun was also reassuring. Zhou Zuoren (1885–1967)—essayist, translator, and literature
professor—later recounted how he had reacted with loathing when Qing

dragon banners replaced the five-color republican flag, and with joy when the five-color flag returned to the streets.[87] His conclusion: the restoration was proof of China's need for an "intellectual revolution"—the task of national reform was not yet complete.[88] Thus the dialectical opposition between monarchism and New Culture ideals continued.

The final, ignominious end to the Qing court came in 1924, but not as a triumph of republican principle. At that time two nominally allied warlords came to blows over control of Beijing. Feng Yuxiang (1882–1948) turned against his superior Wu Peifu (1874–1939) at the beginning of November. Feng had long shown some progressive inclinations.[89] He promptly ordered that Puyi be expelled from the Forbidden City. Feng represented himself first as saving Beijing and the nation from incessant civil war, and only second as saving the Republic.[90]

This final, unedifying chapter of China's imperial history was a necessary epilogue to the unfinished business of the 1911 Revolution. The expulsion of Puyi from the Forbidden City, the cessation of Qing rituals, and the termination of the traditional calendar all marked the final disappearance of the imperial system from Chinese soil. The Revised Articles of Favorable Treatment of 1924 demolished the legal basis of the Qing dynasty. Puyi abandoned his use of the imperial title and would be treated as an ordinary citizen; the imperial household would leave the Forbidden City and find its own place to live. The Revised Articles also promised that the government would maintain some payments to the royal house and poor Manchus; that the Republic would continue to protect the Qing's ancestral temples and imperial tombs; and that the royals could keep their private property, while public property would revert to the Republic. (This last provision was particularly ambiguous.) These controversial "revisions" were soon denounced by Qing loyalists. They provoked a debate—a debate that was really about the nature of the Republic—but the revisions were never rescinded.

The entire incident may be seen as the trivial flotsam of modern Chinese history, whose real currents were being shaped by regional armies, or in places like the streets and classrooms and teahouses of Beijing, the Guomindang's headquarters in Guangzhou, the cabinet office in Tokyo, or anywhere but the Forbidden City. Yet the expulsion did receive considerable press, and its symbolic significance was appreciated by the educated urban population of the day. Some regretted the "mistreatment" of the Qing court. Those speaking on Feng Yuxiang's behalf, however, accused Puyi of planning a restoration, either imminently or eventually.[91] Puyi's mere presence in the Forbidden City encouraged restorationist plots and disturbances, they said. Even thirteen years after his abdication he was still acting like an emperor. He was also hoarding artistic treasures that should belong to the nation.

Various accounts of the expulsion appeared in newspapers at the time and subsequently in memoirs, including Puyi's own memoirs. They differ in detail but all describe a tense situation. On the morning of November 5 Puyi was given an ultimatum to leave or the palaces would be fired upon. He left for his father's mansion in the afternoon. Feng's men took control of the treasures in the Forbidden City. According to his memoirs, Puyi said he looked forward to becoming an ordinary citizen.[92] That was how Feng Yuxiang remembered it as well:

The continued existence of the little court of the former Qing emperor on the territory of the Republic of China—and especially in the very capital of that Republic—not only represented the Republic's shame (everybody who understood anything at this time saw retaining the queue as a mark of shame—what would be more shameful today than if we had left Puyi as a queue on the Republic of China?) but it also formed a real threat by allowing ambitious Chinese and foreigners continuously to make use of it. When we quelled the restoration of 1917, I strenuously argued for getting rid of this weird phenomenon and exterminating the threat, but things did not go according to my wishes. This time, when I entered Beijing, I was determined to abolish it with all my might. After we had agreed on the regency cabinet, I ordered Lu Ruibo [Zhonglin] to carry this out.

He took several guards with him to the palace, and asked Puyi, "So, do you wish to be an ordinary citizen or do you wish to be the emperor? If you wish to be an ordinary citizen, we have ways of dealing with ordinary citizens, but if you wish to be the emperor, then we have means of dealing with emperors!"

Puyi quickly replied, "Of course I should become an ordinary citizen, but I couldn't help having all these people living off of me. They forced me to stay here; otherwise, I would have left sooner."

Lu said, "Since this is the situation, please move out of the palace immediately and from now on become an exemplary ordinary citizen."[93]

The Chinese political establishment, such as it was, and the foreign embassies regarded Feng's action as destabilizing. Ambassadors from the Netherlands, Britain, and Japan (all monarchies) visited the new Foreign Affairs minister to warn him to tread carefully.[94] Feng defended his actions on the grounds that restorationism was an imminent threat.[95] He insisted that the continuation of Puyi's imperial status humiliated the Republic. He pointed out that he was simply enforcing the third clause of the original Articles—that the Qing was to leave the Forbidden City.[96] Above all, the retention of the imperial system in the midst of Beijing "was in great conflict with the popular sentiment of the [republican] political system."[97] Feng's government spoke of its own actions as rooted in loyalty (*zhongai*).[98] And it assured one and all that Puyi would still be treated well.[99] Or as Li Shizeng later put it to a worried Duan Qirui, who was preparing to return to the government: "Louis XVI was killed in the French Revolution, and numerous kings were killed in Britain. The Articles of Favorable Treatment in regard to Puyi are not a foreign relations problem."[100]

The priceless treasures in the court's keeping attracted enormous interest.[101] (The court had been supporting itself for years through the gray-market sales of art works.) Li Shizeng was named head of the Committee for the Readjustment of the Qing Household Affairs. Li said legal scholars and archeologists should determine which items belonged to the Qing house and which to the nation.[102] On November 7, Li met with various representatives of the new government and court officials to discuss procedures.[103] They agreed on five tasks: to inventory the imperial seals; to dismiss lower-grade palace workers; to allow palace residents to remove their personal property only; to allow Puyi and his consorts to remove items of daily use; and to close halls and palaces currently undergoing renovation. Li brought in experts from Peking University, the Historical Museum, and the Capital Library. Reports also stated that police impounded several art works and antiques that eunuchs were trying to sneak out.[104]

The Feng government was to last but a few weeks, but the museumification of the Qing was irreversible. A newspaper editorial in December called for the entire Forbidden City to be turned into an art museum.[105] The editorial promoted the effects of art in almost millennial terms. The essence of the vast Chinese artistic tradition had already been collected by the emperors, so this could be the basis of a national museum like the palace museums of Germany and France. All nations needed the spiritual aid that art could offer. Art even possessed the power to enlighten. After all, the practical power of Buddhism came not from preaching the dharma or reciting sutras but from the ability of its art to move people. And the Christian art of the Renaissance led the way from the depredations of warlords to centuries of cultural and material progress. The editorial concluded that the art of China, which was not limited to religious expression but represented the cultural spirit of the country, could enlighten the populace by spreading culture among them. In the end, the remaining imperial collections of scrolls, jade carvings, porcelain, and thousands of other items were incorporated into the Palace Museum, which opened in 1925.[106]

However, we should also take note of the fact that not all members of the Qing had in fact left on November 5. The last two remaining dowager-consorts (widows of the Tongzhi emperor) had flatly refused to go. The dowager-consorts said they were still in mourning for a third dowager-consort (widow of the Guangxu emperor), who had died October 21 and whose funeral ceremonies were still underway. There were apparently rumors of their deaths, and according to one report, the emperor said the next day, "I don't know what has happened to them. . . . They both threatened to kill themselves if they were turned out by force."[107] In fact, Feng's government left them in place, satisfied for the time being with the expulsion of Puyi and his empress and consort. Newspaper reports said the last two representatives of the Qing house were willing to leave the Forbidden City by mid-November, but were insisting that they not be searched.[108] Li Shizeng said the committee was considering the matter. Finally, on November 21 at 3 PM—a matter of front page news—the dowager-consorts left the palace, without being searched, and entered an automobile, the windows of which were covered by yellow silk.[109] They traveled by police escort and traffic was stopped for their journey. One report did, however, state that an earlier search of their baggage revealed items that the police impounded, such as a large clock from the Qianlong period.[110]

In the meantime, Puyi complained that as his movements were restricted, he was in actuality not being treated like an ordinary citizen.[111] "As I have already said, I am now one member of the Republic of China," Puyi insisted. "Since I am a member of the Republic of China, I should enjoy the same rights [as any citizen]." Negotiations continued over the Revised Articles.[112] With Duan Qirui's entrance into Beijing on November 24, it was reported that "the Qing house regained its liberty."[113] Duan removed the troops from around the mansion of Puyi's father, and Puyi soon made his way to the Japanese concession at Tianjin. Interviewed just after Duan Qirui had dismissed the troops guarding him, Puyi claimed:

For a long time I did not want to go on living in the palace, and also for a long time I favored completely abolishing the Articles of Favorable Treatment. This is because an ex-emperor who has abdicated yet goes on quietly living in this glorious palace in fact becomes an obstacle to republican institutions. Nor has the government been willing to carry out the Articles for some time. Although we still had the piece of paper, its benefits in fact had disappeared, and so it seemed better simply to completely abolish the Articles. Moreover, I was being supported by the populace of the Republic and adding to their burden, earning a salary for doing nothing, and I really apologize for this. But because I was trapped in this environment, I wasn't able to express my true desires. Now, forcible expulsion from the palace may be morally questionable, but in terms of my own position, it has truly given me a great opportunity. . . . I have decided to completely eliminate any imperial taint.[114]

The point is not Puyi's dubious sincerity but that he was contributing to a public debate about the place of the Qing. Intellectuals were not slow to jump on this particular bandwagon. Some still called for the execution of the traitor Puyi.[115] For Zhang Binglin, the expulsion, at least, was long overdue.[116] In a telegram to the leaders of the new government, he congratulated them on removing the Qing "chieftain" from the palace and reducing him to ordinary status. In Zhang's view, the original Articles of Favorable Treatment had been too generous on account of Yuan Shikai's perfidy. In any case, the Articles had been automatically nullified by the 1917 restoration, a traitorous act that left the nation in turmoil and deserved severe punishment. Allowing Puyi to leave the palace alive already signified favorable treatment. Furthermore, Zhang emphasized, the estates belonging to the Qing house had originally been appropriated by force and should be returned to Chinese farmers.[117] The people had not yet benefited from any "virtuous government" (*dezheng*) in the Republic's thirteen years: now was the chance to improve their lives. Zhang was still pushing this argument into December.[118] He also warned that opposition to the expulsion was coming not only from old followers of the Qing but also from Republican officials who wanted to seize the Qing's property for themselves.

The position of Hu Shi was perhaps more surprising. Hu (1891–1962) had emerged as a leading spokesman for the New Culture Movement from his position in the Philosophy Department at Peking University. His communication to Foreign Minister Wang Zhengting was reported in brief as follows: "While I do not support the retention of the imperial title by the Qing house, the Articles of Favorable Treatment represent a relationship that is a kind of international trust or treaty. Treaties may be revised or revoked, but to take advantage of weakness or frailty and carry this out by force is truly the greatest dishonor in the history of the republic."[119] In effect, then, Hu's objection was not to the ends but the means, but it was still an objection. It may be that Hu's personal relations with the emperor played a role in this thinking.[120] He seems to have thought Puyi could become a symbol of the new China if the ex-emperor got away from the stultifying court and studied abroad.

Not all observers agreed that the Articles had the force of a treaty obligation. In a carefully considered article, Ning Xiewan (1881–1946), an old 1911 revolutionary and Japanese-trained lawyer, concluded that they did not.[121] Arguing that treaties by definition only exist between states—that is, political entities possessing territory, people, and sovereignty—Ning posited that the Qing could not possibly be considered a state. Puyi possessed but an "empty title" and the "Qing" had no territory, nor people, nor sovereignty, and so had no standing under international law. With numerous citations, perhaps not always accurate, to modern European history, Ning argued that the Articles were merely a matter of domestic law, and the status of the Qing house rested on no more than a hereditary title. Ning further argued, like Zhang Binglin, that the Articles had in any case already been nullified by the Qing in its 1917 restoration.

Kang Youwei's reaction was, predictably, even stronger than Hu Shi's.[122] He, too, emphasized that the Articles of Favorable Treatment were binding as an international treaty. Kang compared the status of the

Qing house in China to that of the Vatican in Italy—or for that matter to French and Dutch recognition of the native kings of Vietnam and Java.[123] Kang also argued that the Republic owed the Qing a debt of gratitude, since it was Qing military might that conquered Manchuria, Mongolia, and the western parts of China, bequeathing them to the Republic. This was an argument for a kind of victor's memory opposed to Zhang Bing-lin's victim's memory of oppression. Kang said that to strip Puyi of his palace, his wealth, and his imperial title was simply base ingratitude, a violation of the moral requirement to recompense (*bao*) favors. In fact, for Kang, Feng Yuxiang's behavior was even worse than ingratitude: he was a thief bent on stealing the treasures of the Qing for himself. This prompted Kang to accuse Feng of communism, and, for good measure, Sun Yat-sen too. Finally, Kang warned that the Mongols and the Muslims (of the far west) had an interest in the Articles of Favorable Treatment, and the Republic was risking the loss of a large amount of territory by abandoning them.

The only political party to publicly endorse Feng's action was the Guomindang. Its leaders sent Feng a congratulatory telegram on November 11.[124] They trusted that Feng's actions would "permanently cut off any restorationist movements" and check the "politics of tyranny." Sun Yat-sen himself finally made a statement in January 1925 after the Qing's representatives had contacted him to ask for his support for a return to the status quo ante.[125] This was on the grounds that it was Sun, acting as provisional president, who had approved the original Articles of Favorable Treatment in 1912. Sun simply replied that the Qing itself had already voided the Articles by repeatedly violating them over the years.

The last emperors of China were deposed by military force. It is possible to count this way: Puyi in 1912; Yuan Shikai in 1916; and Puyi again in 1917 and 1924. But in each case, military power was not the determining factor. Rather, the popular imagination, or at least mainstream elite imagination, no longer conceived of the state as based on an emperor. The 1911 Revolution hardly turned the Chinese social world upside down. It was soon clear that the victory of "1911" was only partial at best, but it was also irreversible. However the new state would evolve, it would have to be based on the revolution.

In 1915 Zhang Binglin was languishing under house arrest by order of Yuan Shikai. According to his autobiography, Zhang was happy when he heard that Yuan was trying to become emperor, for then "I knew that Yuan's days were numbered."[126] Li Shizeng was living in France at the time, where he had founded a program to bring over Chinese students and workers to broaden their education and aid the war effort (he was also busy with his tofu company and Chinese restaurants). When news of Yuan's monarchical movement reached him, Li wrote to his friend Cai Yuanpei that Yuan had doomed himself.[127] For Li, the monarchical movement was scary, yes. It highlighted the backwardness of the Chinese people and the inadequacies of the revolution, yes, but it was a call to redouble educational efforts more than anything else. Two years later, in the wake of the 1917 restoration attempt, Chen Duxiu said that the emperor was simply another idol whose power stemmed from the people's superstitious belief in him. "But if their state perishes one day, as today Emperor Puyi of the Qing or Nicholas II of Russia [have already perished], they are more pitiful than ordinary people. These rulers of lost states are like clay and wooden idols thrown into the cesspool, and we can see just what supernatural magical powers they have!"[128] Li's and Chen's judgment seems correct. In 1924, in spite of the tut-tuting of political and intellectual elites, as soon as Puyi was out of the Forbidden City, its complete museumification was assured.

Conclusion

MONARCHY OR REPUBLIC? Late Qing intellectuals sometimes posed the question just this starkly. Of course they understood there were countless variations of each option and way stations on the march of progress from the one to the other. But the number of fundamental state forms was limited. Constitutional monarchism was often thought of as a way station, and also as a highly evolved state form in its own right. At the beginning of the nineteenth century, it was essentially impossible to imagine a civilized system of governance outside of the imperial dynasty. By the beginning of the twentieth century, this description remained true for the vast majority of Chinese, but radicalized elites could now imagine lots of non-imperial systems. The political culture—the normative basis and unconscious attitudes underlying rulership and the field of social relations in which rulership operated—seemed to have atrophied in the nineteenth century even as gentry involvement in public affairs grew. The growing role of local gentry and economic elites in the public sphere contributed to the explosion of political activism of the 1890s.

That activism led to the legitimation of revolutionary state-building in the first years of the twentieth century. In this sense, the historical commonplace that the 1911 Revolution was merely one stage of a longer revolutionary process that culminated in the 1949 Communist Revolution—or that "1911" was less important than "1949"—is misleading. The creation of the Republic of China in 1912, whatever its flaws, marked the establishment of modern Chinese national identity. We can see this in the use of the terms "Chinese" and "citizen" and loyalty to the nation-state, and all this implied for the destruction of the old sociopolitical system and the ambiguities of filling that vacuum. This process required "awakening" as John Fitzgerald has shown—awaking of the self, the nation, the masses—and we may add this in turn rested on considerable intellectual work on the problem of what people should be awakened *to*.[1] If modern

Chinese identity is understood as a project, it was not finished in 1912, and it is still not finished today.

No doubt the crisis of the early nineteenth century led, as Philip Kuhn argues, to a new kind of "constitutional" thought.[2] The Self-strengthening Movement of the 1860s expanded the boundaries of the political community by bringing lower-ranking gentry and even commoners into its discussions. It did so, however, within the framework of Confucian social relations, Confucian cosmology, and, in a word, the Confucian monarchy. The Self-strengtheners were rationalists, realists, solid men. It took a utopian dreamer to sever the link between Confucian cosmology and political order, even though he did so by taking a strand of Confucian thought to such an extreme that it broke. This was the result of the peculiar reformism of Kang Youwei.

What I am calling the Confucian monarchy was simply one species of a nearly universal political life-form. Historically, kingship transcended the split of the axial age from pre–axial age cosmologies. Kingship in the enchanted world of the pre–axial age included the universal kingships of Egypt and the Mesopotamian empires, which claimed divine rule over all lands. The Chinese Shang "dynasty" created the same type of polity. The ancient Chinese monarchy thus influenced the creation of the Confucian monarchy in China's axial age. The early Confucian school combined the king's claims to divinity and to ancestral power with claims to moral virtue. The rituals of kingship centered around three motifs, which made visible the unification of the realm and the subjugation of enemies. First, and perhaps at the most ancient level, were claims to the powers inherent in ancestors. Second were cosmological claims of the bequest or Mandate of Heaven and powers that matched cosmic movements. And third were claims of moral supremacy, which in the late imperial era were marked by performances of filiality. In Song Neo-Confucianism, imperial ideology was intimately connected to the Chinese elite's sense of the cosmic rootedness of the social system, centered on the family. In the popular imaginary, the cosmic order was personified by the potency of larger-than-life figures like the sage-kings, Guandi, and the hierarchies of supernatural beings. In the world imagined by the traditional universal kingship, all humans were slotted into more or less hereditary roles. Social reality was never so neat, and Chinese cosmology never denied change—indeed, it reveled in it—yet that the microcosms corresponded to the macrocosm was seldom doubted. Imperial rituals stabilized and synchronized the realm, keeping it in harmony with Heaven. "There is no land under Heaven that does not belong to the ruler," said the ancient *Odes*, a bulwark of gentry education into the twentieth century.

The ideological systems of the Qing may have been plural, as befitted its pluralistic empire, but its claim to unitary rule was universal all the same. Heaven, if not its various peoples, was one. The examination system provided an arena where gentry orthodoxy met imperial ideology, though the Qing's textual authority was never absolute. The seventeenth-century critique of the monarchy was quieted by the Qing, but virtue was a petard by which officials and even the emperor could be hoisted. By the 1860s, a new public sphere emerged that included newspapers, journals and translations, novels, study societies, and schools capable of doing such hoisting. Western learning gradually entered the Chinese knowledge system. At first acquaintance, equality and democracy were found to have ugly connotations, and to have derived from already-rejected ancient Chinese schools of thought. But as the needs of building a modern state impressed themselves on worried intellectuals, equality and democracy were rediscovered via the concepts of citizenship and nation.

Late Qing "egalitarianism" never referred to a sense of atomistic, self-contained persons who are individuals before whatever other roles or places they occupy. For late Qing intellectuals, citizens were still embedded in communities of various kinds, but traditional communities were to be modified in two ways: most directly, the priority of the nation-state; and in general terms, the mutuality of interests and conduct among citizens. Real, existing study societies and schools scarcely lacked hierarchy (any more than the universities of today), but they were exploring an ideal of civil discourse among members who qualified for membership by their skills and their own desire to participate. The intellectual moves involved here and the lived experiences were both extraordinarily liberating. Granted, many students and intellectuals experienced a sense of loss and of fear, and the tensions between new and old value systems were palpable. The conservative reaction of the late 1890s reflected these tensions. But the motif of liberation of one's self and one's people was already clear in the writings of Liang Qichao and especially, in the early twentieth century, the writings of anarchists. By the time of the New Culture Movement, this sense had become widespread.

Already, in the hands of Kang Youwei, New Text Confucianism had reached its subversive potential. Kang attacked the textual basis of the Confucian monarchy, finding forgery everywhere. Beginning in the 1880s, Kang began to suggest that Confucius himself had predicted, justified, and mandated institutional reforms including a written constitution and a parliament. This sounds bizarre today, and sounded no less bizarre at the time. Gradually, however, Kang's vision of the steady progress of civilization and his even more mystical vision of Confucius as a sage-king won followers. Much of Kang's philology and even more of his history was fanciful, but he had breached a bulwark of the imperial state.[3] To turn Confucius the teacher, or even sage-teacher, into the "uncrowned king"—last of the quasi-divine sage-kings—was to make political claims. Kang essentially transferred the charisma surrounding the emperor to Confucius, who in turn legitimated the actions of a strong, reformist emperor if one could be found. The vision of a strong emperor pushing reforms was nearly as much a violation of the existing political order as a purely democratic vision would have been.

Kang's ultimate challenge to the monarchy was to lead itself out of existence. He held that humans made their own history, albeit in a known direction (known to Kang, that is). A sense of the universe as a space in which humans made their own fate was reinforced by the social Darwinism conveyed by Yan Fu. Yan's own root-and-branch attack on the monarchy was based on the presumption that human society was governed by natural laws. There was never a wise sage-king benevolently creating civilized institutions because there never could be such a creature. For Yan, the real, existing emperor was clearly to be judged purely on utilitarian grounds. For both Kang and Yan, the task facing Chinese leaders was to strengthen the state, essentially by whatever means were necessary. That these means would inevitably enlarge the arena of legitimate political action to include the entire world of educated men was taken for granted.

Liang Qichao made an even clearer epistemological break with Confucianism in 1900. When Liang Qichao wrote, "I love Confucius but I love the truth more," he meant that the progress of civilization depended on intellectual freedom.[4] He understood the European Renaissance as the throwing off of religious shackles. While finding some use for Confucianism, he blamed Confucians for restricting the pursuit of knowledge. Liang was rejecting even Kang's approach, because it relied on hermeneutics. Liang had already sketched out his thoroughgoing attack on "despotism" and his plan of replacing it with activist-citizens. He had sought to build national spirit, though still working within the New Text vision of universal public-mindedness. Then, after the turn of the century, as Liang learned more about constitutionalism and clashed with the revolutionaries, he began to sketch out a vision of citizenship firmly within the framework of the disciplinary state. He maintained that the Chinese monarchy—that is, a defanged Qing emperor—could continue to provide a symbol of national unity. Yet the ultimate task was not the creation of a Chinese nation but a new civic state. Although Liang thought that the interests of the people and the state corresponded in every way that counted, he had gradually concluded that nationalism was at best a useful tool for the construction of the state, not the goal of the state. He attacked the narrow nationalism of the revolutionaries, not in the name of a universalism like Kang Youwei's Confucianism, nor yet of a utopian anarchism, but in the name of the state.

By this time, it was clear that states were a product of international politics and that "China" as the "Great Qing" was a project embedded in forced treaty-making. The notion of sovereignty as a duality of domestic power and international position was translated via international law. Liang toyed with the idea that "enlightened autocracy" could whip the Chinese nation into shape, but really he envisioned the disciplinary state as an educational state. Whatever its form, the state represented the highest political good. Like Yan Fu, Liang was alarmed that China had fallen behind in the evolutionary race that led from primitive tribes to military states. In finally turning to a doctrine of the "organic state," Liang was not justifying a version of hierarchy that associated kings with heads and commoners with limbs. On the contrary, his imagination was captured by a sense of the living interconnectedness of all the elements of the people-state: his was an egalitarian vision. The social contract was a universal truth, and it was a binding contract from which there was no withdrawal.

For the generation of 1898, politics was a dangerous game, and the psychological tensions they faced were acute. In other words, they were not playing with exciting new ideas—or not only so playing—but putting their lives on the line. Kang was accused of heresy from the beginning of the 1890s, and Kang and Liang were accused of being traitors to the Qing by 1897. There was a grain of truth in the charge, at least in Liang's case. High politics had been played for high stakes throughout the Qing, and the 1890s were no different. Even if lives had not been at stake, reformers would have felt a tension between their political commitment and the demands of filiality. It was not as if the radical reformers had achieved high positions and were backed by their own political machines. They did indeed envision themselves as fulfilling the highest Confucian ideals as loyal advisers to the emperor. They modeled themselves on standards reiterated from earliest times by Confucius and Mencius. But still, they could not avoid putting their families at risk, much less carry out their responsibilities to care for their parents and other family members. Kang Youwei may have seen his way clear through his messianic instincts, Liang Qichao through a lifelong attempt to work out new values appropriate to the modern age. Liang began to distinguish between private and public morality. The relationship between morality and politics deeply troubled twentieth-century thinkers.[5] This was not an abstract question to the men and women who feared the imminent dismemberment of China.

Moral rage fueled the conservative reaction against the 1890s generation of reformers. Conservative reaction ranged from the moderate traditionalism of Zhang Zhidong to the true reactionaryism of men who saw their most deeply held values under attack. Zhang supported many reform projects, and even the reactionaries had often begun their careers supporting reforms to the schools and the bureaucracy. What they could not tolerate was any talk of the nation, for fear that "democracy" was tantamount to overthrowing the dynasty—as perhaps indeed it was. Certainly an egalitarianism completely at odds with the Three Bonds was in the air. The Hunan reactionaries of 1897 and 1898 articulated a fear that went much deeper than political loyalism. All cultural markers of Confucian civilization and the patriarchal family seemed at risk. The reactionaries believed not only that society needs order but that it depends on nested hierarchies from top to bottom. If China lost the emperor, families would lose their fathers.

Unlike their counterparts in the West, late Qing conservatives never saw the state as the highest good, nor, obviously, could they assign this role to the church. Something more amorphous was at stake. History taught that states, as dynasties, come and go. Loyalism was certainly a virtue, but even in the abstract (regardless of dynasty), it was still not the highest good. Rather, the "rites and music" offered a way to combine political good with the entire social structure, for one could not doubt the "unity of governance and the Teaching" (*zhengjiao heyi*). But reaction was left in ruins by the debacle of the Boxer Uprising, and conservatives felt threatened by the Qing's New Policy reforms. When the Qing tossed the examination system on the rubbish heap of history in 1905, it disenfranchised its natural supporters.

By about 1900 the revolutionary movement was beginning to appeal to intellectuals and especially students. It was dominated by three concepts: a sense of time as linear and progressive, marking the continual improvement of society; a sense of national identity (of the *minzu*) based on racial-cultural consciousness; and a cluster of notions about the good society revolving around "equality" (*pingdeng*), "popular power" (democracy or popular sovereignty, *minquan*), and "human rights." The ideological distinction between revolution and reformism remained surprisingly vague for several years, but the main issue for the revolutionaries was clearly anti-Manchuism. If you supported restoration of the Han race and overthrow of the Manchus, then you favored revolution, republicanism, and possibly some kind of socialism. If you did not think Manchus were the main problem facing China, you still might favor a Han-dominated republic and socialism, but you supported reformist steps to get there. Mostly, though, reformers supported constitutional monarchism, and so came to be called constitutionalists. (Revolutionaries also favored a constitution, of course, and in a few cases might even have supported a constitutional monarchy as long as it was a Han monarchy.) Revolutionaries tended to put race at the core of their vision of the nation, and to derive the state from the nation. They supported their position with the science of race and the laws of historical progress. They traced social evolution from nomadic tribes (such as the Manchus), to organized agrarian civilizations such as the Han Chinese, and finally to military-industrial-imperialist societies represented by the Western powers and Japan.

In their approach to history, the revolutionaries, like Liang Qichao, faced the question of why Chinese progress had seemingly halted too early. Their answer: the Manchus. The Manchus oppressed the Han. In actual fact, this view did not stop the revolutionaries from condemning much longer traditions of Chinese despotism as harshly as did Liang, though they also tried to associate despotism with earlier foreign conquest such as that of the Mongols. Despotism was slavery, and slavery was the racial threat of White domination of Yellow, and Manchu domination of Han. Revolutionaries also claimed that a despotic state was a weak state: when the realm of the public was privatized by a ruler, the state became all the more vulnerable to foreign takeover. The sprouts of democracy visible in the ancient Zhou dynasty were precious markers of Han identity to the revolutionaries. Revolutionaries rooted much of their democratic and egalitarian thought in ancient Han culture and the lines of sage-kings, which combined ethnic and political genealogies. Hence the interest of a Liu Shipei in Zhou institutions.

In this way the revolutionaries displaced some of their fears of Western imperialism onto the Qing, scapegoating Manchus and even identifying on some level with the supposedly more civilized imperialist powers. They thus turned to Western and Japanese models to rethink the nature of the Chinese state, a task the reformers had already begun. Revolutionaries saw their destructive task to be the restoration of the Han people by overthrowing the Qing, and their constructive task to be the establishment of constitutional institutions little different from what reformers were promoting. But one other key difference between the two camps did exist: the revolutionaries wanted to create a true nation-state, where the state was based on an ethnic people (*minzu*). The reformers were not immune to this idea, but essentially thought the state would create the people as citizens (*guomin*). Both groups believed that in practice it was necessary to do considerable educational work among the people. Occasionally, it was even said that the essence of revolution was education.

Much of the revolutionary position was based on traumatic memories of the Manchu conquest of the seventeenth century, rewriting history in

racial terms, and denying the Qing's legitimacy. The trauma of the imminent loss of the Qing state was displaced to the past loss of the Ming. The
anguish felt by so many revolutionaries, not least the protorevolutionary
Tan Sitong, was expressed in rhetorical excess, martyrdom, and suicide.
Pain and humiliation were expressed repeatedly, and it may be that they
even came to be treasured by many intellectuals as part of their identity.[6]
But equally, the moral demand generated by the Confucian sense of public
responsibility motivated intellectuals to take political action at any cost,
which could in turn produce a very dynamic process of self-cultivation.
Both Liang Qichao and Song Jiaoren displayed something of this process.

Whether the 1911 Revolution was to be seen as the creation of a new
state through violence or simply a stage in the evolution of modern Chinese constitutionalism was a subject of struggle and debate in the ensuing
years. Insofar as his legitimacy stemmed from the Qing's abdication, which
referred to the will of Heaven and the people, Yuan Shikai preferred to
emphasize continuity. He was by inclination a constitutional monarchist,
and it is not surprising Liang Qichao tried to work with him. But the Republican government offered a mixed message. The dominant political
ritual of the new Republic was Double Ten, a celebration of revolutionary
change. Yuan was able to capture the symbols of power associated with
the new national day—in particular the new centrality of the military to
Chinese society and polity—but he lost control of its meaning. This was
expressed in the constitution of the Republic of China. After all the political
maneuvering in the wake of the revolution, the provisional constitution of
March 1912 stated that "the Republic of China is formed by the Chinese
people," and that "the sovereignty of the Republic of China is possessed
by the whole people."[7] There was nothing about the will of Heaven or
any relation between Heaven and the people. The constitution of 1916,
written in the wake of Yuan Shikai's downfall, reiterated these principles.[8]

If it seems tempting to dismiss written constitutions as mere words on
paper, it still has to be acknowledged that Double Ten festivities embodied
a certain sense of popular sovereignty. The new calendar, albeit not particularly popular, was the ultimate symbol of new claims to sovereignty.
But in the early years of the Republic, Double Ten celebrations involved
almost all segments of the urban populace. They combined something

like a temple fair with new symbols of the nation-state. These included the flag and other five-colored gestures to racial inclusiveness; national songs; sacrifices to revolutionary martyrs; and most importantly, I think, parades of separately assembled social groups, which simultaneously marked difference and sameness. The state became visible in ways previously walled off from the populace. Double Ten captured something of a double memory: of the ancient line of identity stretching from the sage-kings and of the newness of the republican polity created by revolution. In this context, Yuan's attempts to revive sacrifices to Heaven, in any form, were odd and futile. Heaven had no place, or at least no obvious place, in a formally egalitarian, self-legitimating sovereign state. As an object of sacrifice, Heaven had never had a place outside of imperial ideology.

In 1915 Yuan Shikai was correct in thinking that the ideology and rituals of emperorship continued to resonate among the populace. He was merely wrong—surprisingly enough for a man in his position—in thinking that the opinions of the masses mattered. No regime could claim legitimacy without the acceptance of urban elites who had been educated in a Westernized curriculum and steeped in radical political treatises. In a scientific cosmos, the emperorship lost its point. Nor in spite of the incense-filled rhetoric surrounding the Hongxian reign, did Yuan appear to be particularly virtuous, sagely, or even martial. Yuan was improvising, and he lost his audience. Two years later, the Qing restoration of 1917 was farcical in a way Yuan could never be. Until the expulsion of Puyi from the Forbidden City in 1924, loyalist sentiment remained a mark of cultural identity for many men brought up in the old ways. But the first years of the Republic also saw a great new marker of cultural identity evolving: the institution that would become the National Palace Museum. If Double Ten suggested new forms of political identity, the museum of the objects that had been collected by the Qing emperors marked new national claims to cultural greatness. Imperial art is dead; long live national treasures.

It is possible to imagine alternative histories in which Yuan's presidency was politically stable and a new understanding of Heaven was able to evolve. But it would still have had to evolve away from a cosmology of nested hierarchies. Without an emperor at the top of the human order, the role of Heaven at the top of the cosmic order began to shrink, and even the role of the patriarch at the top of the familial order came under threat. Given the social and economic functions of the family, fathers were not about to disappear, but their role was changing.

The New Culture Movement of 1915 can be seen in part as an expression of intellectuals grappling with the relationship between individual morality and republican polity. This question seemed urgent as republican institutions failed to take root. The old Manchu question had been resolved. The polity question was not. Shocked by Yuan's monarchical movement, many New Culture intellectuals asked, what is wrong with the Chinese? One answer was, Confucianism, which Chen Duxiu was not alone in condemning for infecting the people with a desire for despotism. Even Yuan's demise was not reassuring. New Culture intellectuals came close to blaming the people for being carriers of Confucian germs. They turned to "science" to find a kind of cosmological basis for republicanism. This was not science as methodology or even epistemology but rather as the Un-Confucianism. Yet Confucianism was not dead; it was in fact going through its own democratic stage of development. Liang Qichao, now basing personal morality almost wholly on Confucianism, tried to exemplify civility and political rectitude in the wake of the Yuan monarchy. Followers of Kang Youwei—and other species of Confucians as well—saw no inherent contradiction between an ethics of mutual responsibility and the institutions of republicanism. In the first years of the Republic, Confucians and radicals shared a utopian faith in the perfectibility of society, or at least its near-perfectibility. Li Dazhao's prediction that progress would lead to the replacement of politics with administration was one case of managerial utopianism. The Confucians and the radicals shared a faith that the Chinese people, if they were properly disciplined, would become good citizens. But in fact the task of constructing the new state proceeded with little guidance from moral theory. The old order had been wiped out—as neither Confucians nor radicals yet fully understood. A new language of rights and duties would shape political discourse through the twentieth century.

⸻

Chinese imperial ideology early fastened onto a canon of sacred knowledge that was—unlike, say, Christian or Islamic sacred knowledge—continuously tied to the ideal of emperorship.[9] Institutionally, later emperors and their ministers deliberately followed, to one degree or another, the Qin-Han system founded in 221 BC. After the Sui-Tang reunification in the late sixth century, following centuries of division, the Chinese state was never again thrown into disunity for much more than a generation during violent dynastic transitions. Never again was the heartland of the empire divided between more than two courts. And after the fourteenth century, the empire remained unified under the last two dynasties, and expanded greatly under the Qing. But the empire was not, of course, seamless. Criticisms of the imperial system were coterminous with its self-ideologizing, and a critique of kingship could be traced at least as far back as Zhuangzi (traditionally dated to the Warring States period). There was also a long tradition of realpolitik, a tradition revived in the form of the statecraft school in the late eighteenth century. But the desacralization of the Chinese monarchy did not begin until late in the nineteenth century. The process of desacralization began with Confucian categories, as many scholars have pointed out. This is clearest in the case of Kang Youwei, who was trying self-consciously to work within these categories.[10] Kang also used the non-canonical ancient schools of thought as well as Western models, but he desacralized the emperor by sacralizing Confucius. It was, most notably, Zhang Binglin who desacralized both emperor and Confucius by insisting that the classical canon was essentially a set of historical records; that is, it was a product of magnificent but entirely human institutions. Scholars of the evidential studies school (*kaozhengxue*) of the eighteenth century had shown how the classics were littered with forgeries—later writings attributed to the ancient sages—but done so with the goal of finding the true Truth in the canon. The epistemological shift by Zhang's time could scarcely have been more total.

The anti-Manchuism of the late Qing was thus not only about scape-goating by Han intellectuals impotent to resist the West directly. More immediately, anti-Manchuism represented a way forward in the reformulation of the institutions of state. For all its deep roots in the Chinese soil, anti-Manchuism was simply the flip side of constructing an ethnic-based state. And an ethnic-based state would turn imperial subjects into citizens who felt the mutual bonds of national fellowship. Or so it was imagined. The dissolution of central government in the 1910s and 1920s also served to revive anti-imperialism. The New Culture Movement evolved quickly from skepticism of nationalism to reaffirmation of an embattled China tossed in a hostile sea. Although beyond the scope of this book, it is important to note here that the turn to anti-imperialist nationalism took for granted the construction of the nation-state. This was the preeminent legacy of late Qing intellectuals.

The universalism of much New Culture thought extended the horizontality of society. Women were denied suffrage at the founding of the Republic, but were accepted into the public sphere over the course of just a generation or so. There were limits to this process, which was largely confined to upper-class urban women. But in overthrowing the monarchy, the 1911 revolutionaries were indeed overthrowing the patriarchy, if not quite so dramatically. Filial piety certainly did not disappear, but new ideals of companionate marriage and sometimes free love emerged. Radicals and state-builders targeted popular religion, which among its other crimes as they saw it, provided a reservoir of traditional cosmological hierarchies. The "anti-superstition" movements that persisted through most of the twentieth century attacked not only temples but also ancestral halls. Legal reforms, however slow to take root, marked the growing rights of women and children.

Late Qing intellectuals inserted a concept of human rights into the state-building project. Rights talk spread rapidly because it was a powerful and intuitively satisfying way to highlight the faults of Qing despotism and imagine a key feature of any modern state. In a fashion in some ways parallel to the northern Atlantic world two and three centuries earlier, Chinese intellectuals combined fears of despotism with their commitment to state-building. The New Culture Movement came to condemn imperialism and Western racism in the name of rights. First, however, the New Culture Movement built directly on late Qing foundations to criticize the political conservatism and despotism of the postrevolutionary period. A tradition of liberal dissent was thereby established. However, rights were to have little purchase in the revolutionary ideologies of the Nationalist and the Communist parties. While never entirely abandoning the notion of rights, both parties disqualified certain persons as rights-bearers.[11]

Although the question of "rights" in the Chinese tradition has been well explored, the history of equality in China is complex and remains little known. This is surprising given the centrality of equality to Maoism.[12] It might seem at first glance that this is because Confucian ritual and hierarchy left little space for equality. Indeed, in China, as in other premodern complex societies, there was little interest in equality outside of religious thought. In other words, notions of political, social, and economic equality were at best marginal to mainstream thought and practice. The eighteenth-century crisis that revived interest in finding channels for broader gentry participation in governing had no use for equality talk, nor did the Self-strengtheners of the 1870s and 1880s. Equality talk had to wait for the radical efforts to reform Confucianism in the hands of men like Kang Youwei and Tan Sitong. By the time revolution appeared as a real option, the definition of society centering on the horizontal ties of its members had come to seem inevitable. Yet intellectual elites remained impatient. Claims to speak on behalf of the nation were as much based on a new view of the state as on a new view of the nation. As were demands placed on the nation.

Late Qing intellectuals sought to reform and remake the people in much more totalistic ways than the Confucian governing tradition could supply. During the New Policy reforms, many officials began to imagine a new kind of state in terms of rationalizing its fiscal administration, using the science of statistics to keep track of the population, and disciplining the people though schools and the military and the like. But the totalistic vision of a remade people remained fairly abstract, and the state was not capable of supporting disciplinary institutions. The problem of the state in the late

Qing was inextricable from the problem of sovereignty, that is, the source and exercise of domination. That the state was not reducible to the emperor was quite clear. But the state's relationship to the nation, society, or citizens was less so. The critical importance of a constitution—agreed by reformers and revolutionaries alike—lay in its capacity to delineate the exercise of sovereignty. As sovereignty is exercised domestically, it demands recognition internationally, which was no small issue to late Qing intellectuals. Their concern with constitutions and purposes of government (such as the Three People's Principles) seems at first glance to operate in a sphere far from either the immediate concerns of the people or the nitty-gritty work of governing them. But theoretical debates shaped the rationalities and instruments of government. Statist doctrines came to the fore.

Statism continued to influence Chinese political leaders throughout the twentieth century. Modern Chinese states have taken two views of the nation, either conceiving the Chinese as a multinational people or as assimilating to a single nationality. As Henry Wheaton had suggested in his lawyerly way, there is no such thing as a nation-state: no state, imperial or modern, has ever perfectly mapped onto a nation, whatever precisely that is. But modern states need to clarify who belongs and who does not. Late Qing intellectuals began considering exactly who counted as Chinese, a process of forced inclusion as much as exclusion.

In the wake of 1912, the notion of the "republic of five races" was never very persuasive. Few Chinese in the coastal cities or the agricultural heartlands of central and southern China would have known any non-Han peoples. Sun Yat-sen, in his inaugural address as president in January 1912, spoke of the five races coming together to form a single state and unifying to form a single people.[13] This was the rhetoric of the day, but within a few years Sun was trying to abandon it. He pointed out, correctly enough, that it was absurd to speak of "five races" when there were obviously so many more.[14] But Sun's move was not toward inclusiveness. He dismissed even the Manchus, Mongols, Hui, and Tibetans as tiny minorities compared to the Han. Unlike the Han, they did not deserve their own states. Since their territories were occupied—Manchuria under the control of Japan, Mongolia under Russia, Tibet under Britain—the Han must help them under the umbrella of the Republic of China. Sun's sense of imperialist threats facing China and his new appreciation of Leninism in the 1920s led him back to the United States: a model of assimilationism. By 1921, impatient with the Republic's failure to create a strong Chinese nation, Sun directly called for the absorption of Manchus, Mongols, Hui, and Tibetans into the Han race to form a "unitary nation-state" (*yi minzu zhuyi de guojia*).[15]

Paradoxically, it might be said that Sun Yat-sen had a strong theory of the nation but no theory of the state. In his definitive explanation of the Three People's Principles in 1924, Sun claimed that his first principle, the doctrine of ethnic nationalism (*minzu zhuyi*), was simply a doctrine of the state-nation (*guozu zhuyi*).[16] He argued that this conflation of state and nation was uniquely Chinese. Elsewhere, the state consists of several races or nations, or else one race is dominant in several states. But "in China since the days of the Qin and the Han, the country has been made up of one race (*minzu*)."[17] In other words, the Chinese *people* had a unitary state throughout their history, regardless of changes in the ruling dynasty.[18] Put this way, Sun's proposition, which seems to deny obvious ethnic and cultural differences among the Chinese, perhaps looks more reasonable—but also completely tautological. China = Chinese. Partly, Sun was arguing that both hereditary and cultural factors (such as assimilation) could account for the natural development of Chinese nationality. Sun thus concluded that China was already a nation: it just needed his *minzu* doctrine to break out of its traditional clannishness. Whether Sun's description of China was right or wrong, he conflated the state with the nation. In that sense, he did have a theory of state, but it seems fair to conclude he derived the state entirely from the nation.

Unlike Sun, Mao Zedong thought about the state in theoretical ways. In his 1940 "On New Democracy" Mao emphasized the importance of politics as well as economics. Citing Lenin, he noted, "Any given culture (as an ideological form) is a reflection of the politics and economics of a given society, and the former in turn has a tremendous influence and effect upon the latter; economics is the base and politics is the concentrated expression of economics."[19] As a Marxist, Mao held that the nature of the state was determined by its class structure:

Thus the numerous types of state system in the world can be reduced to three basic kinds according to the class character of their political power: (1) republics under bourgeois dictatorship; (2) republics under the dictatorship of the proletariat; and (3) republics under the joint dictatorship of several revolutionary classes. . . . The first kind comprises the old democratic states. . . . The second kind exists in the Soviet Union, and the conditions for its birth are ripe in the capitalist countries. . . . The third kind is the transitional form of state to be adopted in the revolutions of the colonial and semi-colonial countries.[20]

Yet Mao held it necessary to understand the specific institutions of a government as well as its economic base. "As for the question of the system of government (*zhengti*), this is a matter of how political power is organized, the form in which one social class or another chooses to arrange its apparatus of political power to oppose its enemies and protect itself."[21] In the context of the Anti-Japanese War, Mao saw the Chinese state as transitional. The main point of "new democracy" was to include all anti-imperialist classes, even the bourgeoisie. However, Mao did not turn to the "dictatorship of the proletariat" even in the postwar period. In June 1949, in his "On the People's Democratic Dictatorship," Mao signaled that the new government of the People's Republic of China would be both dictatorial and democratic.[22] He meant it would be dictatorial toward class enemies but democratic for the people. In theory as well as what turned out to be practice, this democratic-dictatorship was a form of statism. At this time, Mao also appears to have been molding his own special role in the future Chinese party-state, looking to Ming Taizu as a model of strong leadership.[23] Ming Taizu had founded a new dynasty and expelled the barbarians through his control of peasant armies. He had, with the advice of his Confucian counselors, been able to bend the bureaucracy to his reformist will. Mao was facing even greater tasks.

The People's Republic of China was founded in 1949 not as a multi-ethnic nation but a multinational state.[24] And not as a nation-state but as a socialist state, ultimately a more advanced stage in the progress of world revolution. Mao foresaw the future abolition of the state (as had Lenin, in a certain mood). Mao's views were based on the understanding of the state as the expression of class power—when classes have disappeared, all the "instruments of class struggle" will also wither away.[25] That is, neither political parties nor the state will be necessary. Indeed, to reach this point was the task of the working class and the Communist Party. However, the time for "Datong" had not yet arrived. As a "democratic dictatorship," the Chinese state would be made up of the "people" (renmin)—that is to say, "the working class, the peasantry, the urban petty bourgeoisie and the national bourgeoisie. These classes, led by the working class and the Communist Party, unite to form their own state and elect their own government."[26] As well, Mao noted that for the foreseeable future China would have to abide by the territorial system of state sovereignty that had been created by Western capitalism and imperialism. For Mao, the institutions of the state, like the international state system, were based on violence, but eventually the evolution of the state would lead to its own abolition. Impatience with the tardiness of the state's "withering away" was evident in some of Mao's calls for "cultural revolution" in the 1960s.

Today, that Marxist dream—and its anarchist counterpart—seem far away. Today's Chinese state, after much turmoil, seems to have replicated the Western model of the state. This model is largely based on nineteenth-century political-legal theory—Bluntschli's is a good example—as reinterpreted by late Qing and Republican intellectuals. That is to say, the state is the representative of the nation, a product of historical progress, and the agent of a civilizing mission. While the notion of a "civilizing mission" has much in common with the traditional dynastic state's task of transforming the people (jiaohua), the Chinese state today is based on technical prowess and professional specialization, not ritual. Today's state remains firmly above society, due not only to its civilizing mission, but to its perceived need to provide scientific management and to guide competing interest groups to a common objective. Specific policies can be criticized, but statism is virtually unchallengeable.

The immediate ancestor of the technocratic self-image of Chinese governmentality that developed at the end of the twentieth century was the vanguard party-state that formed in the century's middle decades. And the shoots of the vanguard party-state grew out of the destruction of the old imperial cosmology at the hands of late Qing intellectuals. These intellectuals began to build a new theory of the state based on an unstable mix of national identity, popular sovereignty, and raison d'état. The modern Chinese concept of the state was constructed on the basis of both Western and traditional intellectual resources. Technocratic ideals themselves owe much to the long development of a quasi-meritocratic bureaucracy since the tenth century.[27] But the traditional bureaucracy remained embedded in a social and political hierarchy of the cosmic order. Today's technocracy, on the contrary, appears self-legitimated because in practice it is embedded in the state.

Statism may or may not provide a stable basis of rule. What we can conclude is that in the early twentieth century it fostered attempts to rebuild the normative and legal foundations of China from the bottom up. It came to the fore through revolution and constitution-making. It was an entirely secular enterprise: that is, it was a matter of humans creating institutions for mutual benefit, and it was seen as such. It had no basis in transcendental principles unless, perhaps, stages of unilinear historical evolution were regarded as a teleology. It is true that Qing officials and some intellectuals continued to refer to Heaven, and even truer that the notion of the hierarchical cosmic order was not erased overnight. But attempts to root constitution-making in such a cosmos—seen in the Qing's constitutionalism of 1905–1910 and in Yuan Shikai's monarchical movement of 1915—had no purchase. The language of sovereignty was secular. Whether sovereignty was said to lie in the "whole people" or was somehow self-produced by the state, it was equally immanent. (Chinese constitutionalists looked to the Meiji, but the Japanese model of the unbroken imperial line could never be applied to China.)

Chinese constitutionalism displayed what might be called Weberian themes: bureaucratic and instrumental rationality; disenchantment (secularization); and the separation of society from the cosmos (even nature). We can also find Foucauldian governmentality: disciplinary and bodily forms of micropower, as well as law and education. Chinese elites assigned themselves the job of remaking popular subjectivity into bounded individuals who would act as members of the state: simultaneously spirited but pliant, creative but receptive, self-directed but industrious. Power was to become a continuous circular flow, not an episodic expression of coercion. Constitutionalism meant, among other things: a new fiscal system under which the people would understand and accept their duty to pay taxes; a new family system in which mothers would serve as teachers of the "rights and duties" of citizens; and, above all, an identification of self-interest with the state. "Society" emerged conceptually coterminous with the state, as both were rooted in the institutions of the late Qing public sphere. The public sphere here refers to the development of the small body of officially ratified gentry into a much larger body of self-ratified cultural elites who participated in public affairs. They acted in a realm of more or less independent self-government organizations, more or less free exchange of views in various media, and more or less egalitarian study societies. It may well be, as Timothy Mitchell has argued, that the state is an "effect" and not ultimately distinct from society.[28] But it is of course a powerful effect (no mere abstraction), and one that late Qing officials desired to strengthen, trying to produce new boundaries around a constitutional government in a way that could encompass society. Cultural elites, for their part, valued constitutionalism because it promised to provide them with a state that would both organize and enfranchise society. The state would stand above all (transcendent) and yet be the common property of all (immanent in the people).

This visionary ideal stemmed from the utopianism of the age that few could entirely resist. The worse things seemed to be for China, the brighter the prospects of an entirely different future. Historians have noted how Liang Qichao and others sought to reconcile apparently opposing interests: local and national, rich and poor, and especially individual (selfishness) and community (public good). Philip Kuhn suggests that this faith in the reconcilability of all within the nation smacked of mysticism.[29] So too did Zhang Binglin's faith that a kind of transcendent state standing above an egalitarian society could be combined with a strong bureaucracy (that was somehow never to be despotic).[30] We can push this "mysticism" farther, I think. In one sense, following Timothy Mitchell, state mysticism is always and everywhere necessary. This is never clearer than at the founding of states. In another sense, Liang's and Zhang's was the *same* mysticism, even though the political systems they were promoting were different. Liang was interested in the messy institutions of a constitutional order; Zhang was simultaneously entranced and repulsed by the operations of power. Yet what they shared was a (mystical) sense of the "one body" of the modern nation-state, opposed to the conflicts and divisions of the traditional imperial state. Ironically, the imperial promise was precisely to unify the state around a clear center, and in their distinct ways Liang and Zhang were attempting a kind of restoration of the center. Nonetheless, the "unity" promised by the new constitutionalism, while owing some of its rhetoric to old Confucian formulas, had more in common with the myth of popular sovereignty. Even for those who believed that sovereignty resided in the emperor, the myth of unity was modern because its target was the nation-state. Notwithstanding the continued belief in some quarters in the efficacy of the Four Books and Five Classics, constitutionalism was designed to replace the discredited textual authority of the past. This was a shift underway by 1898 at the latest. Traditional morality might be useful, but only as it contributed to the civic nation.

The Chinese case was not unique. Kings were disappearing around the world. New states often called themselves republics whether their institutions were particularly republican or not. The founding documents of the United States and the Declaration of the Rights of Man produced in the French Revolution produced a powerful myth—"from subject to citizen"—in the global imagination. But the transition to modern politics was less about popular sovereignty than the loss of belief in any kind of kingly divinity. A new view of the state had arisen by the eighteenth century that, if by no means purely secular, was rather abstract and free of any sense of the king's divine grace.[31] No doubt, this reflected fundamental social changes following from the late Middle Ages and took revolutionary form when the old regimes faced crises.[32] From the eighteenth century to the twentieth century, there was a massive global shift in the constitution of political authority. At the level of ideology, as Edmund Morgan notes, "divine right" is a fiction, and so is the notion that persons "owe obedience to government only if it is their own agent"—these are not facts but "*willingly* suspended disbelief."[33] Nonetheless, when late Qing intellectuals thought popular sovereignty represented the trends of the time, they were right. Between 1905 and 1912 revolution had come to the Ottoman empire, Iran, Mexico, Portugal, and Russia, and other countries also had national and democracy movements that could claim varying degrees of success.

Regardless of the mystical and restorationist aspects of late Qing thought, it was revolutionary in its destruction of the old political and social hierarchies. In the destruction of hierarchy, it was inevitable that society be remade on the basis of the horizontal ties among its members, individuals seen (ideally, again) to have each his or her own unique relationship to the state. Reformist officials, constitutionalists, and revolutionaries alike used the language of public interest. This was inevitably linked to popular participation. Possibly, one could envision the emperor in a constitutional government symbolizing a transcendental state, but that state would still have to represent the people. Revolutionary change had already won insofar as constitutionalist reformers—even officials—acknowledged that the basis of the state was the people. The appeal of the organic conception of the state after the turn of the twentieth century owed much to its seeming logic and naturalness. Perhaps the Confucian premise of the cosmic basis of hierarchical complementarity encouraged the transition to organic thinking. In this logic, relations among individuals and social group reflected the natural working out of cosmic forces. However, social Darwinism fatally wounded any confidence in cosmic order as traditionally understood. This opened up conceptual space for a more—but not an absolutely—egalitarian society. The organic notion of the state in modern China held that within a given society distinct groups supported one another by differentiating their functions. What regulated the organism was rights-and-duties, not filiality and loyalty.

The new Chinese state was thus inevitably secular, in spite of the mystical strains discussed above. Constitutionalism and republicanism in this context had to root out cosmological thinking. Hence the well-documented attempts on the part of elites to eliminate practices they labeled "superstition." Attacks on popular religion were absolutely central to state-building projects from the turn of the twentieth century.[34] The imperial state had long regulated religious activities but also compromised with popular religion. The common ontology shared by state rituals and popular religious practices had been a unifying element in the imperial system. With the New Policy reforms, "superstition" was named, and it was reframed as backward and primitive; a good state should wipe it out. Recent scholars have regarded this turn as the beginning of the state's war on popular religion.[35] To this we can add that the state—that is, political elites in all their own messy differences—was seeking to base itself on a new understanding of the natural order, an understanding that could promote its own founding. As Prasenjit Duara points out, while colonized political elites in different parts of the world turned to religion as an expression of national identity and a strategy of resistance, since China was never fully colonized, Chinese nationalism could be built on an alternative basis.[36] Perhaps all attempts to position sovereignty in the state are ultimately mystical, but the modern Chinese conceptions of the state abandoned religion in the name of science and understood the state as a purely human construct. The new state cosmology, if we can speak of one at all, was immanent in popular sovereignty.

Elites of the late Qing and early Republic essentially sought to create a new civil religion. Their anthropo-historical teleology strongly suggested a common ground of belief: belief in the progressive nature of constitutional political arrangements.[37] The Chinese people had a vocation, in this view, to create a strong state, and the Chinese state equally had the role of creating a strong nation. The ritual, even spiritual components of constitutionalism ranged from sacrifices to revolutionary martyrs and ancient patriots to civic celebrations. Naturally, any new civil religion involved a sense of loss as well as excitement. Perhaps the fears of the dismemberment of China at the hands of the imperialist powers—which look so overwrought today—were a displaced form of psychological terror in response to the breakdown of identities ensured by the traditional empire. Identities carried by family and locality had been inseparable from a textual tradition supported by imperial institutions such as the examination system. These identities might have been a hindrance to the construction of the national subject, but they provided protections as well. In the ritual and textual tradition, the emperor promised a link between the self and cosmic forces, whereas the world of social Darwinism offered little of such comfort. Many intellectuals had looked forward to the demise of the examination system and the monarchy, but could these familiar institutions really be replaced with unmediated access to sovereignty? It is not surprising that a sense of crisis—or at least a sense of the loss—of the entire "orientational order" should ensue.[38] Yet the tasks of construction were an equally powerful force for optimism. Possibly one reason why the collapse of the traditional cosmology was not perceived as a greater loss was that it did not affect the masses until later in the twentieth century.

Proposals for a Confucian church, though politically unsuccessful, nonetheless marked widespread elite faith in the compatibility of Confucianism (suitably denatured) and constitutionalism. Even intellectuals who scorned church-ness sought ways to build modern citizenship on strands of Confucian morality. Only a fairly small if loud group of radicals was entirely immune to this faith. Classical learning—the glue of the old imperial elites—had entered a death spiral, mutating into history, philology, philosophy, and other academic disciplines. Confucian moral principles evolved in the contexts of family and school. But Confucianism had to acknowledge the separate sphere of the state. It was not so much a question of how late Qing intellectuals mixed parts of traditional thought and parts of Western thought like a cocktail, but how the chemistry of the international system of sovereign states exploded in China in the early twentieth century. The global political culture of the nineteenth century was based on disruptive ideologies of race and progress. The world order built in the nineteenth century gave full legitimacy only to so-called nation-states, although it recognized the ontological status of individuals. It tended to delegitimize families and clans, not to mention tribes. All this was reflected in the views of late Qing intellectuals. In attempting to forge a modern state, they necessarily had to forge modern individuals, who, whatever their other roles in life, were to be citizens. The emperor was no longer needed, or at least no longer transcendent. No human (or god) could transcend the people: only the state itself could do that. Yet if the anthropologist Fei Xiaotong was right, some part of imperial ideology fueled the Communist Party. He remarked in an interview in the 1980s, "The people's wishes and needs are for this [honest and capable government]. The idea of the good emperor became collectivized in the Communist Party."[39] This seems a little too simple to me. In a sense, the notion of the good emperor became collectivized in the whole people. The Party spoke of the need "to serve the people" as an ideal for all citizens to attain. And under the Party, the citizen was first and foremost a member of the state, that is, a member of the national community devoted to its interests.

This Rousseauan sentiment lay at the basis of the modern Chinese revolutionary tradition. What was revolutionary about this view was not the notion of serving the people but the identification of the individual with the general interests of the nation, which in turn only the state could execute. The Chinese technocratic state of the twenty-first century no doubt owes much to Qing officialdom. But its normative base has been remade; it can claim no transcendental legitimacy. The struggles over political meaning that began in the late Qing have not yet concluded.

REFERENCE MATTER

List of Characters

aiguo 愛國
An Xiaofeng 安曉峰 (Weijun 維峻)
Ariga Nagao 有賀長雄

Bai Qi 白起
bao 報
bao guojia 保國家
baoguo, baozhong, baojiao
　　保國、保種、保教
Baohuanghui 保皇會
baojiao 保教
baozhong 保種
Bin Fengyang 賓鳳陽
bitan 筆談

Cai E 蔡鍔
Cai Yuanpei 蔡元培
Changsu 長素
Chen Duxiu 陳獨秀
Chen Hanyuan 陳漢元
Chen Huanzhang 陳煥章
Chen Qimei 陳其美
Chen Tianhua 陳天華
Cheng Dequan 程德全
Cheng Yi 程頤
chengxian 成憲
Chi You 蚩尤
chong 寵
Chouanhui 籌安會
Chuanxilu 傳習錄
Chunqiu 春秋
Cixi 慈禧

da Qing 大清
Da Qing huangdi 大清皇帝
Da-Qingmen 大清門
Da Qing qijuzhu 大清起居注
Da Ying junzhu 大英君主
daibiao 代表

daminzu zhuyi 大民族主義
Dao 道
daquan 大權
Datong 大同
Datong shu 大同書
Daxue zhangju xu 大學章句序
dayitong 大一統
de 德
dezheng 德政
difang renmin 地方人民
diguo 帝國
diguo wuzu 帝國五族
Ding Baoshu 丁寶書
ding yu yi 定于一
dingfen zhengming 定分正名
Dong Zhongshu 董仲舒
Duan Qirui 段祺瑞
duli 獨立

en 恩
Enguang 恩光

fa 法
falü zhi zhuren ye 法律之主人也
Fan Zhui 樊錐
faren 法人
fatuan 法團
feng 封
Feng Guifen 馮桂芬
Feng Guozhang 馮國璋
Feng Yuxiang 馮玉祥
fengjian 封建
fengsu guiju 風俗規矩
fu 父
Fu Xi 伏羲
fucong 服從
fumin liguo 福民利國

gaizhi 改制

gangchang 綱常
ganshe 干涉
ge qin qi min er shang tong yu tianzi
　　各親其民而上統於天子
ge you ziyou zizhu zhi dao
　　各有自由自主之道
ge you zizhu zhi quan 各有自主之權
geming 革命
geren jie neng zizhu 各人皆能自主
geren quan 個人權
gewu zhizhi 格物致知
gong 公
Gong jin ou 鞏金甌
gong tianxia 公天下
gong tianxia zhi dayi 公天下之大義
gongchan 公產
gongde 公德
gongfa 公法
gongfashang zhi ren'ge 公法上之人格
gonghe 共和
Gonghe jinianhui 共和紀念會
gonghe zhengti 共和政體
gongli 公理
gongqi 公器
gongquan 公權
Gongyang zhuan 公羊傳
gongyou zhengti 共有政體
Gu Hongming 辜鴻銘
Gu Yanwu 顧炎武
Guandi 關帝
guangfu 光復
Guangxu 光緒
Guanyin 觀音
Guanzi 管子
Guliang zhuan 穀梁傳
guo 國
guo zhi xing 國之形
guocui 國粹
Guocui xuebao 國粹學報
guohao 國號
guoji 國基
guojia 國家
guojia shehui zhuyi 國家社會主義
guojia sixiang 國家思想
guojia tongzhiquan 國家統治權
guojia zhi gongyi 國家之公益
guojia zhi shengcun 國家之生存

guojiao 國教
guojiri 國祭日
guomin 國民
guomin zhi duli 國民之獨立
Guomindang 國民黨
guoqingri 國慶日
guoquan 國權
guoquan shensheng lun 國權神聖論
guoquan zhi zhuti 國權之主體
guoren 國人
guoti 國體
guoxue 國學
guozheng 國政
guozhu 國主
Guozijian 國子監
guozu zhuyi 國族主義
Guwu chenliesuo 古物陳列所
guyou tongzhiquan zhi zhuquan
　　固有統治權之主權
guyou zhi quanli 固有之權力

Haiguo tuzhi 海國圖志
Han (dynasty, people-ethnos) 漢
Han Yu 韓愈
Hanlin 翰林
He Zhen 何震
he zhongmin er cheng jun 合眾民而成君
hepi 闔闢
hezhong 合種
Hong Liangpin 洪良品
Hongxian 洪憲
Hu Hanmin 胡漢民
Hua (Chinese) 華
Huang Xing 黃興
Huang Zongxi 黃宗羲
Huang Zunxian 黃遵憲
Huangdi (Yellow Emperor) 黃帝
Huanghuagang 黃花岡
Huazhong 華種
huguo 護國
Hui 回
huifei 會匪
huifu 恢復

ji 記
jia tianxia 家天下
jian'ai 兼愛

jiao 教

jiaohua 教化

jiguan 機關

jimin er cheng ye 積民而成也

Jimmu (J) 神武

jing 井

jingshen 精神

jingshi 經世

jingtian 井田

jingzuo 靜坐

jinianri 紀念日

jinshi 進士

jinxiao 謹小

jiti 機體

jitian liji 繼天立極

juluan shi 據亂世

jun (ruler) 君

jun (equality) 均

jun pinfu 均貧富

jun zhi siyou 君之私有

junmin 君民

junquan 君權

junquan duzun 君權獨尊

junquan tongyi 君權統一

junquan ze rizun 君權則日尊

juntong 君統

junzhu 君主

junzhu guo 君主國

junzhu neng yu min tong 君主能與民通

junzhu weiquan wu xian 君主威權無限

junzi 君子

juren 舉人

kaise zhi shu 開塞之術

Kang Youwei 康有為

Kangxi 康熙

kaozheng 考證

kaozhengxue 考證學

Katō Hiroyuki 加藤弘之

keji 克己

kokken (J) 國權

kokusui (J) 國粹

kokutai (J) 國體

Kongjiaohui 孔教會

Kongzi gaizhi kao 孔子改制考

Kongzi zhi dadao 孔子之大道

kun 坤

Laozi 老子

li (rites, ritual propriety) 禮

li (principle) 理

Li Dazhao 李大釗

Li Hesheng 李和生

Li Hongzhang 李鴻章

Li Lianying 李蓮英

Li Shizeng 李石曾 (Yuying 煜瀛)

Li Yuanhong 黎元洪

Liang Dingfen 梁鼎芬 (Jie'an 節庵)

Liang Qichao 梁啟超

Liang Shiyi 梁士詒

liangmin 良民

liangzhi 良知

liezhong 劣種

liguo zhi ben 立國之本

Liji 禮記

lijiao 禮教

Lin Xie 林獬

Lin Zexu 林則徐

lishi de renzhong 歷史的人種

Liu Dapeng 劉大鵬

liu junzi 六君子

Liu Shipei 劉師培

liyi 理義

liyue 禮樂

Liyun 禮運

lizhi 立志

Lü Liuliang 呂留良

Lu Ruibo 鹿瑞伯 (Zhonglin 鍾麟)

Lu Xun 魯迅

Lu Zhonglin 鹿鐘麟

luan 亂

lüfa zhangcheng 律法章程

lunli 倫理

Lunyu 論語

Mai Menghua 麥孟華

Man 滿

Meiji 明治

Miao 苗

min 民

min suo guiwang wei zhi wang
民所歸往謂之王

Minbao 民報

minben 民本

minfa 民法

ming (mandate, order, fate) 命
ming (visible, bright; Ming dynasty) 明
Ming Taizu 明太祖
Mingru xue'an 明儒學案
minqi 民氣
minquan 民權
minquan zhengti 民權政體
minsheng 民生
minzei 民賊
minzhu 民主
minzhu guo 民主國
minzu 民族
minzu diguozhuyi 民族帝國主義
minzu zhuyi 民族主義
Mozi 墨子
Mozi 墨子

neng qunmin wei zhi jun 能群民謂之君
Ning Xiewan 甯協萬

Ou Jujia (Qujia) 歐榘甲

Pan Gu 盤古
Pi Jiayou 皮嘉祐
pingdeng 平等
pingmin zhuyi 平民主義
pingquan 平權
Puyi 溥儀

qi yue wangzhe min zhi suo guiwang ye
　　其曰王者民之所歸往也
qian 乾
qiangquan 強權
Qiangxuehui 強學會
qiangzhi 強制
Qianlong 乾隆
Qin (dynasty) 秦
Qing (dynasty) 清
qizhi 氣質
quan 權
quan guiyu zhong 權歸於眾
quanli (powers, rights) 權利
quanli (coercive power, strength) 權力
quanli sixiang 權利思想
quanli zhi zhuti 權力之主體
quanti zhi min 全體之民
qun 群

qunxue 群學

ren (benevolence) 仁
ren (people) 人
rendao 人道
ren'ge 人格
renjun 人君
renlei jihe tuanti 人類集合團體
renmin 人民
renmin tuanti 人民團體
renquan 人權
renren geyou qi zizhu zhi quan
　　人人各有其自主之權
renren you zizhu quanli 人人有自主權利
renxin (humanity, will of the people) 人心
renxin (benevolent heart) 仁心
Renxue 仁學
renyi 仁義
renyu 人欲
renzhu zongzhi 人主總之

san'gang 三綱
sandai 三代
sanshi 三世
santong 三統
seitai (J) 政體
shakai shugi (J) 社會主義
Shang (dynasty) 商
Shang Yang 商鞅
shang zhi yi gong tianwei 上之以共天位
shanggong 尚公
shangshi 尚實
shangwu 尚武
shehui 社會
shehui geming 社會革命
shehui zhuyi 社會主義
shen minquan wu junshang ye
　　伸民權無君上也
Shen Xingong 沈心工
shendao 神道
shendu 慎獨
sheng 聖
shengjiao 聖教
shenglun 聖倫
shengping shi 升平世
shengren 聖人
shengwang 聖王

shengxue 聖學
shengzhi 聖旨
Shennong 神農
shenshi 紳士
shi (gentry, educated man) 士
shi (trend, conditions) 勢
Shiwu bao 時務報
Shiwu xuetang 時務學堂
shixue 實學
Shuihu zhuan 水滸傳
shuken (J) 主權
Shun 舜
shuren siji 庶人私祭
si (self, private) 私
si (thought, to reflect) 思
si wei xinwang ye 斯為新王也
side 私德
siquan 私權
siren 私人
siyou zhi dexing 私有之德性
Sizhouzhi 四洲志
Song (dynasty) 宋
Song Jiaoren 宋教仁
sonnō jōi (J) 尊皇[王]攘夷
Su Yu 蘇輿
Sui (dynasty) 隋
Sun Baoxuan 孫寶瑄
Sun Yat-sen 孫逸仙 (Zhongshan 中山)
Sun Yuyun 孫毓筠
suowei guoquan ji zhi suoyou zhi quanli
    所謂國權既指所有之權利
suwang 素王

Taihedian 太和殿
taiping shi 太平世
Tan Sitong 譚嗣同
Tang (dynasty) 唐
Tang Caichang 唐才常
Tang Hualong 湯化龍
Tang Shaoyi 唐紹儀
Tang Zhen 唐甄
tennōsei (J) 天皇制
ti 體
Tian 天
Tian tong jun 天統君
tianfu 天賦
tianfu quanli 天賦權利

tianfu renquan 天賦人權
tianli 天理
Tianmin 天民
Tianming 天命
tianran zhi fa 天然之法
Tianwei 天威
Tianxia 天下
tianxia wei gong 天下為公
Tianxin 天心
Tianxin zhi juan 天心之眷
Tianyanlun 天演論
Tianyi 天意
Tianze 天則
Tianzi 天子
tong 通
tonghua 同化
Tongmenghui 同盟會
Tongwenguan 同文館
Tongzhi 同治
tongzhi tuanti de quanli 統治團體的權力
tongzhiquan 統治權
Tu Ji 屠寄
Tu Renshou 屠仁守 (Meijun 梅君)
tuanti 團體
tudi guoyou 土地國有

wang 王
Wang Boxin 王柏心
Wang Fuzhi 王夫之
Wang Hui 汪暉
Wang Jingwei 汪精衛
Wang Mang 王莽
Wang Renjun 王仁俊
Wang Tao 王韜
Wang Xianqian 王先謙
Wang Yangming 王陽明
Wang Zhengting 王正廷
wangdao 王道
wangguo 亡國
wangjiao 王教
Wei Tuo 韋陀
Wei Yuan 魏源
weiling 威靈
weiyan dayi 微言大義
weiyi zhi tongzhiquan zhi zhuti
    唯一之統治權之主體
Wen Ti 文悌 (Zhonggong 仲恭)

wenjiao zhi bang 文教之邦
Wenmiao 文廟
Wenming (Bookstore) 文明
wu (property, object) 物
wu (negation, emptiness) 無
wu (martial, war) 武
wu guohao 無國號
Wu Peifu 吳佩孚
Wu Renda 吳人達
Wu Yue 吳樾
Wu Zhihui 吳稚暉
wufu wujun, jie xi wei guran
　　無父無君，皆習為固然
wujun wufu 無君無父
Wumiao 武廟
wuwei 無為
wuxing 五行
wuyishi 無意識

Xia (dynasty) 夏
xiandian 憲典
xianzhu shanwei 賢主禪位
xiao tuanti 小團體
xiaokang 小康
xiaominzu zhuyi 小民族主義
xieshuo 邪說
ximin 細民
xin 心
Xin (dynasty) 新
xing 性
Xing Zhong hui 興中會
xing-Han fuchou 興漢復仇
xingdong 行動
xingfa 性法
Xinminshuo 新民說
xinxue 心學
Xinxue weijingkao 新學偽經考
Xiong Shili 熊十力
Xiongnu 匈奴
xiushen 修身
xiushen jiaokeshu 修身教科書
Xu Shichang 徐世昌
Xue Jingxuan 薛敬軒
xun Hua yirang 勳華揖讓
Xunzi 荀子

Yan Fu 嚴復

yang 陽
Yang Du 楊度
Yang Tingdong 楊廷棟
yanlu 言路
Yao 堯
Yao Zuyi 姚祖義
Ye Dehui 葉德輝
yeren zhi guo 野人之國
yi (righteousness) 義
yi jiao wei zheng 以教為政
yi jun jian shi 以君兼師
yi minzu zhuyi de guojia
　　一民族主義的國家
yihe yipi wei zhi bian 一闔一闢謂之變
Yijing 易經
yili 義理
yin 陰
Yinghuan zhilüe 瀛環志略
yiti 一體
yizhi 意志
yizhong 異種
yong 用
Yongzheng 雍正
Yoshida Shōin 吉田松陰
Yu 禹
yu si Zhongguo zhi renxin
　　欲死中國之人心
Yuan Shikai 袁世凱
Yuandao 原道
Yubei lixian gonghui 預備立憲公會
Yue Fei 岳飛
yun 運

Zaitian 載湉
ze (beneficence) 澤
ze (law, principle) 則
Zeng Guofan 曾國藩
Zeng Qi 曾琦
Zhang Binglin 章炳麟 (Taiyan 太炎)
Zhang Ertian 張爾田
Zhang Jian 張謇
Zhang Shizhao 章士釗
Zhang Xun 張勳
Zhang Zhidong 張之洞
zheng 政
Zheng Guanying 鄭觀應
zhengben 正本

zhengfa 政法
zhengjiao 政教
zhengjiao heyi 政教合一
zhengjiao xiang wei 政教相維
zhengquan 政權
zhengquan zhi yu quyu yi 政權之欲趨於一
zhengti 政體
zhengtong 正統
zhengwei dingming 正位定名
zhengxin 正心
zhengxue 政學
zhi (institutions, rule) 制
zhi (order) 治
zhidu 制度
Zhina wangguo 支那亡國
zhishi 志士
zhong 忠
zhongai 忠愛
zhongbao 中保
Zhongguo 中國
Zhongguo minzu 中國民族
Zhongguo ren 中國人
Zhongguo xiongli yuzhou 中國雄立宇宙
Zhonghua gemingdang 中華革命黨
Zhonghua diguo 中華帝國
Zhonghua minguo 中華民國
Zhonghua minguo guangfu jinian
　中華民國光復紀念
Zhonghua minguo liguo jinian'ge
　中華民國立國紀念歌
Zhonghuamen 中華門
zhongjie 種界
zhongjun 忠君
zhongjun aiguo 忠君愛國
Zhongnanhai 中南海
Zhongxue wei ti, Xixue wei yong
　中學為體，西學為用

zhongyi haozhao he tianxia zhi xin
　忠義號召合天下之心
zhongzu 種族
zhongzu geming 種族革命
Zhou (dynasty) 周
Zhou Zuoren 周作人
zhu 主
Zhu Ciqi 朱次琦
Zhu Xi 朱熹
Zhu Yixin 朱一新
Zhu Zhixin 朱执信
Zhuangzi 莊子
zhuanzheng 專政
zhuquan 主權
zhuquanzhe 主權者
zhuti 主體
zijue 自覺
ziqiang 自強
ziran 自然
zixing 自性
ziyou 自由
ziyou quanli 自由權利
zizhi 自治
zizhu 自主
zizhu zhi quan 自主之權
Zongli yamen 總理衙門
zongyi 總意
Zou Huamin 鄒華民
Zou Rong 鄒容
zu 族
zuigao guyou zhi quanli 最高固有之權力
zuigao zhi quanli 最高之權力
zuigao zhuquan 最高主權
zun bei you ge 尊卑有隔
zun Kong 尊孔
zunhuang rangyi 尊皇攘夷

Notes

DXWC Chen Duxiu. *Duxiu wencun* 獨秀文存. Shanghai: Yadong tushuguan, 1927.

GCXB *Guocui xuebao* 國粹學報. Shanghai, 1905–1912.

KZ *Kongjiaohui zazhi* 孔教會雜誌. Shanghai, 1913.

LSPQJ Liu Shipei. *Liu Shipei quanji* 劉師培全集. Beijing: Zhonggong zhongyang dangxiao chubanshe, 1997.

NCDN *North-China Daily News*. Shanghai, 1850–1924.

PDN *Peking Daily News*. Beijing, 1914–1917.

QXP Zhang Zhidong 張之洞. *Quanxue pian* 勸学篇. Li Zhongxing 李忠兴, ed. and annot. Zhengzhou: Zhongzhou guji chubanshe, 1998.

WLS Song Jiaoren 宋教仁. *Wo zhi lishi* 我之歷史. Taibei: Wenxing shudian, 1962.

XG Zhang Nan 張枬 and Wang Renzhi 王忍之, eds. *Xinhai geming qian shinianjian shilun xuanji* 辛亥革命前十年间时论选集. Beijing: Sanlian shudian, 1963.

YBSHJ Liang Qichao. *Yinbingshi heji* 飲冰室合集. Beijing: Zhonghua shuju, 1995.

YC Su Yu 蘇輿, comp. *Yijiao congbian* 翼教叢編. Yang Ching 楊菁, ed. Taibei: Zhongyang yanjiuyuan Zhongguo wenzhe yanjiusuo, 2005.

ZDNP Kang Youwei. *Kang Nanhai ziding nianpu* 康南海自訂年譜. Taibei: Wenhai, n.d.

ZFGB *Zhengfu gongbao* 政府公報. Taibei: Wenhai, 1971, reprt.

INTRODUCTION

An earlier version of a portion of this chapter has been previously published as "Political Ritual in the Early Republic of China," pp. 149–188, in Kai-wing Chow, Kevin Doak, and Poshek Fu, eds., *Constructing Nationhood in Modern East Asia: Narrative Schemes, Nostalgia, and Ambiguity of Identities* (Ann Arbor: University of Michigan Press, 2001).

1. Reinsch, *An American Diplomat in China*, 25–26. See also "Zhuandian" 專電, *Shibao* 1914.12.24 [dates are given year-month-day, 4; and *Peking Daily News* (hereafter, PDN), 1914.12.24, 4–5. The solstice fell on December 23.

2. Anderson, *Imagined Communities*.

3. Levenson, *Confucian China and Its Modern Fate*. Much as I admire Levenson's work, my point of view, writing half a century later, is naturally different; histories are as much an artifact of their times as any other cultural production.

4. Wang Hui, *Xiandai Zhongguo sixiang de xingqi*. Much as I admire Wang's work, many of his concerns are simply not my concerns, and his position as a Chinese intellectual intimately involved in the debates of his age is not my position.

5. Yü-sheng Lin, *The Crisis of Chinese Consciousness*, 11–18; Hao Chang, *Chinese Intellectuals in Crisis*, 5–8.

6. On the formation of Manchu identity and eighteenth-century Manchu-Han relations, see Crossley, *A Translucent Mirror*; Elliott, *The Manchu Way*.

7. Crossley, *A Translucent Mirror*.

8. Elman, *A Cultural History of Civil Examinations in Late Imperial China*, 230–231, 246–249. See also the brilliant discussion of meritocracy in Woodside, *Lost Modernities*.

9. Of course, this is not to deny enormous changes in ritual performance from dynasty to dynasty and even emperor to emperor. The shifting fortunes of imperial power and its relationship to ritual and classical learning are traced through the early empire in Gan Huaizhen, *Huangquan, liyi yu jingdian quanshi*. The essays in McDermott, ed., *State and Court Ritual in China*, offer examples of strikingly different legitimation technologies. A suggestive overview of the literature of the problem of continuity in Chinese notions of kingship is Crossley, "Review Article: The Rulerships of China."

10. Many polities split the divine and political roles between two leaders. Cf. the functional categories proposed by Geertz, *Negara*, 126.

11. See Weber, "The Sociology of Charismatic Authority" and "The Meaning of Discipline," in Gerth and Mills, trans. and eds., *From Max Weber*, 245–264; and idem, "The Nature of Charismatic Authority and Its Routinization." But see Wallis, "Charisma and Explanation," 167–179; and, highlighting the cross-cultural problems attached to the term, the lucid discussion in Feuchtwang and Wang, *Grassroots Charisma*, 10–21.

12. Feuchtwang, *The Imperial Metaphor*.

13. Bastid, "Sacrifices d'État et legitimité à la fin des Qing."

14. The Roman empire, medieval Europe, modern Europe: the royal presence was direct. "As long as the prince and the estates of the realm 'were' the country and not just its representatives, they could represent it in a specific sense. They represented their lordship not for but 'before' the people." Habermas, *Structural Transformation of the Public Sphere*, 5–10. This tendency was especially developed in France. Louis XIV—the Sun King, Apollo—lived his entire life in public view, creating a persona as the embodiment of power through art, scholarship, religion, and written propaganda—as well as being a hard-working administrator. Marin, *Portrait of the King*. Indeed, earlier French kings were scarcely less attentive to display, which could shore up supporters, cow opposition, and even obfuscate dynastic change. See Brown, *The Monarchy of Capetian France and Royal Ceremonial*.

15. To be used by official historians; preserved for the Qing in the archives as the *Da Qing qijuzhu*.

16. So it was at least by the end of the Kangxi reign (1722); see Rawski, *The Last Emperors*, 211–212.

17. As a matter of geographical reality, during the Qing, the Grand Temple and the Altar of Land and Grain were just to the south of the Forbidden City, the former on the east side and the latter to the west, while the Altar to the Earth was in the suburbs (that is, outside the walls of the Imperial City) to the northeast and the Altar of Heaven in the suburbs to the southeast.

18. Zito, *Of Body & Brush*.

19. Atwood, "'Worshiping Grace.'"

20. Ibid., 103.

21. "Plan for the Prince" is a rather free translation of Huang's title, *Mingyi daifanglu*, which is built on several complex classical allusions. See de Bary, *Waiting for the Dawn*; on the impossibility of translating Huang's title, see ibid., "Introduction," 5–8; and Grieder, *Intellectuals and the State in Modern China*, 35.

22. Struve, "Huang Zongxi in Context"; de Bary, *The Liberal Tradition in China*, 67–90.

23. de Bary, "Introduction," *Waiting for the Dawn*, 20–24.

24. Huang Zongxi, *Mingyi daifanglu*, 27–28. Following de Bary, *Waiting for the Dawn*, 91–92 mod.

25. Ping-chen Hsiung, "T'ang Chen and the Works in Obscurity."

26. Ibid., 118–119 mod.

27. Bastid, "Official Conceptions of Imperial Authority at the End of the Qing Dynasty," 147–186; and idem, "La 'position' dans le ceremonial d'État à la fin de l'Empire."

28. Elman, *From Philosophy to Philology*.

29. Recent work and new perspectives have complicated a story that was once reduced to "failure" and "conservatism," and suggest a more nuanced story, not of unabashed triumph but precisely of dogged institution-building. See Xiong Yuezhi, *Xixue dongjian yu wan-Qing shehui*; Huang Aiping and Huang Xingtao, eds., *Xixue yu Qingdai wenhua*; and Grieder, *Intellectuals and the State*, chaps. 3–4. The standard work, still worth reading, is Wright, *The Last Stand of Chinese Conservatism*.

30. Wang Boxin, "Wang yan," in Sheng Kang, comp., *Huangchao jingshiwen xubian*, 10:3–4.

31. Mittler, *A Newspaper for China?*, 28–30.

32. Eastman, "Ch'ing-i and Chinese Policy Formation during the Sino-French Controversy, 1880–1885," 596–597, 608–610.

33. Recent scholarship has denied that the accomplishments of the Self-strengthening reforms were as desultory as Kang and Liang charged. See Yue Meng, "Hybrid Science versus Modernity"; and Elman, "Naval Warfare and the Refraction of China's Self-strengthening Reforms into Scientific and Technological Failure, 1865–1895." Nonetheless, there was no gainsaying the fact of defeat.

34. Mittler, *A Newspaper for China?* See also the general account in Wagner, "The Early Chinese Newspapers and the Chinese Public Sphere."

35. Bennett, *Missionary Journalist in China*.

36. *Sizhouzhi* 四洲志. See Xiong Yuezhi, *Xixue dongjian yu wan-Qing shehui*, 221–266. Chinese world geographies included Wei Yuan's *The Illustrated Gazetteer on the Sea Kingdoms* (1842, *Haiguo tuzhi*)—see Leonard, *Wei Yuan and China's Rediscovery of the Maritime World*; and Xu Jiyu's *A Short Account of the Maritime Circuit* (1849, *Yinghuan zhilüe*)—see Drake, *China Charts the World*.

37. Xiong Yuezhi, *Xixue dongjian yu wan-Qing shehui*, 8–9, 11–12.

38. The result was a new publishing industry. See Reed, *Gutenberg in Shanghai*.

39. Xiong Yuezhi, *Xixue dongjian yu wan-Qing shehui*, chap. 12. See also Bennett, *John Fryer*.

40. Biggerstaff, *The Earliest Modern Government Schools in China*. See also Rudolph, *Negotiated Power in Late Imperial China*.

41. This was one manifestation of the distinction Joseph R. Levenson drew between emotional commitment to history and intellectual commitment to value—*Liang Ch'i-ch'ao and the Mind of Modern China*, esp. 1–5; see also idem, *Confucian China and Its Modern Fate*, 1:75–78.

42. Xiong Yuezhi, *Xixue dongjian yu wan-Qing shehui*, 723.

43. For overviews, see ibid., 716–723; Hsi-yuan Chen, "The Revelations of the Sacred Scriptures"; and the recent study of the long-term "debate" on the origins question by Lei Zhongxing, *Ming Qing de xixue zhongyuan lun zhengyi*.

44. Huang Zunxian, *Huang Zunxian quanji*, 2:1399–1400.

45. Ibid., 2:1415.

46. Li Huaxing, ed., *Minguo jiaoyu shi*, 55. Such privately established schools might have received support from local officials.

47. Bastid, "Servitude or Liberation," 9.

48. The standard study is Sang Bing, *Qingmo xinzhishijie de shetuan yu huodong*. See also Wakeman, "The Price of Autonomy."

49. In the West, the noun "intellectual" in its modern sense emerged in the course of the Dreyfus affair; in China, the notion of a distinct "intellectual class" was spreading by the 1910s. See Eddy U, "Reification of the Chinese Intellectual."

CHAPTER I

Earlier versions of portions of this chapter have been previously published as "Late Qing Reformism and the Meiji Model: Kang Youwei, Liang Qichao, and the Japanese Emperor," pp. 40–67, in Joshua A. Fogel, ed., *The Role of Japan in Liang Qichao's Introduction of Modern Western Civilization to China* (Berkeley: Institute of East Asian Studies, University of California, 2004); and "The Reform Movement, the Monarchy, and Political Modernity," pp. 17–47, in Rebecca Karl and Peter Zarrow, eds., *Rethinking the Reform Movement of 1898: Political and Cultural Change in Modern China* (Cambridge, MA: Harvard University Asia Center Publications, Harvard University Press, 2002).

1. These were of course partisan accounts, but historians have done much to trace the political and intellectual background of the movement in the archives. For Kang's activities, see works by Kong Xiangji, *Kang Youwei bianfa zouyi yanjiu*; *Wuxu weixin yundong xintan*; and Kong Xiangji, ed., *Jiuwang tucun de lantu*.

2. The background of the 1898 reform movement has received considerable attention, and I will not attempt to compose a bibliography here. Works that have especially influenced my understanding include Hao Chang, "Intellectual Change and the Reform Movement, 1890–8"; Li Zehou, *Kang Youwei Tan Sitong sixiang yanjiu*; Tang Zhijun, *Wuxu bianfa shi luncong*; and Wang Rongzu [Young-tsu Wong], *Wan-Qing bianfa sixiang luncong*. The best general overview in English, if biased in places, is Luke S. K. Kwong, *A Mosaic of the Hundred Days*. Recent scholarship has not attempted a fundamental full-length reappraisal of the movement, but various of its aspects have received new treatment in the articles in Wang Xiaoqiu and Shang Xiaoming, eds., *Wuxu weixin yu Qingmo xinzheng*; Wang Xiaoqiu, ed., *Wuxu weixin yu jindai Zhongguo de gaige*; and Karl and Zarrow, eds., *Rethinking the 1898 Reform Period*.

3. Tang Zhijun, *Wuxu bianfa shi luncong*, 154–221.

4. See Xiong Yuezhi, *Zhongguo jindai minzhu sixiangshi*, 233–243.

5. For a recent overview, see Kuhn, *Origins of the Modern Chinese State*, 2–26. The best detailed yet succinct discussion remains Jones and Kuhn, "Dynastic Decline and the Roots of Rebellion."

6. Population expanded from roughly 100 million when the Qing came to power in 1644 to over 300 million by 1800. This put a severe strain on land holdings, though more land was brought into production and agricultural productivity increased, at least for a time, due to the introduction of American food crops (maize, sweet potatoes) and new cash crops in the sixteenth century. The continued commercialization of the rural economy, engineered in no small part by international trade, encouraged farming families to engage in part-time (or sometimes full-time) handicraft production. The economy was expanding, but strained.

7. Kuhn, *Origins of the Modern Chinese State*, 19–21; for nineteenth-century factionalism, see also Polachek, *The Inner Opium War*. Also there were an increasing number of extra-official jobs in the wake of the Taiping Rebellion—Rankin, *Elite Activism and Political Transformation in China*.

8. Bastid, "Official Conceptions of Imperial Authority at the End of the Qing Dynasty."

9. Though the sheer shock of the defeat should not be underestimated. See Samuel C.

Chu, "China's Attitudes toward Japan at the Time of the Sino-Japanese War." Douglas R. Howland suggests that the Sino-Japanese War had such a major impact on China because it represented the failure of "Civilization" (of which Japan had traditionally been a member) itself—*Borders of Chinese Civilization*, 241. The importance of "preserving Confucianism" (*baojiao*) to the radical reformers, as we will see below, suggests their concerns were not limited to Chinese state-building.

10. Kang's life and thought are incomparably described in Kung-chuan Hsiao, *A Modern China and a New World*. See also Jung-pang Lo, ed., *K'ang Yu-wei*; Hao Chang, *Chinese Intellectuals in Crisis*, 21–65; and Wang Rongzu, *Kang Youwei*.

11. Miles, *The Sea of Learning*.

12. See Elman, *From Philosophy to Philology*; and idem, *Classicism, Politics, and Kinship*.

13. Liang Qichao, "Kang Nanhai zhi Zhongguo zhengce" 康南海之中國政策, YBSHJ wenji 6:87–88.

14. ZDNP. Background on Kang's "chronological autobiography" is given in Jung-pang Lo, ed., *K'ang Yu-wei*, 17–20; translation of the work is 21–174.

15. ZDNP, 8; Jung-pang Lo, ed., *K'ang Yu-wei*, 30.

16. ZDNP, 9–11; Jung-pang Lo, ed., *K'ang Yu-wei*, 32–34.

17. ZDNP, 21; Jung-pang Lo, ed., *K'ang Yu-wei*, 51.

18. ZDNP, 18; Jung-pang Lo, ed., *K'ang Yu-wei*, 47.

19. ZDNP, 27–28; Jung-pang Lo, ed., *K'ang Yu-wei*, 60–61.

20. ZDNP, 18; Jung-pang Lo, ed., *K'ang Yu-wei*, 47.

21. San-pao Li, "K'ang Yu-wei's *Shihli kung-fa chuan-shu*"; and Wang Rongzu, "'Wuxue sasui yicheng.'"

22. Kang Youwei, "Shili gongfa quanshu" 實理公法全書, in idem, *Kang Youwei quanji*, 1:245–306. See Wang Rongzu, "'Wuxue sasui yicheng,'" 53–54.

23. See San-pao Li, "K'ang Yu-wei's *Shihli kung-fa chuan-shu*," 696–708.

24. Kang Youwei, "Shili gongfa quanshu," 708. The idea of choosing the king may echo the "social contract." Rousseau's *Social Contract* had been translated into classical Chinese in Japan in the late 1870s. The notion of mediation seems to have little to do with traditional notions of kingship but resonates with the informal authority of local gentry.

25. Kang Youwei, "Kangzi neiwai pian" 康子內外篇, in idem, *Kang Youwei quanji*, 1:165–200.

26. Ibid., 1:165–166.

27. *Yijing*, "xici" 1:11; I am following Wilhelm, *I Ching: The Book of Change*, 317–318.

28. Kang Youwei, "Kangzi neiwai pian," 1:166.

29. That the term "kaise" reverberates with the chapter title "hepi" may not be an accident.

30. Kang Youwei, "Kangzi neiwai pian," 1:166; citing *Analects* (Lunyu) 8.9.

31. Kang Youwei, "Kangzi neiwai pian," 1:169.

32. Ibid., 1:170. "Sacred relations" was a reference to the Three Bonds (ruler-subject, father-son, husband-wife) or the Five Relationships (emperor-minister, parent-child, husband-wife, elder-younger brother, and friends).

33. Hao Chang, *Chinese Intellectuals in Crisis*, 26–27; Li Sanbao, ed. and trans., "*Kangzi neiwaipian* chubu fenxi," 217.

34. Kang Youwei, "Kangzi neiwai pian," 1:187–188.

35. Ibid., 1:189.

36. Ibid., 1:165.

37. Kung-chuan Hsiao, *A Modern China and a New World*, 80–81.

38. I thus do not agree with the emphasis that Hao Chang (*Chinese Intellectuals in*

Crisis, 29–34) places on the dichotomy between radicalism and conservatism in Kang, but I do find useful the distinction Chang notes between the political and moral layers of Kang's thought. Certainly, there were tensions in Kang's thought, which we will look at further in terms of his utopianism, below.

39. See Wang Rongzu, "'Wuxue sasui yicheng,'" 58; and idem, *Kang Youwei,* 63–90. While Hao Chang and Richard C. Howard emphasize Kang's "conservatism," Wong sees it as a purely instrumental facet of his reformism. Howard stated that Kang saw the monarchy as valid and the emperor as magical—"K'ang Yu-wei [1858–1927]," 308–309. See also Hao Chang, *Chinese Intellectuals in Crisis,* 29: Kang "spoke expansively not only of the cultural glories of the Chinese tradition, but also of the irresistible, absolute moral authority of the Chinese emperor."

40. Kang did of course have many suggestions for reforming a wide range of institutions. These are discussed thoroughly in Kung-chuan Hsiao, *A Modern China and a New World,* 193–207; Kong Xiangji, *Kang Youwei bianfa zouyi yanjiu,* 1–116; and Wang Rongzu, *Kang Youwei,* 41–81.

41. Li Sanbao, "*Kangzi neiwaipian* chubu fenxi," 218.

42. Kang Youwei, "Qing ding lixian kaiguohui zhe" 請定立憲開國會摺, in Jian Bozan et al., eds., *Wuxu bianfa,* 2:236–237.

43. Kang Youwei, "Shang Qing di di er shu" 上清帝第二書, in ibid., 2:152.

44. Kang Youwei, "Qing jun min hezhi Man Han bufen zhe" 請君民合治滿漢不分摺, in ibid., 2:238.

45. Kang Youwei, "Qing ding lixian kaiguohui zhe," in ibid., 2:237.

46. Cf. Wang Hui, *Xiandai Zhongguo sixiang de xingqi,* 2A:932.

47. Kang Youwei, "Jingxie Tianen bing tongchou quanju zhe" 敬謝天恩並統籌全局摺, in idem, *Kang Youwei zhenglunji,* 1:277; cf. Kung-chuan Hsiao, *A Modern China and a New World,* 208.

48. See Price, *Russia and the Roots of the Chinese Revolution, 1896–1911,* 29–61.

49. The Chinese reformers were certainly inspired by the Meiji model but it did not precisely serve, as Lin Mingde has suggested, as a "blueprint" for their own proposals. See Lin Mingde, "Qingmo Minchu Riben zhengzhi dui Zhongguo de yingxiang," 187–191. For a more balanced view of the "influence" of the Meiji Restoration on Chinese reformers, see Hō Takushū, *Chūgoku no kindaika to Meiji isshin,* 1–79, 252–256; and Wang Xiaoqiu, *Jindai Zhong-Ri qishilu,* 69–118.

50. Noriko Kamachi, *Reform in China;* Howland, *Borders of Chinese Civilization.*

51. Kang Youwei, *Riben bianzhengkao* 日本變政考, in idem, *Kang Nanhai xiansheng yizhu huikan,* vol. 10.

52. Kang Youwei, "Riben shumuzhi" 日本書目誌, in idem, *Kang Youwei quanji* 3:585–586. See Kong Xiangji, *Kang Youwei bianfa zouyi yanjiu,* 371–374; Murata Yūjirō, "Kang Youwei de Riben yanjiu jiqi tedian"; and idem, "Kō Yui to 'Tōgaku.'"

53. See inter alia Wang Xiaoqiu, *Jindai Zhong-Ri qishilu,* 192–210; Howard, "Japan's Role in the Reform Program"; and Hō Takushū, *Chūgoku no kindaika to Meiji isshin,* 1–158 passim. For the circumstances of the work's presentation to the emperor, see Kong Xiangji, *Kang Youwei bianfa zouyi yanjiu,* 342–350.

54. Kang Youwei, *Riben bianzhengkao* ("xu"), 10:2.

55. Ibid. ("xu"), 10:1.

56. Ibid. (juan 1), 10:4, 6–7. The Charter Oath of 1868 outlined the Restoration's basic program. According to Kang, the Japanese learned of such pledges from Western investiture practices, though ancient China also knew similar oaths.

57. Ibid. (juan 1), 10:37.

58. Ibid. (juan 4), 10:99; (juan 7), 10:187; (juan 10), 10:244.

59. Ibid. (juan 1), 10:10–11, 19, 39–40; (juan 7), 10:198.

60. Ibid. (juan 1), 10:25.

61. Ibid. (juan 7), 10:196–197; (juan 8), 10:211; (juan 11), 10:306.

62. Ibid. (juan 1), 10:13; (juan 2a), 10:66; (juan 7), 10:118.

63. Wang Xiaoqiu, *Jindai Zhong-Ri qishilu*, 200–201.

64. See Huang Zhangjian, *Kang Youwei wuxu zhen zouyi*, 98. Wang Xiaoqiu notes that Kang wished to strengthen imperial powers as part of a larger process leading to a kind of democratization that Kang, at least, understood in largely Confucian terms—which also informs Kang's emphasis on unity. See Wang Xiaoqiu, *Jindai Zhong-Ri qishilu*, 202–207. However, Wang does not explore the potential contradictions in this scheme; it is not clear if Kang understood how deeply alarmed the Meiji leaders were at the prospects of Japan's democratization following the introduction of constitutional politics in the 1890s, nor how far they were determined to restrict political speech and limit the Diet's powers.

65. Hō Takushū, *Chūgoku no kindaika to Meiji isshin*, 19, 111.

66. Contemporary critics were not slow to impugn his scholarship, and his own disciples rather quickly realized his limitations. Liang Qichao was eventually, in the 1920s, to conclude that Kang suppressed and distorted evidence, drew conclusions that were entirely subjective and arbitrary, and ignored "objective facts," thus failing to found a new school of thought. See Liang Qichao, *Qingdai xueshu gailun*, 126–137. As early as 1901, when Liang wrote a hagiography of the man whose disciple he ostensibly remained, Liang hinted at Kang's intellectual arrogance. "Kang Nanhai zhi Zhongguo zhengce," YBSHJ wenji 6:87–88.

67. Most fully in Kung-chuan Hsiao, *A Modern China and a New World*, 41–189, and Wang Fansen, *Gushibian yundong de xingqi*, 61–208. See also Hao Chang, *Chinese Intellectuals in Crisis*, 25–55; Tang Zhijun, *Kang Youwei yu wuxu bianfa*, 19–79; Wang Hui, *Xiandai Zhongguo sixiang*, 1B:793–820 and 2A:929–935; and Young-tsu Wong, "Philosophical Hermeneutics and Political Reform."

68. Elman, *Classicism, Politics, and Kinship*; and Anne Cheng, "Nationalism, Citizenship, and the Old Text/New Text Controversy in Late Nineteenth-Century China." My summary remarks below are derived from the works cited in this and the preceding note.

69. Even this claim was not original with Kang; he stole it from another scholar, Liao Ping (1852–1932), who, however, had refrained from publically linking his historical speculations with contemporary political issues. See Kung-chuan Hsiao, *A Modern China and a New World*, 65–69.

70. Kang Youwei, *Kongzi gaizhi kao* 孔子改制考.

71. Wang Yeyang, "Kang-Liang yu shixue zhiyong," 204–208.

72. Kang Youwei, *Kongzi gaizhi kao*, 1:1–2.

73. Ibid., 12:283.

74. Ibid., 2:9.

75. Ibid. ("xu"), 7; cf. Kung-chuan Hsiao, *A Modern China and a New World*, 107–108.

76. Kang Youwei, *Datong shu* 大同書; Thompson, *Ta T'ung Shu*. See Tang Zhijun, *Kang Youwei yu wuxu bianfa*, 108–133.

77. Bauer, *China and the Search for Happiness*, cites many utopian visions in the traditional literature, but few were worked out in detail.

78. Reactions to the *Commonweal* perhaps reveal as much about the observer as about Kang. Kung-chuan Hsiao simply judged the work to be highly influential: *A Modern*

China, 497–513. Tang Zhijun dismissed it as reactionary (*Kang Youwei yu wuxu bianfa*, 96–107, 134–171), while Li Zehou found value in its unmasking of feudal society and, in its historical context, a progressive reflection of bourgeois ideals (Li Zehou, *Zhongguo jindai sixiang shilun*, 127–160). Qian Mu made little sense of Kang's profound radicalism—Qian Mu, *Zhongguo jinsanbai nian xueshushi*, 2:644. More recently, Wang Hui has offered a strikingly sympathetic account of Kang's utopianism, pointing not merely to Kang's faith in linear progress and the dialectical relationship between his utopianism and his nationalism, but to how his utopia served as a negation of the once-necessary nation-state. But Wang too sees Kang's "commonweal" notion as contradictory: reflecting the conflict between "the logic of modernity" (i.e., practical state-building reforms in the capitalist world-system) and the logic of "transcending modernity" (i.e., utopian ideals and world administration)—Wang Hui, *Xiandai Zhongguo sixiang*, 2A:747.

79. Hao Chang, *Chinese Intellectuals in Crisis*, 35–41. As Chang acknowledges, there are Buddhist and Western elements in Kang's thought as well.

80. Kang Youwei, *Datong shu* 大同書, 104; Thompson, *Ta T'ung Shu*, 84.

81. Kang Youwei, *Datong shu*, 452–453; Thompson, *Ta T'ung Shu*, 275–276.

82. Fitzgerald, *Awakening China*, 67–76.

83. Hao Chang, *Chinese Intellectuals*, 53–54: "Seen in this light, Kang's evolutionary view of history is obviously not just an ideological instrument to justify his political reformism. . . . Rather, it is a conceptual framework that he finally discovered after years of intellectual search, enabling him to weave together and integrate into an overall synthesis all the major elements of this thinking."

84. Kung-chuan Hsiao, *A Modern China and a New World*, 409.

85. For Kang, the ultimate representative of true kingship was not any historical emperor but Confucius, who created by foretelling the institutions that tended toward perfection. Kang's Confucius was simultaneously a founder of a universal religion, a universalist, and the "sage-king" of China. Cf. Wang Hui, *Xiandai Zhongguo sixiang*, 1B:782–793, 810–820. However, I suspect Kang saw the sage-king of China in a universal rather than particularistic light; again, his true subject was humanity itself.

CHAPTER 2

Earlier versions of portions of this chapter have been previously published as "Late Qing Reformism and the Meiji Model: Kang Youwei, Liang Qichao, and the Japanese Emperor," pp. 40–67, in Joshua A. Fogel, ed., *The Role of Japan in Liang Qichao's Introduction of Modern Western Civilization to China* (Berkeley: Institute of East Asian Studies, University of California, 2004); and "The Reform Movement, the Monarchy, and Political Modernity," pp. 17–47, in Rebecca Karl and Peter Zarrow, eds., *Rethinking the Reform Movement of 1898: Political and Cultural Change in Modern China* (Cambridge, MA: Harvard University Asia Center Publications, Harvard University Press, 2002).

1. Liang's life and thought are one of the best-studied subjects in modern Chinese history, although he was more or less officially dismissed as a bourgeois reactionary in Maoist historiography. He is unique among modern Chinese intellectuals as the subject of four full-length studies in English. Of these, for my purposes, the most useful remains Hao Chang, *Liang Ch'i-ch'ao and Intellectual Transition in Modern China*. In Chinese, Zhang Pengyuan (P'eng-yuan Chang), *Liang Qichao yu Qingji geming*, also remains essential. Chinese (Mainland) scholars rediscovered Liang in the 1980s, producing many specialized monographs, as well as general intellectual biographies such as Huang Minlan, *Zhongguo zhishifenzi diyiren*; Chen Pengming, *Liang Qichao xueshu sixiang pingzhuan*; and Dong

Fangkui, *Qingmo zhengti bianqe yu guoqing zhi lunzheng*. Also to be noted are the essays in Li Xisuo, ed., *Liang Qichao yu jindai Zhongguo shehui wenhua*; Fogel, ed., *The Role of Japan in Liang Qichao's Introduction of Modern Western Civilization to China*; and Hazama Naoki, ed., *Kyōdō kenkyū Ryō Keichō*.

2. Wang Yangming (1472–1529) was a Ming dynasty statesman and philosopher. His school emphasized "innate good knowledge" or moral intuition over textual studies and "the unity of knowledge and action," which could justify political activism. His school dominated late Ming scholarship but was eclipsed for most of the Qing.

3. Liang Qichao, "Baojiao fei suoyi zun Kong lun" 保教非所以尊孔論, YBSHJ wenji 9:50–59.

4. Ibid., 9:53.

5. Ibid., 9:59.

6. Liang Qichao, "Sanshi zishu" 三十自述, YBSHJ wenji 11:15–21.

7. Ibid., 11:16–17.

8. Ding Wenjiang, ed., *Liang Rengong xiansheng nianpu changbian chugao*, 1:43–44.

9. Ibid., 1:20.

10. Ibid., 1:34–35, 22. But see Wang Junzhong, "Jiuguo, zongjiao yi zhexue?" 103–106.

11. Hao Chang, *Liang Ch'i-ch'ao and Intellectual Transition in Modern China*, 59–72.

12. Liang Qichao, "Lun junzheng minzheng xiangshan zhi li" 論君政民政相嬗之理, YBSHJ wenji 2:7–11. Liang's faith in progress through fixed stages was based on New Text prophesy, but it eased his way to an acceptance of social Darwinism by the turn of the century (discussed further below).

13. Liang Qichao, "Du *Chunqiu* jieshuo" 讀《春秋》界說, in idem, *Liang Qichao zhexue sixiang lunwenxuan*, 19–28.

14. Liang Qichao, "Lun Zhongguo yi jiangqiu falü zhi xue" 論中國宜講求法律之學, YBSHJ wenji 1:93–94.

15. Liang Qichao, "Lun junzheng minzheng xiangshan zhi li," YBSHJ wenji 2:7–11.

16. Liang Qichao, "Shuo qun xu" 說群序, YBSHJ wenji 2:3–4. See Hao Chang, *Liang Ch'i-ch'ao and Intellectual Transition in Modern China*, 95–107.

17. Liang cited Kang Youwei's notion that the West was 80–90 percent civilized while China was 10–20 percent; neither had completed the evolutionary trajectory ("Yu Yan Youling xiansheng shu," YBSHJ wenji 1:109). See Xiaobing Tang, *Global Space and the Nationalist Discourse of Modernity*; and Karl, "Creating Asia."

18. Liang Qichao, "Lun Zhongguo yi jiangqiu falü zhi xue," YBSHJ wenji 1:93–94.

19. Liang Qichao, "Bianfa tongyi" 變法通議, YBSHJ wenji 1:1–92.

20. Liang Qichao, "Shanghui yi" 商會議, YBSHJ wenji 4:1.

21. Mai Menghua, "Lun Zhongguo yi zun junquan yi minquan" 論中國宜尊君權抑民權, in Jian Bozan et al., eds., *Wuxu bianfa*, 3:111–113.

22. Liang Qichao, "Bianfa tongyi," YBSHJ wenji 1:80.

23. Ibid., 1:4.

24. Ibid., 1:80, 110. This view was, of course, consonant with the theory of the Three Ages. It is sometimes suggested that "democracy" or "popular power" in writings from this period actually refers to what might be called "gentry democracy" that had no space for the lower classes; however, although it is true that the publicists of the 1898 generation advocated nothing like universal suffrage and could not imagine giving the vote to porters and maids, the reformist vision of "popular power" was not restricted to *gentry* (*shenshi*) in the legal sense of the term but to educated men (*shi*) broadly defined. By the 1890s, there had emerged a strong if inchoate vision that the populace (including women) would eventually

become politically active, if only after they were properly educated. See Li Xiaoti, *Qingmo de xiacengshehui qimeng yundong, 1901–1911*; and Judge, *The Precious Raft of History*.

25. Liang Qichao, "Gu yiyuan kao" 古議院考, YBSHJ wenji 1:95–96.

26. Yan Fu was a reformer just then beginning his career as the preeminent translator of major Western works; we will return to him below.

27. Liang Qichao, "Yu Yan Youling xiansheng shu" 與嚴幼陵先生書, YBSHJ wenji 1:108.

28. Ibid., 1:109; cf. Hao Chang, *Liang Ch'i-ch'ao and Intellectual Transition in Modern China*, 104–105, whose translation of *gong* as "public-minded" I follow here.

29. Liang Qichao, "Yu Yan Youling xiansheng shu," YBSHJ wenji 1:108–109.

30. Liang Qichao, "Lun Zhongguo jiruo youyu fangbi" 論中國積弱由於防弊, YBSHJ wenji 1:96.

31. Ibid., 1:99.

32. Ibid., 1:96.

33. Liang Qichao, "Shuo qun xu," YBSHJ wenji 2:3–4.

34. Liang Qichao, "Lun Zhongguo jiruo youyu fangbi," YBSHJ wenji 1:96–97.

35. Ibid., 1:99. There is a good deal of ambiguity in this use of *quan*, which I explore further below.

36. Liu Guangjing, "Wan Qing renquanlun chutan."

37. Ou Jujia [sometimes Ou Qujia], "Lun dadi geguo bianfa jie you min qi" 論大地各國變法皆由民起, in Jian Bozan et al., eds., *Wuxu bianfa*, 3:152–156. It is perhaps not surprising that in the early 1900s, Ou shifted away from Kang-Liang reformism to the revolutionary camp, supporting provincial-based republicanism in an independent Guangdong. See Price, "Popular and Elite Heterodoxy toward the End of the Qing," 442–444.

38. The locus classicus is from the *Guliang* commentary (*Guliang zhuan*, Zhuang Gong, third year): "What are called Kings are those to whom the people come" (*qi yue wangzhe min zhi suo guiwang ye*).

39. Liang Qichao, "Du *Chunqiu* jieshuo," 19–28.

40. Ibid., 27. *Gongli*, as we have seen in the Introduction, was a key term in late Qing reformist discourse. See Jin Guangtao and Liu Qingfeng, *Guannianshi yanjiu*, chap. 1; Wang Hui, *Xiandai Zhongguo sixiang de xingqi*, 2A. However, in my view *gongli* mostly served as a rhetorical claim to a set of assumptions revolving around truth and justice rather than marking a new epistemological space. In other words, it was seldom articulated as the foundation of a belief system but mostly naturalized in argumentation.

41. Liang Qichao, "Lun Zhongguo yi jiangqiu falü zhi xue," YBSHJ wenji 1:93.

42. Liang Qichao, "Bianfa tongyi," YBSHJ wenji 1:2–3.

43. For discussions of Liang and the Meiji, see Hō Takushū, *Chūgoku no kindaika to Meiji isshin*, 193–264; and Philip Huang, "Liang Ch'i-ch'ao." At a more general level, see Hao Chang, *Liang Ch'i-ch'ao and Intellectual Transition in Modern China*, 73–120 passim, esp. 89–95; and Zhang Pengyuan, *Liang Qichao yu Qingji geming*, 11–80 passim.

44. Liang Qichao, "Bianfa tongyi," YBSHJ wenji 1:8.

45. Or "political learning" (*zhengxue*), ibid., 1:62–63; education is broadly discussed in ibid., 1:21–64.

46. Ibid., 1:1, 4.

47. Ibid., 1:80.

48. Zhang Pengyuan has emphasized the democratic (*minquan*) and radical nature of Liang's thought at this time—Zhang Pengyuan, *Liang Qichao yu Qingji geming*, 48–50, 53–58; see also Hao Chang, *Liang Ch'i-ch'ao and Intellectual Transition in Modern China*, 103–106. However, I would note that although his anti-despotism was certainly

well developed, Liang still granted the sagely emperor a valid and indeed necessary role in the political community.

49. Liang Qichao, "Bianfa tongyi," YBSHJ wenji 1:5. Kangxi (r. 1661–1722) and his son Yongzheng (r. 1722–1735) were indeed innovative and also highly autocratic rulers who consolidated Qing power.

50. Ibid., 1:81.

51. Ibid., 1:8–9.

52. Ibid., 1:27–28. Liang's larger point was that this problem would remain as long as the civil service examination and appointment systems remained unchanged.

53. Ibid., 1:9–10.

54. Ibid., 1:69. See also Hao Chang, *Liang Ch'i-ch'ao and Intellectual Transition in Modern China*, 94–95.

55. Reynolds, *China, 1898–1912*.

56. Liang Qichao, "Da moujun wen Deguo Riben caiyi minquan shi" 答某君問德國日本裁抑民權事, YBSHJ wenji 11:48–57.

57. Ibid., 11:52, 49.

58. Ibid., 11:53–54.

59. Ibid., 11:55–56. A little convolutedly, Liang argued that since in practice even absolute monarchs had to share their powers with officials and eunuchs and the like, they would not lose by sharing their powers with the people instead. The monarchs of states that circumscribed their powers (Britain, Japan) were fortunate men, since they could not be blamed for the government's mistakes.

60. For Liang, see Hao Chang, *Liang Ch'i-ch'ao and Intellectual Transition in Modern China*, 103–107; and Hazama Naoki, "On Liang Qichao's Conceptions of *Gong* and *Si*." For the centrality of *gong* in late Qing political discourse, see Huang Kewu, "Cong zhuiqiu zhengdao dao rentong guozu"; Mizoguchi Yūzō, *Chūgoku no kō to shi*; and Rowe, "The Public Sphere in Modern China."

61. Liang Qichao, "Yu Yan Youling xiansheng shu," YBSHJ 1:108.

62. Liu Shipei, *Zhongguo minyue jingyi* 中國民約精義, in *Liu Shipei quanji* (hereafter, LSPQJ), 1:560–596. Liu is discussed further in Chapter 5.

63. Liang Qichao, "Lun Zhongguo jiruo youyu fangbi," YBSHJ wenji 1:96; see also idem, "Lun jinshi guomin jingzheng zhi dashi ji Zhongguo qiantu" 論近世國民競爭之大勢及中國前途, YBSHJ wenji 4:56.

64. Liang Qichao, "Lun Zhongguo jiruo youyu fangbi," YBSHJ wenji 1:98–99.

65. Liang relates duties, powers, and profit or benefits to one another in several contexts, including his discussions of *quanli*, or "ethically legitimate interests." See Angle, "Should We All Be More English?"

66. See Hao Chang, *Liang Ch'i-ch'ao and Intellectual Transition in Modern China*, esp. chap. 6; and Xiaobing Tang, *Global Space and the Nationalist Discourse of Modernity*, esp. chap. 4.

67. *Xinminshuo* is well discussed in Hao Chang, *Liang Ch'i-ch'ao and Intellectual Transition in Modern China*, 149–295; and Huang Kewu, *Yige beifangqi de xuanze*, 41–60.

68. Liang Qichao, "Lun side" 論私德, in *Xinminshuo* 新民說, YBSHJ zhuanji 4:118–143. In 1903, Liang visited the United States for eight months, publishing "Lun side" upon his return to Japan. It marked Liang's "conservative turn," which was at least in part prompted by his observations of both corruption in American politics and the backwardness of Chinese communities there in spite of their greater freedoms. For this conservative turn, seen in Liang's disillusionment with "democracy" and a sharpening of his attacks on the

revolutionaries, see Hao Chang, *Liang Ch'i-ch'ao and Intellectual Transition in Modern China*, 238–271; Levenson, *Liang Ch'i-ch'ao and the Mind of Modern China*, 153–169; and my discussion in Chapter 3.

69. Liang Qichao, *Xinminshuo*, YBSHJ zhuanji 4:118–119.

70. Ibid., 4:119.

71. Huang Kewu, *Yige beifangqi de xuanze*, 66.

72. Liang Qichao, *Xinminshuo*, YBSHJ zhuanji 4:120–130.

73. Ibid., 4:131.

74. Liang took the notion that freedom of conscience was the root of morality from Kant. See Huang Kewu, "Liang Qichao yu Kangde"; and Max Ko-wu Huang, "Liang Qichao and Immanuel Kant."

75. Liang Qichao, *Xinminshuo*, YBSHJ zhuanji 4:132.

76. Liang attributed Western moral behavior to religion, law, and social pressures (honor, reputation). See ibid., 4:132. But these moral codes would be difficult to import into China—ibid., 4:140.

77. Ibid., 4:138–139.

78. Ibid., 4:139.

79. Yan was also perhaps the most epistemologically daring of the generation of 1890s reformers. The standard English biography of Yan remains Benjamin Schwartz, *In Search of Wealth and Power*, which emphasizes Yan's devotion to the nation-state as the key unit of Darwinian struggle in the contemporary world. The recent Chinese language study by Wang Hui, *Xiandai Zhongguo sixiang de xingqi*, 2A:833–920, emphasizes the modernity of Yan's thought. Two important recent studies of Yan's liberalism, focusing on his translation of John Stuart Mill's *On Liberty*, are Max Ko-wu Huang, *The Meaning of Freedom*; and Howland, *Personal Liberty and Public Good.*

80. See Pusey, *China and Charles Darwin.*

81. Yan Fu, "Pi Han" 闢韓, in idem, *Yan Fu heji*, 1:70–74. Yan's essay was published by Liang Qichao in the newspaper he had helped to found in 1896, the *Shiwu bao.*

82. Han Yu, "Yuandao" 原道, translated as "Essentials of the Moral Way" in de Bary and Bloom, eds., *Sources of Chinese Tradition*, 1:569–573.

83. Mizoguchi Yūzō, *Chūgoku no kō to shi.*

CHAPTER 3

An earlier version of portions of this chapter has been previously published as "Chinese Conceptions of the State during the Late Qing Dynasty (1860–1911)," pp. 235–259, in Takashi Shogimen and Cary J. Nederman, eds., *Western Political Thought in Dialogue with Asia* (Lanham, MD: Lexington Books/Rowman & Littlefield, 2009).

1. Shi Wen and Xu Min, "Wan-Qing shiqi dui guojia qiyuan de sikao he quanshi."

2. Hui Dun 惠顿, *Wanguo gongfa* 万国公法. I have consulted the English edition, Wheaton, *Elements of International Law*. For background, see Lin Xuezhong, *Cong wanguo gongfa dao gongfa waijiao*, esp. chap. 1; and Tian Tao, *Guojifa shuru yu wan-Qing Zhongguo*, esp. chap. 2.

3. Spence, *To Change China*, 130–140.

4. Hui Dun, *Wanguo gongfa*, 24–25; Wheaton, *Elements of International Law*, 29–30.

5. Hui Dun, *Wanguo gongfa*, 29: I back-translate from the Chinese; Wheaton's original text has: "The habitual obedience of the members of any *political society* to a *superior authority* must have once existed in order to constitute a sovereign state"—*Elements of*

International Law, 33–34 (my italics). This is a rare instance where the original sense was substantially changed.

6. Wheaton, *Elements of International Law*, 31; Hui Dun, *Wanguo gongfa*, 27.

7. Wheaton, *Elements of International Law*, 31–32; Hui Dun, *Wanguo gongfa*, 27–28.

8. Hui Dun, *Wanguo gongfa*, 28; Wheaton, *Elements of International Law*, 32. Again, Wheaton's tone is contractarian.

9. Wheaton, *Elements of International Law*, 53; Hui Dun, *Wanguo gongfa*, 37–38.

10. Hui Dun, *Wanguo gongfa*, 14; Wheaton, *Elements of International Law*, 14.

11. For the British in China, especially between 1860 and 1901, see Hevia, *English Lessons*. The classic study is Immanuel C. Y. Hsü, *China's Entry into the Family of Nations*.

12. Succinctly described in Fairbank, *The Great Chinese Revolution*, 87–95, following Fletcher, "The Heyday of the Ch'ing Order in Mongolia, Sinkiang and Tibet"; also see Dong Wang, *China's Unequal Treaties*, 11–12, and chap. 1.

13. Horowitz, "International Law and State Transformation in China, Siam, and the Ottoman Empire during the Nineteenth Century"; Tian Tao, *Guojifa shuyu yu wan-Qing Zhongguo*; idem, "Shijiu shiji xiabanqi Zhongguo zhishijie de guojifa guannian"; Shi Jianxing, "Guojifa de shuru yu Zhongguo jindai guojia zhuquan guannian de faren"; and see Hevia, *English Lessons*, 61–70. The Second Opium War broke out during the massive Taiping Rebellion (1850–1864), which came very close to overthrowing the Qing. The Second Opium War ended after the Qing royals ignominiously fled Beijing and an Anglo-French force burned down the imperial Summer Palace.

14. Dong Wang, *China's Unequal Treaties*, 19–24.

15. Xiaoming Zhang and Chunfeng Xu, "The Late Qing Dynasty Diplomatic Transformation"; Shogo Suzuki, "China's Perceptions of International Society in the Nineteenth Century."

16. The first institutional reformers were the marginal literati of the coastal areas who lacked the status of examination degree-holders. See Cohen, *Between Tradition and Modernity*.

17. Zheng Guanying, "Lun gongfa" 論公法, in *Zheng Guanying ji*, 1:65–68.

18. Zheng Guanying, "Gongfa" 公法, in ibid., 1:387–389.

19. Benton, *Law and Colonial Cultures*, 3.

20. Hevia, *English Lessons*, 57. The British barred the Chinese from using certain terms they considered demeaning, and, more importantly, they used their knowledge of seized Chinese documents as negotiating tools and to demonstrate the xenophobia of Qing officials. The Qing thus "lost control of its own discursive universe in its dealings with Western powers" where it became "effectively 'disenchanted' and drained of authority" (59–60). See also Lydia H. Liu, *The Clash of Empires*.

21. Hevia, *English Lessons*, 69–70, 145–153; Lydia Liu, *Clash of Empires*, chap. 4.

22. Central to any consideration of cross-cultural political theory are the problems and opportunities of translation. Cross-cultural dialogue is not only always situated in specific power relations, but is subject to the problem of incommensurability. A good introduction is Howland, "The Predicament of Ideas in Culture." My approach differs from that of Hevia and Liu in ignoring the admittedly important process of Westerners learning Chinese, and, more importantly, emphasizing the "demand side" on the part of Chinese.

23. Neither *guojia* nor "state" can claim a stable meaning (the English "state" is etymologically derived from the Latin *status*); both terms carry historical baggage. The range of meanings of *guojia* has been determined by Chinese usage over decades. I believe the modern European notion of "state" was *roughly* similar to that already available to nineteenth-century Chinese scholars through Confucian notions of legitimate rule. Both distinguished between state organs and the private interests of the ruler. Qing law and bureaucratic practice, for instance, clearly

distinguished between revenues of the state and those of the imperial household, a practice as old as the Han. The very architecture of the Forbidden City separated the Inner Court of the imperial family and the Outer Court of the bureaucracy. In this chapter, when I cite Chinese usages of "state," I am translating *guojia* and sometimes *guo*; yet I do not invariably take these terms to refer to "state." Context is all. Space constraints make it impossible to discuss translation issues further; they are important and complex, but secondary to figuring out how Chinese thinkers actually used various terms.

24. Fu Lanya 傅蘭雅 [John Fryer], *Zuozhi chuyan* 佐治芻言 (lit. "Humble words in aid of governance"); Chambers and Chambers, *Political Economy for Use in Schools and for Private Instruction*. The Chambers brothers used the terms "state," "nation," and "government" more or less interchangeably; Fryer's translation was also quite free. Chinese readers of the 1880s probably found the Chamberses' political economy easier to make sense of than readers of the 1860s had found Wheaton's law for several reasons; for one, the Chambers brothers told a story while Wheaton analyzed terms.

25. Sun Qing, *Wan-Qing zhi "Xizheng" dongjian ji bentu huiying*, chap. 4.

26. Trescott, "Scottish Political Economy Comes to the Far East."

27. Fu Lanya, *Zuozhi chuyan*, 27–28; Chambers and Chambers, *Political Economy*, 20–21.

28. Fu Lanya, *Zuozhi chuyan*, 28; Chambers and Chambers, *Political Economy*, 21–22.

29. Fu Lanya, *Zuozhi chuyan*, 23; Chambers and Chambers, *Political Economy*, 18.

30. Fu Lanya, *Zuozhi chuyan*, 19–21; Chambers and Chambers, *Political Economy*, 14–16.

31. Fu Lanya, *Zuozhi chuyan*, 28; Chambers and Chambers, *Political Economy*, 22. The *Zuozhi chuyan* translation here differs from the original in one respect. It postulates a clear progress from custom to law, in effect equating the primitive state with customary regulations. The Chambers brothers, however, say they do not know whether the earliest state originated in some kind of rulership (that is, authoritarian command) or in law (that is, mutual regulation), though it probably had both characteristics.

32. Fu Lanya, *Zuozhi chuyan*, 30–31; Chambers and Chambers, *Political Economy*, 24–25. While *Political Economy* terms the second class of government "aristocracy," defined as "rule of a superior hereditary class," in the *Zuozhi chuyan* this became rule of the wise or saintly. Thus did European nobility become Chinese literati.

33. Fu Lanya, *Zuozhi chuyan*, 35; Chambers and Chambers, *Political Economy*, 28–29.

34. Fu Lanya, *Zuozhi chuyan*, 29. I back-translate; the original passage is somewhat less populist in tone.

35. Fu Lanya, *Zuozhi chuyan*, 42; Chambers and Chambers, *Political Economy*, 35. The Chamberses' liberalism was shown in their preference for minimal government: social welfare policies are a mistake since they will discourage work. See Fu Lanya, *Zuozhi chuyan*, 51; Chambers and Chambers, *Political Economy*, 45.

36. Fu Lanya, *Zuozhi chuyan*, 32; Chambers and Chambers, *Political Economy*, 26.

37. Fu Lanya, *Zuozhi chuyan*, 23 (back-translation); cf. Chambers and Chambers, *Political Economy*, 18.

38. Liang Taigen [Yang Taekeun], "Jindai xifang zhishi zai Dongya de chuanbo jiqi gongtong wenben zhi tansuo."

39. The Japanese neologisms to translate key Western political concepts only emerged in stable form toward the end of the Meiji period (1868–1912), after a period of experimentation and development. Howland, *Translating the West*, 61–93, 122–129.

40. Ibid., 138–146.

41. Sōgō Masaaki and Hida Yoshifumi, *Meiji no kotoba jiten*, 164.

42. Suzuki Shūji, *Nihon kango to Chūgoku: kanji bunkaken no kindaika*, 3–21.

43. Legal training grew rapidly as the result of the New Policy educational reforms after 1902, coupled with the abandonment of the traditional civil services examinations in 1905. For legal training, see Lin Xuezhong, *Cong wanguo gongfa*, esp. chap. 2; Zhou Shaoyuan, "Qingmo faxue jiaoyu de tedian"; Zhang Jinfan, *Zhongguo falü de chuantong yu jindai zhuanxing*, 441–442; and Wang Shanping, "Zhang Zhidong yu wan-Qing falü jiaoyu."

44. Late Qing law books certainly paraphrased Japanese legal textbooks and followed similar organizational principles. See, e.g., Kawana Kaneshirō, *Kaitai zōho minpō sōron*; and Tomii Masaakira, *Minpō genron*. But so far as I can determine, the late Qing law books cited here were not direct translations.

45. Zuo xinyi shuju biancuan 作新譯書局編纂, ed., *Xinbian faxue tonglun (wubian)* 新編法學通論(五編), 2–4.

46. The *Xinbian faxue tonglun* 新編法學通論 (183) stressed that "'state's rights' refer to all the rights of the state" (*suowei guoquan ji zhi suoyou zhi quanli*), and not to the rights of rulers, who merely represented (*daibiao*) these rights.

47. In Meiji Japan "state's rights," "people's rights," and the "monarch's rights" played out against one another. See Howland, *Translating the West*, 129–138.

48. Zuo xinyi shuju biancuan, ed., *Xinbian faxue tonglun*, 183–185.

49. Ibid., 189.

50. Ibid., 190.

51. Ibid., 4–5.

52. Ibid., 6.

53. Wu Renda 吳人達, *Falü tonglun* 法律通論. The preface calls this book a translation but does not name a specific source; perhaps Wu abridged and edited several Japanese works.

54. Ibid., 11a.

55. Yang Tingdong 楊廷棟, *Falüxue* 法律學, 49–52, 54–57.

56. Zhou Mian, ed., *Zhongguo liuxuesheng dacidian*, 134. See also Wang Lanping, "Dianjiao xuyan," in Tomii Masaakira, *Minfa yuanlun*, 2; Zhang Pengyuan, *Lixianpai yu Xinhai geming*, 215.

57. Yang Tingdong, *Falüxue*, 54–57.

58. Ibid., 49–52.

59. Ibid., 51.

60. Ibid., 53. In contrast to Yang's insistence on the state's priority, the historical school of law in the German states in the early nineteenth century, a school influential in Japan, claimed that customary law—the entire set of traditions, popular customs, and usages shared by the community as a whole—arose first. It was part of the spirit of the people (*Volkgeist*) or spiritual community (*geistige Gemeinschaft*) that was distinct from both codified laws and the state itself. Such "positive law" as emerged out of customary usage of course was unique to each community, the opposite of the abstract and state-making constitutionalism associated (unfavorably) with the French Revolution and the universal Napoleonic legal code. See Kriegel, *The State and the Rule of Law*, 114–115. The German historical school opposed its story of the origins of the state to "social contract" theory, but both views were influenced by natural law theory.

61. Yang Tingdong, *Falüxue*, 57. Yang's adamant refusal to grant legal personhood to the state was somewhat idiosyncratic. A more mainstream view held that states were indeed legal persons, particularly in the international sphere—see, e.g., Zuo xinyi shuju biancuan, ed., *Xinbian faxue tonglun*, 183, 206.

62. Yang Tingdong, *Falüxue*, 56–58.

63. Ibid., 3, 49.

64. Ibid., 53.

65. Ibid., 52–60.

66. Ibid., 51–52.

67. Bluntschli, a prominent legal thinker of his day, taught at Zurich, Munich, and Heidelberg. To a great extent, Bluntschli followed the historical school of legal thought, emphasizing the law as a product of history rather than purely rational logic. Bluntschli thus concluded that different nations would naturally possess different legal systems (and different state forms). See Bastid-Bruguière, "The Japanese-Induced German Connection on Modern Chinese Ideas of the State," 111–115.

68. Yang Tingdong, *Falüxue*, 62–64. Another such distinction was between personal rights and property rights (65–66).

69. Liang's turn to statism soon after his arrival in Japan is meticulously traced in Zhang Foquan, "Liang Qichao guojia guannian zhi xingcheng," though the exact stages of Liang's political development overlapped one another; Zhang correctly notes that statism influenced the whole of Liang's thought. See also Li Chunfu, "Lun Liang Qichao guojia zhuyi guandian jiqi zhuanbian guocheng"; and Hao Chang, *Liang Ch'i-ch'ao and Intellectual Transition in Modern China*, 238–248. The reasons for Liang's famous "conservative turn" included disillusionment with the revolutionaries and a deeper disillusionment with the capacity of the Chinese people; intellectually, as we will see, Liang's social Darwinist sense of the precariousness of China's position led him to support a stronger state. As well, we cannot ignore Liang's growing acquaintance with Japanese and Western political philosophy.

70. Liang Qichao, "Lun jinshi guomin jingzheng zhi dashi ji Zhongguo qiantu" 論近世國民競爭之大勢及中國前途, YBSHJ wenji 4:57.

71. Liang Qichao, "Aiguolun" 愛國論, Xinminshe, ed., *Qingyibao chuanbian*, vol. 1, 1:16–32.

72. Ibid., 1:22.

73. Ibid., 1:26. Liang distinguished between a vague sort of "democracy" (*minquan*) and a system of strictly republican institutions (*minzhu*). His point was that *minquan* democracy was compatible with constitutional monarchism and was, indeed, first developed in Britain and was then seen in Japan. Liang could therefore argue, as a reformer in the late Qing political context, that *minquan* was not only compatible with the Qing monarchy (albeit a reformed and constitutional one), but would even make the Qing imperial house stronger. Ibid., 1:30–31.

74. Ibid., 1:27–29.

75. Liang Qichao, "Lixianfa yi" 立憲法議, YBSHJ wenji 5:1–7.

76. Feudalism was historically important (as a transitional stage between tribes and centralized states) but no longer found in today's world. See Liang Qichao, "Lun Zhongguo yu Ouzhou guoti yitong" 論中國與歐洲國體異同, YBSHJ wenji 4:61–66.

77. Liang Qichao, "Lun Zhinaren guojia sixiang zhi ruodian" 論支那人國家思想之弱點, *Qingyibao chuanbian*, vol. 1, 2:19–27. In translating *sixiang* as "consciousness," I follow Angle, *Human Rights and Chinese Thought*, 141–162.

78. Liang Qichao, "Lun Zhinaren guojia sixiang zhi ruodian," 2:24–25.

79. Ibid., 2:19.

80. Liang Qichao, "Huobushi xuean" 霍布士學案, YBSHJ wenji 6:89–95.

81. Ibid., 6:89–90.

82. Liang was still feeling his way into Western political theory. He held that Hobbes's notion of the social contract was a bit like Mozi's theory that the people selected leaders to adjudicate their conflicts. But Mozi, unlike Hobbes, at least hypothesized the existence of

Heaven above the emperor, thus providing a check of despotism. Liang Qichao, "Huobushi xuean," YBSHJ wenji 6:94–95.

83. Ibid., 6:92.

84. Liang Qichao, "Lusuo xuean" 盧梭學案, YBSHJ wenji 6:97–110.

85. Ibid., 6:102.

86. Liang Qichao, "Guojia sixiang bianqian yitong lun" 國家思想變遷異同論, YBSHJ wenji 6:12–22.

87. Not equally bound to the laws like his subjects, but not outside of the legal system—Liang Qichao, "Guojia sixiang bianqian," YBSHJ wenji 6:17.

88. Ibid., 6:21–22.

89. Ibid., 6:20.

90. Ibid., 6:19.

91. Liang Qichao, "Zhengzhixue dajia Bolunzhili zhi xueshuo" 政治學大家伯倫知理之學說, YBSHJ wenji 13:67–89. For the source of Liang's text, see Bastid-Bruguière, "The Japanese-Induced German Connection on Modern Chinese Ideas of the State," 117–118; see also Ba Sidi, "Zhongguo jindai guojia guannian suyuan." For Liang's organic view of the state as "statism," see Hao Chang, *Liang Ch'i-ch'ao and Intellectual Transition in Modern China*, 194–195, 252–262.

92. Liang Qichao, "Zhengzhixue dajia Bolunzhili zhi xueshuo," YBSHJ wenji 13:67–68.

93. Ibid., 13:69.

94. Ibid., 13:71–72. In a sense, the state (an advanced structure) comes out of the nation (a natural form of community)—see Bastid-Bruguière, "The Japanese-Induced German Connection on Modern Chinese Ideas of the State," 113–114. But once this happens, the nation becomes a creature of the state.

95. Liang Qichao, "Zhengzhixue dajia Bolunzhili zhi xueshuo," YBSHJ wenji 13:87–88.

96. Ibid., 13:70–71. This was an argument Liang used to attack the revolutionaries' claim that China could adopt the most advanced political form (republicanism), just as it could adopt the most advanced locomotives for its railway system. See Liang's "Kaiming zhuanzhi lun" 開明專制論, YBSHJ wenji 17:59–60.

97. Liang, "Zhengzhixue dajia Bolunzhili zhi xueshuo," YBSHJ wenji 13:88–89.

98. Liang Qichao, "Lun guojia sixiang" 論國家思想, YBSHJ zhuanji 4:1–23.

99. Ibid., 4:23.

100. Ibid., 4:16.

101. Ibid., 4:16–17.

102. Ibid., 4:18–19.

103. Ibid., 4:17.

104. Ibid., 4:20.

105. Liang Qichao, "Lun quanli sixiang," YBSHJ zhuanji 4:36.

106. Ibid., 4:39.

107. Liang, "Lun guojia sixiang," YBSHJ zhuanji 4:21–22.

108. Ibid., 4:21.

109. Wang Hui, *Xiandai Zhongguo sixiang de xingqi*, 2A:981–984; on Liang's statism, see 991–994. The question of Liang's attitudes toward individualism, civil liberties, and rights has been extensively discussed in the scholarly literature and need not detain us here. Scholars agree on the fundamental point that Liang consistently treated individual rights as secondary to collective rights of the nation-state, yet the exact place of individual rights in his political thought remains difficult to pin down.

110. Liang Qichao, "Kaiming zhuanzhi lun," YBSHJ wenji 17:13–83.

111. Ibid., 17:14.

112. Ibid., 17:15–16.

113. Ibid., 17:69–70.

114. Ibid., 17:17–19.

115. Liang tended to see the state as a legal person. As he argued elsewhere, otherwise it would be an object (*wu*): it is in fact the subject (carrier) of rights, not, like property, the object of rights. See "Xianzheng qianshuo" 憲政淺說, YBSHJ wenji 23:44.

116. Liang, "Kaiming zhuanzhi lun," YBSHJ wenji 17:19.

117. Ibid., 17:20.

118. Ibid., 17:21–22.

119. Ibid., 17:31.

120. Ibid., 17:34.

121. Ibid., 17:43–44, 48–49.

122. Ibid., 17:23–25, 35–37.

123. Ibid., 17:26–27.

124. Ibid., 17:28–29.

125. As suggested by Wang Hui, *Xiandai Zhongguo sixiang de xingqi*, 2A:985. My point is not to deny the influence of New Text notions of "grouping" on Liang's mature interpretation of the state but to note that his discussions of morality tended to focus on citizenship and the "new citizen" rather than the state. Indeed, Liang's intellectual trajectory in the decade after the 1898 reforms was to move from a thoroughly moralized Confucian view of the state to a view that de-moralized, or secularized, the state. To a great extent, he was removing morality from the public sphere while reinscribing it in the private.

126. Liang Qichao, "Xianzheng qianshuo," YBSHJ wenji 23:29–46.

127. Ibid., 23:31–33.

128. Ibid., 23:33.

129. Ibid., 23:34.

130. Ibid., 23:37–38.

131. Cai Yuanpei, "Shang huangdi shu" 上皇帝書, *Cai Yuanpei zhengzhi lunzhu*, 12. (Hanlin Bachelor was a post of great prestige that the imperial state bestowed on particularly brilliant *jinshi*, though it consisted more of academic than administrative responsibilities.)

132. Chaohua Wang, "Cai Yuanpei and the Origins of the May Fourth Movement," 232–233.

133. Liang Qichao, "Lun guojia sixiang," 4:16–17.

CHAPTER 4

1. Zhang's formula actually represented a strain of thought found at the beginning of the Self-strengthening Movement; he used it in a discussion of education in 1898. As Joseph R. Levenson points out, *ti-yong* was an intellectual rationalization—*Confucian China and Its Modern Fate*, 1:59–78; more recent discussions include Luke S. K. Kwong, "The T'i-Yung Dichotomy and the Search for Talent in Late-Ch'ing China"; and Weston, "The Founding of the Imperial University and the Emergence of Chinese Modernity," 102–105.

2. Yan Fu, "Yu *Waijiao bao* zhuren shu" 與《外交報》主人書 (1902), in idem, *Yan Fu heji*, 1:273.

3. The incident is described in Seungjoo Yoon, "Literati-Journalists of the *Chinese Progress (Shiwu bao)* in Discord, 1869–1898," 58–62; see Schwartz, *In Search of Wealth and Power*, 82. Yan Fu's essay is discussed above in Chapter 2.

4. Tu Renshou, "Tu Mei jun shiyu zhi Shiwu baoguan bian Pi Han shu" 屠梅君侍御致時務報館辨闢韓書, in Su Yu, comp., *Yijiao congbian* (hereafter, YC), 130–137.

5. Cheng Yi (1033–1107) along with his brother Cheng Hao (1032–1085) was one of the founders of Neo-Confucianism, which was synthesized into a more systematic school of Confucianism by Zhu Xi (1130–1200) and which became the orthodox basis of the examination system from the Yuan dynasty through the Ming and Qing dynasties. In general, the Neo-Confucians looked back to Han Yu as a precursor to their school.

6. YC, 132.

7. YC, 133–134.

8. YC, 136–137.

9. Yan Fu, "Ni shang huangdi shu" 擬上皇帝書, in idem, *Yan Fu heji*, 1:126–147; orig. published in *Guowenbao* 國聞報 (Guangxu 24.1.6–14). While historians have highlighted Yan's political coming out in 1895, this later essay has been neglected.

10. Ibid., 1:129, 134–135.

11. Zhang Zhidong, *Quanxue pian* (hereafter, QXP). As Tze-ki Hon notes, due to his opposition to the 1898 reforms and his ability to get along with Cixi, Zhang has earned a reputation as a conservative. This label slots Zhang into a particular teleology of modernization that neglects his genuine reformism, which Hon argues reached beyond military and technological transfers to include fundamental educational and social change. Tze-ki Hon, "Zhang Zhidong's Proposal for Reform."

12. QXP, 50.

13. QXP, 51.

14. QXP, 58–59.

15. QXP, 50–51.

16. QXP, 70.

17. QXP, 90.

18. QXP, 71.

19. QXP, 70–71.

20. QXP, 87.

21. QXP, 70.

22. QXP, 86.

23. QXP, 85–86.

24. QXP, 86–87.

25. QXP, 87.

26. Huang Zunxian, *Riben guozhi* 日本國志, in idem, *Huang Zunxian quanji*, 2:1399–1400.

27. Ibid., 2:1404–1415. For Huang's views of Meiji Restoration political reforms and the People's Right's Movement, see Noriko Kamachi, *Reform in China*, 79–87.

28. From the *Chunqiu* tradition of the *Gongyang zhuan*, particularly important in New Text learning.

29. Huang Zunxian, *Huang Zunxian quanji*, 2:1414.

30. Ibid., 2:1135.

31. Citing Confucius: *Analects* (Lunyu) 8:9. Exactly what it is that the people may be made to follow is generally understood to be the "Way," but the passage is ambiguous. Other examples of the use of this passage are given below.

32. Huang Zunxian, *Huang Zunxian quanji*, 2:1415.

33. [Huang Zunxian], "Yinbingshi shiyou lunxuejian" 飲冰室師友論學牋, *Xinmin congbao* 13 (7/1902), 55–57.

34. See Ayers, *Chang Chih-tung and Educational Reform in China*.

35. Qu Xingui and Tang Liangyan, eds., *Zhongguo jindai jiaoyushi ziliao huibian*, 534–539.

36. Ibid., 535.

37. Ibid., 536.

38. Gao Buying and Chen Baoquan, *Tongsu guomin bidu*, 1:1a–b.

39. Ibid., 2:15a–b.

40. Liu Jianbai, *Xiaoxue xiushen jiaokeshu*, 1a–2a.

41. Ibid., 45b; see also Li Jiagu, *Mengxue xiushen jiaokeshu*, 34b–35a.

42. Li Jiagu, *Mengxue xiushen jiaokeshu*, 38a.

43. Ibid., 35b.

44. Liu Jianbai, *Xiaoxue xiushen jiaokeshu*, 46a.

45. Lewis, *Prologue to the Chinese Revolution*; a recent overview of the Hunan reform movement is Platt, *Provincial Patriots*, chap. 3.

46. YC, 1.

47. Yang Jing, "Daoyan" 導言, YC, 1–52. See also Ding Yajie, "*Yijiao congbian* de jingdianguan," 31–40; Zhang Jingping, "Cong *Yijiao congbian* kan Ye Dehui de xueshu sixiang"; and Cao Meixiu, "Zhu Yixin yu Kang Youwei." The reformist side of the Hunan conservatives is emphasized in Xiong Qiuliang, "'Yijiao' pai lüelun."

48. He Wenhui, "Shishi de jingying jiqi fankang." (Granted, Zhu Yixin was from Zhejiang, not Hunan, but Zhu had long been a critic of Kang, and his orthodox views suited Su Yu's needs.) For the background, see Hao Chang, "Intellectual Change and the Reform Movement, 1890–8," esp. 300–318; and Lewis, *Prologue to the Chinese Revolution*, 45–68.

49. The exception was Tan Sitong, discussed in the next chapter.

50. See Hirschman, *The Rhetoric of Reaction*.

51. See Hofstadter, *The Paranoid Style in American Politics and Other Essays*, 3–40.

52. YC, 1.

53. YC, 95. Intellectually honest, Ye did note the creation of the new *likin* tax.

54. YC, 13.

55. YC, 13–14.

56. YC, 69.

57. Luo Zhitian posits that Ye was ready to accept democracy as a long-term goal. This may be true but understates Ye's strong conservatism: his opposition to democracy for any kind of foreseeable future. Luo Zhitian, "Sixiang guannian yu shehui jiaose de cuowei," 61–62.

58. YC, 80.

59. YC, 178.

60. YC, 1. "Marking time from Confucius" refers to using a calendar that counted years from Confucius's birth, modeled on the West's Gregorian calendar, rather than dynasty-reign dating.

61. YC, 6–7.

62. YC, 11.

63. YC, 15.

64. YC, 9.

65. YC, 89, 75.

66. YC, 93.

67. YC, 52–53.

68. YC, 53.

69. YC, 55.

70. YC, 53.
71. YC, 54–56.
72. YC, 57–58.
73. YC, 59.
74. YC, 52–53.
75. YC, 30–31. That is, by speaking of knights-errant, extending democracy, establishing political groups, reforming institutions, and even wishing to abolish the rituals of kneeling and the written languages of Manchu and Chinese. The other conservatives discussed in this chapter were ethnically Han, while Wen Ti was a Manchu, but their views were indistinguishable.
76. YC, 80.
77. YC, 142.
78. YC, 13.
79. YC, 14.
80. YC, 96, 95.
81. YC, 178.
82. YC, 9.
83. YC, 11.
84. YC, 1.
85. YC, 1.
86. See, e.g., YC, 141.
87. YC, 144.
88. YC, 155–156.
89. YC, 25.
90. YC, 166. The most important part of the civil service examinations was a highly stylized essay of classical exegesis that was written in eight brief sections—hence called the "eight-legged essay." Reformers had long taken it to be a potent symbol of the reduction of Chinese culture to obscurantist rhetoric.
91. YC, 75.
92. YC, 95.
93. YC, 89.
94. YC, 98, 100–102.
95. Liu Dapeng, *Tuixiangzhai riji*, 144. For a lovely and convincing biography of Liu, see Harrison, *The Man Awakened from Dreams*.
96. Liu Dapeng, *Tuixiangzhai riji*, 74.
97. Ibid., 138.
98. Ibid., 153, 158.
99. Ibid., 130.
100. Enguang, *Qianyuntang riji* 潛雲堂日記, in Li Delong and Yu Bing, eds., *Lidai riji congchao*, 160:1–398.
101. Ibid., 160:134–147ff, 170–179ff.
102. Ibid., 160:190.
103. Ibid., 160:163–164.
104. Kang Youwei, "Kangzi neiwai pian," 1:166; *Analects* (Lunyu), 8:9.
105. Yan Fu, "Min ke shi you zhi buke shi zhi zhi jiangyi" 民可使由之不可使知之講義, *Kongjiaohui zazhi* (hereafter, KZ), 8:1, 5–9.
106. Thus Yan revealed something of a Daoist, rather than Confucian, attitude toward politics. On the question of Yan's "conservatism," see Max Ko-wu Huang, *The Meaning of Freedom*, 18–26.

107. Gugong bowuyuan Ming-Qing dang'anbu, ed., *Qingmo choubei lixian dang'an shiliao*. For the Qing court's moves toward a constitution, see Meienberger, *The Emergence of Constitutional Government in China (1905–1908)*; and Wu Jingxiong and Huang Gongjue, *Zhongguo zhixian shi*, 1–34.

108. See Wang Renbo, *Xianzheng wenhua yu jindai Zhongguo*; Chi Yunfei, "Qingji zhuzhang lixian de guanyuan dui xianzheng de tiren"; Sha Peide, "'Li yu jun, li yu min'"; and Zarrow, "Constitutionalism and the Imagination of the State."

109. Gugong bowuyuan Ming-Qing dang'anbu, ed., *Qingmo choubei lixian dang'an shiliao*, 1:44.

110. Sun Baoxuan, *Wangshanlu riji*, 2:914. Wu Yue (1878–1905) had attempted to assassinate the constitutional commissioners as they were leaving Beijing on their international inspection tours. He was promptly executed, but did delay the tours.

111. Chi Yunfei, "Qingji zhuzhang lixian de guanyuan dui xianzheng de tiren," 15–17.

112. Boli-Bennett, "The Ideology of Expanding State Authority in National Constitutions, 1870–1970"; Arjomand, "Constitutions and the Struggle for Political Order."

113. Or as Kang Youwei's disciple Mai Menghua had urged in the 1898 reform movement: legal reform and dissemination of the laws, local self-government, compulsory universal education, population registers, an efficient tax system, a meritocratic civil service, and a stable currency. Mai Menghua, "Lun Zhongguo yi zun junquan yi minquan" 論中國宜尊君權抑民權, in Jian Bozan et al., ed., *Wuxu bianfa*, 3:111–113.

CHAPTER 5

Earlier versions of portions of this chapter have been previously published as "Liang Qichao and the Conceptualization of 'Race' in Late Qing China," *Bulletin of the Institute of Modern History, Academia Sinica* 52 (June 2006), pp. 113–164; "Old Myth into New History: The Building Blocks of Liang Qichao's 'New History,'" *Historiography East and West*, vol. 1, no. 2 (December 2003), pp. 204–241; and "Historical Trauma: Anti-Manchuism and Memories of Atrocity in Late Qing China," *History and Memory*, vol. 16, no. 2 (Fall/Winter 2004), pp. 67–107.

1. A perennial problem of the agrarian empires and kingdoms of the "central plains"—around the Yellow, Huai, Han, Yangzi, and eventually Pearl Rivers—was threats from the nomads to the north. The term "Han" as a rough ethnic identifier of the peoples of the Central Plains was in use by the sixth century, but over the ensuing centuries it referred to many different peoples and was used by governing elites for various purposes. For the modernity of Han identity, see Leibold, *Reconfiguring Chinese Nationalism*; and Gladney, *Muslim Chinese*, esp. 81–87.

2. Lynch, "Woodrow Wilson and the Principle of 'National Self-Determination'"; Van Alstyne, "Woodrow Wilson and the Idea of the Nation State."

3. Hao Chang, *Chinese Intellectuals in Crisis*, 99–102. This valuable essay highlights Tan's relationship to the Chinese intellectual tradition; however, although I take Chang's point that Tan's vision of humanity was all-inclusive, I cannot agree with the blanket statement that "Tan was not a nationalist" (67)—rather, Tan combined national feelings with a recognition of the common humanity of all persons. See also Zhang Hao, *Lieshi jingshen yu pipan yishi*, 121–127.

4. In addition to the works cited in the note above, see Schäfer, "The People, People's Rights, and Rebellion"; Wang Yue, *Tan Sitong bianfa sixiang yanjiu*, esp. 69–102; and Sin-wai Chan, *Buddhism in Late Ch'ing Political Thought*.

5. Tan Sitong, *Tan Sitong quanji*, 2:337.

6. Ibid., 2:336; cf. Sin-wai Chan, trans., *An Exposition of Benevolence*, 146. Like Yan Fu, Tan criticized Han Yu's understanding of the emperorship.

7. Tan Sitong, *Tan Sitong quanji*, 2:337; cf. Sin-wai Chan, *An Exposition of Benevolence*, 151.

8. Tan Sitong, *Tan Sitong quanji*, 2:338–339; cf. Sin-wai Chan, *An Exposition of Benevolence*, 153–154.

9. For the trope of slavery and "lost country," see Karl, *Staging the World*.

10. Tan Sitong, *Tan Sitong quanji*, 2:348; cf. Sin-wai Chan, *An Exposition of Benevolence*, 173.

11. Williams, *Keywords*. The term for "people" or "nation" (*minzu*) was used in a more or less racial sense—that is, to delineate a group defined by quasi-biological or innate characteristics. See Dikötter, *The Discourse of Race in Modern China*.

12. Pusey, *China and Charles Darwin*; see also Karl, *Staging the World*. Liang Qichao's social Darwinism is well discussed by Hao Chang, *Liang Ch'i-ch'ao and Intellectual Transition in Modern China*, esp. chap. 6; and more recently by Price, "From Might to Right."

13. Whether premodern China (or premodern anybody) used racial categories is a controversial question that need not detain us here. I take "racial science" to be a modern phenomenon that emerged with the development of biology and anthropology (ethnology) as academic disciplines.

14. Crossley, *A Translucent Mirror*; for modern effects of Qing genealogical-racial categories, see 337–361.

15. Gang Zhao, "Reinventing *China*"; Perdue, *China Marches West*, 497–517.

16. Ishikawa Yoshihiro, "Xinhai geming shiqi de zhongzu zhuyi yu Zhongguo renleixue de xingqi"; idem, "Liang Qichao, the Field of Geography in Meiji Japan, and Geographical Determinism." For nuanced analysis of the major intellectual issues involved in racial thinking in modern China, see Lung-kee Sun, *The Chinese National Character*, 3–71; Yuehtsen Juliette Chung, *Struggle for National Survival*; Jing Tsu, *Failure, Nationalism, and Literature*; and Sakamoto Hiroko, "Chūgoku shijō no jinshu kannen o megutte."

17. Sakamoto Hiroko, *Chūgoku minzoku shugi no shinwa*, 28–59; Dikötter, *Discourse of Race in Modern China*, 52–56.

18. Ishikawa Yoshihiro, "Kindai Tō Ajia 'bunmeiken' no seiritsu to sono kyōdō gengo," 26–29.

19. "Ren fen wulei shuo" 人分五類說, *Gezhi huibian*, year 7 (fall), 9a–10b.

20. Ibid., 9b–10a. Ishikawa Yoshihiro argues that early examples of Western anthropological writings in Asia such as "Ren fen wulei shuo" presented Whites in the most favorable terms—see Ishikawa Yoshihiro, "Xinhai geming shiqi de zhongzu zhuyi yu Zhongguo renleixue de xingqi," 999–1000. There is some truth to this view, but in this particular article the main distinction implied is between Caucasians and Mongoloids on the one hand, and Malays, Africans, and Amerindians on the other.

21. Yan Fu, "Yuanqiang" 原強, in idem, *Yan Fu heji*, 1:40–41.

22. Zarrow, "Liang Qichao and the Conceptualization of 'Race' in Late Qing China." Chang P'eng-yuan links Liang's early anti-Manchuism equally to his racial thinking and his democratic thought—see Zhang Pengyuan, *Liang Qichao yu Qingji geming*, 66–104. Yang Suxian convincingly suggests that Liang's use of racial categories was layered on top of his early Datong thinking—see Yang Suxian, "Liang Qichao yu Zhongguo jindai minzu zhuyi." Ishikawa Yoshihiro usefully argues that "race," given scientific imprimatur, became central to Liang's views on history, especially after his exile in Japan and readings of Japanese authors on the subject; less convincing to me is the claim that race formed a "common lan-

guage" that lay at the base of an "East Asian 'cultural sphere,'" although certainly attempts to create such a sphere were made—see Ishikawa Yoshihiro, "Kindai Tō Ajia 'bunmeiken' no seiritsu to sono kyōdō gengo," 25–40.

23. Liang Qichao, "Chunqiu Zhongguo yidi bian xu" 春秋中國夷狄辨序, YBSHJ wenji 2:48–49; see also "Xinxue weijingkao xu" 新學偽經考敘, YBSHJ wenji 2:61–62.

24. Kang Youwei, *Datong shu*, 177–191; Yuehtsen Juliette Chung, *Struggle for National Survival*, 13–14; but see Emma Jinhua Teng, "Eurasian Hybridity in Chinese Utopian Visions."

25. Liang Qichao, "Lun bianfa bi zi ping Man Han zhi jie shi" 論變法必自平滿漢之界始, "Bianfa tongyi," YBSHJ wenji 1:77–83.

26. Liang Qichao, "Lun Zhongguo yu Ouzhou guoti yitong" 論中國與歐洲國體異同, YBSHJ wenji 4:61–67. Later, continuing to surf through the crashing waves of Western intellectual fashion, Liang emphasized the multiple origins of humanity.

27. Liang Qichao, "Zhongguo shi xulun" 中國史敘論, YBSHJ wenji 6:5–7.

28. Ibid., 6:5–7. Liang also stressed the multiracial nature in his "Lun Zhongguo xueshu sixiang bianqian zhi dashi" 論中國學術思想變遷之大勢, YBSHJ wenji 7:4.

29. Liang Qichao, "Lun bianfa bi zi ping Man Han zhi jie shi," YBSHJ wenji 1:77–83.

30. Rhoads, *Manchus and Han*, 3–6. James Pusey, *China and Charles Darwin*, 181–184, treats the essay as an opening salvo of anti-Manchuism, which was continued by the revolutionaries though not by Liang himself. I think the essay is better understood as a critique of Qing policies, though it clearly rested on Liang's adept use of the new racial knowledge. I thus am in basic agreement with Tao Xu's argument that the reformers were fixated on the need for national unity, and so argued for the equality of Manchus and Han. See Tao Xu, *Wan-Qing minzu zhuyi sichao*, 195–203.

31. Sakamoto Hiroko, "The Formation of National Identity in Liang Qichao and Its Relationship to Gender"; Ishikawa Yoshihiro, "Kindai Tō Ajia 'bunmeiken' no seiritsu to sono kyōdō gengo," 33–38; Jiang Jun, "Liang Qichao zaoqi shixue sixiang yu Futian Hemin de *Shixue tonglun*," 31.

32. Liang Qichao, *Xinminshuo*, YBSHJ zhuanji 4:7, 4:10–11.

33. Edward J. M. Rhoads argues that after the turn of the century, Qing leaders began to recognize the need to "equalize" Han and Manchus, abandoning the special privileges that Manchus possessed in law and custom. Yet they failed to pursue reform with sufficient vigor, and both privileges and mandatory markers of the conquest (such as the queue) were maintained. Rhoads, *Manchus and Han*, esp. 132–172. See also Chi Yunfei, "Qingmo zuihou shinian de ping-Man-Han zhenyu wenti."

34. Ishikawa Yoshihiro, "Xinhai geming shiqi de zhongzu zhuyi yu Zhongguo renleixue de xingqi," 2:998–1020; see also Leibold, *Reconfiguring Chinese Nationalism*.

35. The Qing court and provincial governments began sending students to Japan in 1901. More went on their own. The Japanese government was fairly tolerant of Chinese dissidents. Chinese students numbered some 25,000 between 1898 and 1911. Though most were on short-term study programs and had no particular political interests, some forty revolutionary groups were established in 1903–1904, often based on local and provincial ties. Zhang Yufa, *Qingji de geming tuanti*, 13–33; Reynolds, *China, 1898–1912*, 41–49. The topic of the Chinese students in Japan has attracted considerable scholarly interest. The classic study is Sanetō Keishū, *Chūgokujin Nihon ryūgakushi*; see also Harrell, *Sowing the Seeds of Change*; Huang Fuqing, *Qingmo liu Ri xuesheng*; and Shang Xiaoming, *Liuri xuesheng yu Qingmo xinzheng*.

36. Zou Rong, *Gemingjun* 革命軍; Lust, trans. and annot., *The Revolutionary Army*. For the estimate of twenty editions and one million copies, see Ke-wen Wang, ed., *Modern China*, 426.

37. Zou Rong, *Gemingjun*, 26–30; Lust, *Revolutionary Army*, 99–105. See Angle and Svensson, eds., *The Chinese Human Rights Reader*, 29–37; and Abe Ken'ichi, "Zou Rong de *Gemingjun* yu xiyang jindai sixiang."

38. Zou Rong, *Gemingjun*, 29; Angle and Svensson, eds., *Human Rights Reader*, 32–33.

39. Zou Rong, *Gemingjun*, 1, 4; Lust, *Revolutionary Army*, 58, 65.

40. Zou Rong, *Gemingjun*, 18; Lust, *Revolutionary Army*, 80.

41. Zou Rong, *Gemingjun*, 4, 5; Lust, *Revolutionary Army*, 56, 64.

42. Zou Rong, *Gemingjun*, 23, 24–29; Lust, *Revolutionary Army*, 101, 106–110.

43. Revolutionary leaders sometimes distinguished between the awfulness of Qing rulers and the ordinariness of most Manchu people. Sun Yat-sen once remarked, "We don't hate Manchus; we hate those Manchus who harm Han," and "Manchus who do not fight against the revolution will not be hurt"—"Zhonghua minguo wansui" 中華民國萬歲, *Minbao* 10:85. Zhang Kaiyuan argues that a more rationalistic nationalism appealed to educated social elements, while a more emotional nationalism appealed to the masses. This is not convincing, if only because of the clearly emotional elements mixed in with political and philosophical approaches in many highly literate pleas for nationalism (as we will see below). Zhang himself recognizes that rational and emotional appeals were, in practice, mixed. And this would seem to be precisely what allowed anti-Manchuism to play its ultimately positive role (in Zhang's judgment) in the creation of modern Chinese nationalism and, because of its emphasis on bottom-up change (revolution), in the creation of modern Chinese democracy as well. Zhang Kaiyuan, "Xinhai geming shiqi de shehui dongyuan"; and idem, "'Pai-Man' pingyi"; similar views are expressed in Jin Chongji, "Xinhai geming he Zhongguo jindai minzu zhuy"; and Tao Xu, *Wan-Qing minzu zhuyi sichao*, esp. 211–214.

44. Zhu Hongyuan, *Tongmenghui de geming lilun*, 66–68.

45. See, e.g., Ono Shinji, "Shingai kakumei to kakumei senden."

46. Maruyama Masayuki, *Chūgoku kindai no kakumei shisō*, 35–36. Western scholars have tended to take a basically similar position. See Gasster, *Chinese Intellectuals and the Revolution of 1911*, 69–100; Gasster is critical of "racial invective" for inflaming the political atmosphere so that "rational discussion became increasingly difficult" (99). Frank Dikötter has stated that anti-Manchuism was a minor strand compared to fears of the "white race"— *The Discourse of Race in Modern China*, 111–112. This might be true in terms of the overall context of racial thinking in the late Qing, but it is misleading insofar as anti-Manchuism, coupled with frequent and casual racial invective, became central to revolutionary propaganda (curiously, Dikötter fails to connect the construction of the so-called "Han race" with anti-Manchuism). See also Crossley, *Orphan Warriors*, 178–186.

47. The outstanding English-language study remains Gasster, *Chinese Intellectuals and the Revolution of 1911*; see also his "The Republican Revolutionary Movement (1900–13)."

48. Karl, *Staging the World*.

49. Liang doubtless reflected the value placed on unity in the Chinese tradition. See Yang Sixin, "Shilun chuantong 'dayitong' guannian dui Qingmo 'pai-Man' yundong de yingxiang," 160–161; and Gao Qiang and Liu Hailing, "Lun Liang Qichao de 'daminzu zhuyi,'" 76. However, Liang's concept of "great nationalism" also owed much to the West's science of race. Liang did not "transcend the stereotypes of the 'Chinese-barbarian dichotomy' and other ethnic views" (Yang Sixin, 161) so much as move them to the global level.

50. Liang Qichao, "Lun jinshi guomin jingzheng zhi dashi ji Zhongguo qiantu," YBSHJ wenji 4:56–61.

51. Liang Qichao, "Zhengzhi dajia Bolunzhili zhi xueshuo" 政治大家伯倫知理之學說, YBSHJ wenji 13:75–76.

52. Jiang Yi, "Junxian hu? Gonghe hu? Lun Yang Du zhengzhi sixiang de shanbian"; Zhou Xiaoxi and Xiao Honghua, "Lun Yang Du junzhu lixian sixiang." For Yang's life, see He Hanwen and Du Maizhi, *Yang Du zhuan*; Yang Yunhui, *Cong baohuanpai dao mimi dangyuan*; and Platt, *Provincial Patriots*, 130–131.

53. Yang Du, "*Zhongguo xinbao* xu"《中國新報》敘, in idem, *Yang Du ji*, 208–209.

54. Ibid., 210.

55. Yang Du, "Jintie zhuyi shuo" 金鐵主義說, in idem, *Yang Du ji*, 304.

56. Xu Nianci, ed., *Zhongguo dili*, 28a–29b.

57. Tu Ji, ed., *Zhongguo dili jiaokeshu*, 2:7–13.

58. Struve, trans. and ed., *Voices from the Ming-Qing Cataclysm*; and idem, "Confucian PTSD."

59. In psychoanalytical terms, trauma was experienced through secondary witnessing, or a process of transference that could probably only occur when a degree of traumatization was already present. See Zarrow, "Historical Trauma."

60. It is widely recognized that post-traumatic stress disorder (PTSD) is highly subjective, can occur long after the triggering events, and may even occur through "witnessing." See McNally, *Remembering Trauma*, 83–84, 87–89; McCann and Pearlman, "Vicarious Traumatization"; and Pillemer, "Can the Psychology of Memory Enrich Historical Analyses of Trauma?"

61. Excerpts from *Account of Ten Days At Yangzhou* [Wang Xiuchu 王秀楚, "Yangzhou shiri ji" 揚州十日記], in Struve, trans. and ed., *Voices from the Ming-Qing Cataclysm*, 36, 40, 43, 46–47.

62. Wu Lun Nixia, "Xianggang fan-Qing geming xuanchuan baokan jiqi yu Nanyang de lianxi," 418; Ding Wenjiang, ed., *Liang Rengong xiansheng nianpu changbian chugao*, 1:43.

63. Zou Rong, *Gemingjun*, 14–15; Lust, *Revolutionary Army*, 75–76.

64. For Sun's anti-Manchuism, see inter alia Guo Shiyou, "Sun Zhongshan de fan-Man minzu zhuyi sixiang bielun"; and He Lingxu, "Sun Zhongshan suo changdao de mizu zhuyi jiqi shixing zhengce de yanbian." More critical is Zhu Hongyuan, "Zailun Sun Zhongshan de minzu zhuyi." A balanced and well-written account of Sun's life is Bergère, *Sun Yat-sen*; see esp. 103–136.

65. Guo Shiyou, "Sun Zhongshan de fan-Man minzu zhuyi sixiang bielun," 43.

66. Sun Zhongshan [Sun Yat-sen], "Sanmin zhuyi yu Zhongguo minzu zhi qiantu" 三民主義與中國民族之前途, in idem, *Guofu quanji*, 3:18 (emphasis added).

67. Sun Zhongshan, "The True Solution of the Chinese Question," in ibid., 10:87–96 (quote 89).

68. Ziransheng 自然生, "Du yanna liuxuesheng miyu youfen" 讀嚴拿留學生密諭有憤, *Subao* 2846 (1903/6/10).

69. Fu Hanzhong zhe 復漢種者, "Xin guoshilüe" 新國史略, *Jiangsu*, 6 (1903.8.1), 54.

70. That is, using the same Chinese characters. For neo-traditionalist Japanese intellectuals of the 1890s, "national essence" meant something like national character and culture. *Kokusui* became associated with the notion of a unique Japanese polity (*kokutai*).

71. Tze-ki Hon, "National Essence, National Learning, and Culture." See also Zheng Shiqu, *Wan-Qing guocuipai*; Schneider, "National Essence and the New Intelligentsia"; and Tang Zhijun, *Jindai jingxue yu zhengzhi*, 316–325.

72. Liu Shipei, "Lun Kongzi wu gaizhi zhi shi" 論孔子無改制之事, published in GCXB year 2 [1906], nos. 11–12; see LSPQJ 3:194–217. Liu praised Confucius's scholarship but denied he was a religious figure—see "Lun Kongjiao yu Zhongguo zhengzhi wushe" 論孔教與中國政治無涉, LSPQJ 3:307–308.

73. For Zhang, representative monographs include Wang Fansen, *Zhang Taiyan de sixiang*; and Tang Zhijun, *Gailiang yu geming de Zhongguo qinghuai*. In English, see Laitinen, *Chinese Nationalism in the Late Qing Dynasty*; and Young-tsu Wong, *Search for Modern Nationalism*. A comparison between Kang and Zhang is offered in Wang Rongzu, *Kang Zhang helun*; and idem [Young-tsu Wong], *Beyond Confucian China*; and a recent analysis of the relationship between Zhang's understanding of Buddhism and his nationalism is Viren Murthy, *The Political Philosophy of Zhang Taiyan*.

74. Zhang Taiyan [Zhang Binglin], *Qiushu xiangzhu* 訄書詳注. The "qiu" of Zhang's title conveys a sense of compulsion, as well as oppression or persecution.

75. Zhang Taiyan [Zhang Binglin], "Kedi kuangmiu" 客帝匡謬, in *Qiushu xiangzhu*, 1–20.

76. Ibid., 19.

77. Zhang Taiyan [Zhang Binglin], "Zhu Man ge" 逐滿歌 (1906), in Tang Zhijun, ed., *Zhang Taiyan nianpu changbian*, 1:222.

78. Marking not the official fall of the Ming but the defeat of the last Ming remnant fighting in the south. See Feng Ziyou, *Geming yishi*, 1:57–59. Japanese authorities cancelled the meeting.

79. Cited in Young-tsu Wong's *Search for Modern Nationalism*, 61; Feng Ziyou, *Geming yishi*, 1:58.

80. Zhang Taiyan [Zhang Binglin], "Bo Kang Youwei lun geming shu" 駁康有為論革命書, in idem, *Zhang Taiyan quanji*, 4:173–184.

81. Ibid., 4:177.

82. Kang's historical references were to the fighting that occurred at the end of the Warring States period (4th and 3rd centuries BC) and the Qin dynasty (221–206 BC); his point was that earlier political loyalties (or identities) had been superseded by a higher level of unity.

83. Zhang Taiyan [Zhang Binglin], "Bo Kang Youwei lun geming shu," in idem, *Zhang Taiyan quanji*, 4:177.

84. Zhang Taiyan [Zhang Binglin], "Pai-Man pingyi" 排滿平議, in ibid., 4:267–269.

85. See Wang Fansen, *Zhang Taiyan de sixiang*, 68–72, 84–90; also idem, "Qingmo de lishi jiyi yu guojia jiango."

86. Liang Qichao, "Zhongguo shi xulun," YBSHJ wenji 6:1–12; and "Xin shixue" 新史學, YBSHJ wenji 9:1–32. Recent studies have emphasized the pivotal importance of these essays, although Liang was far from alone in his views. See inter alia Xu Guansan, *Xin shixue jiushinian, 1900–*; Chen Feng, "Bumou er he"; Huang Minlan, "Liang Qichao 'Xin shixue' de zhenshi yiyi ji lishixue de wujie"; Wang Yeyang, "Kang-Liang yu shixue zhiyong," 204–218; Duara, *Rescuing History from the Nation*; Xiaobing Tang, *Global Space and the Nationalist Discourse of Modernity*; Wang Fansen, "Wan-Qing de zhengzhi gainian yu 'Xin shixue'"; and Zarrow, "Old Myth into New History."

87. Liang Qichao, "Yao Shun wei Zhongguo zhongyang junquan lanshang kao" 堯舜為中國中央君權濫觴考, YBSHJ wenji 6:22–27.

88. In another essay from this period, Liang described three stages of human progress as: first, tribal chiefs loosely holding individuals together; second, great clans in control of government, their upper levels choosing the king and their lower levels managing the populace; and third, centralized power gradually consolidated under a strong king. The dynamic behind the transitions was outside threat and struggle. Liang Qichao, "Zhongguo shi xulun," YBSHJ wenji 6:1–12.

89. Liang Qichao, "Lun Zhongguo yu Ouzhou guoti yitong," YBSHJ wenji 4:61–67; "Zhongguo zhuanzhi zhengzhi jinhua shilun" 中國專制政治進化史論, YBSHJ wenji 9:59–90.

90. Liang Qichao, "Lun Zhongguo jiruo youyu fangbi," YBSHJ wenji 1:96–100.

91. Liang Qichao, "Zhongguo shi xulun," YBSHJ wenji 6:11; cf. Xiaobing Tang, *Global Space and the Nationalist Discourse of Modernity*, 38.

92. Liang Qichao, "Lun junzheng minzheng xiangshang zhi li," YBSHJ wenji 2:8–9.

93. Liang Qichao, "Xin shixue," YBSHJ wenji 9:1–32.

94. Ibid., 9:1.

95. Liang Qichao, "Shaonian Zhongguo" 少年中國, YBSHJ wenji 5:9. See Chapter 2.

96. Liang Qichao, "Lun Zhongguo yu Ouzhou guoti yitong," YBSHJ wenji 4:63–65.

97. Ibid., 4:66–67. Even in his article on "New Historiography," which stressed the theme of progress, Liang continued to excoriate Chinese kings for "privatizing" the empire, their actions legitimated by false theories of the scholars. Liang Qichao, "Xin shixue," YBSHJ wenji 9:20; see also "Shaonian Zhongguo," YBSHJ wenji 5:9–10.

98. Liang Qichao, "Shaonian Zhongguo," YBSHJ wenji 5:7–12.

99. Liu Shipei, "Huangdi jinian shuo" 黃帝紀年說, LSPQJ 3:467–468.

100. See Shen Songqiao, "Wo yi woxie jian Xuanyuan"; Wang Mingke, "Lun Panfu"; Luo Zhitian, "Baorong ruxue, zhuzi yu Huangdi de guoxue"; Sun Longji [Lung-kee Sun], "Qingji minzu zhuyi yu Huangdi chongbai zhi faming"; Ishikawa Yoshihiro, "20 shiji chunian Zhongguo liu Ri xuesheng 'Huangdi' zhi zaizao"; and Matten, *Die Grenzen des Chinesischen*.

101. Although the theory of descent from the Yellow Emperor was in accord with the traditional ethnocentrism of the seventeenth-century scholar Wang Fuzhi, whom Liu greatly admired, Liu's notions differed from Wang's in several respects. In particular, Liu did not possess Wang's respect for the institution of the monarchy; one of Wang's chief concerns had been to relate descent to the orthodox transmission of the Way and the succession of political authority, a question of no interest to Liu.

102. The general background and appeal of this theory is examined in Tze-ki Hon, "From a Hierarchy in Time to a Hierarchy in Space."

103. The Western origins theory also influenced Japanese historians who provided a model for modern history writing. See Shirakawa Jirō and Kunibu Tanenori, *Shina bunmei shi* (1900; published also in Shanghai in 1903 by the Jinghua shuju), 4, 28–68.

104. Liu Shipei, *Rangshu* 攘書, LSPQJ 2:1–17.

105. Ibid., 2:2.

106. Co-authored with the radical journalist Lin Xie (1874–1926), *Zhongguo minyue jingyi* 中國民約精義, LSPQJ 1:597–626. For discussions of *A Book of Expulsion* (Rangshu) and *Essence of the Social Contract in China* (Zhongguo minyue jingyi), see Bernal, "Liu Shih-p'ei and National Essence," 92–99; Mori Tokihiko, "Minzokushugi to museifushugi"; Onogawa Hidemi, "Ryū Shibai to museifushugi"; and Fang-yen Yang, "Nation, People, Anarchy," 196–227ff.

107. Liu Shipei, *Zhongguo minyue jingyi*, LSPQJ 1:562. Cf. Fang-yen Yang, "Nation, People, Anarchy," 199.

108. Liu Shipei, "Guxue qiyuan lun" 古學起原論, part 1, GCXB year 1, no. 8, 1a.

109. Ibid., 2a–3b.

110. Liu Shipei, "Zhengfaxue shixu" 政法學史敘, GCXB year 1, no. 2.

111. Ibid., 1b, 4a.

112. Originally published in the *National Essence Journal* under the title "The Origins of Ancient Political Formations"—Liu Shipei, "Guzheng yuanshi lun" 古政原始論 (reprinted in LSPQJ 2:34–57).

113. Ibid., GCXB year 1, no. 4, 1b.

114. Ibid., no. 4, 2a. Much the same story, sometimes in the same words, is told in "Zhongguo minzu zhi" 中國民族志, where the Yellow Emperor is labeled the "foundational

ancestor" of the Chinese people: LSPQJ 1:600; and *Zhongguo lishi jiaokeshu* 中國歷史教
科書, LSPQJ 4:276–281.

115. In the fifth essay in the series, Liu more specifically traced agriculture to Shennong
(Divine Farmer), who led the people in giving up nomadism and settling down to farming by
teaching them to burn down the forests to open up new fields, to use fertilizers, to leave fields
fallow, and to practice crop rotation. See "Guzheng yuanshi lun," GCXB year 1, no. 6, 1a–2a.

116. Ibid., no. 4, 3b.

117. In the seventh essay of the series—ibid., no. 6, 6a.

118. Ibid., no. 6, 9b.

119. Ibid., no. 8, 1a.

120. Ibid., no. 8, 3b.

121. Liu's argument from the various terms used for "ruler" directly related his philological
analysis to his historical conclusions; see ibid., no. 4, 4b–5a.

122. Ibid., no. 4, 7a.

123. Ibid., no. 4, 7b–8a.

124. Ibid., no. 4, 10b.

125. Ibid., no. 4, 11a.

126. Ibid., no. 6, 3a.

127. Ibid., no. 6, 2b.

128. Ibid., no. 6, 3a. Other intellectuals understood the well-field system as a type of
socialism (discussed in Chapter 6).

129. See Zarrow, *Anarchism and Chinese Political Culture*, 83–96, 100–114.

130. Zarrow, "The New Schools and National Identity."

131. Qian Zonghan, *Huitu Zhongguo baihua shi*, 1a.

132. Yao Zuyi, *Zuixin gaodeng xiaoxue Zhongguo lishi jiaokeshu*, 1:1a. Again, Yao was
not denying the fact of periods of political disunity but assuming that unity was the normative
condition, a condition maintained at the cultural level regardless of political disruptions.

133. Ibid., 1:2b–3a.

134. Ding Baoshu, *Mengxue Zhongguo lishi jiaokeshu*, 1a–2a.

CHAPTER 6

1. As scholarly consensus has long recognized. See Xiong Yuezhi, *Zhongguo jindai
minzhu sixiangshi*, chap. 7; and Gasster, *Chinese Intellectuals and the Revolution of 1911*, esp.
chaps. 3–4, and his "The Republican Revolutionary Movement (1900–13)," esp. 490–499.

2. Edmund S. K. Fung, *The Military Dimension of the Chinese Revolution*; Esherick,
Reform and Revolution in China; McCord, *The Power of the Gun*, chaps. 1–2.

3. The most comprehensive overview of revolutionary activities remains Zhang Yufa,
Qingji de geming tuanti.

4. Zhang Taiyan [Zhang Binglin], "Bo Kang Youwei lun geming shu," *Zhang Taiyan
quanji*, 4:173–184. I am grateful to Young-tsu Wong for helping me read Zhang's letter.

5. A comprehensive discussion of the founding of the Tongmenghui is Bergère, *Sun
Yat-sen*, chap. 4.

6. Taiyan 太炎 [Zhang Binglin], "Zhonghua minguo jie" 中華民國解, *Minbao* 15
(1907.7.5), 1–17.

7. Taiyan [Zhang Binglin], "Yanshuolu" 演說錄, *Minbao* 6 (1907.1.10), 11–12.

8. Ibid., 9–15.

9. Ibid., 6–9.

10. Ibid., 4–6.

11. Taiyan, "Daiyi ranfou lun" 代議然否論, *Minbao* 14 (1908.10.10), 1–27; and "Zhonghua minguo jie," 11–13. The latter essay is entitled "Gloss on the Republic of China," but it is not entirely clear that Zhang's "Republic" (*minguo*) refers to a republican polity at all, though this had already become an accepted meaning of the term; Zhang's interest lay in the evolution of the Chinese nation, not the state, and he may have used *minguo* to simply refer to the "restoration" of China to its people.

12. "Wuwulun" 五無論, *Minbao* 16 (1907.7.25), 1–22. *Wu*, while conveying "negation" as here translated, was also redolent of the Buddhist notion of "emptiness," suggesting that Zhang was discussing illusions. The essay challenged political theorizing as such. Zhang began by insisting that the state lacked self-nature (*zixing*), or any essential reality. See also Taiyan [Zhang Binglin], "Guojia lun" 國家論 *Minbao* 17 (1907.10.24), 1. As Wang Hui points out, Zhang was concerned with "sovereignty" as a racial and cultural property of the nation, not the territorial state. Wang Hui, "Zhang Taiyan's Concept of the Individual and Modern Chinese Identity," 243–244. However, I cannot agree that Zhang's notion of national sovereignty "was completely racial, not political"—not only did Zhang advocate collective public action but, even while attacking statism, inevitably considered the institutions of collective life precisely to the degree that he accepted the nation.

13. See Zarrow, *Anarchism and Chinese Political Culture*, 182–185.

14. Taiyan [Zhang Binglin], "Zhengwen sheyuan dahui pohuaizhuang" 政聞社員大會破壞狀, *Minbao* 17 (1907.10.24), 2–3; idem, "Daiyi renfou lun" 代議然否論, *Minbao* 24 (1908.10.10), 1.

15. Taiyan, "Zhengwen sheyuan dahui pohuaizhuang," *Minbao* 17 (1907.10.25), 7.

16. Juan Wang, "Imagining Citizenship," 45–47.

17. Jisheng [Wang Dong], "Lun Zhina lixian bi xianyi geming" 論支那立憲必先以革命, *Minbao* 2 (1905.11.26), 1–10.

18. Hanmin [Hu Hanmin], "*Minbao* zhi liu da zhuyi" 民報之六大主義, *Minbao* 3 (1906.4.15), 10.

19. Taiyan, "Daiyi renfou lun," *Minbao* 24 (1908.10.15), 1.

20. Hanmin, "*Minbao* zhi liu da zhuyi," *Minbao* 3 (1906.4.15), 11.

21. Ibid., 9.

22. Jingwei 精衛 [Wang Jingwei], "Bo *Xinmin congbao* zuijin zhi feigeming lun" 駁新民叢報最近之非革命論, *Minbao* 4 (1906.4.28), 1–44; idem, "Zaibo *Xinmin congbao* zuijin zhi feigeming lun" 再駁新民叢報最近之非革命論, *Minbao* 6 (1906.8.23), 79–98; idem, "Zaibo *Xinmin congbao* zhi zhengzhi geming lun" 再駁新民叢報之政治革命論, *Minbao* 7 (1906.9.5), 33–62. For Liang's "enlightened despotism," see Chapter 3.

23. Nor in Wang's view would it lead, as Liang feared, to the foreign conquest of China. Wang essentially argued that revolution (and only revolution) would produce a strong and stable government that could resist further encroachments. See Jingwei [Wang Jingwei], "Bo geming keyi zhao guafen shuo" 駁革命可以召瓜分說, *Minbao* 6 (1906.8.23), 17–39.

24. Jingwei, "Bo *Xinmin congbao* zuijin zhi feigeming lun," 12–14.

25. Ibid., 29–30.

26. Ibid., 31–32.

27. Jingwei, "Zaibo *Xinmin congbao* zhi zhengzhi geming lun," 44.

28. Ibid., 45–48.

29. Jingwei, "Bo *Xinmin congbao* zuijin zhi feigeming lun," 8. See Chapter 3 for the origins of this kind of language.

30. Jingwei, "Zaibo *Xinmin congbao* zhi zhengzhi geming lun," 38–39.

31. Jingwei, "Bo *Xinmin congbao* zuijin zhi feigeming lun," 9, 38.

32. Ibid., 10–11.

33. Jingwei, "Zaibo *Xinmin congbao* zuijin zhi feigeming lun," 89.

34. Ibid., 97.

35. Ibid., 84.

36. Jingwei, "Zaibo *Xinmin congbao* zhi zhengzhi geming lun," 33–37. Wang denied that separation of powers represented a threat to the sovereignty of the state (*guoquan*), arguing that it merely divided the officials who were exercising that sovereignty (i.e., the powers of the state). Ibid., 38–40.

37. For background to the German debates, see Koskenniemi, *The Gentle Civilizer of Nations*, chap. 3; and Kelly, "Revisiting the Rights of Man."

38. Jingwei, "Bo *Xinmin congbao* zuijin zhi feigeming lun," 39–43. (Nor did Wang think much of Liang's Japanese.)

39. Song Jiaoren, *Wo zhi lishi* (hereafter, WLS). References below will be to diary entry date (year.month.day), and original juan and page number. Song Jiaoren kept a diary covering his experiences in Japan from his arrival to 1907. An abridged edition was published in 1919, after his death, and we may assume he did not write it for publication. Song recorded his emotional ups and downs, as well as occasional thoughts. The standard biography remains K. S. Liew, *Struggle for Democracy*; see also Price, "Escape from Disillusionment"; and idem, "Constitutional Alternative and Democracy in the Revolution of 1911."

40. Jing Tsu, *Failure, Nationalism, and Literature.*

41. Haiyan Lee, "All the Feelings That Are Fit to Print."

42. Fitzgerald, "Nationalism, Democracy, and Dignity in Twentieth-Century China."

43. WLS 1905.9.13, 2:35b.

44. WLS 1906.3.14, 3:20a–20b.

45. WLS 1906.8.20, 4:13a.

46. WLS 1906.9.26, 4:35b.

47. WLS 1906.10.1, 5:1.

48. WLS 1906.10.5, 5:3b.

49. A popular novel telling the stories of a brotherhood of outlaws; variously translated under the titles *The Water Margin, Outlaws of the Marsh, All Men Are Brothers*, and *The Marshes of Mount Liang.*

50. Song variously noted that he was reading *Shuihu zhuan* (WLS 1904.11.3, 1:6b) and later that he was moved to tears by the heroic sacrifices of Wu Yue and Chen Tianhua (WLS 1906.9.6, 4:24a).

51. WLS 1904.10.4–5, 1:2b–3a.

52. WLS 1904.9.9, 1:3b–4a, 6–7; 1904.11.3, 1:6b.

53. WLS 1905.1.1, 2:1a.

54. WLS 1905.1.15, 2:2b–3a.

55. WLS 1906.8.16, 4:12a–b.

56. WLS 1906.1.11, 3:3a. Xue Jingxuan (1389–1464) was a leading scholar of the early Ming period and a follower of Cheng-Zhu orthodoxy. The *Mingru xue'an* was Huang Zongxi's biographically based intellectual history of the Ming period.

57. WLS 1906.1.22–27, 3:5a–6b. The *Chuanxilu* consisted of Wang Yangming's instructions to his students and constituted a summary of his "learning of the heart-and-mind" (*xinxue*).

58. WLS 1905.9.9, 2:34b–35a.

59. WLS 1906.2.13, 3:11a–b.

60. WLS 1906.3.26, 3:23b–24a.

61. WLS 1906.2.14–18, 3:11b–12b.

62. WLS 1906.2.21, 3:13a–b.

63. WLS 1906.5.21, 3:32b.

64. Song's complicated and agonizing conflict with his personal friend Li Hesheng may have been a major factor precipitating his hospitalization—see various references from WLS, March and June–August 1906.

65. Liang had fallen in love with a Chinese American he met in Hawaii in 1900: Ding Wenjiang, ed., *Liang Rengong xiansheng nianpu changbian chugao*, 136. In Song's case, his love for a Japanese woman may have been a factor precipitating his hospitalization: WLS 1906.3.14, 3:20a–b; WLS 1906.3.26, 3:23b; see also 1906.3.19, 3:21b–22a.

66. For a more detailed examination of this topic, see Zarrow, "Anti-Despotism and 'Rights Talk.'"

67. Zou Rong, *Gemingjun*, 29; see Angle and Svensson, eds., *The Chinese Human Rights Reader*, 32–33.

68. "Shuo guomin" 說國民, XG 1A:72–77; see also Angle and Svensson, eds., *The Chinese Human Rights Reader*, 3–5.

69. "Shuo guomin," XG 1A:72–73; cf. Angle and Svensson, *Chinese Human Rights Reader*, 3.

70. "Shuo guomin," XG 1A:73; cf. Angle and Svensson, *Chinese Human Rights Reader*, 4.

71. "Shuo guomin," XG 1A:76.

72. See Fang-yen Yang, "Nation, People, Anarchy," 233–249; Zarrow, "Citizenship and Human Rights in Early Twentieth-Century Chinese Thought," 213–218; and the excellent treatment in Angle, *Human Rights and Chinese Thought*, 162–175.

73. Liu Shipei, *Lunli jiaokeshu* 倫理教科書, LSPQJ 4:123–170.

74. Liu Shipei, *Zhongguo minyue jingyi*, LSPQJ 1:566.

75. Liu Shipei, *Lunli jiaokeshu*, LSPQJ 4:137 (28a).

76. Liu Shipei, "Wuzhengfu zhuyi zhi pingdeng guan" 無政府主義之平等觀, XG 2B:918. See Ishikawa Hiroshi, "Byōdō to shittoshin."

77. Shenshu 申叔 [Liu Shipei], "Renlei junli shuo" 人類均力說, *Tianyi bao* 3 (1907.7.10), 24–36.

78. Ibid., 30.

79. "Quanli pian" 權利篇, XG 1A:479–484 (orig. in *Zhishuo* 直說, no. 2, 3/1903). The entire essay is translated in Angle and Svensson, eds., *The Chinese Human Rights Reader*, 15–23. *Zhishuo* was a short-lived journal founded in Japan by students from Zhili at the height of the anti-Russian movement of 1903. See Wang Xiaoqiu, "*Zhishuo*."

80. Yang Tingdong, *Falüxue*, 60–61. See Chapter 3 above.

81. Liang Qichao, "Lun quanli sixiang," YBSHJ zhuanji 4:31–40; see also Angle and Svensson, eds., *The Chinese Human Rights Reader*, 5–15. In taking "sixiang" to refer to a generalized consciousness, I follow Angle, *Human Rights and Chinese Thought*, 141–162.

82. Angle, *Human Rights and Chinese Thought*, 150–157.

83. Liang Qichao, "Lun quanli sixiang," YBSHJ zhuanji 4:38–39; cf. Angle and Svensson, eds., *The Chinese Human Rights Reader*, 13.

84. Jiang Yihua, ed., *Shehui zhuyi xueshuo zai Zhongguo de chuqi chuanbo*.

85. Bernal, *Chinese Socialism to 1907*, 94–99; Yu-ning Li, *The Introduction of Socialism into China*, 12–13.

86. See Fan-shen Wang, "Evolving Prescriptions for Social Life in the Late Qing and Early Republic"; and Michael Tsin, "Imagining 'Society' in Early Twentieth-Century China."

87. Dirlik, "Socialism and Capitalism in Chinese Socialist Thinking: The Origins," in

his *Marxism in the Chinese Revolution*, 17–44; Scalapino and Schiffrin, "Early Socialist Currents in the Chinese Revolutionary Movement."

88. Yan Fu, "Yuanqiang," *Yan Fu heji*, 1:59.

89. Hanmin, "*Minbao* zhi liu da zhuyi," 11–14.

90. See, e.g., Ziyou 自由 [Feng Ziyou 馮自由], "Lu *Zhongguo ribao* minsheng zhuyi yu Zhongguo zhengzhi geming zhi qiantu" 錄中國日報民生主義與中國政治革命之前途, *Minbao* 4 (1906.4.28), 97–122. See also the discussion in Bergère, *Sun Yat-sen*, 167–172.

91. Hanmin, "*Minbao* zhi liu da zhuyi," 12.

92. Xianjie 縣解 [Zhu Zhixin], "Lun shehui geming dang yu zhengzhi geming bingxing" 論社會革命當與政治革命並行, *Minbao* 5 (1906.6.26), 43–66.

93. See for example Liang Qichao, "Bo moubao zhi tudiguoyou lun" 駁某報之土地國有論, YBSHJ wenji 18:1–59; and idem, "Damoubao disihao duiyu *Xinmin congbao* zhi bolun" 答某報第四號對於新民叢報之駁論, YBSHJ wenji 18:59–131.

94. Liang Qichao, "Ganshe yu fangren" 干涉與放任, YBSHJ zhuanji 2:86–87.

95. Xianjie, "Lun shehui geming dang yu zhengzhi geming bingxing," 43.

96. Ibid., 45.

97. Ibid., 59.

98. Xianjie, "Tudi guoyou yu caizheng" 土地國有與財政, *Minbao* 15 (1907.7.5), 67–99; 16 (1907.9.25), 33–71.

99. Taiyan, "Yanshuolu," 12.

100. See Zarrow, *Anarchism and Chinese Political Culture*, chap. 5.

101. Zhen Zhen 震 and Shenshu, "Lun zhongzu geming yu wuzhengfu geming zhi deshi" 論種族革命與無政府革命之得失, *Tianyibao* 6 (1907.9.1), 139.

102. Sun Yat-sen, *Guofu quanji*, 3:9–10.

103. Juan Wang, "Officialdom Unmasked"; idem, "Imagining Citizenship," 29–53.

104. David Der-wei Wang, *Fin-de-Siècle Splendor*, chaps. 2–3, 5.

105. Cited in Juan Wang, "Officialdom Unmasked," 101.

106. As Juan Wang suggests, "In Chinese political culture, where a regime's mandate to rule relies on its moral authority, and where officials were thought to be more important than political institutions, public perceptions of moral degradation would corrode a regime's power." Ibid., 112.

107. Cheng-hua Wang, "The Photographed Images of the Empress Dowager Cixi, *ca.* 1904."

108. "Liang Qichao telai duansong" 梁啟超特來斷送, *Minlibao* 1911.11.16, 3.

109. Esherick, *Reform and Revolution in China*; Rhoads, *Manchus and Han*, chaps. 3–4; Rankin, "Nationalistic Contestation and Mobilization Politics"; Danke Li, "Popular Culture in the Making of Anti-Imperialist and Nationalist Sentiments in Sichuan."

110. Rhoads, *Manchus and Han*, 187–205; Rhoads calls the slaughter "essentially genocide" (204), but does not attempt to estimate the total number killed.

111. Ibid., 189–191.

CHAPTER 7

1. "Teyue lutoudian" 特約路透電, *Minlibao* 1912.10.12, 5509; "Guoqing shengzhong zhi Beijing" 國慶聲中之北京, *Minlibao* 1912.10.14, 5528; "Jinianri zhong zhi jinianri" 紀念日中之紀念日, *Minlibao* 1912.10.18, 5564.

2. "Nanjing guoqing jinianhui zhi jingkuang" 南京國慶紀念會之景況, *Shibao* 1912.10.13, 3; *Minlibao* 1912.10.18, 5564.

3. "Beijing zhuandian" 北京專電, *Minlibao* 1912.10.12, 5526.

4. Judge, "Citizens or Mothers of Citizens?" The first Nanjing assembly and later

Beijing parliaments refused to grant women suffrage—see Edwards, *Gender, Politics, and Democracy*. Although monarchism, the symbiotic twin of patriarchy, had collapsed, the latter survived for the time being, bloodied but unbending.

5. Mouzi 繆子, "Wo suojingguo zhi yida shuangshijie" 我所經過之一打雙十節, *Shenbao* 1924.10.10, 206/663.

6. The literature is extensive. See inter alia Gillis, ed., *Commemorations*; Stråth, ed., *Myth and Memory in the Construction of Community*; and Spillman, *Nation and Commemoration*. The founding studies in this subfield are Anderson, *Imagined Communities*; and Hobsbawm and Ranger, eds., *The Invention of Tradition*. Studies of national rituals moving beyond commemoration include Wilentz, ed., *Rites of Power*; Ozouf, *Festivals and the French Revolution*; and Agulhon, *Marianne into Battle*.

7. As we will see in detail below. See Bell, *Ritual Theory, Ritual Practice*.

8. The premier study of political ritual in this period is Harrison, *The Making of the Republican Citizen*. Harrison emphasizes the links between modern citizenship and national identity as mediated ritually. Relevant studies in Chinese include Chen Hengming, *Zhonghua minguo zhengzhi fuhao zhi yanjiu*; Liu Shichang, "Zhonghua minguo guoqingjie zhi zhiding yu diyige guoqingri zhi jinian"; Zhou Kaiqing, "Guoqing jinianri de youlai," in idem, *Xinzhiji*, 59–72; Wang Gengsheng, *Women de guoqi*; and Sun Zhendong, *Guoqi guoge guohua shihua*.

9. Remembrance was also featured in new postage stamps issued in December 1912, on which was printed: "In Commemoration of the Revolution" in English and "In Commemoration of the Restoration of the Republic of China" in Chinese ("Zhonghua minguo guangfu jinian"). Yu-Chin Huang, "National Identity and Ideology in the Design of Postage Stamps of China and Taiwan, 1949–1979," 16–17. The Qing had established a postal service in the 1880s, and its first stamps featured a dragon motif.

10. Liu Shichang, "Zhonghua minguo guoqingjie," 114.

11. "Wan yuan jinianhui zhi sheng" 皖垣紀念會誌盛, *Shibao* 1912.10.5, 4.

12. See, e.g., "Choubei jinianhui shouxu" 籌備紀念會手續, *Minlibao* 1912.9.24, 5357; "Jinianhui zhi yubei" 紀念會之預備, *Minlibao* 1912.10.2, 5430; Liu Shichang, "Zhonghua minguo guoqingjie," 119.

13. "Zhonghua minguo zhi guoqingri yu jinianri" 中華民國之國慶日與紀念日, *Shibao* 1912.9.24, 3.

14. "Xianyihui jianwenlu" 縣議會見聞錄, *Shibao* 1912.10.5; *Minlibao* 1912.10.5, 5458.

15. "Shanghai guangfu zhi jinianri jinyi" 上海光復之紀念日近矣, *Minlibao* 1912.10.20, 5584; "Difang jinian zhi yishi" 地方紀念之儀式, *Minlibao* 1912.10.25, 5626.

16. "Xin Ningbo zhi jinianri" 新寧波之紀念日, *Minlibao* 1912.10.27, 5646; "Nanjing dianbao" 南京電報, *Minlibao* 1912.10.28, 5652. The Huanghuagang Uprising in Guangzhou was the last of a series of failed uprisings organized by Sun Yat-sen.

17. "Teyue lutoudian," *Minlibao* 1912.10.12, 5509.

18. Liu Shichang, "Zhonghua minguo guoqingjie," 114. In late September, even as they moved to make the Wuchang Uprising anniversary the new national day (on the solar October 10), the assembly also approved Li's request for the dispatch of representatives to Wuchang (for the lunar 19th day of the 8th month). See *Minlibao* 1912.9.25, 5365.

19. "Geming jinianhui faqi yiqushu" 革命紀念會發起意趣書, *Minlibao* 1912.9.12, 5253. The association was formed by Sun Yat-sen and Huang Xing, according to Gao Lao 高勞, "Zhonghua minguo diyijie guoqing jishi" 中華民國第一屆國慶紀事, *Dongfang zazhi* 9.6 (1912.12.2), 5; Liu Shichang, "Zhonghua minguo guoqingjie," 118. By Double Ten, this organization had become the Republican Commemorative Association (Gonghe jinianhui).

20. "Da kewen: geming jinianyue yingyou zhi shengkuang" 答客問：革命紀念月應

有之盛況, *Minlibao* 1912.9.22–23, 5343, 5352; Wu's speech is reprinted in Liu Shichang, "Zhonghua minguo guoqingjie," 115–116. Wu (1865–1953) was an anarchist, but he was close to Sun Yat-sen and later supported Chiang Kai-shek.

21. "Nanjing dianbao," *Minlibao* 1912.10.3, 5436; "Gesheng guoqingri zhi jingxiang" 各省國慶日之景象, *Minlibao* 1912.10.10, 5502.

22. "Guoqing jinianri zhi Shanghai" 國慶紀念日之上海, *Shibao* 1912.10.12; "Minguo diyi guoqingji" 民國第一國慶紀, *Minlibao* 1912.10.12, 5512; "Shuangshijie zhi Nanjing" 雙十節之南京, *Minlibao* 1912.10.12, 5510; "Wuchang qiyi zhounian jinianhui zhi yugao" 武昌起義周年紀念會之預告, *Shibao* 1912.10.19.

23. "Zhuidao zhi zhi xu" 追悼之之序, *Shibao* 1912.10.6; "Guoqingri zhuiji zhu lieshi lijie" 國慶日追祭諸士禮節, *Shibao* 1912.10.12.

24. "Guoqingri daoji zhu lieshi lijie" 國慶日道祭諸烈士禮節, *Shibao* 1912.10.12, 4. See also "Guoqingjie buzhi qingxing" 國慶節布置情形, *Minlibao* 1912.10.7, 5475; "Beijing dianbao" 北京電報, *Minlibao* 1912.10.3, 5436; and "Beijing dianbao," *Minlibao* 1912.10.12, 5508. Offerings of flowers and fruits were generally given gods, not family ancestors, who received full meals.

25. "Gongjie zhi zhudian" 工界之祝典, *Minlibao* 1912.10.10, 5503.

26. "Yuyan zhudian" 預言祝典, *Minlibao* 1912.10.5, 5453.

27. "Guoqing yuebing dadian yuzhi" 國慶閱兵大典預誌, *Shengjing shibao* 1916.10.10, 35/172.

28. "Erbaiwan yuan zhi guoqing jingfei" 二百萬元之國慶經費, *Shengjing shibao* 1916.10.20, 35/212.

29. "Wuzhou guoqing zhisheng" 五周國慶誌盛, *Shengjing shibao* 1916.10.10, 35/180.

30. "Yuzhi guoqing jinian zhi shengkuang" 預誌國慶紀念之盛況, *Shenbao* 1916.10.3, 142/548; "Guoqing jinian zhi yubei" 國慶紀念之預備, *Shenbao* 1916.10.4, 142/5566; 1916.10.7, 142/617; 1916.10.7, 142/620.

31. Harrison, *The Making of the Republican Citizen*, 95.

32. See Yung, Rawski, and Watson, eds., *Harmony and Counterpoint*; and Joseph S. C. Lam, *State Sacrifices and Music in Ming China*.

33. Wang Gengsheng, *Women de guoge*, 11.

34. Ye and Eccles, "Anthem for a Dying Dynasty." See also Pi Houfeng, "Zhongguo jindai guoge kaoshu."

35. *Linshi zhengfu gongbao* 8 (1912.22.5), 164.

36. "Guoge nigao" 國歌擬稿, *Linshi zhengfu gongbao* 22 (1912.2.25), advertising supplement.

37. See Pi Houfeng, "Zhongguo jindai guoge kaoshu," 264.

38. "Zhonghua minguo liguo jinian'ge"; music by Zou Huamin: see Wang Gengsheng, *Women de guoge*, 13; and Pi Houfeng, "Zhongguo jindai guoge kaoshu," 264. These two sources give slightly different versions of the song, the latter referring to the "five peoples," but there are no substantial differences.

39. Wang Gengsheng, *Women de guoge*, 14.

40. Ibid., 14–15.

41. *Linshi zhengfu gongbao* 143 (1912.9.20), 627. An announcement appeared in *Shibao* on 1912.10.8.

42. Wang Gengsheng, *Women de guoge*, 14–15.

43. Ibid., 15–16.

44. Ibid., 15; Pi Houfeng, "Zhongguo jindai guoge kaoshu," 264–265.

45. Wang Gengsheng, *Women de guoge*, 19–20.

46. "Zhongguo xiongli yuzhou": see Wang Gengsheng, *Women de guoge*, 18–19; see also Sun Zhendong, *Guoqi guoge guohua shihua*, 40–45; and Zhou Kaiqing, "Tan guoge" 談國歌, in idem, *Xingzhiji*, 81–85.

47. ZFGB 1915 (1915.5.26), 833.

48. *Zhonghua minguo shishi jiyao* bianji weiyuanhui, ed., *Zhonghua minguo shishi jiyao*, 1915.5.23, 449–451.

49. Zhou Kaiqing, "Tan guoge," 83.

50. Historians have done much to clarify the origins of the Republican flag, and I will focus on the flag debates. See most recently Harrison, *The Making of the Republican Citizen*, 98–106; also Wang Gengsheng, *Women de guoqi*; Sun Zhendong, *Guoqi guoge guohua shihua*, 6–25; and Onodera Shirō, "Shinmatsu minshu no kokki o meguru kōsō to kōsō."

51. Sun Zhendong, *Guoqi guoge guohua shihua*, 24–25. Federalism, though discussed in the 1920s, never had much appeal for most Chinese intellectuals.

52. "Canyiyuan disici kaihui jishi" 參議院第四次開會紀事, *Shengjing shibao* 1912.5.14, 3.

53. *Linshi zhengfu gongbao* 6 (1912.2.3), 6–7.

54. Wang Gengsheng, *Women de guoqi*, 62.

55. "Zhonghua minguo qi zhi lishi" 中華民國旗之歷史, *Shengjing shibao* 1912.3.19, 4. Precisely because Sun stressed its revolutionary pedigree, it is little wonder that the sky-sun flag would have seemed narrowly exclusive to other political actors. Sun's continued use of the sky-sun motif as a flag for his Chinese Revolutionary Party (Zhonghua gemingdang), for the Guangzhou government in the early 1920s, and finally for the Guomindang (without the red background) suggests that it was indeed a partisan flag.

56. "Ge guowuyuan zhi zhengjiang" 各國務員之政見, *Dongfang zazhi* 9.1 (1912.7.1), 21605; see also "Canyiyuan diwuci kaihui jishi" 參議院第五次開會紀事, *Shengjing shibao* 1912.5.17, 4. It was not explained what groups the additional two colors might represent. Perhaps Cai was thinking of the Miao and the Zhuang; I am grateful to Wang Chaohua for this suggestion.

57. ZFGB (unnumbered) 1912.6.7, 90–91.

58. "Zhonghua minguo qi zhi lishi," *Shengjing shibao* 1912.3.19, 22/145.

59. "Zaping er" 雜評二, *Shenbao* 1917.10.11, 685.

60. "Dong Ya zhi qingshi" 東亞之情勢, *Shengjing shibao* 1915.10.17, 32/240; "Guoqi wenti zhi jusong" 國旗問題之聚訟, *Shengjing shibao* 1915.10.29, 32/303; it was not clear what this symbol would be.

61. "Gui de shuangshijie" 鬼的雙十節, *Dagongbao* (Changsha) 1924.10.22 (citation from part 4).

62. Hung Wu, *Remaking Beijing*, 23–24, 60–61.

63. "Teyue lutoudian," *Minlibao* 1912.10.12, 5509.

64. "Guoqingri dayue" 國慶日大閱, *Shibao* 1912.10.12; "Huanghuang daguan zhi guoqingri" 煌煌大觀之國慶日, *Shibao* 1912.10.17, 3.

65. Liu Shichang, "Zhonghua minguo guoqingjie," 120. Yuan's honors list came under general criticism, especially after he seemed to violate republican principles even more directly by "enfeoffing" (*feng*) Mongol princes. The point that Duan and Feng initially opposed the revolutionaries was also raised. See the editorial by "Gufen" 孤憤, "Du guoqingri shangxuan mingling youhuo" 讀國慶日賞勳命令有感, *Shibao* 1912.10.15. An editorial by [Xu] Xue'er [徐]血兒, "Wuhu shanggong" 嗚呼賞功 in *Minlibao* 1912.10.12, 5516, was even more pointed, accusing Yuan of ignoring the men who had sacrificed themselves in revolution. Editorials continued in this vein for a few days, and there were even questions raised in the National Assembly before the issue died down.

66. This description is taken from inter alia "Zongtong zhi fuse" 總統之服色, *Shibao* 1913.10.11, 4; "Bulu choubei guoqing shiwuchu tonggao" 補錄籌備國慶事務處通告, *Shibao* 1913.10.12, 4; and "Guanyu Qinghuangshi daibiao zhi lijie" 關於清皇室代表之禮節, *Shibao* 1913.10.14, 3–4.

67. See also "Zongtong zhi fuse," *Shibao* 1913.10.11, 4.

68. Sartorial Caesarism was adopted from Europe, though. Mosse, "Caesarism, Circuses, and Monuments."

69. "Bulu choubei guoqing shiwuchu tonggao," *Shibao* 1913.10.12, 4.

70. "Zijincheng youji" 紫禁城遊記 *Shibao* 1914.10.18, 4; 1914.10.30, 4.

71. PDN 1914.12.29, 4. For an overview of Yuan's presidency, see Young, *The Presidency of Yuan Shih-k'ai*.

72. Cheng-hua Wang, "The Qing Imperial Collection, circa 1904–1925." The institute's collection consisted of hundreds of thousands of items mostly expropriated from imperial collections, though the rump Qing court retained effective ownership of all the art in the Forbidden City.

73. Reinsch was a political scientist not immune to the Orientalism of the day. His memoirs are Reinsch, *An American Diplomat in China*.

74. Ibid., 4.

75. Ibid., 3–4, 5.

76. Ibid., 1–2.

77. "Ji Tian dali zhi yubei tan" 祭天大禮之預備談, *Shibao* 1914.12.21, 3.

78. Ibid.

79. "Minguo diyijie ji Tian dianli yuwen" 民國第一屆祭天典禮預聞, *Shibao* 1914.12.18, 3.

80. Supposedly, Yuan modestly declined to wear the robes of the Zhou Tianzi (emperor). PDN 1914.1.16, 4.

81. ZFGB 945 (1914.12.21), 208.

82. "Ji Tian dali zhi yubei tan," *Shibao* 1914.12.21, 3; PDN 1914.1.24, 4.

83. ZFGB 631 (1914.2.8), 203–204.

84. NCDN 1914.12.21, 15.

85. "Minguo diyijie ji Tian dianli yuwen," *Shibao* 1914.12.18, 3.

86. ZFGB 631 (1914.2.8), 206.

87. The sacrifices were reported in PDN 1914.12.24, 4–5; and "Choubeizhong zhi ji Tian dadian" 籌備中之祭天大典, *Shibao* 1914.12.23, 4–5; and see Reinsch, *An American Diplomat in China*, 24–26.

88. Reinsch, *An American Diplomat in China*, 25–26.

89. "Mingling" 命令, *Shibao* 1913.6.27, 2; also "Dazongtong fu xuexiao ji Kong mingling" 大總統復學校祭孔命令, KZ 1.6; and "Mingling," *Shibao* 1914.2.10, 2. The Confucian movement is discussed in the next chapter.

90. "Benhui jishi: zonghui" 本會紀事：總會, KZ 1.8; "Guozijian dingji zhi shengyi" 國子監丁祭之盛儀, *Shibao* 1913.9.11, 3.

91. PDN 1914.9.29, 5.

92. Ya-pei Kuo, "'The Emperor and the People in One Body.'"

93. NCDN 1914.11.26, 7–8; Johnston, "Chinese Cult of Military Heroes." For the changing meanings of Guandi, see Duara, "Superscribing Symbols"; and for Yue Fei, see Matten, "The Worship of General Yue Fei."

94. Johnston, "Chinese Cult of Military Heroes," 88–89.

95. Jerome Chen, *Yuan Shih-k'ai*, 159–160.

96. "Yuesheng shangtuan zhu sheng zhi re'nao" 粵省商團祝聖之熱鬧, *Shibao* 1912.10.17, 4;

and "Zaizhi Yuesheng gejie Kongtan zhudian zhisheng" 再誌粵省各界孔誕祝典之盛, *Shibao* 1912.10.18, 3. Confucian ritualism was not a major part of popular culture, but it was integral to schools. Perhaps animosity toward the revolutionary government was motivated by tax issues, while Confucius's birthday provided a vehicle of protest.

97. "Xinshi jinian youpiao" 新式紀念郵票, *Minlibao* 1912.9.23, 5348.

98. See Harrison, *The Making of the Republican Citizen*, 30–40; Weikun Cheng, "Hairdressing and Ethnic Conflict."

99. Laws prohibited women from wearing their hair short on the grounds it represented a kind of transvestitism and therefore harmed public morals. "Jinzhi nüzi jianfa" 禁止女子剪髮, *Shibao* 1913.3.23, 7.

100. See Chen Xiyuan [Hsi-yuan Chen], "Zhongguo yeweimian."

101. "Guoqingri zhi ganyan" 國慶日之感言, *Shengjing shibao* 1916.10.10, 35/168.

102. "Duozai duonan de Zhonghua minguo" 多災多難的中華民國, *Dagongbao* (Changsha) 1924.10.10, 44/436.

103. "Zaping er," *Shenbao* 1913.10.11, 1230/545.

104. Lu Xun, "Zayi" 雜憶, in idem, *Lu Xun quanji*, 1:317–323.

105. All the same, it is important to note that state-building and modernizing projects continued through the presidency of Yuan and even his successors. In the spirit of the New Policies and constitutional reforms of the Qing, at least sporadically government agencies were rationalized; repeated dismissals and re-assembling of parliaments was dispiriting but also preserved something of a public stage for national elites. See Young, *The Presidency of Yuan Shih-k'ai*; and Nathan, *Peking Politics, 1918–1923*.

CHAPTER 8

An earlier version of a portion of this chapter has been previously published as "Political Ritual in the Early Republic of China," pp. 149–188, in Kai-wing Chow, Kevin Doak, and Poshek Fu, eds., *Constructing Nationhood in Modern East Asia: Narrative Schemes, Nostalgia, and Ambiguity of Identities* (Ann Arbor: University of Michigan Press, 2001).

1. Joseph R. Levenson, mocking Yuan's ritualism as both president and would-be emperor, concluded that in 1916 "the parody of a republic yielded (for just a few months) to only a parody of the empire"—*Confucian China and Its Modern Fate*, 2:4. But this seems a little too simple.

2. See Tse-tsung Chow, *The May Fourth Movement*; Schwarcz, *The Chinese Enlightenment*; Lin Yü-sheng, *The Crisis of Chinese Consciousness*; Li Yusheng et al., *Wusi*; Doleželová-Velingerová and Král, *The Appropriation of Culture Capital*; Weston, *The Power of Position*; and Jenco, "'Rule by Man' and 'Rule by Law' in Early Republican China."

3. Jerome Ch'en, *Yuan Shih-k'ai*, 166–176; cf. Young, *The Presidency of Yuan Shih-k'ai*, 215–216.

4. Zhang Xueji, "Lun Youhe Changxiong yu minchu xianzheng de yanbian." Ariga represented a constitutional monarchy, while for the monarchists, Goodnow was a coup, though he may not have known how his essay would be used. Yang Du, "Faqi Chouanhui xuanyanshu" 發起籌安會宣言書, in idem, *Yang Du ji*, 585–586; and see Pugach, "Embarrassed Monarchist"; and Young, *The Presidency of Yuan Shih-k'ai*, 172. Goodnow, professor of law at Columbia University and later president of Johns Hopkins, was a founder of the discipline of political science in the United States. He told Ambassador Reinsch: "Here is a hitherto non-political society which had vegetated along through centuries held together by self-enforced social and moral bonds, without set tribunals or formal sanctions. Now it suddenly determines to take over elections, legislatures, and other elements of our more

abstract and artificial Western system. I incline to believe that it would be infinitely better if the institutional changes had been more gradual, if the system of representation had been based rather on existing social groupings and interests than on the abstract idea of universal suffrage. These political abstractions as yet mean nothing to the Chinese by way of actual experience." Reinsch, *An American Diplomat in China*, 31. The foreigners were but a sideshow, however.

5. In Yan Fu's case, it has been suggested he was more or less strong-armed into providing his name to the Peace Planning Society, and he never actively promoted it. See Schwartz, *In Search of Wealth and Power*, 223–229; and Zhou Zhenfu, "Yan Fu sixiang zhuanbian zhi poxi." Yan's student Hou Yi reported that Yan privately disapproved of the Chouanhui. While Yan fundamentally thought China was best suited to be a constitutional monarchy, since China had become a republic any imposition of monarchism amounted to revolution. Furthermore, "the most important thing that sustains a monarchical system is the charisma of the ruler. But today the ruler's charisma is already spilt water. To restore the old system rashly will only result in further chaos." Hou Yi, *Hongxian jiuwen*, 1:3a.

6. Yang Du, "Junxian jiuguo lun" 君憲救國論, in idem, *Yang Du ji*, 573.

7. Ibid., 568.

8. Yang was alluding to a phrase from the *Mencius* 1A:6: *ding yu yi*. Mencius was advising a king how to pacify the world: the one who will succeed rules by benevolence, not killing.

9. Yang Du, "Jintie zhuyi shuo," 264.

10. Yang Du, "Tan Chouanhui" 談籌安會, in idem, *Yang Du ji*, 613–614.

11. Liu Shipei, "Junzheng fugu lun" 君政復古論, in idem, *Liu Shenshu xiansheng yishu*, zhuan 55.

12. Ibid., shang, 1a.

13. Ibid.

14. Ibid., zhong, 1a, 2a.

15. Ibid., shang, 3b.

16. Ibid., zhong, 1b.

17. See Zarrow, "Liang Qichao and the Notion of Civil Society in Republican China."

18. See Hu Pingsheng, *Liang Cai shisheng yu huguo zhi yi*; *Huguo wenji* bianjizu, ed., *Huguo wenji*; and Zhang Pengyuan, *Liang Qichao yu minguo zhengzhi*, 64–90.

19. Liang Qichao, "Yizai suowei guoti wenti zhe" 異哉所謂國體問題者, YBSHJ zhuanji 33:85–98. There was a certain tone of regret in "How Strange! The So-Called Question of the National Polity," as if Liang still hoped Yuan would return to the correct path of president-for-life. The essay can be read as a kind of remonstrance, as Meng Xiangcai points out. Meng Xiangcai, *Liang Qichao zhuan*, 268–273.

20. ZFGB 1304 (1915.12.25), 987.

21. ZFGB 1293 (1915.12.13), 456.

22. See, e.g., ZFGB 1299 (1915.12.19), 713–714, for Mongol, Tibetan, Qinghai, and Hui representatives.

23. ZFGB 1304 (1915.12.25), 990. The flowery and allusive prose in the memorials and edicts is resistant to translation, but this literary quality was of course a deliberate effect.

24. The term *jitian liji* was taken from Zhu Xi's "Preface to the *Great Learning*" (*Daxue zhangju xu* 大學章句序), referring to the ancient sage-kings, who "carried on for Heaven and established the highest point of excellence." The phrase *jitian* was used to describe rulership in the *Guliang zhuan*, while the phrase *liji* described the ruler in the *Book of Documents* (Shangshu). Gardner, *Chu Hsi and the "Ta-hsueh,"* 78–79.

25. The term *zhengwei* is first found in the *Mencius* 3B:2, describing the "great man" in

terms of something like "abiding in righteousness"—he who "takes his place in the seat of rectitude." Dobson, *Mencius*, 125. The term *dingming* describes the assertion of authority.

26. The term *Tianwei* was found frequently in the classics and non-canonical ancient texts, referring to the awesome powers of Tian. See, e.g., the *Book of Documents*, trans. Legge, *The Chinese Classics*, 3:475; and the *Guanzi*, trans. Rickett, *Guanzi*, 1:341.

27. *Dingfen* was another classical term associated with governance, regulation, and order. *Zhengming* was a fundamental premise of Confucian political and social ethics: the locus classicus is the *Analects* (*Lunyu*), 13:3. Confucius linked the "rectification of names" with true knowledge and administrative effectiveness. *Tianxin zhi juan* is not a classical phrase, but it sounded like one. The cosmological notion of the "mind of Tian" (*Tianxin*) was very ancient.

28. ZFGB 1293 (1915.12.25), 988.

29. *Mencius* 4A:1. Mencius's point here was that benevolence was a necessary but not sufficient aspect of governance, and that governing involved an activist side. In that sense, the allusion was apt.

30. ZFGB 1294 (1915.12.14), 496. The locus classicus of the quotation, long effectively a proverb, is the *Book of Documents*, though the phrase spread into popular consciousness via Confucius and Mencius.

31. Liu Xiaofeng, *Rujiao yu minzuguojia*, 100–115.

32. See, e.g., Wing-tsit Chan, trans. and annot., *"Instructions for Practical Living,"* 96–98; and Angle, *Sagehood*, 55.

33. The Confucian Association was founded in October 1912. Han Hua, *Minchu Kongjiaohui yu guojiao yundong yanjiu*; Gan Chunsong, "Kang Youwei he Kongjiaohui." See also Hsi-yuan Chen, "Confucianism Encounters Religion"; and Goossaert, "Republican Church Engineering," 219–221.

34. See inter alia "Chi Beijing jiaoyuhui pohuai Kongjiao zhi zui" 斥北京教育會破壞孔教之罪, *Shibao* 1913.4.12, 6; "Kongjiao xinwen: shen lun Xushi Shaozhen sitian pei Kong yi" 孔教新聞：申論徐氏紹楨祀天配孔議, KZ 1.4, 6–7; "Lun Cai Yuanpei tiyi xuexiao buji Kongzi" 論蔡元培提議學校不祭孔子, *Shibao* 1912.7.20, 1; and Zhang Ertian, "Yu ren lun changming Kongjiao yi qianggu daode shu" 與人論昌明孔教以強固道德書, KZ 1.5, 21–24.

35. See "Kongjiaohui qingyuanshu," KZ 1.6, 13–14; Chen Huanzhang, "Si Tian yi Kongzi pei yi" 祀天以孔子配議, KZ 1.4, 1–8; "Chi Beijing jiaoyuhui pohuai Kongjiao zhi zui"; and "Faqi Kong Meng zhengxuehui zhi xuanyanshu" 發起孔孟正學會之宣言書, *Shibao* 1912.12.31, 5; Zhang Ertian, "Si Tian fei Tianzi zhi siji kao" 祀天非天子之私祭考, KZ 1.5, 11–19; and "Kongjiao xinwen: si Kong pei Tian zhi yulun" 孔教新聞：祀孔配天之輿論, KZ 1.4, 1–6.

36. Kang Youwei, "Zai Ningyuan xuejie yanshuo" 在寧垣學界演說, in Tang Zhijun, ed., *Kang Youwei zhenglunji*, 2:963.

37. Kang Youwei, "Yi Kongjiao wei guojiao peitian yi" 以孔教為國教配天議, in ibid., 2:843.

38. "Zhiji xianshi jisheng" 致祭先師紀盛, *Shibao* 1913.3.18, 7.

39. "Mingling," *Shibao* 1913.6.27, 2; also "Dazongtong fu xuexiao ji Kong mingling," KZ 1.6, 11–12.

40. Yuan sanctioned state sponsorship of the worship of Confucius as a grand sacrifice on the Ding days of spring and autumn (according to the 60-day cycle of the lunar calendar), with the president serving as chief officiant in Beijing while local officials were to officiate at local ceremonies. "Mingling," *Shibao* 1914.2.10, 2; ZFGB 631 (1914.2.8), 205.

41. "Jiaoyubu xuanshi zun Kong zongzhi" 教育部宣示尊孔宗旨, *Shibao* 1914.7.2, 3.

42. "Zhonghua minguo xianfa an" 中華民國憲法案 (section 3, article 19), in Zhang

Yaozeng and Cen Dezhang, eds., *Zhonghua minguo xianfa shiliao*. When Yuan dissolved parliament, the draft constitution became a dead letter, though it influenced later constitutions. The later 1919 draft constitution used the same wording.

43. Chen's lectures were published at the time in a series of articles, "Lun Kongjiao shi yi zongjiao" 論孔教是一宗教, *Shibao* 1913.10.5–27.

44. See Chen Xiyuan, "'Zongjiao.'"

45. "Lun Cai Yuanpei tiyi xuexiao buji Kongzi," *Shibao* 1912.7.20, 1.

46. Di Yu 狄郁, "Kongjiao pingyi shangpian" 孔教評議上篇, KZ 1.4, 29–36.

47. Di Yu, "Kongjiao pingyi xiapian" 孔教評議下篇, KZ 1.5, 25.

48. Chen Huanzhang, "Si Tian yi Kongzi pei yi."

49. Zhang Ertian, "Si Tian fei Tianzi zhi siji kao."

50. For typical examples, see "Chi Beijing jiaoyuhui pohuai Kongjiao zhi zui," *Shibao* 1913.4.12, 6; "Kongjiao xinwen: shen lun Xushi Shaozhen si tian pei Kong yi"; "Lun Cai Yuanpei tiyi xuexiao buji Kongzi," *Shibao* 1912.7.20, 1; and Zhang Ertian, "Yu ren lun changming Kongjiao yi qianggu daide."

51. "Benhui jishi: zonghui," KZ 1.8, 2.

52. "Kongjiaohui qingyuanshu"; and "Kongjiaohui daibiao Chen Huanzhang, Yan Fu, Xia Zengyou, Liang Qichao, Wang Shitong deng qingding kongjiao wei guojiao chengwen" 孔教會代表陳煥章嚴復夏曾佑梁啟超王式通等請定孔教為國教呈文, *Shibao* 1913.8.18–20, 6.

53. "Shangren zun Kong zhi yiban" 商人尊孔之一斑, *Shibao* 1913.11.4, 8.

54. "Kongjiao wenti zhi sanpaiguan" 孔教問題之三派觀, *Shibao* 1916.12.26, sec. 2, 3.

55. Grieder, *Intellectuals and the State in Modern China*, 204. I cannot consider the full scope of New Culture thought here, but will briefly highlight comments of the movement's leaders on the issues central to previous chapters: the imperial state, revolution, and Confucian reform.

56. See Chen Lai, "Huajie 'chuantong' yu 'xiandai' de jinzhang," 169–170; and Thomas C. Kuo, "Ch'en Tu-hsiu and the Chinese Intellectual Revolution, 1915–1919," 42–43.

57. Chen Duxiu, "Jinggao qingnian" 敬告青年, *Xin Qingnian* 1.1 (Sept. 1915), (reprinted Tokyo: Daiyasu, 1961), 21–26. Translated in Teng and Fairbank, *China's Response to the West*, 240–245.

58. Chen Duxiu, "Xianfa yu Kongjiao" 憲法與孔教, DXWC, 107–111; also see "Fubi yu zun-Kong" 復辟與尊孔, DXWC, 166–167.

59. Chen Duxiu, "Bo Kang Youwei zhi zongtong zongli shu" 駁康有為致總統總理書, DXWC, 100; see also "Jiu sixiang yu guoti wenti" 舊思想與國體問題, DXWC, 149–150; and "Fubi yu zun-Kong," DXWC, 162.

60. Chen Duxiu, "Fubi yu zun-Kong," DXWC, 164–165.

61. Chen Duxiu, "Jiu sixiang yu guoti wenti," DXWC, 148, 149.

62. Chen's strongest critique of nationalism is found in "Aiguoxin yu zijuexin" 愛國心與自覺心, *Chen Duxiu zhuzuoxuan*, 1:113–119.

63. Chen Duxiu, "Jinri zhi jiaoyu fangzhen" 今日之教育方針, DXWC, 17–26 (esp. 22–24).

64. Ibid., 23.

65. Chen Duxiu "Aiguoxin yu zijuexin." See Maruyama Masayuki, *Chūgoku kindai no kakumei shisū*, 201–206.

66. Chen Duxiu, "Yijiu yiliu nian" 一九一六年, DXWC, 41–47.

67. Ibid., 117–118.

68. Chen Duxiu, "Wo zhi aiguo zhuyi" 我之愛國主義, DXWC, 85–94. The Chinese intelligentsia really did think well of the Boy Scouts. Grieder, *Intellectuals and the State in Modern China*, 224.

69. Jenco, *Making the Political*; see also Weston, "The Formation and Positioning of the New Culture Community."

70. For this transition, see Zhang Kaiyuan and Luo Fuhui, "Xinwenhua yundong"; Ying-shih Yu, "The Radicalization of China in the Twentieth Century"; and Meisner, *Li Ta-chao and the Origins of Chinese Marxism*.

71. Li Dazhao, "Zhanhou zhi furen wenti" 戰後之婦人問題, in idem, *Li Dazhao wenji*, 1:635.

72. Li Dazhao, "Laodong jiaoyu wenti" 勞動教育問題, in ibid., 1:632.

73. Li Dazhao, "You pingmin zhengzhi dao gongren zhengzhi" 由平民政治到工人政治, in ibid., 2:502.

74. See, e.g., Li Dazhao, "Pingmin zhuyi" 平民主義, in ibid., 2:596–600.

75. Li Dazhao, "Pingmin zhengzhi yu gongren zhengzhi" 平民政治與工人政治, in ibid., 2:569.

76. Li Dazhao, "You zhengzhi dao gongren zhengzhi," in ibid., 2:502–503. Perhaps Li was as much influenced by Fabianism and John Dewey as by the Russian Revolution. See Tse-tsung Chow, *The May Fourth Movement*, 228–232, for a discussion of Dewey in China.

77. See Rhoads, *Manchus and Han*, esp. 214–230; the 1924 expulsion is discussed 247–250. The events surrounding the expulsion of Puyi are also recently reviewed in Yu Dahua, "'Qingshi youdai tiaojian' xinlun."

78. Lin Zhihong, *Minguo nai diguo ye*.

79. Liu Wangling, *Xinhai geminghou dizhi fubi he fanfubi douzheng*, 63–133.

80. Cited in Johnston, *Twilight in the Forbidden City*, 137–138.

81. Kang Youwei, "Qing Yuan Shikai tuiwei dian" 請袁世凱退位電, in idem, *Kang Youwei zhenglunji*, 2:933–941.

82. Kang Youwei, "Ni fubi dengji zhao" 擬復辟登極詔, in ibid., 2:990–991.

83. Kang Youwei, "Jiuwang lun" 救亡論, in ibid., 2:652–678.

84. Kang Youwei, "Ni Zhonghua minguo xianfa caoan fafan" 擬中華民國憲法草案發凡, in ibid., 2:830–841.

85. That is, the late Qing, Yuan Shikai, and the Puyi restoration. Yang Du, "Yu Wang Shu de tanhua" 與王舒的談話, in idem, *Yang Du ji*, 624; idem, "Fandui Zhang Xun fubi gongdian" 反對張勳復辟公電, in ibid., 620–621. See Li Zenghui, "Cong dizhi huoshou dao Zhonggong dangyuan"; and Jiang Yi, "Junxian hu? Gonghe hu?" 182–183.

86. Weston, *The Power of Position*, 128–131.

87. Zhou Zuoren, *Zhitang huixianglu*, 2:228–229.

88. Ibid., 2:222.

89. Sheridan, *Chinese Warlord*. See also Waldron, *From War to Nationalism*, 181–223.

90. Feng, with the backing of new warlord allies, was able to bring Duan Qirui (1865–1936) into the government. Duan had been one of Yuan Shikai's top generals and after Yuan's death he had served as premier (de facto chief) of several succeeding governments. Duan apparently disapproved of Feng's actions but nonetheless became provisional chief executive on November 24, giving the new regime a certain level of political heft. "Qingdi chugong hou Feng jun jieshou yinxi" 清帝出宮後馮軍接收印璽, *Shengjing shibao* 1924.11.15, 2. See "Qingshi tiaojian fasheng wenti" 清室條件發生問題, *Shengjing shibao* 1924.12.3, 1; see also "Duan Zhang dui Qingshi shijian zhi biaoshi" 段張對清室事件之表示, *Dagongbao* (Changsha) 1924.12.4, 2; and Wang Qingxiang, *Puyi jiaowang lu*, 60.

91. "Chugong zhi jingguo" 出宮之經過, *Shengjing shibao* 1924.11.11, 2; "Feng Yuxiang poling Xuantong chugong zhi jingguo" 馮玉祥迫令宣統出宮之經過, *Dagongbao* (Changsha) 1924.11.13, 3.

92. These events are described in Aixinjueluo Puyi, *Puyi zizhuan*, 158–161; translated (with slight abridgements) by W. J. F. Jenner as *From Emperor to Citizen*, 146–149.

93. Feng Yuxiang, *Wo de shenghuo*, 378.

94. "Xundi beibi chugong xuxun" 遜帝被逼出宮續訊, *Shengjing shibao* 1924.11.9, 2. See also "Feng Yuxiang poling Xuantong chugong zhi jingguo" 馮玉詳迫令宣統出宮之經過, *Dagongbao* (Changsha) 1924.11.13, 3, which attributed the report to foreign sources.

95. "Guanyu Qingshi shijian zhi yaodian" 關於清室事件之要電, *Shengjing shibao* 1924.11.16, 1.

96. "Beijing tonggao Puyi chugong dian" 北京通告溥儀出宮電, *Dagongbao* (Changsha) 1924.11.13, 3.

97. As described in "Chugong zhi jingguo," *Shengjing shibao* 1924.11.11, 2.

98. "Kuaixin zhaiyao" 快信摘要, *Dagongbao* (Changsha) 1924.11.17, 2.

99. See also Johnston, *Twilight in the Forbidden City*, 387–388.

100. "Qingshi tiaojian fasheng wenti," *Shengjing shibao* 1924.12.3, 1; and "Duan Qirui yu youdai Qingshi wenti" 段祺瑞與優待清室問題, *Dagongbao* (Changsha) 1924.12.7, 3.

101. "Xundi beibi chugong xuxun," *Shengjing shibao* 1924.11.9, 2.

102. "Feng Yuxiang poling Xuantong chugong zhi jingguo," *Dagongbao* (Changsha) 1924.11.13, 3.

103. "Qingdi chugong hou Feng jun jieshou yinxi," *Shengjing shibao* 1924.11.15, 2. Of course, Li was himself an appointee of the new government.

104. "Qinggong shanhou zhi xuxun" 清宮善後之續訊, *Shengjing shibao* 1924.11.19, 2.

105. "Gaizao Qinggong yi" 改造清宮議, *Shengjing shibao* 1924.12.17, 1. Such views were common—see inter alia "Jiaoyujie zhuzhang gongkai Qingshi guwu" 教育界主張公開清室古物, *Dagongbao* (Tianjin) 1924.11.23, 2:5; "Qinggong chafeng xuwen" 清宮查封續聞, *Shibao* 1924.11.27, 1:2.

106. Or "Gugong" (Former Palace) Museum. An excellent overview is Barmé, *The Forbidden City*, chaps. 5 and 6. See also Hamlish, "Preserving the Palace"; Lin-sheng Chang, "The National Palace Museum"; and Mingzheng Shi, "From Imperial Gardens to Public Parks."

107. Johnston, *Twilight in the Forbidden City*, 391.

108. "Shicha Qinggong" 視察清宮, *Shengjing shibao* 1924.11.21, 1.

109. "Qingshi liangtaifei chugong" 清室兩太妃出宮, *Shibao* 1924.11.22, 1:1.

110. "Yu, Jin liangfei chugong" 瑜瑨兩妃出宮, *Shengjing shibao* 1924.11.27, 1.

111. "Qingdi chugong hou Feng jun jieshou yinxi," *Shengjing shibao* 1924.11.15, 2.

112. "Puyi chugong hou zhi Qingshi shanhou wenti" 溥儀出宮後之清室善後問題, *Dagongbao* (Changsha) 1924.11.23, 3.

113. "Qingshi fude ziyou" 清室復得自由, *Dagongbao* (Tianjin) 1924.11.26, 1:4; "Qingshi tiaojian fasheng wenti" 清室條件發生問題, *Shengjing shibao* 1924.12.3, 1.

114. "Puyi xiansheng yu jizhe zhi tanhua" 溥儀先生與記者之談話, *Shengjing shibao* 1924.12.3, 2. For Puyi's later recollections of interviews at the time, see below.

115. Zeng Qi 曾琦, "Puyi busha hewei" 溥儀不殺何為, cited in Hu Pingsheng, *Minguo chuqi de fubipai*, 414 (originally published in *Xingshi zhoubao* 醒獅週報, 1924.11.12).

116. "Zhang Taiyan dui Puyi chugong fudian" 章太炎對溥儀出宮復電, *Shenbao* 1924.11.9, 4:14.

117. See also "Zhang Taiyan zai zhi Feng Yuxiang deng dian" 章太炎再致馮玉祥等電, *Shenbao* 1924.11.13, 3:9.

118. "Zhang Taiyan zhi Yi Yincun zhi yifeng shu" 章太炎致易寅村一封書, *Dagongbao* (Tianjin) 1924.12.8, 1:4.

119. "Qingshi wenti yu ge fangmian" 清室問題與各方面, *Shibao* 1924.11.15, 1:1.

The position of Tang Shaoyi—objecting to the means—was similar. See "Tang Shaochuan lun Qingshi yigong shi" 唐少川論清室移宮事, *Shibao* 1924.11.8, 2:4; and "Tang Shaoyi bu zancheng Feng Yuxiang quchu Qingdi" 唐紹儀不贊成馮玉祥驅逐清帝, *Dagongbao* (Changsha) 1924.11.13, 3. Tang was among those who had called for abrogating the Articles in the wake of the Zhang Xun–led restoration of 1917—Rhoads, *Manchus and Han*, 242.

120. Puyi's English tutor, Reginald Johnston, had introduced Puyi to Hu Shi's writings, and when the palace first got a telephone, Puyi called Hu, who later went to the palace for an audience. Hu also visited Puyi in November of 1924, encouraging him to go abroad. Aixinjueluo Puyi, *Puyi zizhuan*, 134–135, 170–171; Jenner, trans., *From Emperor to Citizen*, 127, 157–158; Johnston, *Twilight in the Forbidden City*, 275–276. According to Puyi, in their private meeting after the expulsion, Hu was even more emphatic, stating of Feng Yuxiang's actions, "In the eyes of Europe and America, this is all oriental barbarism." *Puyi zizhuan*, 170.

121. Ning Xiewan, "Qingshi youdai tiaojian shifou guoji tiaoyue" 清室優待條件是否國際條約, *Dongfang zazhi* 22.2, 13–15, cited in Hu Pingsheng, ed., *Fubi yundong shiliao*, 319–322.

122. "Kang shengren yin Puyi shi dama Feng Yuxiang" 康聖人因溥儀事大罵馮玉祥, *Dagongbao* (Changsha) 1924.12.5–6, 3.

123. Ning Xiewan accepted the comparison to the Vatican, but he argued that the Vatican's status was based on an 1871 Italian law and so was not truly sovereign (ignoring the Vatican's recognition in international diplomacy).

124. See "Qingdi chugong hou Feng jun jieshou yinxi," *Shengjing shibao* 1924.11.15, 2.

125. "Zhongshan yu Qingshi yigong shijian" 中山與清室移宮事件, *Dagongbao* (Changsha) 1925.1.16, 2.

126. Zhang Taiyan [Zhang Binglin], *Taiyan xiansheng ziding nianpu*, 25. At the time of the revolution's success, Zhang had favored a strong presidency, but he and Yuan soon became mutually disaffected.

127. Li Yuying, *Li Shizeng xiansheng wenji*, 2:314.

128. Chen Duxiu, "Ouxiang pohuai lun" 偶像破壞論, DXWC, 227–230.

CONCLUSION

An earlier version of a portion of this chapter has been previously published as "Chinese Conceptions of the State during the Late Qing Dynasty (1860–1911)," pp. 235–259, in Takashi Shogimen and Cary J. Nederman, eds., *Western Political Thought in Dialogue with Asia* (Lanham, MD: Lexington Books/Rowman & Littlefield, 2009).

1. Fitzgerald, *Awakening China*.

2. Kuhn, *Origins of the Modern Chinese State*, chap. 1 (on "constitutional dilemmas," 8–24).

3. See Elvin, "The Collapse of Scriptural Confucianism."

4. Liang Qichao, "Baojiao fei suoyi zun Kong lun," YBSHJ wenji 9:59, 55. Writing in 1902, Liang was not rejecting all aspects of Confucianism, but he denied its centrality to the national project.

5. See Angle, *Sagehood*, 179–221.

6. Jing Tsu, *Failure, Nationalism, and Literature*.

7. "Zhonghua minguo linshi yuefa" 中華民國臨時約法, in Zhang Yaozeng and Cen Dezhang, eds., *Zhonghua minguo xianfa shiliao*, articles 1–2.

8. "Zhonghua minguo yuefa" 中華民國約法, in ibid., articles 1–2.

9. By "continuously," I do not mean there was stasis but rather punctuated hermeneutical evolution.

10. Wang Hui has recently emphasized Kang's use of Song cosmological principles. Wang Hui, *Xiandai Zhongguo sixiang de xingqi*, 1B:744–765.

11. The "failure" of rights in China has naturally shaped the discussions of both Chinese and Western historians on the origins of Chinese rights thinking. Chen Lai suggests a tension in Chen Duxiu's thought between "value rationality" (liberty, human rights, and the like as the highest of universal ideals) on the one hand and a more instrumentalist utilitarianism, which gave ultimate priority to strengthening the nation on the other hand—Chen Lai, "Huajie 'chuantong' yu 'xiandai' de jinzhang," 155–158. In his classic study, Li Zehou points to a tension between "national salvation" and "Enlightenment thought"—Li Zehou, "Qimeng yu jiuwang de shuangchong bianzou." However, it may be anachronistic to read later "failure" back into the nationalism, or the communalism, or the utopianism of late Qing thinkers and activists, rather than the state-building process itself. For the "indigenization" of human rights in China, see Zarrow, "Anti-Despotism and 'Rights Talk.'"

12. The wide-ranging work by Zhou Zhongqiu, *Pingdeng guannian de licheng*, a Marxist-inspired survey of both Europe and China across the ages, however, is suggestive.

13. Sun Zhongshan [Sun Yat-sen], "Linshi dazongtong jiuzhi xuanyan" 臨時大總統就職宣言, in idem, *Guofu quanji*, 2:23–24.

14. Sun Zhongshan, "Xiugai zhangcheng zhi shuoming" 修改章程之說明, in ibid., 3:218.

15. Sun Zhongshan, "Sanmin zhuyi zhi juti banfa" 三民主義之具體辦法, in ibid., 3:227.

16. Sun Zhongshan, "Sanmin zhuyi" 三民主義, in ibid., 1:3. See Liu Huaxing and Zhang Yuanlong, "Sun Zhongshan yu Zhongguo jindai guojia guannian de fazhan," 10–21.

17. Sun Zhongshan, "Sanmin zhuyi," 1:4.

18. Cf. Fitzgerald, "The Nationless State," 87–88.

19. Mao Zedong, *Mao Zedong xuanji*, 624. See Knight, "*On Contradiction* and *On New Democracy*."

20. Mao Zedong, *Mao Zedong xuanji*, 636.

21. Ibid., 637–638.

22. Ibid., 1357–1371.

23. Mazur, *Wu Han, Historian*, 345–346.

24. That is, composed of numerous nationalities of which the most numerous were the Han.

25. Cf. Lenin, *The State and Revolution*.

26. Mao Zedong, *Mao Zedong xuanji*, 1364.

27. Woodside, *Lost Modernities*; Elman, *A Cultural History of Civil Examinations*.

28. Mitchell, "The Limits of the State"; also idem, "Society, Economy, and the State Effect," 76–97. The "state effect" in the distinction between state and society is "the defining characteristic of the *modern* political order" (Mitchell, "The Limits of the State," 95, italics added).

29. Kuhn, *Origins of the Modern Chinese State*, 131–132.

30. Pamela Crossley provides a stimulating set of contrasts between Zhang and Liang in terms of the inheritance of Qing nationalist ideologies in Crossley, "Chaos and Civilization."

31. Monad, *The Power of Kings*.

32. Bendix, *Kings or People*; Moore, *Social Origins of Dictatorship and Democracy*; Skocpol, *States and Social Revolutions*.

33. Morgan, *Inventing the People*, 13–15.

34. Duara, "Knowledge and Power in the Discourse of Modernity"; Goossaert, "1898"; Nedostup, *Superstitious Regimes*.

35. As Mayfair Mei-hui Yang notes, "As the state shed its ancient religious and ritual

apparatuses, the category of religion came to be positioned outside it, as a target that helped the state define itself and strengthen its leadership role in modernity"—"Introduction," in Mayfair Mei-hui Yang, ed., *Chinese Religiosities*, 17.

36. Duara, "Religion and Citizenship in China and the Diaspora."

37. This was not, of course, the same thing as the providentialism of the American "civil religion" as proposed by Robert N. Bellah, "Civil Religion in America." But we can see that progressive elites in China were not exactly pure secularists.

38. Yü-sheng Lin, *The Crisis of Chinese Consciousness*, 11–18; Hao Chang, *Chinese Intellectuals in Crisis*, 5–8.

39. Fei Xiaotong [Fei Hsiao-t'ung] (1910–2005) was a founder of anthropology and sociology in China. Quote is from Mazur, *Wu Han, Historian*, 341.

Bibliography

PRIMARY SOURCES

Aixinjueluo Puyi 愛新覺羅‧溥儀. *Puyi zizhuan* 溥儀自傳. Tainan: Jinchuan chubanshe, 1976.

Cai Yuanpei 蔡元培. *Cai Yuanpei zhengzhi lunzhu* 蔡元培政治论著. Gao Pingshu 高平叔, ed. Shijiazhuang: Hebei renmin chubanshe, 1985.

Chambers, William, and Robert Chambers. *Political Economy for Use in Schools and for Private Instruction*. Bristol, Eng.: Thoemmes Press, 1999 [1852].

Chen Duxiu 陳獨秀. *Chen Duxiu zhuzuoxuan* 陈独秀著作选. Ren Jianshu 任建树, Zhang Tongmo 张统模, and Wu Xinzhong 吴信忠, eds. Shanghai: Shanghai renmin chubanshe, 1993.

———. *Duxiu wencun* 獨秀文存. Shanghai: Yadong tushuguan, 1927.

Dagongbao 大公報. Changsha 長沙, 1924.

Dagongbao 大公報. Tianjin 天津, 1912–1924.

Ding Baoshu 丁寶書. *Mengxue Zhongguo lishi jiaokeshu* 蒙學中國歷史教科書. Shanghai: Wenming shuju, n.d. (1905?).

Dongfang zazhi 東方雜誌. Shanghai, 1904–1924.

Feng Yuxiang 馮玉祥. *Wo de shenghuo* 我的生活. Changsha: Yuelu shushe, 1999.

Feng Ziyou 馮自由. *Geming yishi* 革命逸史. Shanghai: Shangwu yinshuguan, 1947.

Fu Lanya [John Fryer] 傅蘭雅, trans. *Zuozhi chuyan* 佐治芻言. Shanghai: Shanghai shudian chubanshe, 2002.

Gao Buying 高步瀛 and Chen Baoquan 陳寶泉. *Tongsu guomin bidu* 通俗國民必讀. Shanghai: Nanyangguan shuju, 1905.

Gezhi huibian 格致彙編. Shanghai, 1892.

Gugong bowuyuan Ming-Qing dang'anbu 故宮博物院明清檔案部, ed. *Qingmo choubei lixian dang'an shiliao* 清末籌備立憲檔案史料, 2 vols. Beijing: Zhonghua shuju, 1979.

Guocui xuebao 國粹學報. Shanghai, 1905–1912.

Hou Yi 侯毅. *Hongxian jiuwen* 洪憲舊聞. N.p.: Yunzaishan fang, 1926.

Hu Pingsheng 胡平生, ed. *Fubi yundong shiliao* 復辟運動史料. Taibei: Zhengzhong shuju, 1992.

Huang Zongxi 黃宗羲. *Mingyi daifanglu* 明夷待訪錄. Taibei: Jinfeng, 1987.

Huang Zunxian 黃遵憲. *Huang Zunxian quanji* 黃遵宪全集. Chen Zheng 陈铮, ed. Beijing: Zhonghua shuju, 2005.

Hui Dun [Henry Wheaton] 惠頓. *Wanguo gongfa* 万国公法. He Qinhua 何勤华, ed. Beijing: Zhongguo zhengfa daxue chubanshe, 2003.

Jian Bozan 翦伯贊 et al., eds. *Wuxu bianfa* 戊戌變法. Shanghai: Shenzhou guoguangshe, 1953.

Jiangsu 江蘇. Taibei: Zhongguo guomindang zhongyang weiyuanhui dangshihui, 1968.

Johnston, Reginald F. *Twilight in the Forbidden City*. New York: D. Appleton-Century, 1934.

Kang Youwei 康有為. *Datong shu* 大同書. Taibei: Longtian, 1979.

———. *Kang Nanhai xiansheng yizhu huikan* 康南海先生遺著彙刊. Jiang Guilin 蔣貴麟, ed. Taibei: Hongye shuju, 1976.

———. *Kang Nanhai ziding nianpu* 康南海自訂年譜. Taibei: Wenhai, n.d.

————. *Kang Youwei quanji* 康有为全集. Jiang Yihua 姜义华 and Wu Genliang 吴根梁, eds. Shanghai: Shanghai guji chubanshe, 1987.

————. *Kang Youwei zhenglunji* 康有为政论集. Tang Zhijun 汤志钧, ed. Beijing: Zhonghua shuju, 1981.

————. *Kongzi gaizhi kao* 孔子改制考. Beijing: Zhonghua shuju, 1958.

Kawana Kaneshirō 川名兼四郎. *Kaitai zōho minpō sōron* 改訂増補民法總論. Tokyo: Kinshi hōryūdō, 1906.

Lenin, V. I. *The State and Revolution*. Peking: Foreign Languages Press, 1973.

Li Dazhao 李大釗. *Li Dazhao wenji* 李大釗文集. Beijing: Renmin wenxue chubanshe, 1984.

Li Jiagu 李嘉穀. *Mengxue xiushen jiaokeshu* 蒙學修身教科書. Shanghai: Wenming shuju, 1905.

Li Yuying 李煜瀛. *Li Shizeng xiansheng wenji* 李石曾先生文集. Zhongguo guomindang dangshi weiyuanhui 中國國民黨黨史委員會, ed. Taibei: Zhongguo guomindang zhongyang weiyuanhui dangshi weiyuanhui, 1980.

Liang Qichao 梁啟超. *Liang Qichao zhexue sixiang lunwenxuan* 梁启超哲学思想论文选. Ge Maochun 葛懋春 and Jiang Jun 蒋俊, eds. Beijing: Beijing daxue chubanshe, 1984.

————. *Qingdai xueshu gailun* 清代學術概論. Taibei: Taiwan shangwu yinshuguan, 1977.

————. *Yinbingshi heji* 飲冰室合集. Beijing: Zhonghua shuju, 1995.

Linshi zhengfu gongbao 臨時政府公報. Taibei: Zhongguo guomindang zhongyang weiyuanhui dangshi shiliao biancuan weiyuanhui, 1968, reprt.

Liu Dapeng 劉大鵬. *Tuixiangzhai riji* 退想齋日記. Taiyuan: Shanxi renmin chubanshe, 1990.

Liu Jianbai 劉劍白. *Xiaoxue xiushen jiaokeshu* 小學修身教科書. Shanghai: Wenmin shuju, 1903.

Liu Shipei 劉師培. *Liu Shenshu xiansheng yishu* 劉申叔先生遺書. N.p., 1934–1938.

————. *Liu Shipei quanji* 劉師培全集. Beijing: Zhonggong zhongyang dangxiao chubanshe, 1997.

Lu Xun 魯迅. *Lu Xun quanji* 魯迅全集. Beijing: Renmin wenxue chubanshe, 1956.

Mao Zedong 毛澤東. *Mao Zedong xuanji* 毛澤東選集. Beijing: Renmin chubanshe, 1969.

Minbao 民報. Zhang Ji 張繼, ed. Beijing: Zhongguo kexueyuan lishi yanjiusuo, 1957, reprt.

Minlibao 民立報. Shanghai, 1910–1913.

Qian Zonghan 錢宗翰. *Huitu Zhongguo baihua shi* 繪圖中國白話史. N.p., 1906.

Qu Xingui 璩鑫圭 and Tang Liangyan 唐良炎, eds. *Zhongguo jindai jiaoyushi ziliao huibian: xuezhi yanbian* 中国近代教育史资料汇编：学制演变. Shanghai: Shanghai jiaoyu chubanshe, 1991.

Reinsch, Paul S. *An American Diplomat in China*. Garden City, NY: Doubleday, Page, 1922.

Shenbao 申報. Shanghai, 1872–1949.

Sheng Kang 盛康, comp. *Huangchao jingshiwen xubian* 皇朝經世文續編. Taibei: Wenhai, 1972.

Shengjing shibao 盛京時報. Shenyang, 1912–1924.

Shibao 時報. Shanghai, 1904–1924.

Shirakawa Jirō 白河次郎 and Kunibu Tanenori 國府種德. *Shina bunmei shi* 支那文明史. Tokyo: Hakubunkan, 1911.

Song Jiaoren 宋教仁. *Wo zhi lishi* 我之歷史. Taibei: Wenxing shudian, 1962.

Su Yu 蘇輿, comp. *Yijiao congbian* 翼教叢編. Yang Ching 楊菁, ed. Taibei: Zhongyang yanjiuyuan Zhongguo wenzhe yanjiusuo, 2005.

Subao 蘇報. Shanghai, 1902–1903.

Sun Baoxuan 孫寶瑄. *Wangshanlu riji* 望山廬日記. Shanghai: Shanghai guji chubanshe, 1983.

Sun Zhongshan [Sun Yat-sen] 孫中山. *Guofu quanji* 國父全集. Qin Xiaoyi 秦孝儀, ed. Taibei: Jindai Zhongguo, 1989.

Tan Sitong 譚嗣同. *Tan Sitong quanji* 譚嗣同全集. Cai Shangsi 蔡尚思 and Fang Xing 方行, eds. Beijing: Zhonghua shuju, 1990.

Tianyibao 天義報. Tokyo, 1907–1908.

Tomii Masaakira 富井政章. *Minfa yuanlun* 民法原论. Trans. Chen Haiying 陈海瀛 and Chen Haichao 陈海超. Beijing: Zhongguo zhenfa daxue chubanshe, 2003.

———. *Minpō genron* 民法原論. Tokyo: Yūhikaku, 1914 [1906].

Tu Ji 屠寄, ed. *Zhongguo dili jiaokeshu* 中國地理教科書. Shanghai: Shangwu yinshuguan, 1905.

Wheaton, Henry. *Elements of International Law*. Richard Henry Dana, Jr., ed. Boston: Little, Brown, 1866, 8th ed.

Wu Renda 吳人達, comp. *Falü tonglun* 法律通論. N.p.: Shanxi fazheng xuetang, 1907/1908.

Xin Qingnian 新青年. Tokyo: Daiyasu, 1961.

Xinmin congbao 新民叢報. Yokohama, 1902–1907.

Xinminshe 新民社, ed. *Qingyibao chuanbian* 清議報全編. Taibei: Wenhai, 1986.

Xu Nianci 徐念慈, ed. *Zhongguo dili: chuji shifan xuexiao jiaokeshu* 中國地理：初級師範學校教科書. Shanghai: Shangwu yinshuguan, 1906.

Yan Fu 嚴復. *Yan Fu heji* 嚴復合集. Wang Qingcheng 王慶成, Ye Wenxin [Wen-hsin Yeh] 葉文心, and Lin Zaijue 林載爵, eds. Taibei: Gugong Liang wenjiao jijinhui, 1998.

Yang Du 楊度. *Yang Du ji* 楊度集. Liu Qingbo 刘晴波, ed. Changsha: Hunan renmin chubanshe, 1986.

Yang Tingdong 楊廷棟. *Falüxue* 法律學. Shanghai: Zhongguo tushu gongsi, 1908.

Yao Zuyi 姚祖義. *Zuixin gaodeng xiaoxue Zhongguo lishi jiaokeshu* 最新高等小學中國歷史教科書. Shanghai: Shangwu yinshuguan, 1904.

Zhang Taiyan [Zhang Binglin] 章太炎. *Qiushu xiangzhu* 訄書詳注. Xu Fu 徐復, annot. Shanghai: Shanghai guji chubanshe, 2000.

———. *Taiyan xiansheng ziding nianpu* 太炎先生自訂年譜. Hong Kong: Lunmen shudian, 1965.

———. *Zhang Taiyan quanji* 章太炎全集. Shanghai renmin chubanshe 上海人民出版社, ed. Shanghai: Renmin chubanshe, 1985.

Zhang Yaozeng 張耀曾 and Cen Dezhang 岑德彰, eds. *Zhonghua minguo xianfa shiliao* 中華民國憲法史料. Taibei: Wenhai chubanshe, 1981.

Zhang Zhidong 張之洞. *Quanxue pian* 劝学篇. Li Zhongxing 李忠兴, ed. and annot. Zhengzhou: Zhengzhou guji chubanshe, 1998.

Zheng Guanying 鄭觀應. *Zheng Guanying ji* 鄭觀應集. Xia Dongyuan 夏東元, ed. Shanghai: Renmin chubanshe, 1982.

Zhengfu gongbao 政府公報. Taibei: Wenhai, 1971, reprt.

Zhou Zuoren 周作人. *Zhitang huixianglu* 知堂回想录. Hefei: Anhui jiaoyu chubanshe, 2008.

Zou Rong 鄒容. *Gemingjun* 革命軍. Shanghai: Zhonghua shuju, 1958.

Zuo xinyi shuju biancuan 作新譯書局編纂, ed. *Xinbian faxue tonglun (wubian)* 新編法學通論(五編). N.p.: Guangzhi shuju, 1902.

SECONDARY SOURCES

Abe Ken'ichi 阿部賢一. "Zou Rong de *Gemingjun* yu xiyang jindai sixiang: yi *minyuelun* ji jinhualun wei zhongxin" 鄒容的《革命軍》與西洋近代思想：以《民約論》及進化論為中心. *Jindai Zhongguo* 近代中國 42 (1984.8), 159–168.

Agulhon, Maurice. *Marianne into Battle: Republican Imagery and Symbolism in France, 1789–1880*. Cambridge, Eng.: Cambridge University Press, 1981.

Anderson, Benedict. *Imagined Communities: Reflections on the Origin and Spread of Nationalism*. London: Verso, 1991.

Angle, Stephen C. *Human Rights and Chinese Thought: A Cross-Cultural Inquiry*. New York: Cambridge University Press, 2002.

———. *Sagehood: The Contemporary Significance of Neo-Confucian Philosophy*. Oxford: Oxford University Press, 2009.

———. "Should We All Be More English? Liang Qichao, Rudolf von Jhering, and Rights." *Journal of the History of Ideas* 61.2 (2000), 241–261.

Angle, Stephen C., and Marina Svensson, eds. *The Chinese Human Rights Reader: Documents and Commentary, 1900–2000*. Armonk, NY: M. E. Sharpe, 2001.

Arjomand, Saïd Amir. "Constitutions and the Struggle for Political Order: A Study in the Modernization of Political Traditions." *European Journal of Sociology* 33.1 (1992), 39–82.

Atwood, Christopher P. "'Worshiping Grace': The Language of Loyalty in Qing Mongolia." *Late Imperial China* 21.2 (Dec. 2000), 86–139.

Ayers, William. *Chang Chih-tung and Educational Reform in China*. Cambridge, MA: Harvard University Press, 1971.

Ba Sidi [Marianne Bastid] 巴斯蒂. "Zhongguo jindai guojia guannian suyuan" 中国近代国家观念溯源. *Jindaishi yanjiu* 近代史研究 1997 (4), 221–232.

Barmé, Geremie R. *The Forbidden City*. Cambridge, MA: Harvard University Press, 2008.

Bastid, Marianne. "Official Conceptions of Imperial Authority at the End of the Qing Dynasty." In Schram, ed., *Foundations and Limits of State Power in China*, 147–186.

———. "La 'position' dans le ceremonial d'État à la fin de l'Empire." *Extrême-Orient, Extrême-Occident* 18 (1996), 51–69.

———. "Sacrifices d'État et légitimité à la fin des Qing." *T'oung Pao* 83 (1997), 162–173.

———. "Servitude or Liberation: The Introduction of Foreign Educational Practices and Systems to China from 1840 to the Present." In Ruth Hayhoe and Marianne Bastid, eds., *China's Education and the Industrialized World: Studies in Cultural Transfer*. Armonk, NY: M. E. Sharpe, 1987, 3–20.

Bastid-Bruguière, Marianne. "The Japanese-Induced German Connection on Modern Chinese Ideas of the State: Liang Qichao and the *Guojia lun* of J. K. Bluntschli." In Fogel, ed., *The Role of Japan*, 105–124.

Bauer, Wolfgang. *China and the Search for Happiness: Recurring Themes in Four Thousand Years of Chinese Cultural History*. New York: Seabury, 1976.

Bell, Catherine. *Ritual Theory, Ritual Practice*. New York: Oxford University Press, 1992.

Bellah, Robert N. "Civil Religion in America." *Daedalus* 96.1 (Winter 1967), 1–21.

Bendix, Reinhard. *Kings or People: Power and the Mandate to Rule*. Berkeley: University of California Press, 1978.

Bennett, Adrian Arthur. *John Fryer: The Introduction of Western Science and Technology into Nineteenth-Century China*. Cambridge, MA: EARC, Harvard University Press, 1967.

———. *Missionary Journalist in China: Young J. Allen and His Magazines, 1860–1883*. Athens: University of Georgia Press, 1983.

Benton, Lauren. *Law and Colonial Cultures: Legal Regimes in World History, 1400–1900*. Cambridge, Eng.: Cambridge University Press, 2002.

Bergère, Marie-Claire. *Sun Yat-sen*. Trans. Janet Lloyd. Stanford, CA: Stanford University Press, 1998.

Bernal, Martin. *Chinese Socialism to 1907*. Ithaca, NY: Cornell University Press, 1976.

———. "Liu Shih-p'ei and National Essence." In Furth, ed., *The Limits of Change*, 90–112.

Biggerstaff, Knight. *The Earliest Modern Government Schools in China*. Ithaca, NY: Cornell University Press, 1961.

Boli-Bennett, John. "The Ideology of Expanding State Authority in National Constitutions, 1870–1970." In John W. Meyer and Michael T. Hannan, eds., *National Development and the World System: Educational, Economic, and Political Change, 1950–1970*. Chicago: University of Chicago Press, 1979, 222–237.

Brown, Elizabeth A. R. *The Monarchy of Capetian France and Royal Ceremonial.* Aldershot, Eng.: Variorum, 1991.

Cao Meixiu 曹美秀. "Zhu Yixin yu Kang Youwei: yi jingxue xiangguan wenti wei taolun zhongxin" 朱一新與康有為——以經學相關問題為討論中心. *Zhongguo wenzhe yanjiu jikan* 中國文哲研究集刊 28 (Mar. 2006), 219–256.

Chadwick, Owen. *The Secularization of the European Mind in the Nineteenth Century.* Cambridge, Eng.: Cambridge University Press, 1975.

Chan, Sin-wai. *Buddhism in Late Ch'ing Political Thought.* Hong Kong: Chinese University Press, 1985.

———, trans. *An Exposition of Benevolence: The* Jen-hsueh *of T'an Ssu-t'ung.* Hong Kong: Chinese University Press, 1984.

Chan, Wing-tsit, trans. and annot. *"Instructions for Practical Living" and Other Neo-Confucian Writings by Wang Yang-ming.* New York: Columbia University Press, 1963.

Chang, Hao. *Chinese Intellectuals in Crisis: Search for Order and Meaning, 1890–1911.* Berkeley: University of California Press, 1987.

———. "Intellectual Change and the Reform Movement, 1890–8." In Fairbank and Liu, eds., *The Cambridge History,* vol. 11, 274–338.

———. *Liang Ch'i-ch'ao and Intellectual Transition in Modern China.* Cambridge, MA: Harvard University Press, 1971.

Chang, Lin-sheng. "The National Palace Museum: A History of the Collection." In Wen C. Fong and James C. Y. Watt, eds., *Possessing the Past: Treasures from the National Palace Museum, Taipei.* New York: Metropolitan Museum of Art, 1996, 3–25.

Ch'en, Jerome. *Yuan Shih-k'ai.* Stanford, CA: Stanford University Press, 1972.

Chen Feng 陈丰. "Bumou er he: 'nianjian pai' he Liang Qichao de xin shixue sixiang" 不谋而合：「年鉴派」和梁启超的新史学思想. *Dushu* 读书 177 (1993), 42–47.

Chen Hengming 陳恆明. *Zhonghua minguo zhengzhi fuhao zhi yanjiu* 中華民國政治符號之研究. Taibei: Taiwan shangwu yinshuguan, 1986.

Chen, Hsi-yuan. "Confucianism Encounters Religion: The Formation of Religious Discourse and the Confucian Movement in Modern China." Ph.D. dissertation, Harvard University, 1999.

———. "The Revelations of the Sacred Scriptures: The Christian New/Old Testaments and the Reconstruction of the Confucian New/Old Text Schools in Modern China." Paper presented at the conference "Encounters and Transformations: Cultural Transmission and Knowledge Production in a Cross-literary and Historical Perspective 1850–1960." Cambridge University, Sept. 28–29, 2009.

Chen Lai 陳來. "Huajie 'chuantong' yu 'xiandai' de jinzhang: wusi wenhua sichao de fansi" 化解「傳統」與「現代」的緊張：五四文化思潮的反思. In Lin Yusheng et al., *Wusi,* 151–185.

Chen Pengming 陈鹏鸣. *Liang Qichao xueshu sixiang pingzhuan* 梁启超学术思想评传. Beijing: Beijing tushuguan chubanshe, 1999.

Chen Qi'nan 陳其南. *Chuantong zhidu yu shehui yishi de jiegou: lishi yu renleixue de tansuo* 傳統制度與社會意識的結構：歷史與人類學的探索. Taibei: Yunchen wenhua, 1998.

Chen Xiyuan [Hsi-yuan Chen] 陳熙遠. "Zhongguo yeweimian: Ming Qing shiqi de Yuanxiao, yejin yu kuanghuan" 中國夜未眠——明清時期的元宵、夜禁與狂歡. *Zhongyang yanjiuyuan lishi yuyan yanjiusuo jikan* 中央研究院歷史語言研究所集刊 75.2 (2004), 283–329.

———. "'Zongjiao': yige Zhongguo jindai wenhuashi shang de guanjianci" 「宗教」——一個中國近代文化史上的關鍵詞. *Xin shixue* 新史學 13.4 (2002), 37–66.

Cheng, Anne. "Nationalism, Citizenship, and the Old Text/New Text Controversy in Late Nineteenth-Century China." In Fogel and Zarrow, eds., *Imagining the People*, 3–38.

Cheng, Weikun. "Hairdressing and Ethnic Conflict: The Queue-Cutting Movement after the 1911 Revolution." *Chinese Historians* 4.2 (June 1991), 1–26.

Chi Yunfei 迟云飞. "Qingji zhuzhang lixian de guanyuan dui xianzheng de tiren" 清季主张立宪的官員对宪政的体认. *Qingshi yanjiu* 清史研究 2000 (1), 14–22.

———. "Qingmo zuihou shinian de ping-Man-Han zhenyu wenti" 清末最後十年的平满汉畛域问题. *Jindaishi yanjiu* 近代史研究 2001 (5), 21–44.

Chow, Tse-tsung. *The May Fourth Movement: Intellectual Revolution in Modern China.* Stanford, CA: Stanford University Press, 1960.

Chu, Samuel C. "China's Attitudes toward Japan at the Time of the Sino-Japanese War." In Akira Iriye, ed., *The Chinese and the Japanese: Essays in Political and Cultural Interactions.* Princeton, NJ: Princeton University Press, 1980, 74–95.

Chung, Yuehtsen Juliette. *Struggle for National Survival: Eugenics in Sino-Japanese Contexts, 1896–1945.* New York: Routledge, 2002.

Cohen, Paul A. *Between Tradition and Modernity: Wang T'ao and Reform in Late Ch'ing China.* Cambridge, MA: CEAS, Harvard University Press, 1987.

Cohen, Paul A., and Merle Goldman, eds. *Ideas across Culture: Essays on Chinese Thought in Honor of Benjamin I. Schwartz.* Cambridge, MA: CEAS, Harvard University Press, 1990.

Crossley, Pamela Kyle. "Chaos and Civilization: Imperial Sources of Post-Imperial Models of the Polity." *Si yu yan* 思與言 36.1 (1998.3), 119–190.

———. *Orphan Warriors: Three Manchu Generations and the End of the Qing World.* Princeton, NJ: Princeton University Press, 1990.

———. "Review Article: The Rulerships of China." *American Historical Review* 97.5 (Dec. 1992), 1468–1483.

———. *A Translucent Mirror: History and Identity in Qing Imperial Ideology.* Berkeley: University of California Press, 1999.

de Bary, Wm. Theodore, trans. *Waiting for the Dawn: A Plan for the Prince—Huang Tsung-hsi's "Ming-i-tai-fang lu."* New York: Columbia University Press, 1993.

———. *The Liberal Tradition in China.* Hong Kong: Chinese University Press, 1983.

de Bary, Wm. Theodore, and Irene Bloom, eds. *Sources of Chinese Tradition.* New York: Columbia University Press, 1999, 2nd ed.

Dikötter, Frank. *The Discourse of Race in Modern China.* London: Hurst, 1992.

Ding Wenjiang 丁文江, ed. *Liang Rengong xiansheng nianpu changbian chugao* 梁任公先生年譜長編初稿. Taibei: Shijie shuju, 1988.

Ding Wenjiang, and Zhao Fengtian 赵丰田, eds. *Liang Qichao nianpu changbian* 梁启超年谱长编. Shanghai: Shanghai renmin chubanshe, 1983.

Ding Yajie 丁亞傑. "*Yijiao congbian* de jingdianguan" 《翼教丛编》的经典观. *Hunan daxue xuebao (shehui kexue ban)* 湖南大学学报(社会科学版) 18.4 (July 2004), 31–40.

Dirlik, Arif. *Marxism in the Chinese Revolution.* Lanham, MD: Rowman & Littlefield, 2005.

———. *The Origins of Chinese Communism.* New York: Oxford University Press, 1989.

Dobson, W. A. C. H. *Mencius.* Toronto: University of Toronto Press, 1969.

Doleželová-Velingerová, Milena, and Oldrich Král, eds. *The Appropriation of Culture Capital: China's May Fourth Project.* Cambridge, MA: HUAC, Harvard University Press, 2001.

Dong Fangkui 董方奎. *Qingmo zhengti biange yu guoqing zhi lunzheng: Liang Qichao yu lixian zhengzhi* 清末政体变革与国情之论争：梁启超与立宪政治. Wuchang: Huazhong shifan daxue chubanshe, 1991.

Drake, Fred W. *China Charts the World: Hsu Chi-yü and His Geography of 1848.* Cambridge, MA: EARC, Harvard University Press, 1975.

Duara, Prasenjit. "Knowledge and Power in the Discourse of Modernity: The Campaigns against Popular Religion in Early Twentieth-Century China." *Journal of Asian Studies* 50.1 (Feb. 1991), 67–83.

———. "Religion and Citizenship in China and the Diaspora." In Mayfair Mei-hui Yang, ed., *Chinese Religiosities*, 43–64.

———. *Rescuing History from the Nation: Questioning Narratives of Modern China.* Chicago: University of Chicago Press, 1995.

———. "Superscribing Symbols: The Myth of Guandi, Chinese God of War." *Journal of Asian Studies* 47.4 (Nov. 1988), 778–795.

Eastman, Lloyd. "Ch'ing-i and Chinese Policy Formation during the Sino-French Controversy, 1880–1885." *Journal of Asian Studies* 24.4 (Aug. 1965), 595–611.

Edwards, Louise. *Gender, Politics, and Democracy: Women's Suffrage in China.* Stanford, CA: Stanford University Press, 2008.

Edwards, R. Randle, Louis Henkin, and Andrew J. Nathan. *Human Rights in Contemporary China.* New York: Columbia University Press, 1986.

Elliott, Mark C. *The Manchu Way: The Eight Banners and Ethnic Identity in Late Imperial China.* Stanford, CA: Stanford University Press, 2001.

Elman, Benjamin A. *Classicism, Politics, and Kinship: The Ch'ang-chou School of New Text Confucianism in Late Imperial China.* Berkeley: University of California Press, 1990.

———. *A Cultural History of Civil Examinations in Late Imperial China.* Berkeley: University of California Press, 2000.

———. *From Philosophy to Philology: Intellectual and Social Aspects of Change in Late Imperial China.* Cambridge, MA: CEAS, Harvard University, 1984.

———. "Naval Warfare and the Refraction of China's Self-strengthening Reforms into Scientific and Technological Failure, 1865–1895." *Modern Asian Studies* 38.2 (May 2004), 283–326.

Elverskog, Johan. *Our Great Qing: The Mongols, Buddhism and the State in Late Imperial China.* Honolulu: University of Hawai'i Press, 2006.

Elvin, Mark. "The Collapse of Scriptural Confucianism." *Papers on Far Eastern History* 41 (1990), 45–76.

Esherick, Joseph W. *Reform and Revolution in China: The 1911 Revolution in Hunan and Hubei.* Berkeley: University of California Press, 1976.

Fairbank, John K., ed. *The Cambridge History of China: Late Qing, 1800–1911*, vol. 10. New York: Cambridge University Press, 1978.

———. *The Great Chinese Revolution: 1800–1985.* New York: Harper & Row, 1987.

Fairbank, John K., and Kwang-ching Liu, eds. *The Cambridge History of China: Late Qing, 1800–1911*, vol. 11. Cambridge, Eng.: Cambridge University Press, 1980.

Feuchtwang, Stephan. *The Imperial Metaphor: Popular Religion in China.* London: Routledge, 1992.

———. "School-Temple and City God." In G. William Skinner, ed., *The City in Late Imperial China.* Stanford, CA: Stanford University Press, 1977, 581–608.

Feuchtwang, Stephan, and Mingming Wang. *Grassroots Charisma: Four Local Leaders in China.* London: Routledge, 2001.

Fitzgerald, John. *Awakening China: Politics, Culture, and Class in the Nationalist Revolution.* Stanford, CA: Stanford University Press, 1996.

———. "Nationalism, Democracy, and Dignity in Twentieth-Century China." In Sechin

Y. S. Chien and John Fitzgerald, eds., *The Dignity of Nations: Equality, Competition, and Honor in East Asian Nationalism*. Hong Kong: Hong Kong University Press, 2006, 94-114.

———. "The Nationless State: The Search for a Nation in Modern Chinese Nationalism." *Australian Journal of Chinese Affairs* 33 (Jan. 1995), 75-104.

Fletcher, Joseph. "The Heyday of the Ch'ing Order in Mongolia, Sinkiang and Tibet." In Fairbank, ed., *The Cambridge History of China*, vol. 10, 351-408.

Fogel, Joshua A., ed. *The Role of Japan in Liang Qichao's Introduction of Modern Western Civilization to China*. Berkeley: Institute of East Asian Studies, University of California–Berkeley, Center for Chinese Studies, 2004.

Fogel, Joshua A., and Peter Zarrow, eds. *Imagining the People: Chinese Intellectuals and the Concept of Citizenship, 1890-1920*. Armonk, NY: M. E. Sharpe, 1997.

Fu Jinquan 傅金泉. "Zhonghua minguo kaiguo dianzhang" 中華民國開國典章. *Shaanxi wenxian* 陝西文獻 44 (Jan. 1981), 4-5.

Fung, Edmund S. K. *The Military Dimension of the Chinese Revolution: The New Army and Its Role in the Revolution of 1911*. Vancouver: University of British Columbia Press, 1980.

Furth, Charlotte, ed. *The Limits of Change: Essays on Conservative Alternatives in Republican China*. Cambridge, MA: Harvard University Press, 1976.

Gan Chunsong 干春松. "Kang Youwei he Kongjiaohui: Minguo chunian rujia fuxing nuli jiqi cuozhe" 康有为和孔教会：民国初年儒家复兴努力及其挫折. *Qiushi xuekan* 求是学刊 29.4 (2002), 110-114.

Gan Huaizhen 甘懷真. *Huangquan, liyi yu jingdian quanshi: Zhongguo gudai zhengzhishi yanjiu* 皇權、禮儀與經典詮釋：中國古代政治史研究. Taibei: Taiwan daxue chuban zhongxin, 2004.

Gao Qiang 高强 and Liu Hailing 刘海玲. "Lun Liang Qichao de 'daminzu zhuyi'" 论梁启超的"大民族主义." *Baoji wenli xueyuan xuebao (shehui kexue ban)* 宝鸡文理学院学报(社会科学版) 22.1 (Mar. 2002), 75-80.

Gardner, Daniel K. *Chu Hsi and the "Ta-hsueh": Neo-Confucian Reflection on the Confucian Canon*. Cambridge, MA: CEAS, Harvard University Press, 1986.

Gasster, Michael. *Chinese Intellectuals and the Revolution of 1911*. Seattle: University of Washington Press, 1969.

———. "The Republican Revolutionary Movement (1900-13)." In Fairbank and Liu, eds., *The Cambridge History*, vol. 11, 463-534.

Geertz, Clifford. *Negara: The Theatre State in Nineteenth-Century Bali*. Princeton, NJ: Princeton University Press, 1980.

Gillis, John R., ed. *Commemorations: The Politics of National Identity*. Princeton, NJ: Princeton University Press, 1994.

Gladney, Dru. *Muslim Chinese: Ethnic Nationalism in the People's Republic*. Cambridge, MA: Harvard University Press, 1991.

Goossaert, Vincent. "1898: The Beginning of the End for Chinese Religion?" *Journal of Asian Studies* 65.2 (May 2006), 307-335.

———. "Republican Church Engineering: The National Religious Associations in 1912 China." In Mayfair Mei-hui Yang, ed., *Chinese Religiosities*, 209-232.

Grieder, Jerome B. *Intellectuals and the State in Modern China*. New York: Free Press, 1981.

Guo Shiyou 郭世佑. "Sun Zhongshan de fan-Man minzu zhuyi sixiang bielun" 孙中山的反满民族主义思想别论. *Qingshi yanjiu* 清史研究 1994 (4), 40-49.

Habermas, Jürgen. *The Structural Transformation of the Public Sphere: An Inquiry into a Category of Bourgeois Society*. Trans. Thomas Burger. Cambridge, MA: MIT Press, 1989.

Hamlish, Tamara. "Preserving the Palace: Museums and the Making of Nationalism(s) in Twentieth-Century China." *Museum Anthropology* 19.2 (1995), 20–30.

Han Hua 韩华. *Minchu Kongjiaohui yu guojiao yundong yanjiu* 民初孔教会与国教运动研究. Beijing: Beijing tushuguan chubanshe, 2007.

Harrell, Paula. *Sowing the Seeds of Change: Chinese Students, Japanese Teachers, 1895–1905*. Stanford, CA: Stanford University Press, 1992.

Harrison, Henrietta. *The Making of the Republican Citizen: Political Ceremonies and Symbols in China, 1911–1929*. Oxford: Oxford University Press, 2000.

———. *The Man Awakened from Dreams: One Man's Life in a North China Village, 1857–1942*. Stanford, CA: Stanford University Press, 2005.

Hauf, Kandice. "The Community Covenant in Sixteenth Century Ji'an Prefecture, Jiangxi." *Late Imperial China* 17.2 (Dec. 1996), 1–50.

Hazama, Naoki. "On Liang Qichao's Conceptions of *Gong* and *Si*: 'Civic Virtue' and 'Personal Virtue' in the *Xinmin shuo*." Trans. Matthew Fraleigh. In Fogel, ed., *The Role of Japan*, 205–221.

Hazama Naoki 狭间直树, ed. *Kyōdō kenkyū Ryō Keichō: Seiyō kindai shisō juyō to Meiji Nihon* 共同研究梁啓超：西洋近代思想受容と明治日本. Tokyo: Misuzu shobō, 1999.

He Hanwen 何汉文 and Du Maizhi 杜迈之. *Yang Du zhuan* 杨度传. Changsha: Hunan renmin chubanshe, 1979.

He Lingxu 賀淩虛. "Sun Zhongshan suo changdao de minzu zhuyi jiqi shixing zhengce de yanbian" 孫中山所宣導的民族主義及其施行政策的演變. *Jindai Zhongguo* 近代中國 107 & 108 (1995.6–8), 196–216, 290–314.

He Wenhui 何文辉. "Shishi de jingying jiqi fankang: wuxu qianhou Hunan xinjiu zhi zheng de zhengzhixue fenxi" 失势的菁英及其反抗：戊戌前後湖南新旧之争的政治學分析. *Beijing xingzheng xueyuan xuebao* 北京行政学院学报 2004 (5), 82–86.

Hevia, James L. *English Lessons: The Pedagogy of Imperialism in Nineteenth-Century China*. Durham, NC: Duke University Press, 2003.

Hirschman, Albert O. *The Rhetoric of Reaction: Perversity, Futility, Jeopardy*. Cambridge, MA: Belknap Press, 1991.

Hō Takushū [Peng Zezhou] 彭澤周. *Chūgoku no kindaika to Meiji isshin* 中國の近代化と明治維新. Kyoto: Dōbōsha, 1976.

Hobsbawm, Eric, and Terence Ranger, eds. *The Invention of Tradition*. Cambridge, Eng.: Cambridge University Press, 1983.

Hofstadter, Richard. *The Paranoid Style in American Politics and Other Essays*. New York: Vintage Books, 1967.

Hon, Tze-ki. "From a Hierarchy in Time to a Hierarchy in Space: The Meanings of Sino-Babylonianism in Early Twentieth-Century China." *Modern China* 36.2 (Mar. 2010), 139–169.

———. "National Essence, National Learning, and Culture: Historical Writings in *Guocui xuebao*, *Xueheng*, and *Guoxue jikan*." *Historiography East and West* 1.2 (2003), 242–286.

———. "Zhang Zhidong's Proposal for Reform: A New Reading of the *Quanxue pian*." In Karl and Zarrow, eds., *Rethinking the 1898 Reform Period*, 77–98.

Horowitz, Richard S. "International Law and State Transformation in China, Siam, and the Ottoman Empire during the Nineteenth Century." *Journal of World History* 15.4 (Dec. 2004), 445–486.

Howard, Richard C. "Japan's Role in the Reform Program." In Jung-Pang Lo, ed., *K'ang Yu-wei*, 280–312.

———. "K'ang Yu-wei [1858–1927]: His Intellectual Background and Early Thought." In

Arthur Wright and Denis Twitchett, eds., *Confucian Personalities*. Stanford, CA: Stanford University Press, 1962, 294–316.

Howland, Douglas R. *Borders of Chinese Civilization: Geography and History at Empire's End*. Durham, NC: Duke University Press, 1996.

———. *Personal Liberty and Public Good: The Introduction of John Stuart Mill to Japan and China*. Toronto: University of Toronto Press, 2005.

———. "The Predicament of Ideas in Culture: Translation and Historiography." *History and Theory* 42.1 (Feb. 2003), 45–60.

———. *Translating the West: Language and Political Reason in Nineteenth-Century Japan*. Honolulu: University of Hawai'i Press, 2002.

Hsiao, Kung-chuan. *A Modern China and a New World: K'ang Yu-wei, Reformer and Utopian, 1858–1927*. Seattle: University of Washington Press, 1975.

Hsiung, Ping-chen. "T'ang Chen and the Works in Obscurity: Life and Thought of a Provincial Intellectual in Seventeenth Century China." Ph.D. dissertation, Brown University, 1983.

Hsü, Immanuel C. Y. *China's Entry into the Family of Nations*. Cambridge, MA: Harvard University Press, 1960.

Hu Pingsheng. *Liang Cai shisheng yu huguo zhi yi* 梁蔡師生與護國之役. Taibei: Guoli Taiwan daxue wenxueyuan, 1976.

———. *Minguo chuqi de fubipai* 民國初期的復辟派. Taibei: Taiwan Xuesheng shuju, 1985.

Huang Aiping 黃爱平 and Huang Xingtao 黃兴涛, eds. *Xixue yu Qingdai wenhua* 西学与清代文化. Beijing: Zhonghua shuju, 2008.

Huang Fuqing 黃福慶. *Qingmo liu Ri xuesheng* 清末留日學生. Taibei: Zhongyang yanjiuhuan jindaishi yanjiusuo, 1983.

Huang Kewu [Max Ko-wu Huang] 黃克武. "Cong zhuiqiu zhengdao dao rentong guozu—Mingmo zhi Qingmo Zhongguo gong si guannian de chongzheng" 從追求正道到認同國族——明末至清末中國公私觀念的重整. In Huang Kewu and Zhang Zhejia 張哲嘉, eds., *Gong yu si: jindai Zhongguo geti yu qunti zhi chongjian* 公與私：近代中國個體與群體之重建. Taibei: Zhongyang yanjiuyuan jindaishi yanjiusuo, 2000, 59–112.

———. "Liang Qichao yu Kangde" 梁啟超與康德. *Zhongyang yanjiuyuan jindaishi yanjiusuo jikan* 中央研究院近代史研究所集刊 30 (Dec. 1998), 101–148.

———. *Yige beifangqi de xuanze: Liang Qichao tiaoshi sixiang zhi yanjiu* 一個被放棄的選擇：梁啟超調適思想之研究. Taibei: Zhongyang yanjiuyuan jindaishi yanjiusuo, 1994.

Huang, Max Ko-wu. "Liang Qichao and Immanuel Kant." In Fogel, ed., *The Role of Japan*, 125–155.

———. *The Meaning of Freedom: Yan Fu and the Origins of Freedom*. Hong Kong: Chinese University Press, 2008.

Huang Minlan 黃敏兰. "Liang Qichao 'Xin shixue' de zhenshi yiyi ji lishixue de wujie" 梁启超《新史學》的真实意义及历史学的误解. *Jindaishi yanjiu* 近代史研究 1994 (2), 219–235.

———. *Zhongguo zhishifenzi diyiren: Liang Qichao* 中国知识分子第一人：梁启超. Hankou: Hubei jiaoyu chubanshe, 1999.

Huang, Philip. "Liang Ch'i-ch'ao: The Idea of the New Citizen and the Influence of Meiji Japan." In David C. Buxbaum and Frederick W. Mote, eds., *Transition and Permanence: Chinese History and Culture—A Festschrift in Honor of Dr. Hsiao Kung-ch'uan*. Hong Kong: Cathay Press, 1972, 71–102.

Huang, Yu-chin. "National Identity and Ideology in the Design of Postage Stamps of China and Taiwan, 1949–1979." Ph.D. dissertation, School of Oriental and African Studies, University of London, 2007.

Huang Zhangjian 黃彰健. *Kang Youwei wuxu zhen zouyi* 康有為戊戌真奏議. Taibei: Zhongyang yanjiuyuan lishi yuyan yanjiusuo, 1974.

Huguo wenji bianjizu 《护国文集》编辑组, ed. *Huguo wenji* 护国文集. Shijiazhuang: Hebei jiaoyu chubanshe, 1988.

Ishikawa Hiroshi 石川洋. "Byōdō to shittoshin—Ryū Shibai no anakizumu ni tuite no ikkōsatsu" 平等と嫉忌心——劉師培のアナキズムについての一考察. *Chūgoku tetsugaku kenkyū* 中國哲學研究 (Tokyo University) 21 (Nov. 2005), 1–27.

Ishikawa, Yoshihiro. "Liang Qichao, the Field of Geography in Meiji Japan, and Geographical Determinism." In Fogel, ed., *The Role of Japan*, 156–176.

Ishikawa Yoshihiro 石川禎浩. "20 shiji chunian Zhongguo liu Ri xuesheng 'Huangdi' zhi zaizao: pai-Man, xiaoxiang, xifanqiyuanlun" 20世紀初年中国留日学生"黃帝"之再造——排满、肖像、西方起源论. *Qingshi yanjiu* 清史研究 2005 (4), 51–62.

———. "Kindai Tō Ajia 'bunmeiken' no seiritsu to sono kyōdō gengo—Ryō Keichō ni okeru 'jinshu' o chūshin ni" 近代東アジア"文明圏"の成立とその共同言語——梁啟超における「人種」お中心に. In Hazama Naoki, ed., *Seiyō kindai bunmei to Chūka sekai* 西洋近代文明と中華世界. Kyoto: Kyōto daigaku gakaujitsu shuppankai, 2001, 24–50.

———. "Xinhai geming shiqi de zhongzu zhuyi yu Zhongguo renleixue de xingqi" 辛亥革命时期的种族主义与中国人类学的兴起. In Zhongguo shixuehui 中国史学会, ed., *Xinhai geming yu 20 shiji de Zhongguo* 辛亥革命与20世纪的中国. Beijing: Zhongyang wenxian chubanshe, 2002, 2:998–1020.

Jenco, Leigh K. *Making the Political: Founding and Action in the Political Theory of Zhang Shizhao*. Cambridge, Eng.: Cambridge University Press, 2010.

———. "'Rule by Man' and 'Rule by Law' in Early Republican China: Contributions to a Theoretical Debate." *Journal of Asian Studies* 69.1 (Feb. 2010), 181–203.

Jenner, W. J. F., trans. *From Emperor to Citizen: The Autobiography of Aisin-Gioro Pu Yi*. Beijing: Foreign Languages Press, 1979.

Jiang Jun 蒋俊. "Liang Qichao zaoqi shixue sixiang yu Futian Hemin de *Shixue tonglun*" 梁启超早期史学思想与浮田和民的《史学通论》. *Wenshizhe* 文史哲 (1993) 5, 28–32.

Jiang Yi 江轶. "Junxian hu? Gonghe hu? Lun Yan Du zhengzhi sixiang de shanbian" 君宪乎？共和乎？论杨度政治思想的嬗变. *Chuanshan xuekan* 船山学刊 75 (2010.1), 180–184.

Jiang Yihua 姜义华, ed. *Shehui zhuyi xueshuo zai Zhongguo de chuqi chuanbo* 社会主义学说在中国的初期传播. Shanghai: Fudan daxue chubanshe, 1984.

Jin Chongji 金冲及. "Xinhai geming he Zhongguo jindai minzu zhuyi" 辛亥革命和中国近代民族主义. *Jindaishi yanjiu* 近代史研究 2001 (5), 1–20.

Jin Guangtao 金觀濤 and Liu Qingfeng 劉青峰. *Guannianshi yanjiu: Zhongguo xiandai zhongyao zhengzhi shuyu de xingcheng* 觀念史研究：中國現代重要政治術語的形成. Hong Kong: Chinese University Press, 2008.

Johnston, R. F. "Chinese Cult of Military Heroes." *New China Review* 3.2 (April 1921), 79–91.

Jones, Susan Mann, and Philip A. Kuhn. "Dynastic Decline and the Roots of Rebellion." In Fairbank, ed., *The Cambridge History of China*, vol. 10, 107–162.

Judge, Joan. "Citizens or Mothers of Citizens? Gender and the Meaning of Modern Chinese Citizenship." In Merle Goldman and Elizabeth J. Perry, eds., *Changing Meanings of Citizenship in Modern China*. Cambridge, MA: Harvard University Press, 2002, 23–43.

———. *The Precious Raft of History: The Past, the West, and the Woman Question in China*. Stanford, CA: Stanford University Press, 2008.

Kamachi, Noriko. *Reform in China: Huang Tsun-hsien and the Japanese Model*. Cambridge, MA: Harvard University Press, 1981.

Karl, Rebecca E. "Creating Asia: China in the World at the Beginning of the Twentieth Century." *American Historical Review* 103.4 (Oct. 1998), 1096–1118.

———. *Staging the World: Chinese Nationalism at the Turn of the Twentieth Century*. Durham, NC: Duke University Press, 2002.

Karl, Rebecca E., and Peter Zarrow, eds. *Rethinking the 1898 Reform Period: Political and Cultural Change in Late Qing China*. Cambridge, MA: HUAC, Harvard University Press, 2002.

Kelly, Duncan. "Revisiting the Rights of Man: Georg Jellinek on Rights and the State." *Law and History Review* 22.3 (Fall 2004), 493–529.

Kertzer, David I. *Ritual, Politics, and Power*. New Haven, CT: Yale University Press, 1988.

Knight, Nick. "*On Contradiction* and *On New Democracy*: Contrasting Perspectives on Causation and Social Change in the Thought of Mao Zedong." *Bulletin of Concerned Asian Scholars* 22.2 (April–June 1990), 18–34.

Kong Xiangji 孔祥吉, ed. *Jiuwang tucun de lantu: Kang Youwei bianfa zouyi jizheng* 救亡圖存的藍圖：康有為變法奏議輯證. Taibei: Lianhebao xi wenhua jijinhui, 1998.

———. *Kang Youwei bianfa zouyi yanjiu* 康有为变法奏议研究. Shenyang: Liaoning jiaoyu chubanshe, 1988.

———. *Wuxu weixin yundong xintan* 戊戌维新运动新探. Changsha: Hunan renmin chubanshe, 1988.

Koskenniemi, Martti. *The Gentle Civilizer of Nations: The Rise and Fall of International Law, 1870–1960*. Cambridge, Eng.: Cambridge University Press, 2002.

Kriegel, Blandine. *The State and the Rule of Law*. Trans. Marc A. LePain and Jeffrey C. Cohen. Princeton, NJ: Princeton University Press, 1995.

Kuhn, Philip A. *Origins of the Modern Chinese State*. Stanford, CA: Stanford University Press, 2002.

Kuo, Thomas C. "Ch'en Tu-hsiu and the Chinese Intellectual Revolution, 1915–1919." *Chinese Studies in History* 25.3 (Spring 1992), 40–56.

Kuo, Ya-pei. "'The Emperor and the People in One Body': The Worship of Confucius and Ritual Planning in the Xinzheng Reforms, 1902–1911." *Modern China* 35.2 (Mar. 2009), 123–154.

Kwong, Luke S. K. *A Mosaic of the Hundred Days: Personalities, Politics, and Ideas of 1898*. Cambridge, MA: CEAS, Harvard University Press, 1984.

———. "The T'i-Yung Dichotomy and the Search for Talent in Late-Ch'ing China." *Modern Asian Studies* 27.2 (1993), 253–279.

Laitinen, Kauko. *Chinese Nationalism in the Late Qing Dynasty: Zhang Binglin as an Anti-Manchu Propagandist*. London: Curzon, 1990.

Lam, Joseph S. C. *State Sacrifices and Music in Ming China: Orthodoxy, Creativity and Expressiveness*. Albany: State University of New York Press, 1988.

Lee, Haiyan. "All the Feelings That Are Fit to Print: The Community of Sentiment and the Literary Public Sphere in China, 1900–1918." *Modern China* 27.3 (July 2001), 291–327.

Legge, James. *The Chinese Classics*. Taibei: SMC Publishing, 1991.

Lei Zhongxing 雷中行. *Ming Qing de xixue zhongyuan lun zhengyi* 明清的西學中源論爭議. Taibei: Lantai, 2009.

Leibold, James. *Reconfiguring Chinese Nationalism: How the Qing Frontier and Its Indigenes Became Chinese*. New York: Palgrave Macmillan, 2007.

Leonard, Jane Kate. *Wei Yuan and China's Rediscovery of the Maritime World*. Cambridge, MA: CEAS, Harvard University Press, 1984.

Levenson, Joseph R. *Confucian China and Its Modern Fate*. Berkeley: University of California Press, 1965.

———. *Liang Ch'i-ch'ao and the Mind of Modern China*. Berkeley: University of California Press, 1970.

Lewis, Charlton M. *Prologue to the Chinese Revolution: The Transformation of Ideas and Institutions in Hunan Province, 1891–1907*. Cambridge, MA: EARC, Harvard University Press, 1976.

Li Chunfu 李春馥. "Lun Liang Qichao guojia zhuyi guandian jiqi zhuanbian guocheng" 论梁启超国家主义观点及其转变过程. *Qingshi yanjiu* 清史研究 2004 (2), 46–60.

Li, Danke. "Popular Culture in the Making of Anti-Imperialist and Nationalist Sentiments in Sichuan." *Modern China* 30.4 (Oct. 2004), 470–505.

Li Delong 李德龙 and Yu Bing 俞冰, eds. *Lidai riji congchao* 歷代日記叢鈔. Beijing: Xueyuan chubanshe, 2006.

Li Huaxing 李华兴, ed. *Minguo jiaoyu shi* 民国教育史. Shanghai: Shanghai jiaoyu chubanshe, 1997.

Li Sanbao [San-pao Li] 李三寶, trans. and ed. "*Kangzi neiwaipian* chubu fenxi—Kang Nanhai xiancun zuizao zuopin" 《康子內外篇》初步分析——康南海現存最早作品. *Qinghua xuebao* 清華學報 11.1–2 (Dec. 1975), 213–247.

Li, San-pao. "K'ang Yu-wei's *Shihli kung-fa chuan-shu* (A complete book of substantial truths and universal principles)." *Zhongyang yanjiuyuan jindaishi yanjiusuo jikan* 中央研究院近代史研究所集刊 7 (June 1978), 683–725.

Li Xiaoti 李孝悌. *Qingmo de xiacengshehui qimeng yundong, 1901–1911* 清末的下層社會啟蒙運動, 1901–1911. Taibei: Zhongyang yanjiuyuan jindaishi yanjiusuo, 1992.

Li Xisuo 李喜所, ed. *Liang Qichao yu jindai Zhongguo shehui wenhua* 梁启超与近代中国社会文化. Tianjin: Tianjin guji chubanshe, 2005.

Li, Yu-ning. *The Introduction of Socialism into China*. New York: Columbia University Press, 1971.

Li Zehou 李泽厚. *Kang Youwei Tan Sitong sixiang yanjiu* 康有为谭嗣同思想研究. Shanghai: Renmin chubanshe, 1958.

———. "Qimeng yu jiuwang de shuangchong bianzou" 啟蒙與救亡的雙重變奏. In idem, *Zhongguo xiandai sixiang shilun*, 1–54.

———. *Zhongguo jindai sixiang shilun* 中国近代思想史论. Beijing: Renmin chubanshe, 1986.

———. *Zhongguo xiandai sixiang shilun* 中國現代思想史論. Taibei: Fengyun shidai chuban gongsi, 1991.

Li Zenghui 李增辉. "Cong dizhi huoshou dao Zhonggong dangyuan: Yang Du wannian sixiang zhuanbian yuanyin qianxi" 从帝制祸首到中共党员——杨度晚年思想转变原因淺析. *Zhongxue lishi jiaoxue cankao* 中学历史教学参考 2002 (9), 39–40.

Liang Taigen [Yang Taekeun] 梁台根. "Jindai xifang zhishi zai Dongya de chuanbo jiqi gongtong wenben zhi tansuo: yi *Zuozhi chuyan* wei li" 近代西方知識在東亞的傳播及其共同文本之探索——以《佐治芻言》為例. *Hanxue yanjiu* 漢學研究 24.2 (Dec. 2006), 323–351.

Liew, K. S. *Struggle for Democracy: Sung Chiao-jen and the 1911 Chinese Revolution*. Berkeley: University of California Press, 1971.

Lin Mingde 林明德. "Qingmo Minchu Riben zhengzhi dui Zhongguo de yingxiang" 清末民初日本政制對中國的影響. In Yue-him Tam, ed., *Sino-Japanese Cultural Interchange: The Economic and Intellectual Aspects*. Hong Kong: Institute of Chinese Studies, Chinese University of Hong Kong, 1985, 3:187–213.

Lin Xuezhong 林学忠. *Cong wanguo gongfa dao gongfa waijiao* 从万国公法到公法外交. Shanghai: Guji chubanshe, 2009.

Lin, Yü-sheng. *The Crisis of Chinese Consciousness: Radical Anti-traditionalism in the May Fourth Era*. Madison: University of Wisconsin Press, 1979.

Lin Yusheng [Yü-sheng Lin] 林毓生 et al. *Wusi: duoyuan de fansi* 五四：多元的反思. Hong Kong: Sanlian shudian, 1989.

Lin Zhihong 林志宏. *Minguo nai diguo ye: zhengzhi wenhua zhuanxingxia de Qingyimin* 民國乃敵國也：政治文化轉型下的清遺民. Taibei: Lianjing, 2009.

Liu Guangjing 劉廣京. "Wan Qing renquanlun chutan: jianlun Jidujiao sixiang zhi yingxiang 晚清人權論初探——兼論基督教思想之影響. *Xin shixue* 新史學 5.3 (Sept. 1994), 1–22.

Liu Huaxing 刘华兴 and Zhang Yuanlong 张元隆. "Sun Zhongshan yu Zhongguo jindai guojia guannian de fazhan" 孙中山与中国近代国家观念的发展. In Jiang Zhongxiao 江中孝 and Wang Jie 王杰, eds., *Kuashiji de jiedu yu shenshi: Sun Zhongshan yanjiu lunwen xuanji (1996–2006)* 跨世纪的解读与审视：孙中山研究论文选辑 (1996–2006). Tianjin: Tianjin guji chubanshe, 2006, 10–21.

Liu, Lydia H. *The Clash of Empires: The Invention of China in Modern World Making*. Cambridge, MA: Harvard University Press, 2004.

Liu Shichang 劉世昌. "Zhonghua minguo guoqingjie zhi zhiding yu diyige guoqingri zhi jinian" 中華民國國慶節之制定與第一個國慶日之紀念. *Guoli bianyiguan guankan* 國立編譯館館刊 1 (Oct. 1971), 113–122.

Liu Wangling 刘望龄. *Xinhai geminghou dizhi fubi he fanfubi douzheng* 辛亥革命后帝制复辟和反复辟斗争. Beijing: Renmin chubanshe, 1975.

Liu Xiaofeng 刘小枫. *Rujiao yu minzuguojia* 儒教与民族国家. Beijing: Huaxia chubanshe, 2007.

Lo, Jung-pang, ed. *K'ang Yu-wei: A Biography and a Symposium*. Tucson: University of Arizona Press, 1967.

Lu, Weijing. *True to Her Word: The Faithful Maiden Cult in Late Imperial China*. Stanford, CA: Stanford University Press, 2008.

Luo Zhitian 罗志田. "Baorong ruxue, zhuzi yu Huangdi de guoxue: Qingji shiren xunqiu minzu rentong xiangzheng de nuli" 包容儒學、諸子與黃帝的國學：清季士人尋求民族認同象徵的努力. *Taida lishi xuebao* 台大歷史學報 29 (June 2002), 87–105.

———. "Sixiang guannian yu shehui jiaose de cuowei: Wuxu qianhou Hunan xinjiu zhi zheng zaisi—cezhong Wang Xianqian yu Ye Dehui" 思想观念与社会角色的错位：戊戌前後湖南新旧之争再思——侧重王先谦与叶德辉. *Lishi yanjiu* 历史研究 1998 (5), 56–76.

Lust, John, trans. and annot. *The Revolutionary Army: A Chinese Nationalist Tract of 1903*. The Hague: Mouton, 1968.

Lynch, Alan. "Woodrow Wilson and the Principle of 'National Self-Determination': A Reconsideration." *Review of International Studies* 28 (2002), 419–436.

Mair, Victor H. "Language and Ideology in the Written Popularizations of the *Sacred Edict*." In David Johnson, Andrew J. Nathan, and Evelyn S. Rawski, eds., *Popular Culture in Late Imperial China*. Berkeley: University of California Press, 1985, 325–359.

Marin, Louis. *Portrait of the King*. Trans. Martha M. Houle. Minneapolis: University of Minnesota Press, 1988.

Maruyama Masayuki 丸山松幸. *Chūgoku kindai no kakumei shisō* 中国近代の革命思想. Tokyo: Kenbun shuppan, 1982.

Matten, Marc Andre. *Die Grenzen des Chinesischen—Nationale Identitätsstiftung im China des 20. Jahrhunderts*. Wiesbaden: Harrassowitz-Verlag, 2009.

———. "The Worship of General Yue Fei and His Problematic Creation as a National Hero in Twentieth-Century China." *Frontiers of History in China* 6.1 (Mar. 2011), 74–94.

Mazur, Mary G. *Wu Han, Historian: Son of China's Times*. Lanham, MD: Lexington Books, Rowman & Littlefield, 2009.

McCann, I. L., and L. A. Pearlman. "Vicarious Traumatization: A Framework for Understanding the Psychological Effects of Working with Victims." *Journal of Traumatic Stress* 3 (1990), 131–149.

McCord, Edward A. *The Power of the Gun: The Emergence of Modern Chinese Warlordism.* Berkeley: University of California Press, 1993.

McDermott, Joseph P., ed. *State and Court Ritual in China.* Cambridge, Eng.: Cambridge University Press, 1999.

McNally, Richard J. *Remembering Trauma.* Cambridge, MA: Belknap Press, Harvard University Press, 2003.

Meienberger, Norbert. *The Emergence of Constitutional Government in China (1905–1908): The Concept Sanctioned by the Empress Dowager Tz'u-Hsi.* Bern: Peter Lang, 1980.

Meisner, Maurice. *Li Ta-chao and the Origins of Chinese Marxism.* New York: Atheneum, 1973.

Meng Xiangcai 孟祥才. *Liang Qichao zhuan* 梁启超传. Beijing: Beijing chubanshe, 1980.

Meng, Yue. "Hybrid Science versus Modernity: The Practice of the Jiangnan Arsenal, 1854–1897." *East Asian Science, Technology, and Medicine* (Tübingen, Germany) 16 (1999), 13–52.

Miles, Steven B. *The Sea of Learning: Mobility and Identity in Nineteenth-Century Guangzhou.* Cambridge, MA: HUAC, Harvard University Press, 2006.

Mitchell, Timothy. "The Limits of the State: Beyond Statist Approaches and Their Critics." *American Political Science Review* 85.1 (Mar. 1991), 77–96.

———. "Society, Economy, and the State Effect." In George Steinmetz, ed., *State/Culture: State-Formation after the Cultural Turn.* Ithaca, NY: Cornell University Press, 1999, 76–97.

Mittler, Barbara. *A Newspaper for China? Power, Identity, and Change in Shanghai's News Media, 1872–1912.* Cambridge, MA: HUAC, Harvard University Press, 2004.

Mizoguchi Yūzō 溝口雄三. *Chūgoku no kō to shi* 中国の公と私. Tokyo: Kenbun shuppan, 1995.

Monad, Paul Kléber. *The Power of Kings: Monarchy and Religion in Europe, 1589–1715.* New Haven, CT: Yale University Press, 1999.

Moore, Barrington, Jr. *Social Origins of Dictatorship and Democracy: Lord and Peasant in the Making of the Modern World.* Boston: Beacon, 1966.

Morgan, Edmund S. *Inventing the People: The Rise of Popular Sovereignty in England and America.* New York: W. W. Norton, 1988.

Mori Tokihiko 森時彦. "Minzokushugi to museifushugi—kokugaku kyō shi Ryū Shibai no kakumei ron" 民族主義と無政府主義——國学の徒、劉師培の革命論. In Onogawa Hidemi and Shimada Kenji, eds., *Shingai kakumei no kenkyū,* 135–184.

Mosse, George L. "Caesarism, Circuses, and Monuments." *Journal of Contemporary History* 6.2 (1971), 167–182.

Murata Yūjirō 村田雄二郎. "Kang Youwei de Riben yanjiu jiqi tedian: *Riben bianzhengkao Riben shumuzhi* guanjian" 康有为的日本研究及其特点——《日本变政考日本书目志》管见. *Jindaishi yanjiu* 近代史研究 1993 (1), 27–40.

———. "Kō Yui to 'Tōgaku': 'Nihon shomoku shi' o megutte" 康有為と「東学」——「日本書目志」をめぐって. *Chūgoku kyōshitsu ronbunshū* 中国教室論文集 (University of Tokyo) 40 (1992.5), 1–42.

Murthy, Viren. *The Political Philosophy of Zhang Taiyan: The Resistance of Consciousness.* Leiden: Brill, 2011.

Nathan, Andrew J. *Peking Politics, 1918–1923: Factionalism and the Failure of Constitutionalism.* Berkeley: University of California Press, 1976.

Nedostup, Rebecca. *Superstitious Regimes: Religion and the Politics of Chinese Modernity*. Cambridge, MA: HUAC, Harvard University Press, 2010.

Ono Shinji 小野信爾. "Shingai kakumei to kakumei senden" 辛亥革命と革命宣伝. In Onogawa Hidemi and Shimada Kenji, eds., *Shingai kakumei no kenkyū*, 37–88.

Onodera Shirō 小野寺史郎. "Shinmatsu minshu no kokki o meguru kōsō to kōsō: seiten hakujitsu ki to goshiki ki ni tsuite" 清末民初の國旗おめめぐる構想と抗争：清田白日旗と五色旗について. *Rekishigaku kenkyū* 歴史学研究 803 (2005.7), 33–48.

Onogawa Hidemi 小野川秀美. "Ryū Shibai to museifushugi" 劉師培と無政府主義. *Tōhō gakuhō* 東方學報 36 (1964), 695–720.

Onogawa Hidemi, and Shimada Kenji 島田虔次, eds. *Shingai kakumei no kenkyū* 辛亥革命の研究. Tokyo: Chikuma shoten, 1978.

Ozouf, Mona. *Festivals and the French Revolution*. Trans. Alan Sheridan. Cambridge, MA: Harvard University Press, 1988.

Perdue, Peter C. *China Marches West: The Qing Conquest of Central Eurasia*. Cambridge, MA: Belknap Press, Harvard University Press, 2005.

Pi Houfeng 皮后锋. "Zhongguo jindai guoge kaoshu" 中国近代国歌考述. *Jindaishi yanjiu* 近代史研究 1995 (2), 260–271.

Pillemer, David B. "Can the Psychology of Memory Enrich Historical Analyses of Trauma?" *History & Memory* 16.2 (Fall/Winter 2004), 140–154.

Platt, Stephen R. *Provincial Patriots: The Hunanese and Modern China*. Cambridge, MA: Harvard University Press, 2007.

Polachek, James. *The Inner Opium War*. Cambridge, MA: CEAS, Harvard University Press, 1992.

Price, Don C. "Constitutional Alternative and Democracy in the Revolution of 1911." In Cohen and Goldman, eds., *Ideas across Culture*, 234–260.

———. "Escape from Disillusionment: Personality and Value Change in the Case of Sung Chiao-jen." In Richard J. Smith and D. W. Y. Kwok, eds., *Cosmology, Ontology, and Human Efficacy: Essays in Chinese Thought*. Honolulu: University of Hawai'i Press, 1993, 217–236.

———. "From Might to Right: Liang Qichao and the Comforts of Darwinism in Late-Meiji Japan." In Fogel, ed., *The Role of Japan*, 68–102.

———. "Popular and Elite Heterodoxy toward the End of the Qing." In Kwang-ching Liu and Richard Shek, eds., *Heterodoxy in Late Imperial China*. Honolulu: University of Hawai'i Press, 2004, 431–461.

———. *Russia and the Roots of the Chinese Revolution, 1896–1911*. Cambridge, MA: Harvard University Press, 1974.

Pugach, Noel. "Embarrassed Monarchist: Frank J. Goodnow and Constitutional Development in China, 1913–1915." *Pacific Historical Review* 42.4 (1973), 499–517.

Pusey, James Reeve. *China and Charles Darwin*. Cambridge, MA: CEAS, Harvard University Press, 1983.

Qian Mu 錢穆. *Zhongguo jinsanbai nian xueshushi* 中國近三百年學術史. Shanghai: Shangwu, 1937.

Rankin, Mary B. *Elite Activism and Political Transformation in China: Zhejiang Province, 1865–1911*. Stanford, CA: Stanford University Press, 1986.

———. "Nationalistic Contestation and Mobilization Politics: Practice and Rhetoric of Railway-Rights Recovery at the End of the Qing." *Modern China* 28.3 (July 2002), 315–361.

Rao Zongyi 饒宗頤. *Zhongguo shixueshang zhi zhengtong lun: Zhongguo shixue guannian tantao zhi yi* 中國史學上之正統論——中國史學觀念探討之一. Taibei: Zongqing tushu gongsi, 1979.

Rawski, Evelyn S. "The Creation of an Emperor in Eighteenth-Century China." In Yung, Rawski, and Watson, eds., *Harmony and Counterpoint*, 150–174.

———. *The Last Emperors: A Social History of Qing Imperial Institutions*. Berkeley: University of California Press, 1998.

Reed, Christopher A. *Gutenberg in Shanghai: Chinese Print Capitalism, 1876–1937*. Vancouver: University of British Columbia Press, 2004.

Reynolds, Douglas R. *China, 1898–1912: The Xinzheng Revolution and Japan*. Cambridge, MA: CEAS, Harvard University Press, 1993.

Rhoads, Edward J. M. *Manchus and Han: Ethnic Relations and Political Power in Late Qing and Early Republican China, 1861–1928*. Seattle: University of Washington Press, 2000.

Rickett, W. Allyn. *Guanzi: Political, Economic, and Philosophical Essays from Early China*, vol. 1. Princeton, NJ: Princeton University Press, 1985.

Rowe, William T. "The Public Sphere in Modern China." *Modern China* 16.3 (July 1990), 309–329.

Rudolph, Jenifer M. *Negotiated Power in Late Imperial China: The Zongli Yamen and the Politics of Reform*. Ithaca, NY: Cornell University Press, 2008.

Sakamoto, Hiroko. "The Formation of National Identity in Liang Qichao and Its Relationship to Gender." In Fogel, ed., *The Role of Japan*, 272–289.

Sakamoto Hiroko 坂元ひろ子. *Chūgoku minzoku shugi no shinwa: jinshu, shintai, jendā* 中国民族主義の神話：人種、身体、ジェンダー. Tokyo: Iwanami shoten, 2004.

———. "Chūgoku shijō no jinshu kannen o megutte" 中国史上の人種概念をめぐって. In Takesawa Taiko 竹沢泰子, ed., *Jinshu kannen no futsūsei tou: Seiyō teki paradaisu o koete* 人種概念の普遍性を問う：西洋的パラダイムを越えて. Kyoto: Jinbun shoin, 2005, 182–204.

Sanetō Keishū さねとう・けいしゅう. *Chūgokujin Nihon ryūgakushi* 中国人日本留学史. Tokyo: Kuroshio shuppan, 1981, 2nd ed.

Sang Bing 桑兵. *Qingmo xinzhishijie de shetuan yu huodong* 清末新知识界的社团与活动. Beijing: Sanlian shudian, 1995.

Scalapino, Robert A., and Harold Schiffrin. "Early Socialist Currents in the Chinese Revolutionary Movement: Sun Yat-sen versus Liang Ch'i-ch'ao." *Journal of Asian Studies* 18.3 (May 1959), 321–342.

Schäfer, Ingo. "The People, People's Rights, and Rebellion: The Development of Tan Sitong's Political Thought." In Fogel and Zarrow, eds., *Imagining the People*, 82–112.

Schneider, Laurence A. "National Essence and the New Intelligentsia." In Furth, ed., *The Limits of Change*, 57–89.

Schram, S. R., ed. *Foundations and Limits of State Power in China*. London: School of Oriental and African Studies, 1987.

Schwarcz, Vera. *The Chinese Enlightenment: Intellectuals and the Legacy of the May Fourth Movement of 1919*. Berkeley: University of California Press, 1986.

Schwartz, Benjamin. *In Search of Wealth and Power: Yen Fu and the West*. Cambridge, MA: Belknap Press, Harvard University Press, 1964.

Sha Peide [Peter Zarrow] 沙培德. "'Li yu jun, li yu min': Wan-Qing guanyuan dui lixiang zhi yilun" 「利於君，利於民」：晚清官員對立憲之議論. *Zhongyang yuanjiuyuan jindaishi yanjiusuo jikan* 中央研究院近代史研究所集刊 42 (Dec. 2003), 47–71.

Shang Xiaoming 尚小明. *Liuri xuesheng yu Qingmo xinzheng* 留日学生与清末新政. Nanchang: Jiangxi jiaoyu chubanshe, 2003.

Shen Songqiao 沈松僑. "Wo yi woxie jian Xuanyuan: Huangdi shenhua yu wan-Qing de guozu jian'gou" 我以我血薦軒轅——黃帝神話與晚清的國族建構. *Taiwan shehui yanjiu jikan* 台灣社會研究季刊 28 (Dec. 1997), 1–77.

Sheridan, James E. *Chinese Warlord: The Career of Feng Yu-hsiang.* Stanford, CA: Stanford University Press, 1966.

Shi Jianxing 施建兴. "Guojifa de shuru yu Zhongguo jindai guojia zhuquan guannian de faren" 国际法的输入与中国近代国家主权观念的发轫. *Nanping shizhuan xuebao* 南平师专学报 22.1 (Mar. 2003), 46–50.

Shi, Mingzheng. "From Imperial Gardens to Public Parks: The Transformation of Urban Space in Early Twentieth-Century Beijing." *Modern China* 24.3 (July 1998), 219–254.

Shi Wen 史文 and Xu Min 许敏. "Wan-Qing shiqi dui guojia qiyuan de sikao he quanshi" 晚清时期对国家起源的思考和诠释. *Wuhan daxue xuebao (Renwen kexue ban)* 武汉大学学报(人文科学版) 59.1 (Jan. 2006), 56–61.

Skocpol, Theda. *States and Social Revolutions: A Comparative Analysis of France, Russia, and China.* Cambridge, Eng.: Cambridge University Press, 1979.

Sommerville, John C. *The Secularization of Early Modern England: From Religious Culture to Religious Faith.* Oxford: Oxford University Press, 1992.

Sōgō Masaaki 惣郷正明 and Hida Yoshifumi 飛田良文. *Meiji no kotoba jiten* 明治のことば辞典. Tokyo: Tōkyōdō, 1998.

Spence, Jonathan. *To Change China: Western Advisers in China, 1620–1960.* Boston: Little, Brown, 1969.

Spillman, Lyn. *Nation and Commemoration: Creating National Identities in the United States and Australia.* Cambridge, Eng.: Cambridge University Press, 1997.

Stråth, Bo, ed. *Myth and Memory in the Construction of Community: Historical Patterns in Europe and Beyond.* Brussels: PIE Lang, 2000.

Struve, Lynn A. "Confucian PTSD: A Teenager's Traumatic Memory of 1651–1652." *History & Memory* 16.2 (Fall/Winter 2004), 14–31.

———. "Huang Zongxi in Context: A Reappraisal of His Major Writings." *Journal of Asian Studies* 47.3 (Aug. 1988), 474–502.

———, trans. and ed. *Voices from the Ming-Qing Cataclysm: China in Tigers' Jaws.* New Haven, CT: Yale University Press, 1993.

Sun Longji [Lung-kee Sun] 孫隆基. "Qingji minzu zhuyi yu Huangdi chongbai zhi faming" 清季民族主义与黄帝崇拜之发明. *Lishi yanjiu* 历史研究 2000 (3), 68–79.

Sun, Lung-kee. *The Chinese National Character: From Nationhood to Individuality.* Armonk, NY: M. E. Sharpe, 2002.

Sun Qing 孙青. *Wan-Qing zhi "Xizheng" dongjian ji bentu huiying* 晚清之 "西政" 东渐及本土回应. Shanghai: Shanghai shudian chubanshe, 2009.

Sun Zhendong 孫鎮東. *Guoqi guoge guohua shihua* 國旗國歌國花史話. N.p., 1981.

Suzuki, Shogo. "China's Perceptions of International Society in the Nineteenth Century: Learning More about Power Politics?" *Asian Perspectives* 28.3 (Fall 2004), 115–144.

Suzuki Shūji 鈴木修次. *Nihon kango to Chūgoku: kanji bunkaken no kindaika* 日本漢語と中國：漢字文化圏の近代化. Tokyo: Chūōkōronsha, 1981.

Tang, Xiaobing. *Global Space and the Nationalist Discourse of Modernity: The Historical Thinking of Liang Qichao.* Stanford, CA: Stanford University Press, 1996.

Tang Zhijun 汤志钧. *Gailiang yu geming de Zhongguo qinghuai: Kang Youwei yu Zhang Taiyan* 改良與革命的中國情懷：康有為與章太炎. Taibei: Taiwan shangwu yinshuguan, 1991.

———. *Jindai jingxue yu zhengzhi* 近代经学与政治. Beijing: Zhonghua shuju, 1989.

———. *Kang Youwei yu wuxu bianfa* 康有为与戊戌变法. Beijing: Zhonghua shuju, 1984.

———. *Wuxu bianfa shi luncong* 戊戌变法史论丛. Shanghai: Renmin chubanshe, 1957.

———, ed. *Zhang Taiyan nianpu changbian* 章太炎年谱长编. Beijing: Zhonghua shuju, 1979.

Tang Zuodong 唐作棟. "Yuannian yuandan kaiguo shihua" 元年元旦開國史話. *Shaanxi wenxian* 陝西文獻 44 (Jan. 1981), 2–4.

Tao Xu 陶绪. *Wan-Qing minzu zhuyi sichao* 晚清民族主义思潮. Beijing: Renmin chubanshe, 1995.

Taylor, Charles. *Modern Social Imaginaries*. Durham, NC: Duke University Press, 2004.

———. *A Secular Age*. Cambridge, MA: Belknap Press, Harvard University Press, 2007.

Teng, Emma Jinhua. "Eurasian Hybridity in Chinese Utopian Visions: From 'One World' to 'A Society Based on Beauty' and Beyond." *positions* 14.1 (Spring 2006), 131–163.

Teng, Ssu-yü, and John K. Fairbank. *China's Response to the West: A Documentary Survey, 1839–1923*. Cambridge, MA: Harvard University Press, 1979.

Thompson, Laurence G. *Ta T'ung Shu: The One-World Philosophy of K'ang Yu-wei*. London: George Allen & Unwin, 1958.

Tian Tao 田涛. *Guojifa shuru yu wan-Qing Zhongguo* 国际法输入与晚清中国. Ji'nan: Ji'nan chubanshe, 2001.

———. "Shijiu shiji xiabanqi Zhongguo zhishijie de guojifa guannian" 19世纪下半期中国知识界的国际法观念. *Jindaishi yanjiu* 近代史研究 2000 (2), 102–135.

Trescott, Paul B. "Scottish Political Economy Comes to the Far East: The Burton-Chambers *Political Economy* and the Introduction of Economic Ideas into Japan and China." *History of Political Economy* 21.3 (1989), 481–502.

Tsin, Michael. "Imagining 'Society' in Early Twentieth-Century China." In Fogel and Zarrow, eds., *Imagining the People*, 212–231.

Tsu, Jing. *Failure, Nationalism, and Literature: The Making of Modern Chinese Identity, 1895–1937*. Stanford, CA: Stanford University Press, 2005.

U, Eddy. "Reification of the Chinese Intellectual: On the Origins of *Zhishifenzi*." *Modern China* 35.6 (July 2009), 604–631.

Van Alstyne, Richard W. "Woodrow Wilson and the Idea of the Nation State." *International Affairs* 37.3 (July 1961), 293–308.

Wagner, Rudolf G. "The Early Chinese Newspapers and the Chinese Public Sphere." *European Journal of East Asian Studies* 1.1 (2001), 1–33.

Wakeman, Frederick, Jr. "The Price of Autonomy: Intellectuals in Ming and Ch'ing Politics." *Daedalus* 101.2 (Spring 1972), 55–67.

Waldron, Arthur. *From War to Nationalism: China's Turning Point, 1924–1925*. Cambridge, Eng.: Cambridge University Press, 1995.

Waley, Arthur. *The Analects of Confucius*. New York: Vintage Books, 1938.

Wallis, Roy. "Charisma and Explanation." In Eileen Barker, James A. Beckford, and Karel Dobbleaere, eds., *Secularization, Rationalism, and Sectarianism: Essays in Honour of Bryan R. Wilson*. Oxford: Clarendon Press, 1993, 167–179.

Wang, Chaohua. "Cai Yuanpei and the Origins of the May Fourth Movement: Modern Chinese Intellectual Transformations, 1890–1920." Ph.D. dissertation, University of California, Los Angeles, 2008.

Wang, Cheng-hua. "The Photographed Images of the Empress Dowager Cixi, *ca.* 1904." Unpublished paper.

———. "The Qing Imperial Collection, circa 1904–1925: National Humiliation, Heritage Preservation, and Exhibition Culture." In Hung Wu, ed., *Reinventing the Past: Archaism and Antiquarianism in Chinese Art and Visual Culture*. Chicago: Center for the Art of East Asia, University of Chicago, 2010, 320–341.

Wang, David Der-wei. *Fin-de-Siècle Splendor: Repressed Modernities of Late Qing Fiction, 1849–1911*. Stanford, CA: Stanford University Press, 1997.

Wang, Dong. *China's Unequal Treaties: Narrating National History*. Lanham, MD: Lexington Books, Rowman & Littlefield, 2005.

Wang, Fan-shen. "Evolving Prescriptions for Social Life in the Late Qing and Early Republic: From *Qunxue* to Society." In Fogel and Zarrow, eds., *Imagining the People*, 258–278.

Wang Fansen [Fan-shen Wang] 王汎森. *Gushibian yundong de xingqi: yige sixiangshi de fenxi* 古史辨運動的興起：一個思想史的分析. Taibei: Yunchen wenhua, 1987.

———. "Qingmo de lishi jiyi yu guojia jiango: yi Zhang Taiyan weili" 清末的歷史記憶與國家建構：以章太炎為例. *Si yu yan* 思與言 34.3 (1996.9), 1–18.

———. "Wan-Qing de zhengzhi gainian yu 'Xin shixue'" 晚清的政治概念与"新史学." In Luo Zhitian 罗志田, ed., *Ershi shiji de Zhongguo: xueshu yu shehui—shixuejuan* 20 世纪的中国：学术与社会——史学卷. Ji'nan: Shandong renmin chubanshe, 2001, 1:1–30.

———. *Zhang Taiyan de sixiang (1868–1919) jiqi dui ruxue chuantong de chongji* 章太炎的思想(1868–1919)及其對儒學傳統的衝擊. Taibei: Shibao wenhua gongsi, 1985.

Wang Gengsheng. *Women de guoge* 我們的國歌. Taibei: Zhangyang wenwu gongyingshe, 1981.

———. *Women de guoqi* 我們的國旗. Taibei: Guoli bianyiguan, 1981.

Wang Hui 汪晖. *Xiandai Zhongguo sixiang de xingqi* 现代中国思想的兴起, 4 vols. Beijing: Sanlian shudian, 2004.

———. "Zhang Taiyan's Concept of the Individual and Modern Chinese Identity." In Wen-hsin Yeh, ed., *Becoming Chinese: Passages to Modernity and Beyond*. Berkeley: University of California Press, 2000, 231–259.

Wang, Juan. "Imagining Citizenship: The Shanghai Tabloid Press, 1897–1911." *Twentieth-Century China* 35.1 (Nov. 2009), 29–53.

———. "Officialdom Unmasked: Shanghai Tabloid Press, 1897–1911." *Late Imperial China* 28.2 (Dec. 2007), 81–128.

Wang Junzhong 王俊中. "Jiuguo, zongjiao yi zhexue? Liang Qichao zaonian de foxueguan jiqi zhuanzhe (1891–1912)" 救國、宗教抑哲學?——梁啟超早年的佛學觀及其轉折. *Zhongguo lishi xuehui shixue jikan* 中國歷史學會史學集刊 (Taibei) 31 (June 1999), 93–116.

Wang, Ke-wen, ed. *Modern China: An Encyclopedia of History, Culture, and Nationalism*. New York: Garland, 1998.

Wang Mingke 王明珂. "Lun Panfu: Jindai Yan Huang zisun guozu jian'gou de gudai jichu" 論攀附：近代炎黃子孫國族建構的古代基礎. *Zhongyang yanjiuyuan lishi yuyan yanjiusuo jikan* 中央研究院歷史語言研究所集刊 73.3 (2002), 583–624.

Wang Qingxiang 王庆祥. *Puyi jiaowang lu* 溥仪交往录. Beijing: Dongfang chubanshe, 1999.

Wang Renbo 王人博. *Xianzheng wenhua yu jindai Zhongguo* 宪政文化与近代中国. Beijing: Falü chubanshe, 1997.

Wang Rongzu [Young-tsu Wong] 汪榮祖. *Kang Youwei* 康有為. Taibei: Dongda tushu gongsi, 1998.

———. *Kang Zhang helun* 康章合論. Taibei: Lianjing, 1988.

———. *Wan-Qing bianfa sixiang luncong* 晚清變法思想論叢. Taibei: Lianjing, 1990.

———. "'Wuxue sasui yicheng': Kang Youwei zaonian sixiang xilun" 「吾學卅歲已成」：康有為早年思想析論. *Hanxue yanjiu* 漢學研究 12.2 (Dec. 1994), 51–62.

Wang Shanping 王姍萍. "Zhang Zhidong yu wan-Qing falü jiaoyu" 张之洞与晚清法律教育. *Guizhou wenshi congkan* 贵州文史丛刊 2006 (2), 17–20.

Wang Xiaoqiu 王晓秋. *Jindai Zhong-Ri qishilu* 近代中日启示录. Beijing: Beijing chubanshe, 1987.

———, ed. *Wuxu weixin yu jindai Zhongguo de gaige: wuxu weixin yibai zhounian guoji xueshu taolunhui lunwenji* 戊戌维新与近代中国的改革：戊戌维新一百周年国际学术讨论会论文集. Beijing: Shehui kexue wenxian chubanshe, 2000.

———. "*Zhishuo*" 《直說》. In Ding Shouhe 丁守和, ed., *Xinhai geming shiqi qikan jieshao* 辛亥革命时期期刊介绍. Beijing: Renmin chubanshe, 1982, 1:259–268.

Wang Xiaoqiu, and Shang Xiaoming 尚小明, eds. *Wuxu weixin yu Qingmo xinzheng: wan-Qing gaigeshi yanjiu* 戊戌维新与清末新政：晚清改革史研究. Beijing: Renmin chubanshe, 1998.

Wang Yeyang 王也扬. "Kang-Liang yu shixue zhiyong" 康、梁与史学致用. *Jindaishi yanjiu* 近代史研究 1994 (2), 204–235.

Wang Yue 王樾. *Tan Sitong bianfa sixiang yanjiu* 譚嗣同變法思想研究. Taibei: Taiwan xuesheng shuju, 1990.

Weber, Max. *From Max Weber: Essays in Sociology.* Trans. and ed. H. H. Gerth and C. Wright Mills. New York: Oxford University Press, 1946.

———. "The Nature of Charismatic Authority and Its Routinization." In S. N. Eisenstadt, ed., *Max Weber on Charisma and Institution Building.* Chicago: University of Chicago Press, 1968, 48–65.

Weston, Timothy B. "The Formation and Positioning of the New Culture Community." *Modern China* 24.3 (July 1998), 255–284.

———. "The Founding of the Imperial University and the Emergence of Chinese Modernity." In Karl and Zarrow, eds., *Rethinking the 1898 Reform Period*, 99–123.

———. *The Power of Position: Beijing University, Intellectuals, and Chinese Political Culture, 1898–1929.* Berkeley: University of California Press, 2004.

Wilentz, Sean, ed. *Rites of Power: Symbolism, Ritual and Politics since the Middle Ages.* Philadelphia: University of Pennsylvania Press, 1985.

Wilhelm, Richard, trans. *I Ching: The Book of Change: The Richard Wilhelm Translation.* Trans. Cary F. Baynes. London: Routledge & Kegan Paul, 1983.

Williams, Raymond. *Keywords: A Vocabulary of Culture and Society.* New York: Oxford University Press, 1985.

Wong, Young-tsu. *Beyond Confucian China: The Rival Discourses of Kang Youwei and Zhang Binglin.* New York: Routledge, 2010.

———. "Philosophical Hermeneutics and Political Reform: A Study of Kang Youwei's Use of Gongyang Confucianism." In Ching-i Tu, ed., *Classics and Interpretations: The Hermeneutic Traditions in Chinese Culture.* New Brunswick, NJ: Transaction Publishers, 2000, 383–407.

———. *Search for Modern Nationalism: Zhang Binglin and Revolutionary China, 1869–1936.* Hong Kong: Oxford University Press, 1989.

Woodside, Alexander. *Lost Modernities: China, Vietnam, Korea and the Hazards of World History.* Cambridge, MA: Harvard University Press, 2006.

Wright, Mary Clabaugh. *The Last Stand of Chinese Conservatism: The T'ung-chih Restoration, 1862–1874.* Stanford, CA: Stanford University Press, 1957.

Wu, Hung. *Remaking Beijing: Tiananmen Square and the Creation of a Political Space.* London: Reaktion, 2005.

Wu Jingxiong 吳經熊 and Huang Gongjue 黃公覺. *Zhongguo zhixian shi* 中國制憲史. Shanghai: Shangwu yinshuguan, 1937.

Wu Lun Nixia 吳倫霓霞. "Xianggang fan-Qing geming xuanchuan baokan jiqi yu Nanyang de lianxi" 香港反清革命宣傳報刊及其與南洋的聯繫. *Xianggang Zhongwen daxue Zhongguo wenhua yanjiusuo xuebao* 香港中文大學中國文化研究所學報 19 (1988), 407–422.

Xiong Qiuliang 熊秋良. "'Yijiao' pai lüelun" "翼教"派略论. *Hunan shifan daxue shehui kexue xuebao* 湖南师范大学社会科学学报 28 (1999), 90–94.

Xiong Yuezhi 熊月之. *Xixue dongjian yu wan-Qing shehui* 西学东渐与晚清社会. Shanghai: Renmin chubanshe, 1994.

———. *Zhongguo jindai minzhu sixiangshi* 中国近代民主思想史. Shanghai: Shanghai shehui kexueyuan chubanshe, 2002.

Xu Guansan 許冠三. *Xin shixue jiushinian, 1900–* 新史學九十年：一九０ 0 –. Hong Kong: Zhongwen daxue chubanshe, 1989.

Yang, Fang-yen. "Nation, People, Anarchy: Liu Shih-p'ei and the Crisis of Order in Modern China." Ph.D. dissertation, University of Wisconsin, 1999.

Yang, Mayfair Mei-hui, ed. *Chinese Religiosities: Afflictions of Modernity and State Formation.* Berkeley: GAIA, University of California Press, 2008.

———. "Introduction." In Mayfair Mei-hui Yang, ed., *Chinese Religiosities*, 1–40.

Yang Sixin 杨思信. "Shilun chuantong 'dayitong' guannian dui Qingmo 'pai-Man' yundong de yingxiang" 试论传统"大一统"观念对清末"排满"运动的影响. *Zhongzhou xuekan* 中州学刊 118 (July 2000), 159–163.

Yang Suxian 楊蕭獻. "Liang Qichao yu Zhongguo jindai minzu zhuyi: 1896–1907" 梁啟超與中國近代民族主義：一八九六~一九０七. *Shiyuan* 史原 9 (1979), 129–148.

Yang Yunhui 杨云慧. *Cong baohuanpai dao mimi dangyuan: huiyi wo de fuqin Yang Du* 从保皇派到秘密党员：回忆我的父亲杨度. Shanghai: Shanghai wenhua chubanshe, 1987.

Ye, Xiaoqing, and Lance Eccles. "Anthem for a Dying Dynasty: The Qing National Anthem through the Eyes of a Court Musician." *T'oung Pao* 93.4/5 (2007), 433–458.

Yoon, Seungjoo. "Literati-Journalists of the *Chinese Progress* (*Shiwu bao*) in Discord, 1869–1898." In Karl and Zarrow, eds., *Rethinking the 1898 Reform Period*, 48–76.

Young, Ernest P. *The Presidency of Yuan Shih-k'ai: Liberalism and Dictatorship in Early Republican China.* Ann Arbor: University of Michigan Press, 1977.

Yu Dahua 喻大华. "'Qingshi youdai tiaojian' xinlun: jiantan Puyi qianwang donbei de yige yuanyin" 「清室优待条件」新论：兼探溥仪潜往东北的一个原因. *Jindaishi yanjiu* 近代史研究 1994 (1), 161–177.

Yu, Ying-shih. "The Radicalization of China in the Twentieth Century." *Daedalus* 122.2 (Spring 1993), 125–150.

Yung, Bell, Evelyn S. Rawski, and Rubie S. Watson, eds. *Harmony and Counterpoint: Ritual Music in Chinese Context.* Stanford, CA: Stanford University Press, 1996.

Zarrow, Peter. *Anarchism and Chinese Political Culture.* New York: Columbia University Press, 1990.

———. "Anti-Despotism and 'Rights Talk': The Intellectual Origins of Modern Human Rights Thinking in the Late Qing." *Modern China* 34.2 (April 2008), 179–209.

———. "Citizenship and Human Rights in Early Twentieth-Century Chinese Thought: Liu Shipei and Liang Qichao." In Wm. Theodore de Bary and Weiming Tu, eds., *Confucianism and Human Rights.* New York: Columbia University Press, 1998, 209–233.

———. "Constitutionalism and the Imagination of the State: Official Views of Political Reform in the Late Qing." In idem, ed., *Creating Chinese Modernity: Knowledge and Everyday Life, 1900–1940.* New York: Peter Lang, 2006, 51–82.

———. "Historical Trauma: Anti-Manchuism and Memories of Atrocity in Late Qing China." *History & Memory* 16.2 (Fall/Winter 2004), 67–107.

———. "Liang Qichao and the Conceptualization of 'Race' in Late Qing China." *Zhongyang yanjiuyuan jindaishi yanjiusuo jikan* 中央研究院近代史研究所集刊 52 (June 2006), 113–164.

———. "Liang Qichao and the Notion of Civil Society in Republican China." In Fogel and Zarrow, eds., *Imagining the People*, 232–257.

———. "The New Schools and National Identity: Chinese History Textbooks in the late Qing." In Tze-ki Hon and Robert J. Culp, eds., *The Politics of Historical Production in Late Qing and Republican China*. Leiden: Brill, 2007, 21–54.

———. "Old Myth into New History: The Building Blocks of Liang Qichao's 'New History.'" *Historiography East and West* 1.2 (Dec. 2003), 204–241.

Zhang Foquan 張佛泉. "Liang Qichao guojia guannian zhi xingcheng" 梁啟超國家觀念之形成. *Zhengzhi xuebao* 政治學報 1 (Sept. 1971), 1–66.

Zhang Hao [Hao Chang] 張灝. *Lieshi jingshen yu pipan yishi: Tan Sitong sixiang de fenxi* 烈士精神與批判意識：譚嗣同思想的分析. Taibei: Lianjing, 1988.

Zhang Jinfan 张晋藩. *Zhongguo falü de chuantong yu jindai zhuanxing* 中国法律的传统与近代转型. Beijing: Falü chubanshe, 1997.

Zhang Jingping 张晶萍. "Cong *Yijiao congbian* kan Ye Dehui de xueshu sixiang" 从《翼教丛编》看叶德辉的学术思想. *Hunan daxue xuebao (shehui kexue ban)* 湖南大学学报 (社会科学版) 18.4 (July 2004), 41–48.

Zhang Kaiyuan 章开沅. "'Pai-Man' pingyi: dui Xinhai geming qianhou minzu zhuyi de zairenshi" 「排滿」平議：對辛亥革命前後民族主義的再認識. *Guoshiguan guankan* 國史館館刊 16 (1994.6), 125–143.

———. "Xinhai geming shiqi de shehui dongyuan—yi 'pai-Man' xuanchuan wei shili" 辛亥革命時期的社会动员——以"排满"宣传为实例. *Shehui kexue yanjiu* 社会科学研究 1996 (5), 93–99.

Zhang Kaiyuan and Luo Fuhui 罗福惠. "Xinwenhua yundong: minzhuxing zhengzhi wenhua de fazhan yu zhuanbian" 新文化运动：民主型政治文化的发展与转变. In Zhongguo shehui kexueyuan keyanju 中国社会科学院科研局 and Zhongguo shehui kexue zazhishe 中国社会科学杂志社, eds., *Wusi yundong yu Zhongguo wenhua jianshe: wusi yundong qishi zhounian xueshu taolunhui lunwenxuan* 五四运动与中国文化建设：五四运动七十周年学术讨论会论文选. Beijing: Shehui kexue wenxian chubanshe, 1989, 1:353–373.

Zhang Nan 张枬 and Wang Renzhi 王忍之, eds. *Xinhai geming qian shinianjian shilun xuanji* 辛亥革命前十年间时论选集. Beijing: Sanlian shudian, 1963.

Zhang Pengyuan [Chang P'eng-yuan] 張朋園. *Liang Qichao yu minguo zhengzhi* 梁啓超與民國政治. Taibei: Hansheng chubanshe, 1992.

———. *Liang Qichao yu Qingji geming* 梁啓超與清季革命. Taibei: Zhongyang yanjiuyuan jindaishi yanjiusuo, 1982, 1999.

———. *Lixianpai yu Xinhai geming* 立憲派與辛亥革命. Taibei: Zhongyang yanjiuyuan jindaishi yanjiusuo, 1983.

Zhang, Xiaoming, and Chunfeng Xu. "The Late Qing Dynasty Diplomatic Transformation: Analysis from an Ideational Perspective." *Chinese Journal of International Politics* 1.3 (Summer 2007), 405–445.

Zhang Xueji 张学继. "Lun Youhe Changxiong yu minchu xianzheng de yanbian" 论有贺长雄与民初宪政的演变. *Jindaishi yanjiu* 近代史研究 2006 (3), 54–75.

Zhang Yufa 張玉法. *Qingji de geming tuanti* 清季的革命團體. Taibei: Zhongyang yanjiuyuan jinshisuo yanjiusuo, 1975.

Zhao, Gang. "Reinventing *China*: Imperial Qing Ideology and the Rise of Modern Chinese National Identity in the Early Twentieth Century." *Modern China* 32.1 (Jan. 2006), 3–30.

Zheng Shiqu 郑师渠. *Wan-Qing guocuipai: wenhua sixiang yanjiu* 晚清国粹派：文化思想研究. Beijing: Beijing shifan daxue chubanshe, 1993.

Zhonghua minguo shishi jiyao bianji weiyuanhui 《中華民國史事紀要》編輯委員會, ed. *Zhonghua minguo shishi jiyao* 中華民國史事紀要. Taibei: Zhonghua minguo shiliao yanjiu zhongxing, 1981.

Zhou Kaiqing 周開慶. *Xingzhiji* 行知集. Taibei: Changliu banyuekanshe, 1975.

Zhou Mian 周棉, ed. *Zhongguo liuxuesheng dacidian* 中国留学生大辞典. Nanjing: Nanjing daxue chubanshe, 1999.

Zhou Shaoyuan 周少元. "Qingmo faxue jiaoyu de tedian" 清末法学教育的特点. *Fashang yanjiu* 法商研究81 (Jan. 2001), 138–144.

Zhou Xiaoxi 周小喜 and Xiao Honghua 肖红华. "Lun Yang Du junzhu lixian sixiang" 论杨度君主立宪思想. *Changsha daxue xuebao* 长沙大学学报 23.4 (July 2009), 53–54.

Zhou Zhenfu 周振甫. "Yan Fu sixiang zhuanbian zhi poxi" 嚴復思想轉變之剖析. *Xuelin* 學林 13 (Jan. 1941), 113–133.

Zhou Zhongqiu 周仲秋. *Pingdeng guannian de licheng* 平等观念的历程. Haikou: Hainan chubanshe, 2002.

Zhu Hongyuan 朱浤源. *Tongmenghui de geming lilun: "Minbao" gean yanjiu* 同盟會的革命理論：《民報》個案研究. Taibei: Zhongyang yanjiuyuan jindaishi yanjiusuo, 1995.

———. "Zailun Sun Zhongshan de minzu zhuyi" 再論孫中山的民族主義. *Zhongyang yanjiuyuan jindaishi yanjiusuo jikan* 中央研究院近代史研究所集刊 22 (June 1993), 327–357.

Zito, Angela. *Of Body & Brush: Grand Sacrifice as Text/Performance in Eighteenth-Century China*. Chicago: University of Chicago Press, 1997.

Index

Academy of Current Affairs (Shiwu xuetang), 58, 59, 158, 246
Account of Ten Days at Yangzhou, 161–63
Account of the Jiading Massacre, 162–63, 241
Africa, 69
agriculture, 310n6; and Shennong, 170, 177, 335n115. *See also* well-field (*jingtian*) system
American Revolution, 196, 259, 292–93; July 4, 218, 219
anarchism, 185, 186, 198, 201, 205, 260, 275, 276, 341n20; of Liu Shipei, 168, 178, 197, 200, 206
Angle, Stephen, 199
anti-American boycott of 1905, 207
anti-Japanese War, 288
anti-Manchuism, 14, 17, 25, 154, 165, 214, 241, 284, 329n22, 339n106; and attitudes regarding Qing conquest, 160–64, 279–80; of Liang Qichao, 76, 152, 329n22, 330n30; of Liu Shipei, 173; among revolutionaries, 157–58, 181, 182, 205, 207, 210–11, 278, 330n30, 331nn43,46; of Sun Yat-sen, 162–63, 183, 206, 331n43; of Tan Sitong, 147, 149, 280; of Zhang Binglin, 166–68; of Zou Rong, 156
anti-Russian student campaign of 1903, 155, 190, 338n79
Ariga Nagao, 243, 344n4
aristocracy, 6, 11, 98, 102, 184, 186, 320n32; Liang Qichao on, 60, 64, 74, 116, 169, 170, 204
Aristotle, 114
Articles of Favorable Treatment, 213, 261–62, 266, 268, 269–70, 350n119

autocracy, 105, 214, 223, 244–45, 259, 276; Kang Youwei on, 39, 40, 43, 45, 251

Bai Qi, 167
Baks, 173–175
Bary, Theodore de, 15
Bastid, Marianne, 28
Beijing: Imperial Academy, 237; Institute for Exhibiting Antiquities, 233, 343n72; Tiananmen, 230, 231, 232; Zhonghuamen, 230; Zhongnanhai, 233–34. *See also* Forbidden City; National Palace Museum; Peking University
Bellah, Robert N., 352n37
benevolence (*ren*), 62, 129, 148, 228, 254; Kang Youwei on, 33, 36, 37, 38, 40, 51, 52–53, 69; Mencius on, 248, 345n8, 346n29
Bentham, Jeremy, 144
Bin Fengyang, 141
Bluntschli, Johann Kaspar, 103, 106, 108, 109, 110, 189, 289, 322n67
Bodin, Jean, 114–15
Book of Documents, 174, 175, 345n24, 346n30
Book of Rites (Liji), 50, 163
Bornhak, Conrad, 188, 189
Boxer Uprising, 3, 72, 92, 145, 235, 278
Brown, Elizabeth A. R., 308n14
Buddhism, 8, 14, 21, 35, 84, 122, 148, 201, 205, 208, 267; egalitarianism of, 36, 141, 184, 201, 205–6; and Kang Youwei, 31, 36, 52, 314n79; and Liang Qichao, 58, 59; and Zhang Binglin, 166, 183, 184, 336n12

Cai E, 229–30, 246

in, 334n103; Jimmu, 172; Meiji period, 26, 35, 41–45, 69–74, 81, 98–99, 113, 126, 127, 128, 166, 168, 185, 193, 244, 259, 279, 291, 312nn49,56, 313n64, 320n39, 321n47; People's Rights Movement in, 126, 127; relations with imperial China, 19, 24, 28, 29, 42, 46, 59, 121, 151, 181, 310n9; relations with Republic of China, 2, 242, 287; and Shandong, 240; socialism in, 201; Tokugawa shogunate, 70; during WWI, 240, 242
Jellinek, Georg, 189
Jenco, Leigh, 259–60
jeopardy thesis, 133
Jesus, 148, 149, 166, 172
Jiading massacre, 162–63, 164, 241
Jiangnan Arsenal, 20
jiao, 57
Johnston, Reginald, 350n120
journals, 26

Kang Youwei, 29–41, 172, 286, 309n33, 333n82; on autocracy, 39, 40, 43, 45, 251; on benevolence (*ren*), 33, 36, 37, 38, 40, 51, 52–53, 69; *Book of the Commonweal* (Datong shu), 47, 51–52, 59, 205, 313n78; on boundaries, 52, 53, 197; and Buddhism, 31, 36, 52, 314n79; "chronological autobiography," 31; *A Complete Book of Substantial Truths and Universal Principles*, 32–33; and Confucian Association, 250; on Confucianism and republicanism, 143, 251, 282; on Confucius as reformer, 48–49, 123, 136, 148, 275; on Confucius as uncrowned king, 46, 48, 68, 136, 141, 166, 275, 314n85; criticisms of, 87–88, 123, 130–31, 132, 134, 135–36, 138, 141–42, 165, 276, 314n78; on Datong (Great Harmony), 47, 50, 51, 52, 53, 56, 87–88, 135, 141, 165, 201, 236, 249, 289, 314n78, 329n22; on democracy, 33, 39–40, 48, 50, 52, 135, 313n64; on equality, 33, 36, 37, 51, 52, 123,

135, 138–39, 141, 286–87; *Esoteric and Exoteric Essays of Master Kang*, 33–36, 41; *An Examination of the Forged Classics of the Xin Dynasty*, 48; on expulsion of Puyi, 269–70; on imperial charisma, 18, 36, 37, 38; on imperial power, 34–38, 41, 45, 313n64; on individual autonomy, 33; influence of contractarian theory on, 89; on institutions, 25, 33, 38, 39–40, 48, 49, 50, 136, 168; interpretation of Confucian classics, 38, 46–53, 135–36, 276, 313nn66,69; on king as mediator (*zhongbao*), 33; vs. Liang Qichao, 56, 57, 58–59, 60, 61, 62, 68, 69, 70, 71, 76, 87–88, 89, 165, 276, 277, 315n17; on Meiji Japan, 41–45, 69, 71, 312n56; on monarchy, 8, 33–38, 63, 263, 275, 283, 311n24, 312n39, 314n85; motivation of, 31; on national unity, 39, 43, 44, 52, 313n64; and New Text school, 30, 39, 46–47, 48–50, 53, 54, 56, 76, 87, 135–36, 165, 249, 275; on Peter the Great, 41; on politics, 70, 71; on progress, 46–47, 48, 49–53, 54, 59, 61, 62, 74, 76, 87–88, 249, 314nn78,83, 315n17; on race, 152, 167; and reform movement of 1898, 8, 24–25, 28, 31, 32, 39, 40–41, 46, 53, 71–72, 166; relationship with Liang Qichao, 8, 24, 30, 56, 58; relationship with Ou Jujia, 67; relationship with Yuan Shikai, 263; relationship with Zhang Binglin, 182; relationship with Zhu Ciqi, 31; during restoration of Qing in 1917, 262–63; on righteousness (*yi*), 36, 38, 69; on ruler-subject relationship, 33, 36, 39–40, 43, 44, 64; on sage-kings, 36–37, 40, 48, 50–51, 55, 62, 68, 70, 71, 251, 275, 314n85; self-image as sage, 31, 32; and Society to Protect the Emperor, 31, 154, 182; *Study of Japan's Reforms*, 42–45; and Study Society for Strengthening, 22; on suffering, 34, 35, 51–52;

315n24, 328n113; Empress Dowager
Cixi during, 8, 24, 25–26, 28, 72; failure of, 8, 19, 24, 26, 29, 31, 32, 59,
71–72, 76, 87–88, 117, 126–27, 145,
154; and Guangxu emperor, 8, 19,
24–25, 39, 40–41, 42, 43; and Kang
Youwei, 8, 24–25, 28, 31, 32, 39,
40–41, 46, 53, 71–72, 166
Reinsch, Paul, 1, 233–34, 343n73
Renaissance, European, 276
republicanism, 2, 3–4, 8, 149, 154, 156,
164–65, 181, 196–97, 198, 209, 278,
294; and Confucianism, 143–45,
249–55, 282, 293; Hu Hanmin on,
185–86; Liang Qichao on, 64, 76,
118, 185, 245, 322n73, 323n96; of
Ou Jujia, 316n37; Wang Jingwei on,
187–88; Yang Du on, 158, 159, 243,
244, 263; Ye Dehui on, 139; Zhang
Binglin on, 168, 183, 184, 185,
336n11. *See also* anti-Manchuism;
democracy; rituals, republican; Sun
Yat-sen; Tongmenghui
Republic Commemoration Society (Gonghe jinianhui), 214
Republic of China: citizenship in, 214,
216–17, 241; constitution of, 236,
247n42, 252, 280; disillusionment
with, 216, 240–41; Double Ten
commemoration, 214–22, 223, 228,
229–30, 232, 238, 239–40, 280–81,
340n18, 342n65; education in, 252;
freedom of religion in, 251, 254–55;
government of, 212; militarization
in, 231, 232, 237–38, 254, 262, 280;
Ministry of Education, 222, 224,
236, 252; as multinational state, 5,
289, 351n24; national anthem, 216,
222–28, 341n38; National Assembly, 217, 218, 220, 224, 227, 228,
230–31, 247n42, 339n4, 340n18,
342n65; national flag, 216, 217,
226–30, 264, 281, 342n55; national
identity in, 215, 216, 217; parliament, 213; postage stamps, 238,
340n9; solar calendar used by, 213,
217, 219, 262, 264, 280; territory of,

226–27, 270; unity of the five peoples
in, 214, 225, 226–27, 229–30, 235,
281, 287, 341n38; women in, 215,
284–85, 291, 339n4, 344n99. *See
also* rituals, republican
restoration (*guangfu*), 164, 165, 166, 206,
238–39, 279
revenge (*fuchou*), 163–64, 166, 167, 168,
210, 241
Revised Articles of Favorable Treatment,
264, 268
Revive China Society (Xing Zhong hui),
162
Revolution of 1911, 8, 118, 142–43, 259,
260; vs. Communist Revolution, 272;
as irreversible, 2–3, 4, 246, 249, 270–
71; martyrs of, 214–15, 216, 218,
220, 228, 232, 237–38, 240, 281,
294–95; and modern Chinese identity,
272–73; and political modernity, 5;
role of New Army in, 181, 208–9;
role of racial consciousness in, 154–
60, 161, 162–64, 166–67, 167, 180,
210–11, 278–80, 331n46; Wuchang
Uprising, 208–10, 214, 217–18, 219,
223, 225, 230, 340n18
Rhoads, Edward J. M., 330n33, 339n110
righteousness (*yi*), 134, 135, 136, 140, 142,
228, 254; Kang Youwei on, 36, 38, 69
rights (*quanli*), 96, 156, 188, 195, 196–
200, 197, 256, 282, 291, 294, 351n11;
and autonomy, 66–67, 75, 156; Liang
Qichao on, 75, 111–12, 199–200,
317n65, 323n109, 324n115, 338n81;
Liu Shipei on, 197–98; relationship to
citizenship, 4, 156, 188, 196–97, 199;
rights consciousness (*quanli sixiang*),
199–200, 338n81; states' rights (*guoquan*), 99, 111, 321nn46,47. *See also*
human rights (*renquan*); natural rights
(*tianfu renquan*)
rituals, imperial, 1–2, 3, 9, 10, 12–13,
134, 139, 142, 216, 231, 234–37,
251, 264, 274, 281, 294, 308n9;
grand sacrifices, 13, 234, 237, 253,
308n17; worship of Confucius, 234,
236–37, 253

The authorized representative in the EU for product safety and compliance is:
Mare Nostrum Group
B.V Doelen 72
4831 GR Breda
The Netherlands

www.ingramcontent.com/pod-product-compliance
Lightning Source LLC
Chambersburg PA
CBHW020451270326
41926CB00008B/561